ARCHAEOLOGY

CULTURE HISTORY	FANTASTIC TALES	NEW WORLD ORIGINS	SOUTHWESTERN ARCHAEOLOGY
		1972 MacNeish, PIKIMACHAY CAVE	
		1965 Meggers & Evans, VALDIVIA	1965 SOUTHWEST ARCHAEOLOGICAL RESEARCH GROUP
1958 Willey & Phillips, METHOD AND THEORY			
1955 Steward, THEORY OF CULTURE CHANGE			
Braidwood, ORIGINS OF DOMESTICATION			
1950 RADIOCARBON DATING			
1949 Steward, CULTURE CAUSALITY	1947 Gladwin		
1948 Taylor, STUDY IN ARCHAEOLOGY			
PALYNOLOGY BEGINS			
1932 Kidder, PLEA FOR BETTER REPORTING & PUBLICATION, ARTIFACTS OF PECOS	1931 Churchward	1932 CLOVIS	1932 PECOS CLASSIFICATION
1924 DENDRO DATING	1925 Spense	1927 FOLSOM	1924 PECOS CONFERENCE
1917 Moorhead, SAW ARTIFACTS AS A CLASS			1916 Nelson, TAOS CERAMICS
1910 Boas	1910 G.E. Smith		
Reisner, METHODOLOGICAL CARE, ASWAN DAM SURVEY			
Petrie, SERIATION AND CROSS-DATING		1906 Marquis de Nachaillac, PREHISTORIC INDIANS	
Pitt-Rivers, DIG EVERYTHING, TYPICAL OBJECT IS BEST	1878 Le Plongeon	1880 Wetherill Brothers	
Morgan, UNILINEAR EVOLUTION		Bandelier, ETHNOGRAPHIC ANALOGY	
Tylor			
Lepsius, EGYPT		1841 Stephens & Catherwood	
Mariette, EGYPT			
Worsaae			
Wilson, TERM "PREHISTORY"			
1836-Thomsen, 3 AGES; FUNCTIONAL CLASSES			
1784 Jefferson, DIG WITH PURPOSE, STRATIFICATION, DIG TO SOLVE PROBLEMS			
1750 Weber, METICULOUS WORK AT HERCULANEUM			

Introduction to Archaeology

Introduction to Archaeology

James J. Hester
University of Colorado

HOLT, RINEHART AND WINSTON   New York   Chicago   San Francisco   Atlanta
Dallas   Montreal   Toronto   London   Sydney

Library of Congress Cataloging in Publication Data

Hester, James J.
  Introduction to archaeology

  1.   Archaeology.   I.   Title
CC165.H45   930.1   75-1410
ISBN 0-03-080179-6

Acknowledgments

For permission to reprint from copyrighted materials, the author is indebted to the following:

Aldine Publishing Company: For Figs. 6–6, 7–10, 7–11, 7–12, 9–1, and Tables 6–1 and 7–2 from Butzer, K., Environment and Archaeology. By permission of the publisher. For Fig. 8–2 from Oakley, K., Frameworks for Dating Fossil Man. By permission of Aldine Publishing Company and Weidenfeld & Nicolson, London.
Aldine Publishing Company and Edinburgh University Press: For Figs. 9–2, 10–2, 10–3, 10–18, 10–19, 10–21, 12–2, 12–3, 12–4, 12–7, 12–8, 12–9, 12–10, 12–12, 12–13a, b, and c, 12–14, and 12–15 from Ancient Europe by Stuart Piggott. © Stuart Piggott 1965. By permission of Aldine Publishing Company and Edinburgh University Press.
American Geophysical Union: For Fig. 3–4 from Suess, Hans E., Journal of Geophysical Research, Vol. 70, p. 5950, Fig. 4, 1965, copyright by American Geophysical Union.
Anderson, Adrienne, for the front endpaper.
Anthropological Society of Washington: For an extract from Flannery, Kent V. "Archeological Systems Theory and Early Mesoamerica," reproduced by permission of the Anthropological Society of Washington from Anthropological Archeology in the Americas, 1968.
Biological-Archaeological Institute of the University at Groningen, the Netherlands: For Fig. 2–8, photograph in DeLaet, S. J. The Low Countries.
Cambridge University Press: For Table 7–1 from World Prehistory: An Outline, by J. G. D. Clark, 2d ed., 1971. For Table 9–2 from Excavations at Star Carr, by J. D. G. Clark, 1971. For Fig. 10–22 and 10–23 from The Neolithic Cultures of the British Isles by Stuart Piggott, 1954. For Fig. 11–18 from The Indus Civilization, by M. Wheeler. All of the above by permission of Cambridge University Press.
Carnegie Institute of Washington: For Fig. 15–23 from Morris, E. H., "Temple of the Warriors at Chichén Itzá, Yucatan," Carnegie Institute of Washington Publications, No. 406, 1931. By permission of the publisher.
Thomas Y. Crowell Company, Inc.:   For Figs. 11–1, 11–2, 11–6, 11–7, 11–15, and 11–19 from The First Civilization by Glyn Daniel. Copyright © 1968 by Glyn Daniel, with permission of Thomas Y. Crowell Company, Inc., publisher.
Doubleday & Company, Inc.:   For Fig. 9–5 from Bordaz, J., Tools of the Old and New Stone Age. Copyright © 1970 by Doubleday & Company, Inc. By permission of the publisher. For Figs. 12–5 and 12–6 from Stonehenge Decoded, copyright © 1965 by Gerald S. Hawkins and John B. White. Reprinted by permission of Doubleday & Co., Inc. and Souvenir Press, Ltd., London. For Fig. 15–28 from Mexico before Cortez: Art, History, and Legend by Ignacio Bernal, trans. by Willis Barnstone.

Copyright © 1963 by Doubleday & Company, Inc. Reproduced by permission of the copyright holder.
Fort Burgwin Research Center: For Fig. 13–10 from Blackwater Locality No. 1: A Stratified, Early Man Site in Eastern New Mexico, by J. J. Hester. Publication of the Fort Burgwin Research Center No. 8.
Hawthorn Books, Inc.:   For Fig. 1–2 from The Concise Encyclopedia of Archeology, edited by L. Cottrell. Copyright © 1960 by Leonard Cottrell. All rights reserved. By permission of Hawthorn Books, Inc.
Holt, Rinehart and Winston: For Fig. 2–4 from An Introduction to Prehistoric Archeology, 3d ed., by Frank Hole and Robert F. Heizer. Copyright © 1965, 1969, 1973 by Holt, Rinehart and Winston, Inc. Reprinted by permission of Holt, Rinehart and Winston, Publishers. For Fig. 7–9 from Atlas of Fossil Man by C. Loring Brace, Harry Nelson, and Noel Korn. Copyright © 1971 by Holt, Rinehart and Winston, Inc. Reprinted by permission of Holt, Rinehart and Winston, Publishers.
Leroi-Gourhan, André: For Figs. 8–8, 8–10, 8–12, 8–13, 8–14, and 8–15 from Treasures of Prehistoric Art by André Leroi-Gourhan. By permission of the author and Editions d'Art Lucien MAZENOD, Paris.
McGraw-Hill Book Company: For Figs. 7–1, 7–2, 7–3, 7–4, 7–5, 7–6, 8–4, 8–5, 8–6, 8–7, and 8–9 from The Old Stone Age by François Bordes. Translation © George Weidenfeld & Nicolson Limited 1968. Used with permission of McGraw-Hill Book Company and Weidenfeld &Nicolson. For Table 14–1 and Fig. 14–4 from Prehistory of North America by J. D. Jennings. Copyright © 1968 by McGraw-Hill Book Company. Used with permission of McGraw-Hill Book Company.
Masson & Cie: For Fig. 7–13 from "Observations sur les faunes du Riss et du Würm I," by F. Bordes and F. Prat, l' Anthropologie 69:31–46 (1966) Masson & Cie, Paris.
The M.I.T. Press: For Figs. 11–9, 11–10, 11–11, and 11–12 from Architecture in Ancient Egypt and the Near East by A. Badawy by permission of The M.I.T. Press, Cambridge, Mass. Copyright © 1966 by The M.I.T. Press.
The New American Library, Inc.:   For Fig. 7–14 from The Prehistory of East Africa by Sonia Cole Copyright © 1963 by Sonia Cole. Reprinted by arrangement with The New American Library, Inc., New York, N.Y., and The Macmillan Company, New York, N.Y.
Penguin Books Ltd.:   For Fig. 11–13 from Edwards, I.E.S., The Pyramids of Egypt. By permission of Penguin Books Ltd.
Prentice-Hall, Inc.:   For Figs. 13–9, 14–2, 14–3, 14–17, 15–1, 15–4, 15–5, and 15–12 from Willey, Gordon R., An Introduction to American Archaeology. Volume One: North and Middle America, © 1966. By permission of Prentice-Hall, Inc., Englewood Cliffs, New Jersey. For Figs. 13–15, 14–2, 16–1, 16–2, 16–3, 16–4, 16–5a, 16–9, and extracts from Willey, Gordon R., An Introduction to American Archaeology, Volume Two: South America, © 1971. By permission of Prentice-Hall, Inc., Englewood Cliffs, New Jersey. For Figs. 14–1,

Preface

Introduction to Archaeology is a text for the beginning college course in archaeology or world prehistory. It provides a balanced survey of world prehistory with generous treatment of both Old World and New World archaeology. While the approach is primarily descriptive, emphasizing what has been found—by whom and in what manner—the major aim of the volume is to reconstruct prehistoric lifeways as fully and convincingly as possible given the limitations of the evidence available to archaeologists.

Because this book evolved from the teaching of a freshman course at the University of Colorado, the needs and interests of students have largely shaped the author's view of what it should contain and how the message should be gotten across. Students are primarily interested in the way people lived in other times and other places—not in detailed descriptions of bones and artifacts nor in the scholarly controversies of professional archaeologists. Also, students of today have grown up with television and with often more visual than verbal modes of communication and learning. The author has therefore attempted a free-flowing narrative style of exposition with much supplementary detail provided in over 200 illustrations that are packed with information about site locations, chronology, and cultural relationships.

The book emphasizes no professional fads and proposes no new integrative schemes since these, though important to the professional archaeologist, tend not to be of interest to the freshman student who comes to an archaeology course with no required prerequisites. Also, students thought it less confusing to use such terminology as Lower Paleolithic, Mesolithic, Neolithic, and so on for chapter headings, and again, in the students' interest, these have been retained.

Part I, The Nature of Archaeology, presents a working definition of archaeology including the nature of archaeological data, the methods and techniques of archaeology, and the conceptual and analytic tools that allow archaeologists to create plausible descriptions of prehistoric cultures. Part II, Cultural Data Revealed by Archaeology, describes the development of prehistoric man on this planet with a balanced treatment of prehistoric cultures across the world.

Each chapter is designed to include material for a week's concentration in an eighteen-week course. Shorter courses can cover the material more rapidly. The book's major objective is to introduce freshman students to a body of information that may, if the student chooses, serve as a basis for more detailed exposure to methodological and theoretical issues in advanced courses.

I am indebted to those who have read this book in manuscript form and who have given their critical comments. My thanks are hereby expressed to James Grady, William Haviland, Frank Hole, David Thomas, and Linda Williams. I often incorporated their suggestions into the final version of the text, and my gratitude to these colleagues is deep and sincere.

J. J. H.

Contents

THE NATURE
OF ARCHAEOLOGY

PART

Introduction: Some Definitions and Observations about Archaeology

The development of archaeology as a discipline is recent, most of its current form, interests, and methods having originated within the past 100 years. On the other hand, man's interest in man's past is common to all societies. Evidence of such interest in the past dates back to the last days of Babylon, 555–538 B.C. (Hole and Heizer 1969:5). The earliest excavations to find ancient artifacts that we know of were conducted by Nabonidus, the last king of Babylon. How then do we differentiate the modern science from its historical antecedents, and if we do so, to what purpose?

Perhaps our question can be answered by defining who an archaeologist is or what the archaeologist does that is unique. The modern archaeologist would draw a distinction between the simple collector of antiquities and the archaeologist. He would also define some students of ancient objects as philologists, epigraphers, or art historians but not archaeologists. What then are the criteria by which we define archaeology? Practically every archaeologist has tried his hand at definitions so I will not quote here an exhaustive series of them. One usable definition is that of Grahame Clark in his *Archaeology and Society* (1969:17).

Archaeology may be simply defined as the systematic study of antiquities as a means of reconstructing the past. For his contributions to be fruitful the archaeologist has to possess a real feeling for history, even though he may not have to face what is perhaps the keenest challenge of historical scholarship, the subtle interplay of human personality and circumstance. Yet he is likely to be involved even more deeply in the flow of time. The prehistoric archaeologist in particular is confronted by historical changes of altogether greater dimensions than those with which the historian of literate civilizations is concerned, and has to face demands on his historical imagination of a commensurate order, further, at a purely technical level he is likely to be met with much greater difficulties of decipherment, difficulties which can as a rule only be surmounted by calling on scientists and scholars practiced in highly specialized branches of knowledge.

In my own definition, I consider archaeology to be the study of man's past cultural behavior within the specific historical and ecological frameworks in which it occurred. The methodology includes the finding of evidences of this past cultural activity and then establishing the relationship of these findings to the temporal and spatial locale in which they occurred. Also of importance is the fact that these findings are not of themselves cultural behavior but are the *result* of behavioral patterns; thus the behavioral patterns themselves must be inferred. For example, the presence of a potsherd on a site provides a major opportunity for such inferences. The sherd may be painted, its interior shows scraping marks, and the clay it was made from has a distinctive temper (the crushed rock, sand, or other material placed within the clay to inhibit cracking). From the painted decoration we learn something of the design style. We may even be able to infer that the design is symbolic, as it may have religious, calendrical, or mnemonic meaning. The interior scraping will be typical of either handmade or wheel-made pottery. The temper may be identifiable to a specific place where it was obtained. The design style may have chronological significance. The form of the sherd may suggest the shape of the vessel that it is from, and thus we may infer the former uses of the vessel.

If we can learn so much from a single potsherd, then what possibilities await our study of the other remnants of man's past? Here lies the core of interest that makes archaeology so appealing to young and old. Beneath the next shovelful of dirt may lie something hitherto unknown to history, an object the like of which no one living today has ever seen. We have thus bound up in one field the glamor of a treasure hunt, a sense of creativity equal to that of the artist, and the vision into the unknown of the scientist. It is the excitement of the treasure hunt which so appeals to the common man. Everywhere I go, when people learn that I am an archaeologist, they say, "How fascinating, I'm sure your work must be exciting!" The truth of the matter is that frequently archaeology is not all that exciting. It has its share of drudgery because digging is hard work, usually carried out in a hot dusty cave, in the rain, or in a cloud of gnats. Normally you are too busy labeling sample bags, drawing profiles, or taking photographs to notice everything that comes out of the trenches. Therefore, you lose or at least temporarily forget your sense of that excitement which is so typical of the nonprofessional. However, there are times when it suddenly comes back to you and you realize that you are the treasure hunter after all, only somewhat disguised by scientific motives and methodology. I remember the time I was excavating an 11,000-year-old (that is, 11,000 years Before Present) mammoth killsite in New Mexico. In the trench wall of the Clovis level a workman had exposed what in profile looked like a human skull. Immediately I planned what steps I would take. I would first obtain a highway patrolman to guard the specimen in place and then would notify the press of this momentous find—the earliest human remains found to date in the New World. Fortunately I decided to dig just a little bit more around the skull to be sure what it was and it turned out to be a large turtle shell! Another example concerns our work in the Egyptian desert south of Aswan. We were driving across an open sandy plain some 5 or 6 miles west of the Nile. Suddenly we noticed two cut stone columns, about a foot in diameter and 5 feet in height, lying on the sand. They were obviously of some antiquity but we could not understand why they were at that particular place. We photographed them and then drove on. A day later in the same area we found another such set of columns. This time we realized their presence was not accidental. We drove in a straight line toward the first set we had located and began to find additional sets at intervals of about one mile. Obviously they were some kind of road markers. We eventually traced the former road for about 30 miles, finding 22 sets of columns en route. We found that some of the markers had Roman numerals on them and that the interval between sets was about 4800 feet, the distance of the Roman mile. We had discovered the first Roman roads in southern Egypt; such roads had been long known in Tripolitania but not in Egypt. The point I wish to make here is that *we had made an exciting discovery, but did not realize it until later.*

We have established that the archaeologist studies remains of past cultures and from these remains attempts to infer the nature of prior behavioral patterns. The subject thus includes: a methodology for the recovery of objects and other kinds of information, a body of data already known with which new finds may be compared, a set of concepts to organize the data in meaningful terms, and a variety of ancillary techniques of laboratory analysis such as radiocarbon dating, archaeomagnetic studies, and so forth. Specific details of each of these parts of archaeology will be treated in later chapters.

The entire study of archaeology is made possible by accidents of preservation. Durable items such as stone tools, pottery, or stone architecture are usually preserved, even if broken or disarranged. Items of perishable materials also may be preserved in certain kinds of environments of deposition. Dry caves and sites below the water table are both excellent environments for the preservation of fibers, wood, cloth, leather, and other perishable materials.

Often the items we find are preserved through some unique circumstance such as the volcanic eruption at Pompeii or the accidental loss of a ship at sea. In addition, most of our finds are items that were broken in antiquity and discarded by their users. Our task is thus made more difficult. We must reconstruct the nature of past cultures from those remnants which have been preserved no matter how fragmentary or incomplete they are. However, I do not mean to suggest that archaeological remains are rare, for they occur almost everywhere, including portions of continental shelves now below sea level and in deserts now completely uninhabited. Archaeological remains per se are common; there are probably some archaeological remains within a mile of the homes of most of us. What is characteristic of archaeological sites is that wherever they occur, and no matter what their size, they contain only a portion of the material culture of the people that occupied the site. A major portion of the original materials have been destroyed by burning, erosion, organic decay, or chemical alteration. Therefore, the archaeologist's task is twofold: he must reconstruct the original nature of the objects he finds and in addition, infer their role in a prehistoric society. A helpful device employed by archaeologists is the recording of the position of each item found in a site. The relationship of items to each other may give clues as to their former uses and associations. By such means we may learn that items of vastly different form were used together in the past. An example would be the parts of a composite tool such as a harpoon. The harpoon head might be slotted for the insertion of a chipped stone point. You could infer from such a harpoon head that it had possessed a point, but finding one example with a point in place would constitute archaeological "proof" that the two items were associated in their use. A more abstract example could be a cluster of small items utilized in a religious ceremony. By their form there might be no way to guess that they were associated. Finding them together in one group establishes evidence that they were used together in the past. An outstanding example is the series of human figurines made of jade found at the Olmec site at La Venta on the east coast of Mexico (Fig. 1–1). The figurines had been placed vertically in a semicircle. Facing the semicircular group was a single figurine. From the association the excavators inferred that the group had been purposefully buried in that position to represent a specific past ceremony.

Although the field techniques for the recovery of archaeological materials are fairly standardized, the types of intellectual inquiry possible through examination of archaeologically obtained specimens are infinitely varied. Obvious divisions include those governed by the major time-space divisions. Some special interests depend upon study of techniques used; for example, weaving or pottery manufacture. Historical concerns afford another approach, such as the development of specific architectural features in cities or the development of social systems associated with specific economies.

These problems or interest areas have culminated in a series of specialities within archaeology. As a result the average archaeologist today does not attempt to master the entire body of knowledge relative to past human cultural

Fig. 1–1   Human figurines of jade found within a pyramid at La Venta, Tabasco, Mexico. Their arrangement represents a prehistoric ceremony. (Hester photograph, courtesy Mexican National Museum of Anthropology.)

activity but instead specializes in one or more areas. He may also specialize in a specific technique or method for the recovery of data, but that is a subject we will cover later. We will now review some of the major topical areas in greater detail.

MAJOR TOPICS OF ARCHAEOLOGICAL INTEREST

EVOLUTION   the development of culture through time. Historically, evolution was the archaeological subject that first attracted attention. With the discoveries of stone tools in gravel pits in France by Boucher de Perthes in the late 1830s, the scientific world first became aware of the fact that such flaked objects were of regular intentional form made by ancient men. Of help in understanding these finds were the tools collected by Europeans from contemporary aboriginal peoples (William Haviland, personal communication). These discoveries were linked with contemporaneous innovations in geological thinking. Charles Lyell published between 1830 and 1833 a revolutionary geological concept termed *uniformitarianism* which attributed the thickness and variety of earth strata to the action of geologic processes of erosion and deposition similar to those at work today but at work over a very long period of time. Such humble beginnings in the study of prehistory had a long way to go, for several generations elapsed before the last doubters were convinced that: 1. these primitive stone tools were indeed made by men and 2. the age of the earth dated far back in time beyond the biblical concept of its origin, interpreted by Bishop Ussher as occurring in 4004 B.C. However, once these major mental blocks to the understanding of man's cultural development had been removed, then archaeological activity focused on human cultural evolution. A major breakthrough came when an archaeologist named Thomsen, working in the Danish National Museum, grouped artifacts by their materials—stone, bronze, and iron. He described these as indicative of a Stone Age, a Bronze Age, and an Iron Age. Later excavations confirmed this sequence, and the names have remained in use to this day. With the development of such a preliminary classification scheme, archaeologists became increasingly concerned with the identification of new stages of human cultures and the fitting of these new manifestations into an overall scheme of classification. This concern with evolutionary relationships has continued with intermittent enthusiasm to the present.

HUMAN PALEONTOLOGY   the study of human biological evolution. In this field the evidence consists of fragments of bones and teeth of both humans and prehumans. The exciting aspect of this study is that every new find may be a missing link, such as the famous Java man *(Homo erectus)* remains discovered by Eugene Dubois in the 1890s. Owing to a variety of problems, the pattern of human physical evolution is still somewhat unclear; therefore, research in this area is as fascinating as ever. For example, human evolution may not have featured an unidirectional sequence of forms but instead may have included numerous dead-ends and cases of parallel or convergent evolution. Another complicating factor is that the finds are never made in a simple chronological order but are mixed, with later materials being known years before their antecedents are found, or vice versa. Further complications are introduced by the fact that different portions of the human skeleton evolved at different rates which makes it difficult to correlate changes in tooth size and complexity with changes in cranial capacity or some other aspect of the skeleton. These complications however only serve to make human paleontology the fascinating study that it is.

CULTURAL ECOLOGY   the study of man's relationship to his environment. A basic and unique fact relative to man is his development of culture. With tools and the accumulated and transmitted knowledge of how to use them, man has been able to provide protection for himself against the harsher aspects of his environment. He has been able to inhabit a wider range of habitats through his use of cultural means. He utilized fire and clothing to keep warm, his weapons enabled him to kill animals larger and more swift than himself, and his development of food preparation and storage techniques allowed him to devote more time to leisure activities. The archaeologist interested in the study of cultural ecology collects data on the nature of the past environments that man inhabited. He then studies the distribution of sites and the implements preserved in them as a means of assessing man's adaptation to each environment. A major aspect of this approach is the *settlement pattern* study. The archaeologist observes within a specific region every different topographic feature which man could have utilized. He then locates the actual occurrence of prehistoric sites on terraces, flood plains, and other such natural features. The pattern of past human use thus revealed tells the archaeologist a great deal about how the prehistoric inhabitants viewed the environment in which they lived.

TECHNOLOGY   The archaeologist may be primarily concerned with how stone tools were manufactured. Termed *technology,* this approach focuses on the actual steps involved in the transition of a natural rock into a finished stone tool. First is the systematic removal of the exterior of a cobble through the striking off of a series of trimming flakes. This is followed by the removal of a specially prepared flake, the so-called primary flake, which is then further modified into a tool by the removal of chips from the edge. The series of manufacturing steps or processes constitutes the prehistoric stone technology.

TYPOLOGY   The shape of the finished implements made by the same technology is variable and the tools can be grouped into various form classes, such as points, bifaces, flakes, and so on. Such a grouping is termed a *typology,* and it is basic to our organization of individual stone tool *assemblages* (the tools found at one site or in one level) into larger units of classification. Every archaeologist is involved in these kinds of analyses to some degree, but some are specialists in these studies and are known as typologists.

CULTURAL DYNAMICS   Other archaeologists are concerned with the overall major developments in human culture history. This interest in *cultural dynamics* is evidenced in studies that attempt to understand the nature of cultural processes—how and why major revolutions or changes in culture took place. What were the underlying causes? Were they environmental or did they result from technological innovations or social factors? Were they the result of a cumulative effect, with each change the result of prior changes, with none of them being really major in scope? A major subdivision of this area is the subject of *culture change.* As an example, the culture change specialist may isolate for study smaller cultural units such as design styles in a series of ceramic types. He then describes the changes that occurred in this portion of culture through time in a search for cultural regularities—patterns of change that will enable him to better understand the nature of cultural changes in general.

HISTORICAL ARCHAEOLOGY Specialists in *historical archaeology* work with the remains of cultures possessing written historical records. Some of the contributions of the archaeologist lie in his ability to find evidence of cities, buildings, and other structures identified in historical documents. In this way he is able to cross-check and verify the historical records. Another focus of interest concerns the everyday life of the people. Frequently mundane affairs such as the method of construction of houses for the common people or the manufacture of cooking pots and other utilitarian objects are not recorded in historical documents. When excavating in a historical site, the archaeologist thus has the opportunity to reveal new and interesting details about the daily life of a group. Even though that group may be well known historically, our knowledge from historical sources may be primarily in terms of wars, religion, and the activities of a ruling class. Therefore, archaeological studies of historically known cultures can provide unique new information.

By this time I suspect you have come to the conclusion that archaeologists are interested in everything concerning man's past, which is the point that I am trying to make. There are archaeologists who specialize in dating techniques, ceramic analysis, tracing of ancient trade routes, the deciphering of ancient languages, verification of the Bible, underwater archaeology, and many more specialized endeavors. In short, the archaeologist is anyone who studies the remains of the past collected through use of archaeological field methods. These methods are more or less standardized while the point of view of the archaeologist toward the remains he studies varies with his own particular bias or interest. Thus we perceive that the unifying elements that bind these rather diverse studies together are: 1. it is the remains of ancient cultures that are studied and 2. these remains were collected through use of standardized archaeological methods.

A BRIEF HISTORY OF THE DEVELOPMENT OF ARCHAEOLOGY

We have already narrowed our field of interest by stating that archaeologists study ancient remains as a means of reconstructing past cultural behavior. This limitation has by no means always been in effect. Archaeology has evolved over the past 2500 years, and during this interval the study of antiquities has had a number of different emphases. The first concern with objects from the past was displayed by tomb robbers. Tomb robbing is a long standing tradition in Egypt which continues to the present. We have no idea when the earliest such occurrence took place, but we do know that by 1120 B.C. the practice was so widespread that an investigation was held. At a somewhat later date Nabonidus excavated at Ur, brought his findings back to Babylon, and placed them in a museum (Hole and Heizer 1973:41). Other early incidents involving the planned or accidental finding of antiquities are known. In most cases these demonstrate only a limited concern for the past, and frequently the motivation was purely financial, with the objects recovered being sold.

In the fifth century B.C. the Athenians opened some graves which they adjudged to be Carian because they included artifacts which were similar to those still used by the Carians. Julius Caesar's soldiers robbed the graves at Corinth and sold the bronze vessels. Another Roman emperor collected ancient Greek coins, but even he was centuries ahead of his time, for the collecting of antiquities as a special interest did not develop until the fifteenth century A.D. It is difficult to coin a term for this early historic period, in which tomb robbing was a major aspect. Occasionally there were other concerns, but these could be categorized as curiosity seeking rather than a true interest in the ancient cultures themselves.

Associated with the Renaissance was the development of interest in the collecting of art treasures. This practice began in Italy in the fifteenth century and rapidly became a widespread custom, with wealthy men and officials of the church decorating their homes and establishments with ancient statuary. Alexander VI, who was pope between 1492 and 1503, initiated the practice of excavating to obtain such treasures. Pompeii and Herculaneum were principal cities which were "mined" in an extractive sense rather than being excavated to obtain information. The collector's spirit spread to other parts of Europe, especially England where wealthy individuals such as Thomas Howard made periodic visits to Italy to purchase antiquities. Soon the practice included the remains of other ancient civilizations, those of the Middle East and Egypt. Claudius Rich was one such collector. Residing in Bagdad as part of Britain's diplomatic corps, he was an assiduous collector of ancient coins, manuscripts, and clay tablets for 25 years (Daniel 1967). At his death in 1821, 7000 pounds of these antiquities were deposited in the British Museum. Another Englishman, Henry Creswick Rawlinson, traveled the length and breadth of Iran in his search for examples of ancient writing. He then spent years in the decipherment of cuneiform script. Of special help in his quest were the inscriptions on Behistun rock in three languages, Old Persian, Babylonian, and Susian (Fig. 1–2). He worked on the texts from 1835 to 1847 at which time he was able to publish a full translation.

An interest in Egyptian antiquities became widespread after Napoleon's invasion of Egypt in 1789. With the troops were archaeological specialists, and from this initial contact developed the French Institute in Cairo. The most important find was that of the Rosetta Stone in 1799, which was transported to the British Museum after the British victory in 1801. Giovanni Belzoni (1778–1823) was the most famous collector of Egyptian antiquities. An Italian, he went to Egypt to work on irrigation projects, but when that did not work out, he worked for the British Consul collecting antiquities. A former circus strong man, Belzoni collected papyri, mummies, statues, and anything else he could move. In 1820 he held an exhibition in the Egyptian Hall in Piccadilly. He also published a book, *Narrative of the Operations and Recent Discoveries Within the Pyramids, Temples, Tombs and Excavations in Egypt and Nubia* (1820), one of the earliest works devoted to antiquities.

During this period the collector specialized in antiquities from the great civilizations and collected them to resell to art lovers. Men, such as Rawlinson,

Fig. 1–2 Sir Henry Creswicke Rawlinson deciphered Mesopotamian writing through the study of this text on Behistun rock carved in three ancient languages. The Behistun inscription was carved in 516 B.C. on the orders of Darius the First. (Cottrell 1960:Plate 25.)

who maintained serious scholastic interest in the objects they obtained were rare. By categorizing periods of interest, I do not mean to imply that we have a neat sequence of steps in the evolution of archaeology. For example, the collecting phase is still with us. However, it is usually possible to attribute the efforts of individuals to the specific intellectual interests of the times in which they lived.

In seventeenth- and eighteenth-century England there developed a series of gentlemen with a strong interest in the cultures of ancient Britain. For the first time in history, the inquiry shifted from the nature of the ancient objects to the nature of their makers. The outstanding pioneer in this field was William Camden (1551–1623), a school headmaster, who traveled over England studying antiquities. In 1586 he published *Britannia* which was the first general guide to the archaeology of England. He described the antiquities and provided illustrations of them. His writings not only included descriptions of barrows (prehistoric burial mounds) and other architectural remains but sought to explain why they were so constructed. John Aubrey (1626–1697), writing between 1659 and 1670, was another of the English antiquarians. The following description by him indicates that intellectual inquiries were becoming increasingly discerning.

Let us imagine then what kind of countrie that was in the time of the ancient Britons. By the nature of the soil, which is sour woodsere land, very natural for the production of akes especially, one may conclude that this North Division was a shady dismal wood; and the inhabitants almost as savage as the Beasts whose skins were their only rayment (Quoted in Daniel 1967:37).

Edward Lhwyd (1660–1708), the first keeper of the Ashmolean Museum at Oxford, published a catalogue of fossils and in 1707 the first volume of his *Archaeologia Britannica,* in which he discoursed on the histories and customs of the original inhabitants of Great Britain. One of his major concerns was to lay to rest the myth that stone implements were shot from the sky by elves. As Lhwyd states, "But for my part I must crave leave to suspend my faith, until I see one of them descend" (Daniel 1967:39). Other antiquaries, Henry Rowlands (1655–1723) and William Stukeley (1687–1765), were deeply concerned with the nature of pre-Roman Britain, especially the Druid cult and the sites of Avebury and Stonehenge.

The foundations of the true discipline of archaeology were established in the first half of the nineteenth century with two major developments, one in Denmark and the other in England. The Danish contribution is known as the *three age system:* the categorization of artifacts into periods or ages according to their characteristic components—stone, bronze, or iron. The English contribution was in the field of stratigraphic geology with the principle of uniformitarianism defined and linked with new concepts as to the true age of earth strata.

The three age system was the first truly archaeological theory, for it predicated that one could determine the relative age of an artifact merely by knowing the material it was made from without any other kind of corroborative information.

At first the tools and weapons of the earliest inhabitants of Scandinavia were made of stone or wood. Then the Scandinavians learnt to work copper and then to smelt it and harden it . . . and then latterly to work iron. From this point of view the development of their culture can be divided into a Stone Age, a Copper Age and an Iron Age. These three ages cannot be separated from each other by exact limits for they encroach on each other. Without any doubt the use of stone implements continued among the more impoverished groups after the introduction of copper, and similarly objects of copper were used after the introduction of iron. . . . Artifacts of wood have naturally decomposed, those of iron are rusted in the ground; it is those of stone and copper which are the best preserved (Daniel 1967:90–91).

The theoretical statements concerning the Stone, Copper, Iron sequence were further implemented by practical application. In 1806 Professor Rasmus Nyerup, of the University of Copenhagen, proposed the establishment of a Danish National Museum for antiquities. The following year the Danish government set up a royal committee for that purpose. In 1816 Christian Jurgensen Thomsen was appointed the museum's first curator. He set to work arranging the exhibits on the basis of the three age system, and the museum was opened in 1819. The first systematic description of artifacts classified according to this system was published in a guidebook to the National Museum in 1836. Shortly thereafter the museum staff was augmented by the addition of Jens Jacob Asmussen Worsaae (1821–1885) who may properly be termed the first professional archaeologist. His monumental work, *The Primeval Antiquities of Denmark,* first published in 1843 when he was only 22 years old, contained several major concepts basic to the development of the true discipline of archaeology. He detailed the need for the three age scheme of classification; he outlined the use of the comparative method of analysis and methods of excavation, and he stressed the need for a public awareness of the values of archaeology. Brief extracts from his work will serve to indicate the nature of his concerns.

In order that the Danish memorials may appear in their true light and connection, it will be of importance to enquire in what regions of other countries similar monuments of antiquity have been observed. Without such a general examination it would scarcely be possible to derive satisfactory historical conclusions from the enquiry . . . (Daniel 1967:101–102).

In general, it is not to be desired that the ancient barrows belonging to the times of paganism, should be either opened, or removed. It is true they occur, in certain parts of the country, in such numbers as to offer serious impediments to agriculture; while they contain beside large masses of stone, which in many cases might be used with advantage. Still they deserve to be protected and preserved, in as great a number as possible. They are national memorials, which may be said to cover the ashes of our forefathers; and by this means constitute a national possession, which has been handed down for centuries, from race to race. Would we then unconcernedly destroy these venerable remains of ancient times, without any regard to our posterity? Would we disturb the peace of the dead, for the sake of some trifling gain (Daniel 1967:103–104).

If a barrow must, of necessity be removed, a complete description of its external form, its height, and circumference should first be made. This description should explain whether it is surrounded, or enclosed, with large stones; whether it has borne any peculiar name; whether any traditions are associated with it; and finally whether there are similar memorials in the same district and what is their number. If the description were accompanied with drawings of the appearance of the barrow, it would naturally be an advantage. As it is of importance to know what is the internal condition of the barrow, and what may be the relation between the tomb itself, and the objects deposited within it, the tomb must now be examined with all possible precaution. If the barrow is one of the usual conical kind, it will be best to cut through it from southeast to north-west, with a trench of about eight feet broad, which, in more complete investigations may again be intersected by a similar trench from southwest to northeast. It will often be sufficient so to excavate the barrow from the top, as to form a large round cavity as far as the bottom of the mound, which is always on a level with the surrounding field; for it is in the middle of this base, that the most important tombs are usually situated. In this proceeding it is, however, advisable to form a trench from the cavity in the middle, to the southeast side of the barrow, since tombs are often found here, and it might otherwise be extremely difficult to bring up the earth from the central cavity, when such cavity had obtained a depth of several feet.

As soon as the trench is begun, and the first covering of grass and heath removed, we must examine whether vessels of clay with burnt bones and ashes, are not to be met with under such stones. These vessels, from their great antiquity, are so extremely fragile, that it is only with the greatest care they can be brought from the barrow in an uninjured state. When the surrounding stones are carefully removed, the best and safest mode of extracting the urns, is by introducing a board beneath them, then placing them in the open air, and after a few hours the clay becomes firm again . . . Skeletons, and in particular sculls, must be preserved; and even the bones of those animals, which have been interred with the deceased may have a value for science . . . (Daniel 1967:104–105).

The importance of Worsaae's work was recognized in Scandinavia, and from his time on, it is appropriate to speak of a true archaeological discipline. However the significance of his writings was slow to influence the efforts of researchers in other parts of Europe. In England and France other developments independently formed the antecedents of a true archaeological tradition. Fore-most among these developments were the concepts of the new geology. Based on the concept of *uniformitarianism*—the principle that the present is the key to the past—the new views of the antiquity of the earth stressed that all geologic features are the result of geological processes at work in the present. Therefore, the variety and great thickness of geologic sediments could be explained only by extremely minute causal factors carried out over a long period of time. A major integral portion of these ideas was the concept of *stratigraphy:* the layers of the earth were laid down sequentially, and unless there had been dramatic subsequent tectonic action, the oldest layers were those on the bottom of each sequence, and each layer was somewhat younger than the layer immediately beneath it. These new concepts were initiated by William "Strata" Smith (1769–1839) who described the strata of England. An alternative view was that termed *catastrophism*. First proposed by Jacque Cuvier (1769–1832) from his studies of fossil vertebrates, the theory empha-sized the catastrophic destruction of one fauna and the subsequent creation of another. The publication of Charles Lyell's *Principles of Geology* (1830–1833) led to acceptance of the uniformitarian approach.

The papers delivered in 1858 and 1859 by Darwin and Wallace at the Royal Society, the Linnean Society, and the Society of Antiquaries of London outlined the principles of *evolution*, which could be used to explain the origins of man.

At approximately the same time there were major findings of artifacts that led to increased interest in man's past, as well as speculations concerning the manner in which these implements came to be deposited. In 1849 Boucher de Perthes published his findings at Abbeville, France. Within undisturbed beds of sand and gravel in the Somme River terraces, he had uncovered stone implements in association with extinct mammals. The major facts revealed were that these items were undoubted artifacts of deliberate manufactured form. They were in undisturbed strata and associated with animals now extinct; therefore they must have great antiquity. In addition to numerous field trips on which Boucher de Perthes convinced some of his colleagues of the importance of his finds, the remains were also interpreted by geologists. In 1863 Sir Charles Lyell published *The Geological Evidences of the Antiquity of Man* in which he reviewed the prehistoric evidence available. He included the Somme tools as well as the Neanderthal skeleton found near Düsseldorf in 1856.

Another outstanding find was made during the very dry winter of 1853–1854 in Switzerland. A. Morlot, professor at the Academy of Lausanne, and Dr. Ferdinand Keller of Zurich examined the remains of ancient peoples revealed by the lowering of lake levels. Along the shores of these lakes they found villages with houses that had been built over the water on pilings. The remains of these villages, including stone axes, antler artifacts, pottery, and so forth, revealed that the three age sequence developed in Scandanavia could be adapted to the Swiss remains.

We may thus conclude that by 1870 there existed in several parts of Europe an intellectual tradition which we may term archaeological. Major theoretical and methodological advances were yet to come, but the discipline itself had been established. The last third of the nineteenth century featured widespread efforts by European archaeologists to extend their knowledge through the systematic excavation and documentation of the remains of ancient civilizations. It is in this period that discovery of the unknown past became a common profession with increasingly rigorous methodologies. In no way will I attempt to detail this period, since other works are available with such coverage. During this period we had the excavations at Troy by Schliemann, the discovery of paleolithic cave art in France and Spain, the beginnings of scientific excavations in Mesopotamia with Layard's work at Nimrud, Fiorelli's excavations at Pompeii, excavations by Flinders Petrie in Egypt where he worked out his famous sequence dating of graves, and General Pitt-Rivers' work on Roman and ancient British remains on his estate. Some of the latter's statements on methods are as pertinent today as when they were written:

Excavators, as a rule, record only those things which appear to them important at the time, but fresh problems in archaeology and anthropology are constantly arising, and it can hardly fail to have escaped the notice of anthropologists, especially those who, like myself, have been concerned with the morphology of art, that on turning back to old accounts in search of evidence, the points which would have been most valuable have been passed over from being thought uninteresting at the time. Every detail should, therefore, be recorded in the manner most conducive to facility or reference, and it ought at all times to be the chief object of an excavator to reduce his own personal equation to a minimum.

I have endeavoured to record the results of these excavations in such a way that the whole of the evidence may be available for those who are concerned to go into it . . . (Daniel 1967:238).

Pitt-Rivers also had designed a special medal, dated and inscribed "opened by A. Pitt-Rivers, F.R.S.," which he placed in the bottom of his test pits. These medals were to inform future excavators that the site had already been investigated.

Sir Flinders Petrie, whose professional life spanned not only the last third of the nineteenth century but the first 40 years of the twentieth century, is credited with a number of firsts in archaeological techniques. In 1877 he described his practice of precise measurements of ancient earthworks and architecture, in this case remains in southern England. In 1880 he went to Egypt to measure the pyramids and there found his life's work. In excavations conducted almost annually until 1926, he pioneered the use of potsherds in dating, revealed that systematic excavation could lead to a rigorous interpretation of past events, set up the sequence dating of graves at Naqada, trained his workmen to dig with professional care, stressed the cultural importance of minor objects ignored by treasure hunters, had the materials of which the various objects were made carefully analyzed, and in every way pioneered the development of a rigorous science of archaeology.

We have described in some detail the history of archaeology in Europe. To some degree there was a separate development of archaeology in the United States. In America an outstanding pioneer was the third President of the United States, Thomas Jefferson. In 1780, overcome with curiosity as to the constitution of some mounds on his plantation, he ordered one of them to be trenched. His findings, published in his *Notes on the State of Virginia*, were that the mound was probably of recent Indian manufacture and had been built up as a sequence of four layers deposited at different times. The work was descriptively sound and was equivalent to excavation techniques utilized a century later. Unfortunately Jefferson's findings went largely unnoticed at the time and made little contribution to the development of archaeology as a discipline. A second pioneer, William Henry Harrison, examined the mounds near Cincinnati in 1793. In 1838 he wrote *A Discourse on the Aborigines of the Valley of Ohio* for the Historical Society of Ohio. His approach was less descriptive and more philosophical than Jefferson's; another of the major differences was that Harrison ascribed great antiquity to the mounds.

In 1799 Baron Alexander von Humboldt received permission from Charles IV, the king of Spain, to have unlimited access to the Spanish colonies in the New World to engage in scientific investigations. Everything was of interest to him—the geography, climate, flora, fauna, people, and antiquities. His five-year trek took him across South America, Cuba, Mexico, and part of the United States. His first scientific work, *Vuesde Cordilleres et Monuments des Peuples Indigenes de l'Amerique* (1814), contained numerous illustrations and descriptions of pyramids, codices, and stone sculpture. Much more influential than either the work of Jefferson or Harrison, Humboldt's book stimulated later scholars of American antiquities, including John Lloyd Stephens, William H. Prescott, the Abbe Brasseur de Bourbourg, and Edward Seler. Humboldt investigated pictographs in the Amazon, the Archaic period occupation sites (now termed Formative) in the Valley of Mexico, the pyramids at Teotihuacan, Inca masonry and roads, calendrical inscriptions in Columbia, among other findings. His interests were only partially devoted to antiquities, but nonetheless his efforts were the earliest to awaken other students to the world of America's past.

Perhaps the first "American" professional archaeologist was E. George Squier (1821–1888). His initial efforts consisted of a monumental survey of ancient mounds in the eastern United States, *Ancient Monuments of the Mississippi Valley,* coauthored by E. H. Davis and published by the Smithsonian Institution in 1848. The work describes the hundreds of mounds they personally investigated, mapped, and measured, as well as illustrates the artifacts they recovered. Their approach was descriptive and pragmatic without any reliance on conjecture as to origins. Soon after, his work came to the attention of William H. Prescott, the famous historian of the conquests of Mexico and Peru. With Prescott's help Squier was appointed U.S. charge d'affaires in Central America in 1849. He transferred his interests to the antiquities of Central America and later to Peru. Once his assigned duties were taken care of, he set off on an 18-month journey which covered most of Peru, his mission being to describe, photograph, excavate, and survey sites. He was the first to map the massive ancient city of Chan Chan, a project which only today is being completed. Squier's Peruvian book published in 1877, *Peru Illustrated: Incidents of Travel and Exploration in the Land of the Incas,* was the capstone of a distinguished career.

John Lloyd Stephens was a traveler and explorer whose book on Arabia and the Holy Land was a best seller in 1837. He became interested in new fields to explore, and Central America with its reputed stone cities attracted his attention. With Frederick Catherwood, an English architect and draftsman, he landed in British Honduras in 1839. Their goal was the ruined city of Copan, an ancient Mayan city. Their first glimpse of the ancient city is described in *Incidents of Travel in Central America, Chiapas, and Yucatan* (1843):

The massive stone structures before us had little the air of belonging to a city, the intrenchment of which could be broken down by the charge of a single horseman. . . .

The wall was of cut stone, well laid, and in a good state of preservation. We ascended by large stone steps, in some places perfect, and in others thrown down by trees which had grown up between the crevices, and reached a terrace, the form of which it was impossible to make out, from the density of the forest in which it was enveloped. Our guide cleared a way with his machete, and we passed, as it lay half buried in the earth, a large fragment of stone elaborately sculptured, and came to the angle of a structure with steps on the sides, in form and appearance, so far as the trees would enable us to make it out, like the sides of a pyramid. Diverging from the base, and working our way through the thick woods, we came upon a square stone column, about fourteen feet high and three feet on each side, sculptured in very bold relief, and on all four of the sides, from the base to the top. The front was the figure of a man curiously and richly dressed, and the face, evidently a portrait, solemn, stern, and well fitted to excite terror. The back was of a different design, unlike anything we had ever seen before, and the sides were covered with hieroglyphics. This our guide called an "Idol;" and before it, at a distance of three feet, was a large block of stone, also sculptured with figures and emblematical devices, which he called an altar. The sight of this unexpected monument put at rest at once and forever, in our minds, all uncertainty in regard to the character of American antiquities, and gave us the assurance that the objects we were in search of were interesting, not only as the remains of an unknown people, but as works of art, proving, like newly-discovered historical records, that the people who once occupied the continent of America were not savages (Wauchope 1965:80–83).

Equal to and even surpassing the quality of Stephens' prose were the illustrations prepared by Catherwood. In their beauty and clarity they are outstanding, and are my favorite illustrations of archaeological monuments. Photographic in detail, they combine artistic beauty with precise objectivity in such a way that the inscriptions unintelligible to Catherwood nonetheless can be deciphered today. This attention to detail is remarkable, considering that untold numbers of other European trained artists, when presented with the opportunity to paint American aborigines, portrayed them with European physical traits and in some cases even in allegorical scenes drawn from Greek mythology.

The Central American journeys of Stephens and Catherwood, as described in Stephens' books, were popular fare reprinted in a number of different editions. America was becoming aware of its archaeological past. With the pattern of exploration of Central America and Yucatan established by Stephens and Squier, the latter half of the nineteenth century witnessed numerous followers in their footsteps. Their efforts were succeeded by those of Arthur Morelet, Desire Charnay, Alfred P. Maudsley, and Teobert Maler. The jungles kept their secrets well hidden, and repeated exploration was necessary to gradually reveal its wealth of antiquities. The general pattern was the penetration of the jungle in search of a reported ruin which upon occasion was located. The process is still being continued with the most outstanding recent find being the painted temple of Bonampak, located in 1947.

A contrasting approach to Mayan archaeology was that of Edward H. Thompson. He purchased the plantation which included the ruined city of Chichén Itzá, and began its systematic exploration. His outstanding feat was the dredging of the sacred cenote. He recovered quantities of gold ornaments, jade, human skeletal remains, and copal incense. The finds were spectacular in themselves, but of most importance was the fact that Thompson undertook the dredging to determine if the ancient legends of human sacrifice were true; therefore his motives were scientific as well as object oriented.

During the last half of the nineteenth century other areas became of increasing archaeological interest. The sites in the eastern United States received attention with the beginning of full-scale excavations of some mound groups. Frederick W. Putnam (1839–1915), curator of the Peabody Museum of American Archaeology and Anthropology at Harvard, excavated the Turner Mound group of Moundsville, Ohio, as well as numerous other Ohio mounds. He was also personally responsible for the preservation of Serpent Mound in Ohio as a state park. The wealth of artifacts in these mounds stimulated extensive excavation for the recovery of effigy stone pipes, cutout decorations of mica and copper, engraved shell, and thousands of fresh water pearls. Men such as Gerard Fowke and W. K. Moorehead devoted their life energies to such excavations.

Pioneering in another direction led to the discovery of further evidences of man's past in the Americas. Geographical exploration of the American Southwest received major impetus from the Hayden Survey, organized by Ferdinand V. Hayden, Professor of Geology at the University of Pennsylvania and the first director of the Geographical Surveys, later to become the U.S. Geological Survey. William Henry Jackson, pioneer photographer of the American West, began an association in 1870 with Hayden's survey of the Yellowstone country. Four years later, guided by a local prospector, Jackson and his men visited Mancos Canyon in southwestern Colorado and became the first men in recent history to explore the ancient Puebloan cliff dwellings. Back in Washington, after Jackson's return, Professor Hayden viewed the photographs and descriptions of the ruins with interest. He dispatched Jackson back to the Southwest in 1875 and again in 1876 and 1877. The result was the constant acquisition of information on these cliff houses in a scientific manner. The knowledge gained was transmitted to the Smithsonian Institution and Bureau of American Ethnology, two pioneer scientific institutions concerned with American antiquities.

Ernest Ingersoll, correspondent for the *New York Tribune,* was with Jackson in 1874 at the time of the first discovery of a cliff dwelling. Ingersoll's article bears repeating.

There seven hundred measured feet above the valley, perched on a little ledge only just large enough to hold it, was a two-story house made of finely cut sandstone, each block about 14 by 6 inches, accurately fitted and set in mortar now harder than the stone itself. The floor was the ledge upon which it rested, and the roof of the overhanging rock. There were three rooms upon the ground floor, each one 6 by 9 feet, with partition walls of faced stone. Between the stories was originally a wood floor, traces of which still remained, as did also the cedar sticks set in the wall over the windows and door . . . Each of the stories was six feet in height, and all the rooms, upstairs and down, were nicely plastered and painted what now looks a dull brick-red color, with a white band along the floor like a base-board. There was a low doorway from the ledge into the lower story, and another above, showing that the upper chamber was entered from without. The windows were large, square apertures, with no indication of any glazing or shutters. They commanded a view of the whole valley for many miles. Near the house several convenient little niches in the rock were built into better shape, as though they had been used as cupboards or caches; and behind it a semi-circular wall inclosing the angle of the house and cliff formed a water-reservoir holding two and a half hogsheads ... Searching further in this vicinity we found remains of many houses on the same ledge, and some perfect ones above it quite inaccessible. The rocks also bore some inscriptions—unintelligible hieroglyphics for the most part ... All these facts were carefully photographed and recorded (Quoted in Deuel 1967).

It was not until 1888 that the nearby, more spectacular ruins in the Mesa Verde were discovered. Richard Wetherill, a local rancher, accompanied by his cousin, was pursuing stray cattle when they came upon the remains of an ancient village, now part of Mesa Verde National Park. Their name "Cliff Palace," was appropriate, since the site contained 200 rooms and 23 kivas. The Wetherills found Spruce Tree House the following day. Public recognition of their finds revived interest in Southwestern ruins.

During the 1890s numerous eastern museums sent expeditions to the Southwest to locate and excavate ruins and bring their findings back for exhibit. Men such as A. F. Bandelier, J. W. Fewkes, W. H. Holmes, Walter Hough, Victor Mindeleff, George H. Pepper, Byron Cummings, and Baron Gustav Nordenskiold began the systematic recovery of archaeological information which provided the background of our present knowledge of Southwestern archaeology.

Archaeology in the Americas does not seem to have had the long period of intellectual development that it experienced in Europe. In part this was due to transatlantic intellectual contacts; for example, John Lloyd Stephens had traveled in the Holy Land and Egypt prior to his American explorations and undoubtedly had discussed his interests with other Europeans intrigued with remains of the past. On the other hand, the American remains were of a different character. Those of most interest at an early date were spectacular architectural monuments, impossible to ignore, and as was the case with the mounds of Ohio, sufficient in themselves to stimulate excavation simply to satisfy one's curiosity. Less spectacular remains such as Stone, Bronze, or Iron Age implements and paleolithic hand axes found in European river gravels, required greater intellectual skills in order to interpret their relevance to human prehistory. Also of importance to the development of American archaeology was the influence of William H. Prescott. With Prescott as a guide, later investigators had little difficulty relating their archaeological findings in Mexico and Peru to the ancient civilizations of the Aztec and Inca. In fact, some of these associations were in error, but nonetheless they had at hand a ready-made intellectual framework into which they could fit archaeological findings.

Another major intellectual development occurred nearly simultaneously in both England and the United States. The writings of E. B. Tylor and Lewis H. Morgan laid the groundwork for the science of anthropology—a discipline concerned with the development of cultural patterns as manifest in all human societies, past and present. In Tylor's *Anthropology,* the first text by that name, he states:

The student who seeks to understand how mankind came to be as they are, and to live as they do, ought first to know clearly whether men are newcomers on the earth, or old inhabitants. Did they appear with their various races and ways of life ready-made or were these shaped by the long, slow growth of ages? (1881).

On the American side of the Atlantic, Morgan published in 1877 *Ancient Society or Researches in the Lines of Human Progress from Savagery through Barbarism to Civilization.* In that work he offered the following definitions:

I. Lower Status of Savagery
This period commenced with the infancy of the human race, and may be said to have ended with the acquisition of a fish subsistence and of a knowledge of the use of fire. Mankind were then living in their original restricted habitat, and subsisting upon fruits and nuts. The commencement of articulate speech belongs to this period. . . .

II. Middle Status of Savagery
It commenced with the acquisition of a fish subsistence and a knowledge of the use of fire, and ended with the invention of the bow and arrow. Mankind, while in this condition, spread from their original habitat over the greater portion of the earth's surface. . . .

III. Upper Status of Savagery
It commenced with the invention of the bow and arrow, and ended with the invention of the art of pottery. . . .

IV. Lower Status of Barbarism
The invention or practice of the art of pottery, all things considered, is probably the most effective and conclusive test that can be selected to fix a boundary line, necessarily arbitrary, between savagery and barbarism . . . All such tribes, then, as never attained to the art of pottery will be classed as savages, and those possessing this art but who never attained a phonetic alphabet and the use of writing will be classed as barbarians. . . .

V. Middle Status of Barbarism
It commenced with the domestication of animals in the Eastern hemisphere, and in the Western with cultivation by irrigation and with the use of adobe-brick and stone in architecture. Its termination may be fixed with the invention of the process of smelting iron ore. . . .

VI. Upper Status of Barbarism
It commenced with the manufacture of iron, and ended with the invention of a phonetic alphabet, and the use of writing in literary composition. Here civilization begins. . . .

VII. Status of Civilization
It commenced, as stated, with the use of a phonetic alphabet and the production of literary records, and divides into Ancient and Modern. As an equivalent, hieroglyphical writing upon stone may be admitted.

With Morgan's classification, which was also utilized in modified form by Tylor, we have developed a theoretical scheme encompassing the entire cultural development of mankind, whether or not the specific culture being studied made tools of stone, iron, bronze, or some other substance. The fledgling scientific discipline of anthropology provided for the first time an intellectual framework relative to which all antiquities could be classified and understood. Thus by the end of the nineteenth century, archaeology as a discipline possessed full-time professional practitioners in both the Old and New World. A variety of kinds of prehistoric and historic remains of past societies had been discovered, and some of these had been sufficiently studied so that their general development and chronological position was understood. In addition, there were in existence the general evolutionary schemes of Thomsen and Worsaae, Tylor and Morgan, Darwin, and Lyell, which aided the archaeologists in understanding their findings. Specific, archaeologically developed theoretical schemes and new methods for the recovery of data from ancient sites were to come in the twentieth century.

REFERENCES

Belzoni, G., 1820, *Narrative of the Operations and Recent Discoveries within the Pyramids, Temples, Tombs, and Excavations in Egypt and Nubia,* 2 vols. London: J. Murray.

Clark, G., 1969, *Archaeology and Society: Reconstructing the Prehistoric Past.* New York: Barnes & Noble.

Coe, M. D., 1967, *Mexico.* New York: Praeger.

Cottrell, L., (ed.), 1960, *The Concise Encyclopedia of Archaeology.* New York: Hawthorn Books.

Daniel, G., 1967, *The Origins and Growth of Archaeology.* New York: Crowell. (Paperback ed., Baltimore: Penguin.)

Deuel, L., 1967, *Conquistadors without Swords: Archaeologists in the Americas.* New York: St. Martin's.

Harrison, W. H., 1838, *A Discourse on the Aborigines of the Valley of Ohio.* Columbus: Historical Society of Ohio.

Hole, F., and R. Heizer, 1969, *An Introduction to Prehistoric Archeology,* 2d ed. New York: Holt, Rinehart and Winston, Inc.

———, 1973, *An Introduction to Prehistoric Archeology,* 3d ed., rev. New York: Holt, Rinehart and Winston, Inc.

Hutton, James, 1785, *Theory of the Earth.* London: Cadell, Jr., and Davies.

Lyell, C., 1872, *Principles of Geology,* 11th ed., 2 vols. New York: Appleton.

Morgan, L. H., 1877, *Ancient Society or Researches in the Lives of Human Progress from Savagery through Barbarism to Civilization.* New York.

Squier, E. G., 1877, *Peru Illustrated. Incidents of Travel and Exploration in the Land of the Incas.* New York: Hurst and Co.

Stephens, J. L., 1843, *Incidents of Travel in Central America, Chiapas, and Yucatan,* 2 vols. New York: Harper & Row. (Reprint of one volume, *Incidents of Travel in Yucatan,* with introduction by V. von Hagen (ed.). Norman: University of Oklahoma Press, 1962.)

Tylor, E. B., 1881, *Anthropology.* London.

Von Humboldt, A., 1814, *Researches Concerning the Institutions and Monuments of the Ancient Inhabitants of America, with Descriptions and Views of Some of the Most Striking Scenes in the Cordillieras,* 2 vols. London: Longmans. (French title cited in text.)

Wauchope, R., 1965, *They Found the Buried Cities.* Chicago: The University of Chicago Press.

Worsaae, J. J. A., 1849, *Primeval Antiquities of Denmark.* London.

2

The Nature of
Archaeological
Data

Archaeological data includes those items which were manufactured by the members of a past society, those items which they collected and used, any alterations in the natural landscape resulting from man's activities, the bodies of the former inhabitants, and the relationships between any of these factors that are the result of human activity. We will discuss each of these in turn. We may further divide archaeological data into a number of categories based on other considerations. For example, stone tools are almost indestructable and therefore are commonly found, while perishable items are found only under the most favorable circumstances of preservation. Also of concern is whether the particular prehistoric society had cities, towns, isolated farmsteads, or campsites and whether they practiced irrigation, built temples or pyramids, or occupied caves. Because of these inherent differences in archaeological data, it is tempting to lose sight of the larger goals of culture history and become interested in the nature of specific items. What we must always bear in mind is that the archaeological data we find are evidences of the past cultural practices of a particular society. No matter how simple or how complex these remains are, they can and should be utilized as a means of inferring past patterns of human behavior. This point of view, probably more than any other characteristic, serves to distinguish between the professional archaeologist and the amateur or antiquarian; the former is interested in antiquities as sources of information, while the latter is more interested in the objects themselves.

What are the typical objects, and what do they reveal about the past? Stone tools are the most common items, exceeded in frequency by pottery after it was invented. Probably next in frequency are bone tools, with wooden tools, cordage, basketry, gourds, and other perishable items less common. In most sites, even more common than the tools are bones, shells, plant parts, and other food remains. Perhaps next in importance are structural remains; these vary from the least permanent—slight indentations in the ground sometimes with an associated firepit or post holes—to multistory buildings of cut stone. The grouping of individual structures or the clustering of contiguous rooms can be segregated into types, and these types then form the basis of inferences as to family, band, or tribal size and social organization.

In addition to the objects themselves, there is another order of data which we may obtain by precisely recording the association of the objects one to another. Associational data of this type provides a means whereby we may infer that several separate objects which do not fit together, at least in form, were utilized together in a particular cultural practice. A modern example would be the finding together of a tin can and a can opener. Their occurrence together strengthens our belief that they were used together.

There are other situations in which archaeological inferences may be made. For example, large stones occurring in fine grained lacustrine sediments which obviously could not have been placed there by water action or other geological processes may be the result of human activity, even though the stones themselves show no modification, evidence of use, or pattern. Obviously, human footprints or handprints constitute another category of data.

Finally, we rely in great part on data recorded by scientists skilled in other disciplines. Geologists, paleontologists, botanists, palynologists, geochronologists, and others study the natural as well as cultural materials recovered from archaeological sites. Their results aid our understanding of the age of the sites as well as the nature of the environment that man was occupying at the time, and give us clues as to how man had modified and adapted to his environment.

All archaeological data is dependent upon the degree of its preservation in terms of weathering, corrosion or other modification of the objects. In addition, there may have been alteration in the physical association of the objects one to the other, brought about through erosion and other geological processes. Before we can make valid interpretations about the nature of archaeological sites, we must have some knowledge of geological processes in order to properly attribute the association of objects to either cultural or natural causes.

Another generalization is that archaeological remains are not randomly distributed over the earth's surface; they are concentrated in those areas which formerly provided the optimum conditions for human occupation. In addition, with the refinements in cultural technology that man had effected through time, he was able to gradually expand into more hostile or marginal environments.

Finally, we must concede that our knowledge is in part limited by the extent of prior archaeological investigations. During the combined Prehistoric Expedition's work in 1963–1965 (part of the Aswan Dam Salvage program), we found hundreds of sites in the Egyptian Sahara in an area which today is uninhabited. Until our work the area had not been investigated for archaeological evidence. There is no doubt that many such areas which are archaeologically unknown at present will reveal major evidence of past occupation once they are studied.

ARTIFACTS

Stone Tools

Implements of stone are one of the most common cultural items found on sites. Their study is of importance to the archaeologist in a number of ways. They occur throughout the archaeological record from early to late, and for large numbers of sites they are practically the only cultural material preserved. Stone tools may be classified as: those pieces of stone that were modified to a specific form by man prior to use and those that were modified by use. Those stones that were imported to sites by man but show no evidence of use have been termed *manuports*.

Tool use is not limited to man but is also a characteristic of some anthropoids as well as the sea otter and a few other animals. In addition, naturally broken stones can resemble man-made implements; thus the identification of valid early man-made tools is difficult. Toward the end of the nineteenth century this problem resulted in the formulation of the concept of an "Eolithic" or Dawn Stone Age. This idea was first published by an Englishman, Prestwich, in 1891 as a means of explaining the presence of peculiarly shaped flints found in English beach gravels. The "Eolithic" was considered to represent a phase in human cultural evolution represented by the simplest of all possible tools made from broken flints. The idea has not stood the test of time for several reasons. The eoliths were found to be indistinguishable from flints naturally broken by geologic processes such as wave action on a beach and the rolling of stones in stream beds (Fig. 2–1). Another part of the concept was the belief that the simpler the tool was in form the older it must be. This point of view has subsequently been proved erroneous through use of absolute dating methods and the comparison of stone tools made by modern aborigines with archaeological industries. Finally, "proof" that such stones of nondiagnostic

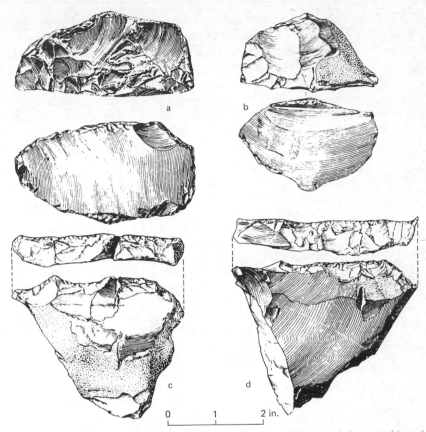

Fig. 2-1 "Eoliths" and accidents of nature: a. and c. are eoliths; b. and d. were chipped by natural agencies. (Oakley 1972:Fig. 2.)

form were used as artifacts can be demonstrated only by their occurrence on a verifiable living floor, a place where the splintered food bones and other evidences of human occupation also occur.

While the "Eolithic" cannot be proved to have existed, we can at least examine the earliest evidence definitely attributed to man. At present the earliest stone industry known is from Olduvai Gorge in East Africa. Dated by the Potassium-argon radioactivity decay method at 1.75 million years of age, this industry has been named the Oldowan by its finders, the Leakeys. What is remarkable about the Oldowan stone industry is that it is not simple; most of the implements are battered pebbles and utilized flakes which can be divided into 10 or more distinct form categories. There may have been an even earlier, simpler use of stones which has not been located to date; so the search goes on.

Stone tools are frequently the only remains that have been preserved. As a result they have been subjected to detailed analysis to determine, if possible, how they were made and what functions they performed. Critical to such studies is the distinction between naturally broken stones and those that were deliberately broken by men to be manufactured into tools. This is, I believe, the most confusing factor in archaeology for the nonarchaeologist to comprehend. The most common question people ask me is, "How can you *tell* that this piece of stone is a tool?" By way of answer, I would like to quote from Kenneth Oakley's *Man the Tool-Maker,* for I believe he has clarified the situation more than any other author. Within this quotation the figure references have been changed to correspond with the figures in this chapter Oakley (1956:9–12).

Wherever it was available to him, Stone Age man made tools of flint or flint-like rock. Flint and similar hard homogeneous rocks break somewhat after the fashion of glass. A sharp blow directed vertically at a point on the surface of a slab of glass or flint knocks out a solid cone (resembling a limpet-shell in shape), with the apex or origin at the point of impact (Fig. 2–2a). Fracture of this type is called conchoidal (from Κόγχη, Greek for shell). When a blow is directed obliquely near the edge of a slab of material which breaks conchoidally, a chip or *flake* is detached (Fig. 2–2b, b'). The fractured face of the flake looks like a musselshell; it has a half-formed *cone of percussion* at the point of impact, passing into a salient, or swelling, called the *positive bulb of percussion,* followed by low concentric ripples. There is a corresponding rippled hollow, or *flake-scar,* with *negative bulb of percussion,* on the parent lump, or core (Fig. 2–2c). The bulb of percussion on a large flake struck by a sharp blow commonly shows a miniature scar or *eraillure,* near the centre (Fig. 2–2b').

One of the chief accidental agencies by which stones are flaked is thermal change. Rapid changes of temperature cause unequal expansion or contraction of the surface of the stone or rock relative to its interior. In deserts, for example, the exposed surfaces of some types of rock are continually flaking as a result of the difference between the day and night temperature. In cold regions flakes are commonly split off by frost—the outer layer of the stone expanding through the freezing of absorbed water. A flake or flake-scar due to frost or other thermal fracture is easily recognized, for the surface of fracture has either a roughish, blank appearance, or shows ripples concentric about a central point (the stresses set up by the thermal change being concentrated *within* the outer layer). On the other hand, the surface of a fracture due to a sharp external blow appears clean-cut, and shows a definite bulb of percussion with faint radial fissures and ripples originating at a point on the edge of the flake or flake-scar. Flakes split from a lump of flint by frost action are often round in outline and are commonly referred to as "potlids" (Fig. 2–2d). When the residual frost-pitted lump (Fig. 2–2e) happens to be of appropriate shape it is easily mistaken for an implement or weapon; but its natural origin is usually obvious on closer inspection. Thermal changes sometimes cause flint to break like starch, for example into prisms resembling blade-cores (Fig. 2–2f–h), but the lines of this form of thermal fracture have probably been determined in advance by strains set up by slow internal shrinkage. Stones splintered by fire, or faceted by sandstorms (ventifacts or dreikanters) are occasionally mistaken for the work of man (Fig. 2–2j).

Flakes struck by man show a well-defined bulb of percussion. The geologist H. B. Woodward remarked in 1878: "I was astounded to pick out of the stone bed of the Norwich Crag a flake containing a good bulb of percussion." He evidently believed that he was on the track of Pliocene Man. However, heavy stones hurled by the sea against

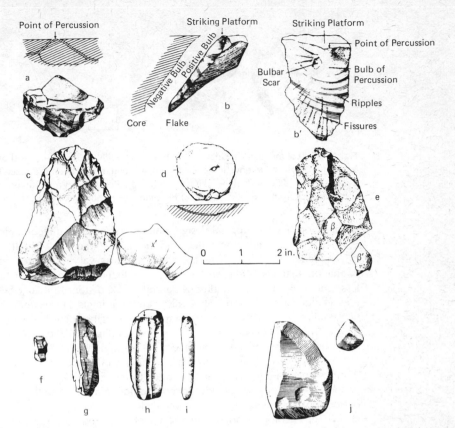

Fig. 2–2 Characteristics of humanly worked flints and natural forms sometimes mistaken for artifacts: *a.* complete cone of percussion in flint; *b., b'.* flint flake struck by man (two views); *c.* flint handaxe (Palaeolithic core tool), and one of the waste flakes (at χ = flake scar with negative bulb of percussion, χ' = waste flake with positive bulb); *d.* rounded spall of flint ("potlid") split from nodule by frost action; *e.* lump of flint pitted by the intersecting scars (at β), of frost spalls (at β'); *f.* shrinkage prism of starch. *g.* flint showing prismatic, or starch fracture; *h.* prismatic core of volcanic glass from which blades (such as *i.*) have been struck, Chalcolithic, Crete; *j.* ventifacts of dreikanter type, pebbles of jasper faceted by windblown sand, Carnac, Brittany. (Oakley 1972:Fig. 4.)

flints firmly fixed in a beach commonly detach flakes showing bulbs; while bulbar flakes are produced also by the powerful pressure of one stone against another in a gravel which is disturbed by an overriding glacier, or by subsidence on a disintegrating bedrock, or by cliff-falls. But usually the flakes produced in such ways show flatter and more diffuse bulbs of percussion than those produced by purposeful blows.

A fair proportion of the flakes struck by man, even in primitive industries, have their edges dressed. But the edges of thin pieces of stone are very liable to become chipped through friction against other stones, such as occurs in soil-creep (solifluxion), in torrent action, or when stony deposits are caught up in the bottom layer of an ice-sheet. As a general rule naturally chipped flints are easily distinguished from the works

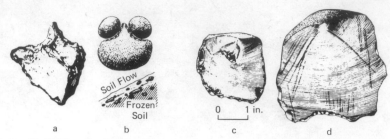

Fig. 2-3 "Eoliths" and accidents of nature: *a.* "eolith" from river gravel at Piltdown, Sussex; *b.* diagram to illustrate how an "eolith" such as *a* could have been produced by soil-creep under periglacial conditions; *c.* flint flake from Sub-Crag Stone Bed, West Runton, Norfolk; *d.* flake of siliceous rock from glacial desposits of Permian Age in South Africa. (Oakley 1972:Fig. 3.)

of man, for they lack logical design, flake-scars occur in uneconomical profusion, the edges have a bruised appearance, and the flake-surfaces are usually scratched.

Frequently, also, there are signs (such as varying degrees of weathering or patination) that the flake-scars have been produced at several different dates. Nevertheless, under exceptional conditions naturally flaked stones occur which, if seen out of their geological context, might be mistaken for artifacts. For example, large numbers of broken flints with neatly chipped scraper-like margins occur in the Bullhead Bed under nearly 30 feet of Eocene sand at Grays in Essex (Fig. 2–1b, d). The flint nodules in this bed touch one another and they have been crushed together during the slow subsidence of the Eocene formation, which rests on a surface of Chalk which is undergoing solution. Again, stones flaked by glacial action into forms showing a remarkable resemblance to artifacts have been found in Pleistocene boulder clays, and in the Permian glacial beds of South Africa, some 180 million years old (Fig. 2–3d).

Thus geologists are inclined to adopt a cautious attitude with regard to crudely chipped stones resembling artifacts, particularly if they occur in situations where natural flaking cannot be ruled out. By contrast even the most crudely chipped pieces of quartz found with the remains of Peking Man in the Choukontien caves can be accepted as implements merely on account of their situation.

Identification of a stone fragment as being man-made is only the first step in the analysis. Subsequent steps include their classification into the major categories of tools and debitage or waste. The tools are then divided into form classes—core tools and flake tools—which are then subdivided in terms of morphology: overall shape, shape of edge, type and amount of retouch, and so forth. In some cases such forms are given specific names which imply a function, for example, knife, scraper, and point. In other cases the name is descriptive, for example, truncated flake or denticulate, without function being implied. The classification of stone tools by type provides one means whereby we can describe specific assemblages, for example, 14.4 percent of the tools from a particular site are side scrapers. Comparison of the tool types from other sites helps determine the degree of similarity between site collections.

Another procedure is to identify the specific manufacturing techniques that were used and to determine their order. These technological studies provide another method of describing ancient cultural practices. Through such studies archaeologists attempt to reconstruct every manufacturing step from the quarrying of the original raw material to the completion of the finished artifact.

Pottery

Pottery appears much later in the cultural record than tools of stone, wood, bone, or shell. Where pottery is present, no other artifacts are as informative, with the exception of written records; even in this field the first writing was on clay tablets. Different kinds of information provided by pottery include the details of the manufacturing processes and the sources of clay utilized. Design styles provide insight into cultural beliefs as well as a means of chronological ordering, for once invented, pottery was such a flexible media that its form and decoration were constantly being modified. Since continuous changes through time are characteristic of pottery, we can identify archaeological periods on the basis of these changes. Another outstanding characteristic of pottery is its near indestructability. Whole vessels are fragile and easily broken, but once broken, the smaller potsherds are likely to be preserved, since they can be destroyed only by severe erosion. Fire changes only their color and they are almost impervious to chemical decay.

   The characteristics of pottery are numerous; in some cases as many as 60 or 70 separate attributes can be identified within a specific assemblage of potsherds. The basic features include shape, method of manufacture, and base color. Either the coiling method, the paddle and anvil method, or the wheel is used in the manufacture. Base color is determined by the clay and whether it was fired in a reducing or oxidizing atmosphere. The base color may be covered with a thin wash of clay, called a slip, or it may be painted with a variety of colors. Decoration may further be added by pinching, punching, incising, engraving, and the addition of applique (small pieces of clay pressed on). Pottery may also be cast in molds. In some cases, such as the Mochica culture of Peru, most of what we know about their past cultural practices has been learned from studying their pottery.

Bone Artifacts

Artifacts of bone are less informative than pottery or stone because usually they are utilitarian objects of simple form. However, bone is a durable material, and because of man's early reliance on game animals for food, it was easily available. The earliest presumed bone tools are those termed the *Osteodonto-keratic culture*. These are objects of bone, teeth, and horn that, according to their describer, Raymond Dart, were used as simple tools by the earliest hominids, the Australopithecines of South Africa. In most cultures items of bone are of relative unimportance; however in a few cultures, such as the Eskimo, where other materials suitable for tool manufacture are rare, bone was widely used, replacing stone or wood as a manufacturing material. Bone, of course, can also be carved, and it is in bone that we perceive one of man's earliest artistic expressions, small carvings of humans and animals in the Upper Paleolithic period some 20,000–30,000 years ago. Bone tools can also be studied to determine what functions they performed and the manufacturing methods employed—cutting, grinding, engraving, and so on. Tools of bone are frequently combined with portions of wood or stone to form composite tools. In normal instances bone tools are small, usually of a size to be conveniently hand held. Large bones are used rarely; although, for example, whalebones were used for construction materials in Eskimo houses. The most common occurrence of bone is as food debris.

Wooden Objects

Tools of wood were undoubtedly among the very first implements to be used by men. We know, for example, that the simplest form of tool using by modern apes consists of the picking up or tearing off of limbs, stripping off the leaves and twigs, and then using the stick as a club, missile, or item to poke into holes or dig. There can be no doubt such tools have been in use since the dawn of culture. Unfortunately, wood is a perishable material and these early tools have not been preserved. To my knowledge, the earliest wooden implements found to date are from Kalambo Falls in Rhodesia and are about 55,000 years of age. They have been identified as digging sticks, a throwing stick, and the point of a spear (Cole 1965: 158). Those specimens were recovered from a waterlogged level where bacterial decay was inhibited. The other major depositional environment where wood may be preserved are dry caves. Any environment which is alternately subjected to wetting and drying will result in decay of wood and other perishable materials. Such decay is a major limitation to archaeology because most environments are of this type and few environments are either waterlogged or extremely dry. One other technique for recovering the form of wooden objects is to make a plaster cast. In rare circumstances while digging, you encounter holes in the soil which are the result of a piece of wood having rotted away. Usually such holes are postholes, but occasionally they are the result of decay of wooden artifacts. The most famous such find was the ancient Sumerian harp which Sir Leonard Woolley recovered by pouring plaster into the holes (Fig. 2–4). Imagine his delight after excavation of the hardened plaster cast to find attached to the plaster the metal ornaments that had originally decorated the harp.

Most wooden items were either simple tools or the hafts of tools such as spears, knives, and axes. It is only within the last few thousand years that major constructions of wood, such as ships, forts, houses, and pile villages, were built. In rare instances, examples of these have been recovered archaeologically. The Sutton Hoo ship (Fig. 2–5) can be reconstructed from its impression in the earth, and the warship Vasa, which sunk on its maiden voyage, has been

Fig. 2–4 Reconstruction of Sumerian harp found at Ur achieved by pouring plaster of paris down holes left from the rotting away of the wooden harp frame. (Hole and Heizer 1973:105.)

salvaged. The Swiss Lake dwellings are another example of preserved structures of wood. The most outstanding recovery of ancient furniture is from the tomb of the Egyptian Pharoah Tutankhamen (Fig. 2–6).

One of the most important uses of wood in archaeology is in dating. Radiocarbon analysis is possible with both wood and charcoal. Even more impressive is the fact that in certain areas pieces of wood or charcoal with more than 25 annual rings can be correlated with a master chronology, and thereby the individual specimens can be dated to the exact year in which the last ring was deposited. The method has its limitations because only certain species of trees produce distinctive annual rings. A further qualification is that the regional climate must possess fluctuations in annual rainfall which are reflected in the differential widths of growth in the annual rings. If these conditions are present, then it is possible to work out a master chronology. The

Fig. 2–5 Excavation of the ancient ship at Sutton Hoo, England. The ship was found in 1939 and dates to the seventh century A.D. (Trustees of the British Museum (Natural History) 1959.)

best known area for tree ring studies is the American Southwest where it originated. However, it has also been attempted in the American Plains, the North American Arctic, Egypt, Turkey, New Zealand, and Chile.

Shell Objects

Items of shell are rare in early sites because they do not seem to have been important to Paleolithic man. Later peoples used shells for ornaments, such as beads, pendants, and bracelets. The utilitarian use of shells seems to have been a late development, with shells being used for cutting implements, horns, fish hooks, and occasionally as currency. Shells occur in great frequency in many sites as food debris. While unaltered and thus not artifacts, they provide much information about prehistoric diet.

Other Materials

A wide variety of other materials have been utilized by ancient cultures. These include pearls, pitch, amber, glass, precious stones, quartz crystals, mica, and many other exotic and unusual materials. Foremost in importance among these is metal because it is malleable and may be hammered or cast into any form.

Fig. 2–6 Wooden furnishings from the tomb of the Pharaoh, Tutankhamen. (Photographs by Harry Burton, the Metropolitan Museum of Art.)

Metal is also fairly durable. It will rust or corrode, but in many cases such decay has not completely destroyed the item, and through use of specialized techniques these items may be recovered and restored.

TYPES OF SITES

The recovery of individual specimens is only part of the archaeologist's concern. The larger context in which the items were found is especially important, since the sites are the remains of ancient communities and specialized use areas. The *site* is the basic unit of study of interest to the archaeologist. He attempts to learn everything possible about the particular site, its size, type, plan, the architectural style of the buildings, relationships that existed between units of the site, the position of every artifact recovered, and lastly the relationships of that site to the local environment and similar sites in the region.

Types of sites are myriad; however, there are only a few major categories. The largest subdivisions are those termed *open sites* and *cave sites.* Open sites occur on the surface of the natural landscape. Cave sites pertain to those caves or rock shelters that were used as occupation sites by men. Open sites are subdivided into lesser categories: sherd areas, killsites, campsites, quarry sites, and workshops.

A *sherd area* is any area in which potsherds occur on the surface. In some cases buried structures may be present. In other cases, the evidence of prior occupation is entirely on the surface, either because the site was not occupied for long or because subsequent erosion has removed the soil. Surface sites also may have architectural remains which vary from the smallest storage bin to elaborate cities.

A *killsite* is any location at which an animal was killed and butchered. The stampede was a favorite hunting technique of ancient man. The animals were either driven into some type of natural trap, a swamp, pond, creek, or draw, or were driven over a cliff. The result consists of a welter of bones of dismembered carcasses on the top of the pile, with more articulated and occasionally whole carcasses toward the bottom of the bone pile. The ambush was another hunting technique. The ancient hunters hid near waterholes, salt licks, game trails, or other natural points of animal concentration. As the animals approached they were speared, clubbed, or shot, and then butchered on the spot. The pit trap was another favorite hunting technique.

A *campsite* is any place where the inhabitants lived for any length of time, prepared and ate their food, manufactured tools, and carried out everyday activities. Frequently, killsites occur at some distance from the campsite, with the meat being carried back to the base camp for consumption. Occasionally the people camped at the kill and thus we have both kinds of evidence at the same place. Both open sites and cave sites were used as campsites or habitation sites. However, it is rare that we find that a kill took place within a cave.

A *quarry site* is the place at which suitable stone for the manufacture of tools was acquired. Frequently preliminary shaping of the selected stone was accomplished at the quarry. A *workshop* is somewhat different in nature; here the tools were manufactured from the selected quarry material. In some cases workshops occur in isolation; in other cases they occur at the quarry or on the campsite. The archaeologist identifies the kinds of activities carried out at each site by means of his detailed analyses of its particular components. He studies the percentages of each type of stone tool, the frequency and type of waste flakes, the occurrence of fire hearths and food bones, and so forth.

Sites with architecture form one of our largest categories. An inclusive classification of all possible kinds of structures is beyond the scope of this book; however, it is possible to describe the more common types of units and the ways in which they are grouped together in communities.

Individual house units are the most common architectural elements. Their size varies from a tiny hut or single room to extended longhouses up to 100 feet in length by 30 feet in width. The size of the individual house unit is dependent in part upon the environment. For example, the availability of certain building materials may limit house size. A second variable concerns the social organization of the group building the houses. Those with a nuclear family structure—husband, wife, and children—most likely would build smaller units than a group with an extended family structure, which could include grandparents, aunts, uncles, and cousins, in addition to the nuclear family.

House types include the following:

1. Pithouses are partially subterranean or semisubterranean rooms of either round or square form with walls of poles or logs and either a flat or beehive shaped roof made of logs.

2. Masonry structures may be of any form, although a rectangular form is most common. Walls frequently have window and door openings with stone or wooden lintels. Roofs are commonly of logs or planks, but stone slabs are also used. Most masonry units are above ground, although a few specialized structures, such as kivas, or chamber graves, are subterranean. Masonry units also are easily added onto or subdivided by the addition of cross walls; as a result masonry is one of the major building materials used in larger structures. A major variable in masonry structures is the pattern of the stonework itself. Walls may be with or without mortar; they may or may not be plastered. In some cases the walls are layered, with cut stone facing on the interior and exterior and a core of loose rubble. Although masonry units are usually well preserved, the archaeologist has to reconstruct their original height and configuration, for usually all wooden beams have decayed, walls have collapsed, and the cut stone facing may have been robbed for use in later buildings.

3. Walls of adobe may be made either of sun-dried mud brick or of puddled or poured courses of mud called tapia. The bricks may be of almost any form, contrary to what you might have thought; they are usually rectangular but may also be round, conical, or shaped like a loaf of bread. The ample

use of mortar gives form to the structure apart from the actual shape of the bricks. Tapia walls are laid up in courses with the mud being patted into shape. The mud is put up in as dry a form as possible and can be piled to a height of a foot to 15 inches. Above that height the weight of the wet mud causes it to slump. Therefore each course must be allowed to dry before the next course can be added. The use of adobe permits the construction of units of any form. Remodeling is easy; all that is necessary is to cut a hole for a new window or door. In dry environments adobe is an excellent building material because, if kept dry, it will last for hundreds of years.

4. Wood is a common building material; wherever wood is present it is used, even in the Arctic where the only available wood is driftwood. Houses of wood are most often of logs, but plank houses are also common. An interesting variant is the earth lodge, consisting of a beehive-shaped unit of logs covered over with grass and earth. Wood is more often used for single-family dwellings than for communal structures, although such were used by the Iroquois and tribes of the Northwest Coast in British Columbia. The Swiss lake dwellings represent one of the most elaborate uses of wood, with the entire village being built on wooden pilings.

5. Jacal, also called wattle and daub, is a building type consisting of walls made of poles interwoven with twigs or grass and then plastered with mud. Typical of dry climates, jacal is most common in individual family units because for larger structures it is not particularly strong. Another common usage is for dividing walls within structures.

6. Thatch houses are common the world over. Made of grass, palm fronds, or other pliable material woven over a pole framework, they represent one of man's most frequent house types. Unfortunately such structures are almost never preserved. What may be found archaeologically are the scattered remains of the poles and thatch if they had been preserved—usually by having been burned, since charcoal is resistant to decay.

Normally house units are grouped near each other or are physically connected. Such a grouping consists of the settlement type or prehistoric community. Modern archaeologists are interested in settlement patterns, for the nature of the specific communities and their distribution within the natural environment provide information concerning social organization as well as the environmental adaptation of the specific prehistoric culture. The basic types of settlements include: individual houses, small house clusters, small agglutinated villages (in which the individual rooms or houses are tied together into one unit), nucleated villages (in which groups of houses or housing units are united with streets or other connective devices), towns (larger nucleated settlements), and finally cities (those urban centers which have a high population as well as reciprocal relationships with outlying communities). However, in fact these community types are arbitrary divisions of a continuum.

Special use areas are set apart on the basis of function. They may occur within the confines of a village, town, or city, adjacent to these, or occur separately. Such use areas include cemeteries, fields, terraces, roads, wells,

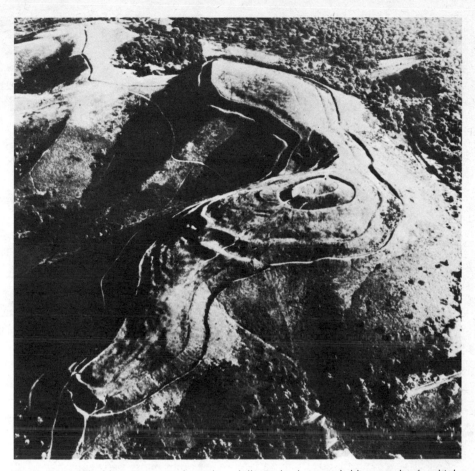

Fig. 2–7 Herefordshire Beacon in the Malvern hills, England; a remarkable example of multiple occupation. The hill fort dates back to the Iron Age, later it had a medieval castle built upon it, and the hill top was finally adapted as a bailey in the Middle Ages. (Charles-Picard 1972:333)

irrigation canals, sacred places and fortresses (Fig. 2–7). Sacred places range from areas where offerings are deposited (where spirits reside) to complex ceremonial centers. Temples, residences of priests, altars, and other sacred structures may be grouped within a restricted area of the community or may also be built as separate centers.

Miscellaneous site types include rock faces decorated by pecking or painting. Termed *petroglyphs* and *pictographs,* this rock art is commonly found where suitable natural rock exposures occur.

Another category consists of sites that occur underwater. The sites are of many different types and occur underwater for a variety of reasons. Such sites include shipwrecks, sites on fossil beaches now submerged by a rising sea level, wells or springs into which offerings were tossed, and situations where earthquakes caused a local change in sea level. Underwater sites are classed

Fig. 2–8 Evidence of human burials preserved as stains in the soil. (De Laet 1958:Fig. 17.)

together because a similar set of excavation techniques is used in their study rather than because they are similar in nature.

Finally, archaeological data include human burials; physical type as evidenced by the skeletons or mummies; cultural practices as revealed by mutilation or alteration of the bodies either before or after death; the method of burial—inhumation, cremation, bundle burial, group burial, and so on; and beliefs connected with the afterlife as evidenced by the cultural objects placed with the bodies. Such objects are informative in helping define the individual's role in life—whether he was a farmer, warrior, or priest, or whether she was a weaver, potter, or other worker. Group burials provide information as to family structure or other details of nonmaterial culture, such as warfare.

The nature of archaeological data is almost infinitely variable, and it is not my purpose here to present a catalog of these data. I have summarized the most common kinds of evidence, but other kinds that I have not mentioned are often of equal importance; for example, samples for dating or pollen analysis, charred plant remains, or stains in the soil (Fig. 2–8). What is important to bear in mind is that the archaeologist's primary interest is not in the specific items that he finds but in the information they provide concerning the cultural patterns of prehistoric peoples and the nature of the environments they inhabited.

REFERENCES

Charles-Picard, Gilbert, (ed.), 1972, *The Larousse Encyclopedia of Archaeology.* New York: Putnam.

Cole, S., 1965, *The Prehistory of East Africa.* New York: Mentor.

Daniel, G., 1968, *Man Discovers His Past.* New York: Crowell.

Dart, R. A., 1926, "Taungs and Its Significance," *Natural History,* 26:315–330.

De Laet, S. J., 1958, *The Low Countries.* London: Thames and Hudson.

Oakley, K. P., 1972, *Man the Tool-Maker,* 6th ed. London: British Museum. (First published 1950.)

Trustees of the British Museum (Natural History), 1959, *The Sutton Hoo Ship Burial.* London.

Woolley, L., 1954, *Digging Up the Past.* Baltimore: Penguin.

3

Stratigraphy, Chronology, and Dating Techniques

STRATIGRAPHY

Stratigraphy is one of the cornerstones of archaeological methodology. Without an understanding of the natural sequence of strata in a site, we would have no framework to which we could relate the objects found within it. In its simplest form, stratigraphy is the sequence of layers in a site, each of which is older than the layer above it. Once this principle is understood, it is possible to describe the sequence of accretion of individual sites. The sequence of strata is an historical record which permits the archaeologist to describe the sequence of events which occurred at that particular site. Without any other means of dating, the archaeologist can determine from the strata a *relative* sequence. He knows which items occur in which levels, and thus he can state the age of each specimen relative to that of other specimens from the same site. At this point he has no knowledge of their exact age in terms of years but can order their occurrence from early to late. We may also assume, normally, that all items found within a layer were deposited there during the formation of that unit; therefore those items are of approximately the same age. However, we must always be alert to the possibility of earlier or later specimens being introduced into a layer. Several factors can contribute to the overturning of entire layers which results in inverted stratigraphy, the oldest levels being those on the top. One of the most common causes of such a situation in a site is prior excavation. Unknown to the current excavator, at an earlier date someone, either another archaeologist or a relic hunter, has excavated at the site. As he dug, he piled the excavated earth by the side of the pit, each older layer excavated is then piled on top of the younger material that was previously removed from the pit. After a short time the rearranged layers may resemble in form an undisturbed stratigraphic sequence, the only difference being that the sequence of layers has been reversed. A similar situation could occur in antiquity with the excavation of burial pits, especially if the burial pits were dug into layers of food debris or other cultural strata. Erosion through geologic action is another method whereby strata may be rearranged and redeposited. In this case the true age of the strata are usually recognized through study of the included fossils and other chronological indicators. However, it is common for the artifacts in such a deposit to be derived from several sources of different age; therefore the resultant grouping of artifacts is chronologically mixed. If we do not already have some knowledge of the age of the artifact types present, we may assume that because they were found together in the same layer, they are of the same age.

It is also a frequent occurrence that objects are *accidentally* introduced into strata of older age. One of the most common culprits is the lowly gopher. The archaeologist is always alert to the possibility of such postdepositional alteration of a site because the finding of a single artifact in a layer where it should not occur can cause the archaeologist mental anguish when he begins reconstructing the sequence of events that occurred at the site. Later artifacts may be introduced into earlier layers by the trampling of feet and excavations by the prehistoric inhabitants. The latter situation is not much of a problem if the prior existence of a pit is demonstrated by careful excavation; however, if the pit is not recognized, then the archaeologist may record false information.

The development of layers in a site is the result of two factors: geologic processes and cultural activity. The layers themselves vary from purely natural, noncultural deposits to purely cultural ones. However, most layers in a site are the result of both of these factors in operation at the same time. In addition, deposition of layers may have been continuous as in lakes or bogs, or it may have been interrupted by periods of nondeposition or erosion. In the case of geologic processes, local nondeposition is normally associated with erosion, with deposits being built up somewhere else. The effect on the site of interest is the development of an erosion surface. Such a surface could have lying upon it all those objects which were too large to have been swept away by water or wind action. If later deposition were to cover this erosion surface, the objects found on that surface might all be considered to be of the same age—which might be a fallacious assumption. Therefore, it is important for the archaeologist to record every detail of the strata in order to understand how they and associated artifacts came to be deposited. Interruptions in cultural deposition may occur simply because the inhabitants moved elsewhere.

Strata differ markedly in type. Some represent long periods of essentially unchanging conditions of deposition; others record frequent fluctuations. In

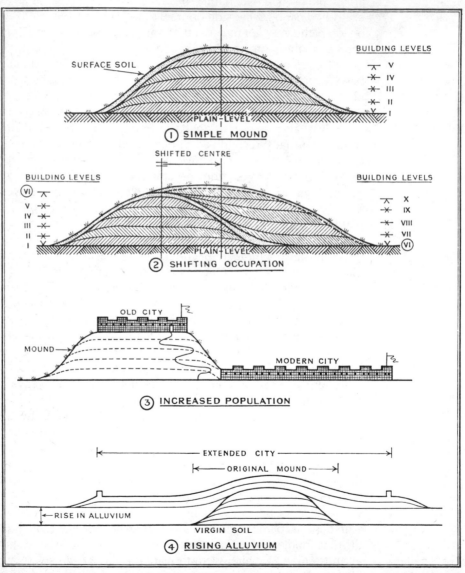

Fig. 3–1 Sequences of accumulation of layers to form mounds of similar outward shapes but differing stratigraphic histories. (Lloyd 1963:Fig. 10.)

one example, the thin layers deposited as a result of glacial melt called varves are annual with a lighter and darker component, each the result of the melt during the summer or winter.

One contrast between natural and cultural stratigraphy is that the latter is normally restricted to a small area. One technique is to put down test pits beyond the site to reveal the sequence of layers present without any human influence. Such tests can then aid the understanding of the cultural sequence. Figure 3–1 illustrates a series of typical situations in the accumulation of occupation layers to form stratigraphic sequences.

In those situations where natural stratigraphic layers are not easily followed, the archaeologist may excavate the site by arbitrary levels. Such a methodology does not replace analysis of natural layers as a means of reconstructing the sequence of events at the site. However, arbitrary levels provide one means whereby the individual objects can be assigned specific provenience within the site. This methodology thereby achieves a relative sequence for purposes of dating the objects in the absence of natural stratigraphic units.

CHRONOLOGY

The establishment of a sequence of cultures for a region is one of the major tasks of archaeology. These regional sequences may then be correlated with each other to provide areal or even continental chronologies. Critical to the establishment of chronologies is the ability to date individual objects and the levels in which they occur. However, prior to the discovery of various dating techniques, which provide absolute dates in terms of years, archaeologists had to devise other methods which would permit the establishment of chronologies. The techniques so developed are basic to all archaeology and are still in use. We have discussed the role of stratigraphy in the formulation of *relative sequences*. Another basic archaeological tool is the concept of *index fossil*. Derived from paleontology, this usage relies upon three related principles: 1. Certain fossils or specimens are distinctive in form. 2. They are widespread in their distribution. 3. They were in existence for a short period of time. One of the first things archaeologists noticed was that certain prehistoric implements were of distinctive and similar form. It was apparent during the earliest excavations that objects of similar form were common in some levels and did not occur in others. This is of course the underlying principle which led to the development of the Three Age scheme of classification of ancient cultures. With such a concept at hand, it is only a small step further to utilize index fossils in cross-dating. If an object has a brief span of time in which it was utilized, it can be used for dating, wherever it is found. However, it must occur in primary association with other objects and not secondarily deposited at a later date through geologic or other causes.

We have briefly reviewed the use of the archaeological index fossil. The definition of such an item is based upon the *type* concept. Prehistoric objects are considered as having been made according to a preconceived idea on the part of the manufacturer (Deetz 1967). Items of the same artifactural class, such as projectile points, scrapers, and so on, will therefore have a similar form. While these items will vary in some attributes, they will feature a central core of shared attributes. This core or modal tendency is typical for that group of artifacts. Such a description of the "type" is an abstraction, since few individual artifacts possess exactly the same attributes as the idealized type description. Nonetheless the concept is useful, for it provides a means whereby we may classify individual objects into form classes. This assignment provides one method of categorizing items from a particular level; for example, 45 percent of the projectile points are type A and 25 percent are type B. In addition, if the types are distinctive, the presence of a single example may indicate the relative age of that level. It should be added that form is not the only relative criterion. Technology and material are among other characteristics which could provide the core attributes of a type.

Stratigraphy is our primary tool for the construction of regional sequences. Once established, the individual regional sequences are then dated through use of index fossils.

Cultural items change slowly but continuously in form through time. When we wish to pinpoint a specific item in time, we may identify its position on the entire continuum of change in that class of items. This is the concept termed *seriation*. Potsherds, for example, have a large number of constituent attributes, such as paint, color, line width, design style, slip, paste, and temper. As these attributes change through time, lines become wider or narrower, paint changes from one to several colors, design styles change from naturalistic to geometric or vice versa. These specific attributes change at different times and at different rates. However, by examining the totality of attributes present in each potsherd, we can usually assign it a position on the total cultural continuum of which it forms a part. Once so ranked, it may also be used as an index fossil. A further refinement in seriation consists of quantifying the occurrence of items in a level in percentile terms. Once this has been done, it is possible to arbitrarily subdivide cultural sequences on the basis of changes in these frequencies. For example, at a point where a pottery type we term Mancos Black on White becomes less common than the type we term Mesa Verde Black on White, we can state that there has been a transition to the Mesa Verde period. Such a division of the archaeological record should be recognized as arbitrary; nonetheless, it is one method whereby we may subdivide the regional archaeology into convenient space-time units.

Chronology is frequently confused by the layman with techniques of dating. The two subjects are related but they are not synonymous. Chronology consists of the construction of a conceptual framework with space-time dimensions into which the specific content of cultural levels can be fitted. Dating techniques provide chronological *data* in the sense that dates can be assigned to individual specimens or levels. Since construction of a chronology is based on intellectual concepts, it is appropriate to define our terms in a rigorous manner; these terms are defined in Chapter 5.

DATING TECHNIQUES

Techniques utilized in dating may be classified in terms of the types of dates obtained. A simple classification includes relative dates, absolute dates, and age estimates. By no means are all dates the same. Some are given in terms of years; others in years with a probable error also stated; others as older than or younger than a particular level or item, and finally we have age estimates which are really not dates at all.

Relative Dates

Relative dating includes all those techniques which provide us with information as to the age of an object or level as compared with the age of some other object or level. Thus dates are older, younger, or contemporaneous. Chronological sequence building is one of the major applications of this method. If, for example, we have excavated three sites and have identified levels in these sites according to their diagnostic artifacts, then we may compare and arrange their respective levels into a chronology (Fig. 3–2). The chronology to be established would include levels 0, 1, 1A, 2, 3, 4, 5 in that order from late to early. Note that level 1A occurs between levels 1 and 2 and is therefore bracketed in time; its relative age has been established. Level 0 is later than 1, since it is superimposed above 1. However, from the stratigraphic evidence, we have no knowledge of how much of a time gap exists between levels 0 and 1, or for that matter how much elapsed time is present between any two of the other levels.

CHEMICAL DATING   Buried bones gradually absorb fluorine from the groundwater. Such absorption is dependent upon the composition of the local groundwater. Inasmuch as the quantity of such absorption depends upon the length of time the bone has been buried, it is possible to measure the fluorine in two bones from the same deposit and determine if there is any significant difference in their relative age. The quantity of fluorine can be determined either through chemical analysis or with the x-ray crystallographic method. Nitrogen provides another measurement of relative age. By contrast to fluorine, nitrogen in bone decreases with the length of time it has been buried. The two techniques utilized together can provide information as to the relative age of bone specimens. Such techniques are especially important when we wish to establish whether all the bone specimens in a level are of the same age or whether they are of different ages and their association in the level is due to secondary deposition.

Stones, either buried in the ground or lying on the surface for a length of time, undergo chemical alteration. Such alteration, termed *patina,* is manifest in a milky colored coating on the surface of the stones. Flints that have been lying on the ground with the same side uppermost through time may be heavily patinated on the bottom and only lightly patinated on the upper surface. Whatever the causes of patination, it is a local phenomena not useful for regional comparisons. However, if in comparing objects from different levels in

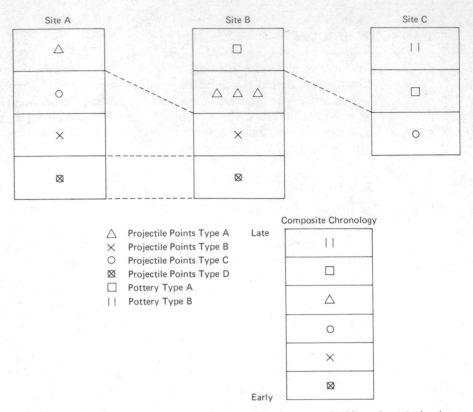

Fig. 3–2 Model illustrating the method of archaeological sequence building where site levels are correlated on the basis of included artifacts of distinctive form. The total sequence established is thus an abstraction, not precisely represented at any single site, but assumed to be representative of the culture sequence of the region.

a single site or comparing different objects from the surface of a site, differences in degree of patination are noted, these differences may be assumed to represent differences in relative age.

Absolute Dates

Dates termed *absolute* are really of two separate categories. Those which are stated in terms of years in our calendar are true absolute dates. The other category consists of techniques which yield dates expressed in years with an associated probability factor, or the dates are referred to a floating chronology which has yet to be correlated with our calendar.

True absolute dates may be derived from tree rings, ancient calendrical systems, coins, and varves where traced directly back in time from the present. What is essential for an absolute date is that there must be no equivocation— the date must be exactly correct to the year. As we will see, such accuracy is seldom available to the archaeologist.

TREE-RING DATING It is possibly our best example of absolute dating. Trees sensitive to fluctuations in rainfall or other climatic factors lay down annual growth rings of varying width. Over a period of 25 to 50 years such a sequence of ring widths establishes a pattern which is not exactly duplicated by any other such sequence of rings. The sequence can then be correlated with a master chronology of ring widths extending from the present back in time. In the American Southwest the master chronology covers approximately the past 8000 years. Such correlation can thus provide a date for the year in which the last ring on our specimen was laid down. This is an absolute date. However, we must bear in mind that the outside ring on our specimen may not be the year that the tree was cut or died, for the exterior may be eroded or it may have been cut off when the log was modified for use, burned, or altered in some other fashion.

Another inherent limitation in the method is that in years of severe climatic stress, no ring may be deposited or it may be of microscopic size. This leads to missing rings in the chronology, or rings that are termed *locally absent* because they occur on only a portion of the circumference of the specimen. Careful dating of such specimens should provide the correct date. Careless analysis could provide a date in error by one or more years. It is also true that the date pertains to the last year that the specimen was growing. Such a date cannot automatically be applied to the archaeological site from which it was obtained for a variety of reasons. The log may have been salvaged from an earlier dwelling and reused, or the tree may have stood dead for a number of years before it was cut and used. What must be established before the date can be utilized is the archaeological provenience of the specimen; in what way was the log used and what was its association in the site? For example, if all of the roof beams in a room date within one or two years of each other, then we may assume that those dates bracket the period of construction. On the other hand, one early date in such a group of dates would suggest reuse of an older beam. It is possible to determine the sequence of room building from wall abutments. If the associated tree-ring dates are in a similar sequence then it is possible to rely on those dates with greater confidence even if only one or two dates per room is available. Dates obtained on charcoal in a firepit or on burned logs lying on a floor may also be correlated with the use of the room or its construction.

The development of a tree-ring chronology is dependent upon the presence of the correct tree species—species that produce annual rings sensitive to some climatic factor such as temperature or rainfall. A second major factor is that the climate must be variable in order to cause the formation of tree rings of varying widths. Regions such as the Hawaiian Islands or the coast of British Columbia have climates that are too constant, thus producing unvarying ring widths termed *complacent*. Areas too desertic, too wet, or too cold are also eliminated; however, many of the temperate regions of the world have suitable conditions and tree-ring chronologies have been developed for some of those regions.

In brief, the method is capable of producing absolute dates for certain regions. However the use of such dates is dependent upon our understanding of the position of the dated specimen in the sequence of events recorded at the specific site. The method is accurate but its application is dependent upon the accuracy of our observations in the field and the skill by which the specimens were excavated.

Radiocarbon Dating

The radioactive decay of the isotope carbon-14 provides another method of dating termed "absolute." The dates are given in terms of years with a statistical statement as to the amount of probable error; for example, 4200 years Before Present plus or minus 200 years. The probability statement means that the true date is 4200 years B.P. ± 200 with a reliability of one standard deviation or sigma. Translation of this statistical statement means that in 68 percent of such cases the true date would fall between 4000 and 4400 years B.P. If we wish to be more exact, we can utilize two sigmas in which case there is a 95 percent probability that the true date falls between 3800 and 4600 years B.P. Three sigmas would provide a 99 percent probability that the true date would fall between 3600 and 4800 years B.P. It must also be pointed out that there are no limits within which the true age lies with *absolute* certainty. "Before Present" is also arbitrarily defined as years prior to A.D. 1950. I hope to have dispelled the impression that simply because radiocarbon dates are published in terms of years they are *absolute* dates.

The principle behind the radiocarbon method is that neutrons produced by cosmic radiation enter the earth's atmosphere and react with the isotope nitrogen-14. This reaction produces an isotope of carbon, C-14, which readily mixes with the oxygen in the atmosphere. From the atmosphere the C-14 isotope eventually enters all living organisms as part of the oxygen exchange process. The individual organism continues to incorporate C-14 as long as it is living. After the organism dies, it no longer receives atoms of C-14 but instead begins the process of radioactive decay. The C-14 is continually being reduced at a fixed rate. Termed *half-life,* such a reduction is described as the length of time necessary for the radioactive substance to lose one half of its radioactive isotopes. The half-life of C-14 has been calculated by counting the number of beta emissions per minute per gram of samples of known age. A wide variety of specimens of known age were counted to establish the C-14 half-life as being 5568 ± 30 years. Samples included wood and mummified flesh from pharaonic tombs, dated tree ring specimens, living trees, and other materials of known age. By demonstrating that dates obtained by counting C-14 isotopes could be correlated with objects of known age, it was proved the method had value. However the half-life so established had only theoretical significance because it was still only an average of determinations. In addition, the entire concept depended upon several major assumptions:

1. The rate of cosmic radiation has remained constant through time.
2. C-14 is evenly distributed throughout the atmosphere and all living matter.

3. The concentration of C-14 in the reservoir of exchangeable carbon on the earth and in the atmosphere has not changed.

Research on the above assumptions has demonstrated that the natural concentration of C-14 in the atmosphere has varied for certain periods. The primary variable seems to have been variations in solar activity. Since it has not been possible to explain this variation by theoretical considerations, scientists have had to check the veracity of the C-14 dates by systematic dating of dated tree ring specimens. The result has suggested that the original computation of the half-life was in error and that a figure of 5730 ± 40 is more nearly correct.

The actual counting of the samples was accomplished first by Willard Libby, the inventor of the method, who converted the organic sample to elemental carbon which was then smeared on the inner surface of a steel cylinder. The cylinder was surrounded by a ring of geiger counters to record the emissions from the sample. Cosmic radiation reaching the counters would also be recorded; therefore, this "background count" was screened out by enclosing the entire counting mechanism in a thick-walled lead vault. The method had drawbacks in that it was time-consuming and the possibilities for error were relatively high. Within a few years more modern methods were developed in which the carbon is changed to a gas, either carbon dioxide, acetylene, or methane which is then counted in a proportional counter. The gas method is more reliable inasmuch as the sample is not handled after it has been prepared for conversion to gas. A second advantage of the gas counting method is that reliable dates may be obtained from smaller samples. Currently minimum sample sizes recommended are: charcoal, 8 to 12 grams; wood, 10 to 30 grams; shell, 30 to 100 grams; peat, 10 to 25 grams; and bone, 20 to 100 grams. Other carbonaceous materials suitable for dating include: soot, burned bone, antler or tusk, calcareous tufa, lake mud, parchment, dung, flesh, hide, hair, any preserved vegetal material such as grass, twigs, or bark, and any other substances from a once-living organism. The sample collected need not represent the remains of a single organism; for example, a number of small shells could be dated as one sample. The sample may also combine particles found separate from each other. Some of our most valuable dates were obtained by the painstaking picking of tiny charcoal flecks scattered throughout a stratigraphic layer. The date so derived would represent an average date for that geologic unit.

A serious concern of both the archaeologist and the radiocarbon dating analyst is the possibility of sample contamination. Samples may be contaminated while they are in the ground, during the collection process, or in the dating laboratory. I will not attempt to outline in detail all of the possible sources of contamination, since it is a highly complex subject. Contamination may result in a date being either too young or too old. For example, an older date may be obtained by dating shells which have incorporated inactive (radioactively dead) carbon during their growth. Both younger or older dates may be the result of groundwater activity. Leaching of carbon from a sample would yield an older date, while enrichment could occur if there is a nearby source of more recent carbon. Samples may contain recent rootlets, another source of younger carbon. Sample collection requires care, for contamination may be introduced by the wrapping material used, such as cotton. The coating of fragile specimens with preservatives such as shellac can introduce modern carbon almost impossible to remove in the laboratory. In recent years dating laboratories have become increasingly conscious of contamination problems. As a result, they now routinely prepare the samples by a rigorous cleaning. Samples are picked under a microscope; they are then washed in strong acid and alkali solutions and then burned. Furthermore the samples after being prepared are stored in tight containers for several weeks before dating in order to permit the radioactive decay of tritium and other isotopes with a short half-life.

Radiocarbon dating is the single best dating technique available to date specimens with ages within the past 50,000 years, which is the practical limit of the technique. However, with elaborate preparation methods, it is possible to enrich the quantity of isotopes available for dating within a sample. This technique pushes back the theoretical limit of the process to 70,000 years. Isotopic enrichment deals with the concentration of very small amounts of carbon-14. Therefore the introduction of only a very small percentage of modern carbon would result in serious contamination making the date erroneous.

If contamination is such a problem, then how is it possible to use radiocarbon dates with confidence? The most important fact to bear in mind is that radiocarbon dates are archaeological dates. They were collected from archaeological sites, and their isolation, recovery, and identification to provenience are the result of standard archaeological methods. Reused beams and intrusions (such as burials) into earlier levels are among the many problems which the archaeologist must decipher from his excavation notes before he submits a radiocarbon sample for dating. Therefore, if we have dated a single date from each of eight successive stratified levels, it is expectable that the dates will form a single sequence from early to late. Any deviation from such an expected sequence would have to be explained. Presented with an anomalous date, the archaeologist can date other samples from the same level, or he can reexamine his site excavation notes to be sure that he did not miss an archaeological feature such as a burial pit or other cause of the inappropriate date. It is also possible that in some cases the archaeologist has an age estimate in mind for a level which may be revealed by C-14 to have been erroneous. In such cases the archaeologist may refuse to believe that the C-14 date is accurate, since it does not support his prior bias. After all, archaeologists have normal human failings.

An excellent example of the resolution of an archaeological problem through use of radiocarbon dates is the dating of the sequence of construction of the North Acropolis at Tikal (Stukenrath, Coe, and Ralph 1966). The archaeological problem was simple: the dating of the long constructional sequence of a major architectural feature in a Classic Mayan ceremonial center. The resolution of the problem was far from simple as the researchers demonstrated. Twenty-five radiocarbon dates were obtained, primarily on samples of charcoal collected from the constructional fill between finished platform surfaces. The researchers describe the North Acropolis, its constructional sequence, and the problems attendant with sample collection as follows:

It [the North Acropolis] consists essentially of a series of great superimposed platforms, each of which sustains various buildings of a ceremonial nature. The majority of radiocarbon samples considered here are charcoals recovered from the fills employed in construction. Such charcoals occur in fill as randomly as potsherds and other cultural material. The true source of this charcoal is difficult if not impossible to isolate. This is basically true of the actual fills. We assume that the cultural detritus and charcoal found in such fills ultimately derive from household middens, workshop scrap, and from other accumulations of trash resulting from daily living at Tikal. The fill matrix ranges from limestone rubble, to demolished prior constructions, marl scraped from bedrock, and earths and clays. A serious drawback in assessing sources is the extent to which the old was demolished to make way for the new at Tikal. . . .

The point is simply that the content of a fill matrix at Tikal cannot be assumed to express contemporary reality, ceramic, or otherwise. A pot must be broken, a hearth extinguished and cold before the products of both are available as constructional fill. This requires that we date a fill in terms of having been collected and laid down no earlier than the time of the latest material within it. In submitting charcoal to a laboratory for radiocarbon determination, we are aware of how limited our control of the sample is. Granted, we may well control a sample in terms of its sequential or stratigraphic provenience and we often know the nature of the pottery with which it is physically associated. However, there remain a number of clearcut, potentially significant variables that can color the radiocarbon results treated in this paper (Stuckenrath, Coe, and Ralph 1966:372).

Specific dating problems posed by the charcoal samples are identified as follows (Stuckenrath, Coe, and Ralph 1966:372–374):

1. Post-sample error—this is the interval of time between the "death" of the organic source of the sample and the "death" of the organic matrix of the source. A common example is the differential age between pith wood and the cambial layer, in some cases a difference of several hundred years.
2. Placement history—the interval between the death carbonization of the source and the final archaeological placement of the sample. This gap must be assessed through archaeological means—the range of variation in age of associated artifacts, stratigraphy, etc. Of importance is the fact that the PH gap may range from nonexistent to as much as 1000 years.
3. Average death-rate—if the sample is made up of mixed botanical elements, the date assigned represents an *average* age.
4. Contamination—rootlets, groundwater leaching, etc., are problems inherent to all radiocarbon samples.
5. Sigma—the true age, as we have discussed earlier, lies within a statistical range of the ± factor given; *i.e.*, the exact age lies within the ± factor (1 sigma) given in only 2 out of 3 cases. The chances are that even 2 sigmas from the mean includes only 19 out of 20 true ages.

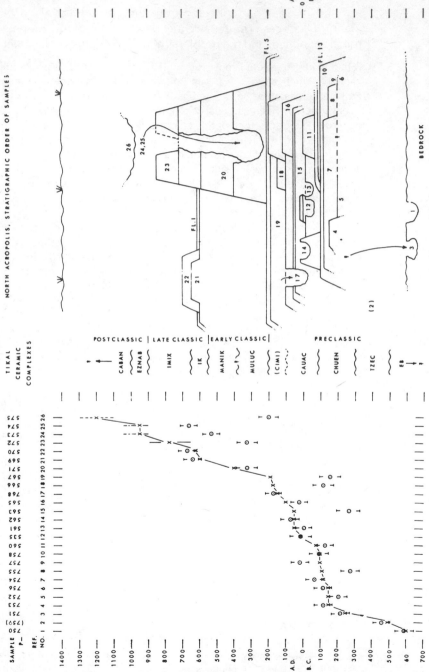

Fig. 3–3 Radiocarbon chronology of the North Acropolis, Tikal, Guatemala. (*Left*) Dates: x's are C-14 dates; o's, expected dates. (*Right*) stratigraphy. (Stuckenrath, Coe, and Ralph 1966:375.)

6. Half-life—the exact half-life used will affect the dates assigned. The Tikal dates are based on a 5568 year half-life whereas 5730 is now more commonly used. The 5730 figure would result in dates some 240 years earlier.

The dating of the North Acropolis was facilitated through the exact placement of the samples in the constructional sequence (Fig. 3–3). The next step was the assigning of expected ages to the levels based on ceramic cross-dating of the associated potsherds, the stratigraphic sequence, the contemporaneity of specific samples, and the estimated age of the architectural features. These estimated ages are plotted in Figure 3–3 by the symbol X; departures from this expected age are plotted as circles.

The significance of the technique employed is obvious. Only about one half of the dates are reasonably close to their predicted age. The authors resign themselves to these facts: the samples are no better than any other archaeological remains; their stratigraphic location is the result of numerous factors many of which are chronologically significant. The authors state:

The point is that somewhat less than 50% of the North Acropolis samples make the depositional sense expected of all. This may be a useful statistic; it may be that at other complex sites half the results on charcoal are merely useful for detecting error in the other half (Stukenrath, Coe, and Ralph 1966:383).

In conclusion, the authors also point out that even with samples which they personally excavated and for which they found no evidence of archaeological error, the dated results clearly indicate that a substantial PH error was in fact present. The results are humbling for all those interested in dating the events of the past.

The early efforts at radiocarbon dating were based on theoretical assumptions concerning the rate of radioactive decay of carbon-14. The decay rate was based upon the rate of cosmic radiation reaching the earth, which was assumed to have been constant through time. Proof of these assumptions could be obtained only through the radiocarbon dating of specimens of known archaeological age. Tests were run on ancient specimens from pharaonic Egypt, specimens attributed to specific dynasties with a known age. The results were supportive—the radiocarbon dates agreed with the archaeological data. We were therefore assured that the radiocarbon chronology was accurate; one radiocarbon year was equivalent to one calendar year. Further clarification of this relationship has been made possible in recent years by the radiocarbon dating of tree ring samples, each of 10-year length, covering the last 8000 years (Ferguson 1972). When these precisely dated tree ring specimens were dated in a series of 312 radiocarbon runs, it was determined that radiocarbon years were not directly equivalent to calendar years but in fact fluctuate through time by being either too young or too old depending on the age of the specimen (Fig. 3–4). The results are of extreme importance to all of the historical sciences. We now know more precisely the true age of samples dated by radiocarbon. We further have verified that cosmic radiation has fluctuated through time.

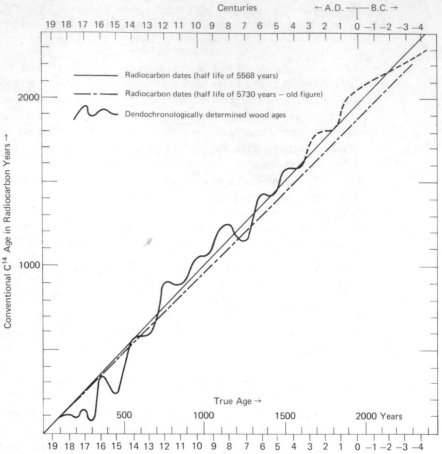

Fig. 3–4 Graph of correlation between radiocarbon years and calendar years showing the effects of recalibration. (Suess 1965:Fig. 4.)

The Oxygen 16/18 Ratio

The Oxygen 16/18 technique provides climatic data, primarily a record of fluctuations in past temperature. Nonetheless this method may be used by extrapolation for the dating of Pleistocene events. The primary application of the method has been in the analysis of deep-sea cores, although ice cores have also been studied. Deep-sea cores are made up of the layered ooze on the sea floor which accumulates at a very slow rate, one to several centimeters per 1000 years. The components of the *Globigerina* ooze are clay and from 30 to 90 percent of calcium carbonate derived from the shells of Foraminifera. The ocean temperature at the time these Foraminifera were living can be assessed by the ratio of the two stable isotopes Oxygen 16 and Oxygen 18 in the calcium carbonate of their shells. The temperature graph so determined is of little value for short-term fluctuations because of the reworking of bottom sediments by burrowing sea floor fauna. For long-term fluctuations it is reliable and presents us with a temperature curve adjusted to that of the oceanic surface. The oceanic curve may then be correlated with continental phenomena, primarily glacial advances and retreats. The resultant curve is therefore a record of Pleistocene climatic fluctuations, the later portion of which has been precisely dated by the C-14 and Pa^{231}/Th^{230} methods. By extrapolation the deep-sea core curve may be used to estimate the duration of Pleistocene events beyond the range of precise dating techniques (Emiliani 1969).

Calendars

Ancient calendrical systems would appear to be capable of yielding exact dates which could be correlated with our present calendar. The occurrence of calendars is limited in archaeology, since their development is associated with a high level of cultural attainment. The ancient civilizations of Greece, Rome, Egypt, Carthage, Mesopotamia, and Yucatan are examples. Most of the cultures studied by archaeologists developed neither calendrical observations nor writing, and thus other methods of dating have to be employed. For those cultures that possessed calendars several qualifications must be pointed out. All calendars of concern to the archaeologist are subject to slight modifications because of the difference between the astronomical year and the 365-day tropical year. Such a correlation is handled by our present Gregorian calendar with the addition of an extra day every fourth year. Early calendars coped with such variation in a number of ways, and we must know which method was used in order to permit an exact correlation with our present system. It is also possible to have an exact calendar, which, because its use was discontinued in antiquity, has become a floating chronology. The Mayan calendar is such an example. Their calendar contained two systems, the extremely accurate Long Count, correct to the day over 374,440 years, and the abbreviated and much less accurate Short Count, correct only within 256¼ years. By the time of European contact the Short Count was the only system still in use; thus we have Short Count dates for which the corresponding Gregorian equivalents are known. However, the next step of correlating the Mayan Short Count with the Mayan Long Count has led to two different correlations. Respectively termed the Goodman, Thompson, Martinez correlation and the Spinden correlation, after the men who described them, they differ in their correlation with our present calendar by 260 years. In recent years the correlation controversy has been resolved by the radiocarbon dating of wooden door lintels which had dates in the Mayan Long Count system carved on them. The result suggests that the GTM correlation is the more accurate. Thus finally Mayan calendrical dates may be assigned modern equivalents.

Probably the major restriction on use of calendrical dates is that they are inscribed on objects subject to all the vicissitudes of time that all other archaeological specimens encounter. If the date is struck on a coin, then the presence of the coin in a site does not necessarily date the site to that year. After all, coins are in circulation for a number of years after they are minted, so the dated coin only provides a minimal date for that level in the site. The introduction of the coin into the level could not have occurred *earlier* than its mint date. Application of archaeological methods is again in order because the position of dated specimens in a site must be explained in terms of site accretion as determined by excavation. Coins occurring in groups with closely clustered dates are better evidence that their presence in the site dates shortly after the latest date in the group. Occasionally, when freshly minted coins are found in large quantity, it is possible to assume that their presence in the site is the result of an event which occurred almost immediately after minting. Other dated objects, such as stelae and building blocks, must also be viewed with some caution. Were the stones introduced into a structure on the date inscribed, was the building begun or completed on that date, and so forth? One only has to bear in mind the construction history of medieval cathedrals in Europe to realize that a dated stone might differ considerably in age from the date of completion of the building in which it occurs. Thus calendars can provide exact dates for specimens but their chronological meaning in the history of a site must be assessed after consideration of the total body of archaeological information available.

Potassium-Argon Dating

Radioactive decay is a principle that provides a mechanism for the dating of numerous kinds of specimens. To be of value to archaeology the isotopes being counted must have a half-life in the correct time span to provide dates applicable to human prehistory. Some isotopes decay in a matter of hours or days, obviously too short a time to be of value; others cover too great a span of time. One usable ratio is that resulting from the decay of potassium 40 to the gas, argon 40. The half-life of 1.3 billion years is much longer than that of C-14. With the K/A method, the age of rocks, including chronological marker beds such as volcanic ash falls, can be measured. Rocks as found in a site should not be dated by this method because the age of the rock probably is much greater than the time of its use as an implement. The principle application of the method would be in dating rocks which occur in a stratigraphic sequence that includes human cultural materials. In such a case the K/A age relative to the cultural items can be established. It is through use of this method that the oldest dates associated with human remains have been obtained. When first published, the age of 1.75 million years for the oldest cultural level at Olduvai Gorge, Tanzania, was thought to be unreasonably old; however, at this writing our views on man's antiquity have been revised to include these K/A dates.

Archaeomagnetic Dating

Through time the angle of declination between magnetic north and true north and the angle of dip of a magnetic needle fluctuate. Such fluctuations have been recorded for over 400 years, and they vary in a systematic way which may be plotted as a series of curves. These cycles are repeated at specific intervals. All that is needed to date a specimen within a particular cycle is to have preserved information as to the direction of magnetic north at the time the specimen was manufactured. This may seem unlikely, but the key to the whole method is the fact that items of fired clay have fixed permanently, by the firing process, the declination of magnetic north as it was when the specimen was fired. The field techniques employed in collecting an archaeomagnetic sample are relatively easy. The sample—a portion of a fire hearth or burned floor is best—is isolated as a small block in place. It is then surrounded with plaster of pairs, which, as it is setting, has inscribed upon it magnetic north and true north. After these determinations are made and the plaster is set, the specimen is removed from the ground. Back in the laboratory, the permanent magnetism in the specimen is measured, thus enabling the plotting of the magnetic declination as it was at the time the specimen was fired. This measurement does not yield a date, since the specific 400-year-long cycle to which the sample belongs has yet to be identified. The declination measurement only tells us where within such a cycle the specimen fits. Identification of a sample to a specific cycle depends upon the establishment of the relative age of the sample through archaeological methods. First we must date the hearth through associated potsherds or other artifacts as belonging to a specific 400-year period. Then the archaeomagnetic method can be utilized to further date the specimen within a 20-year segment of this magnetic cycle.

When I first took archaeology as a beginning student, archaeomagnetic dating was discussed as a theoretically promising method for the dating of archaeological materials. Today the method has been refined by Robert Dubois and Daniel Wolfman of the University of Oklahoma to the point where there is an established chronology for the American Southwest. Additional chronologies are being worked out for Mesoamerica and Peru. A final aspect of current research on archaeomagnetism is that the archaeologically obtained specimens will provide additional data on the nature of prior magnetic cycles whose configuration has been determined on the basis of theoretical considerations.

Thermoluminescence

The principle upon which thermoluminescent dating is based is that objects, such as pottery or stones, which have been heated in the past will release energy in the form of light when reheated. The amount of light emitted by a specimen is dependent upon the length of time since the specimen was last fired. In addition, the glow curve also permits the measurement of the temperature at which the specimen was originally fired.

First announced in 1960 by two physicists, Kennedy and Knopff, the concept seemed theoretically sound. The method was received with enthusiasm by archaeologists for the raw material to be dated was potsherds, the principle single artifact class previously used by archaeologists for sequence building. If the relative sequences established with potsherd analyses could be tied to absolute dates, the entire chronological foundations of archaeology could be dramatically improved. Furthermore it was suggested that the dating of an individual sample would be relatively inexpensive, on the order of a couple of dollars each.

Unfortunately all these good predictions have to some degree failed to materialize with the actual practical application of the theoretical principles. It is now apparent that there are a number of relevant variables which have inhibited the production of reliable dates. Consequently the enthusiasm on the part of both the archaeologists and physicists has cooled. However, systematic research on the method is continuing, and it is hoped that it will be successful.

Obsidian Hydration

A freshly broken surface of obsidian exposed to the atmosphere absorbs water to form a visible surface layer. Termed a hydration layer, it increases in thickness at a fixed rate. We thus have available another natural clock for the precise measurement of elapsed time. Inasmuch as a great many stone implements were made from obsidian, the potential of such a method is indeed great. The application of the method is rather simple. First a small, thin section is removed from the specimen with a diamond lapidary saw. The sample is mounted on a microscope slide and then examined with a polarizing petrographic microscope. The polarized light makes the hydration layer visible, and its thickness in microns may be directly measured. However, it is not possible to compare this measurement with a universal thickness standard because hydration does not occur at the same rate in every region. There seems to be a correlation with temperature and other environmental factors which suggests that regional rates of hydration are possible. Lists of dates have been prepared for various selected areas, and they show promise of an acceptable reliability. Problems limiting the method are variable chemical composition of different obsidians, modification in the surface of the obsidian by burning, sand blasting, or surface exposure, or frequent variations in temperature and precipitation. A final problem is reuse of obsidian implements. In spite of these limitations, the method has merit where the specimens dated are of a similar variety of obsidian and all the specimens have been buried in a similar environment since use.

Varves

Varves are laminated layers of sediments which are deposited in lakes near a glacial margin. Each varve is made up of two layers, a coarse, thick, usually lighter colored layer on the bottom and a thin, fine-grained, darker-colored layer on top. The two layers together represent the deposition from one year's glacial melt. The coarse layer may be correlated with the summer melt and the thin layer with the winter's runoff. Varves are variable in thickness, but this is not a problem in their use for dating. A major restriction is that varves occur only in glaciated regions and therefore are absent in most of the world. Their most outstanding occurrence is in Scandinavia where they have been traced continuously back in time from the present to 17,000 years ago. Varve sequences were first described by Gerhard De Geer on the basis of the Scandinavian evidence (De Geer 1912, 1940). Subsequently varve analysis has been applied in certain areas of North America, South America, and Africa. In these areas varve sequences are not continuous because of the intermittent presence of glaciers in the past. Thus we have had the description of floating chronologies. Ernst Antevs has worked in both Scandinavia and North America and has attempted a correlation of these sequences. Probably Antevs' work has suitable accuracy; what is more of a drawback is the fact that varve sequences can seldom be correlated with an archaeological sequence. In recent years the varve sequences have been further dated by radiocarbon.

Age Estimates

In certain situations where no other dating techniques have been applicable, archaeologists have relied upon simple guesses termed *age estimates*. The method has little to recommend it, although there are unique situations where such guesses were later shown to be reasonably correct. One of the most outstanding was the age assigned to the Folsom bison killsite. When first discovered in 1927, this hitherto undocumented association of man with animals now extinct was guess-dated at 10,000 years of age. In recent years C-14 determinations on samples of Folsom age reveal that such dates concentrate between 10,200 and 9800 years ago. Quite a remarkable accuracy for a guess-date! On the other hand, when I first took an introductory course in archaeology, the age of the earliest humans was guess-dated at approximately 500,000 to 1,000,000 years of age. The K/A dates at Olduvai Gorge now suggest that man's antiquity is approximately twice this earlier guess.

Rather than pick a date out of thin air and assign it to a site or cultural level, archaeologists have long used a more rigorous method. By assuming a certain rate of deposition in a site—for example, one foot per thousand years—they have attempted to quantify site accumulation. While several attempts have been made (Cosgrove and Cosgrove, 1932:100–103; Gifford 1916; Cook 1946; Vaillant 1935:166–167, 257–258), especially with cave deposits and shell middens, the results have not always agreed with dates obtained by other methods. In short, archaeological deposits accumulate at different rates and no standard is likely to be applicable.

REFERENCES

Cook, S. F., 1946, "A Reconstruction of Shell Mounds with Respect to Population and Nutrition," *American Antiquity* 12:51–53.

Cosgrove, H. S., and C. B. Cosgrove, 1932, *The Swarts Ruin.* Peabody Museum Papers 15, No. 1.

Deetz, J., 1967, *Invitation to Archaeology.* New York: Doubleday.

De Geer, G., 1912, A Geochronology of the Last 12,000 years. *Cong. Geol. Internat. Compte Rendu.* Stockholm, 1910, pp. 241–253.

De Geer, G., 1940, Geochronologia Suecica Principles. Stockholm: Svenska Vetenskaps-akademiens, Handlingar, Vol. 18, No. 6.

Emiliani, C., 1970, "The Significance of Deep-Sea Cores," in D. Brothwell and E. Higgs (eds.), *Science in Archaeology*. New York: Praeger, pp. 109–117.

Ferguson, C. W., 1972, "Dendrochronology of Bristlecone Pine Prior to 4000 B.C." Paper presented at the International Radiocarbon Dating Conference, Wellington, New Zealand.

Gifford, E. W., 1916, "Composition of California Shellmounds." University of California Publications in American Archaeology and Ethnology 12:1–29.

Lloyd, S., 1963, *Mounds of the Near East*. Edinburgh: Edinburgh University Press.

Stuckenrath, R., Jr., W. R. Coe, and E. K. Ralph, 1966, "University of Pennsylvania Radiocarbon Dates IX," *Radiocarbon* 8:348–385.

Suess, Hans E., 1965, "Secular Variations of the Cosmic-ray Produced Carbon-14 in the Atmosphere," *Journal of Geophysical Research* 70:5950.

Vaillant, G. C., 1935, "Excavations at El Argolillo." American Museum of Natural History Anthropological Papers 35, Part 2.

Willey, G. R., and P. Phillips, 1958, *Method and Theory in American Archaeology*. Chicago: The University of Chicago Press.

4

Techniques in Archaeological Investigation

SITE SURVEY

How does the archaeologist locate the sites that he will study? First of all we must define what the archaeologist looks for when he begins his field work. The basic unit is the *site,* which may be defined as any location which exhibits evidence of past human activity. While such a definition may seem to be too general, we must have a term equally adequate for areas on which a few potsherds occur—perhaps the result of the accidental breaking of a single pot—to those of the size and complexity of a city of several hundred thousand people. By keeping his definition of a site flexible, the archaeologist reserves the right to study any evidence of past culture that he wishes. For example, he may want to record every item, no matter how small. On the other hand, his interest may pertain only to sites with a certain level of complexity, such as those with architecture. With a general approach to site definition the archaeologist remains free to study whatever he wishes.

63

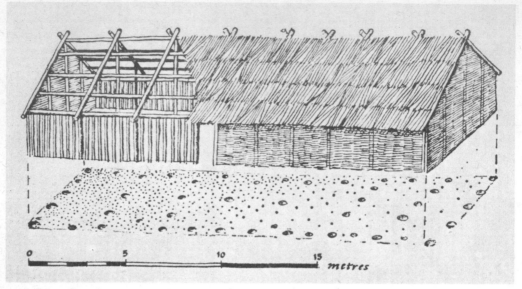

Fig. 4–1   House outline revealed by the pattern of ancient postholes. (Piggott 1968:350.)

The next most common questions that puzzle the nonarchaeologist are: How can you tell that you have found a site and how did you know where to look? Sites are revealed by their unique character. They are places where evidence of past human activity is present. The site area commonly will have either stone tools, pottery fragments, or both lying on the surface. Buried sites may be revealed in cutbanks. Another technique is to examine closely those areas which experience has shown you were the most frequently occupied. An example is the edge of a bluff overlooking a river valley. Once you have discovered which specific portions of an area most commonly have sites, it is not difficult to find other sites. A final method of site location is simply to look everywhere. This is a valid technique used by the professional archaeologist. If he does not know anything about an area, he simply starts looking until he finds a few sites. Once these are located, he notes carefully the features of the terrain in which they occur and then searches similar locales for more sites. Sites are also indicated by evidence of human modification of the local environment. The site area may have been cleared of vegetation in prehistoric times, and therefore the modern vegetation differs from that adjacent to the site. There may be ruined walls or other architectural features present. Suspicious looking mounds may be man-made. Even depressions of regular form—shapes which do not normally occur in nature—are likely man's responsibility. Excavation of the latter frequently reveals patterns of postholes indicating former houses (Fig. 4–1).

Once the site has been located then the archaeologist normally makes out a survey form (Fig. 4–2). He systematically records the location of the site on a map and describes all the features of the site, such as the presence of

Site No_____,_____County,_____State_____Drainage

1· Prior No./Name_____Used By_____

2·Elevation_____3_____U.S.G.S· Quad   4 Other Map_____

5· **LOCATION**_____

_____

_____, U·T·M· Grid_____
 ⁰⁄₀SEC_____TOWNSHIP_____, RANGE_____

6·Owner_____ 7·Address_____

8·Tenant_____ 9·Prior Owner(s)_____

10·Informant_____ 11·Address_____

12· **NEAREST WATER**_____permanent_____,season_____

13· Distance to 12_____ 14·Elevation of 12_____

15· **LOCALE VEGETATION**_____

16·**SITE TYPE**_____ 17·Cultural Affiliation (if known)_____

18· Description_____

_____

_____

19·Size_____ 20·Faces to (cardinal direction)_____

21· Depth & Character of Deposits_____

_____

22·Material Observed or Reported_____

_____

23·Material Collected_____

_____

24·Condition_____

25· **RECOMMENDATIONS**_____

_____

_____

26·Photograph Nos·_____ 27· Recorded By_____

28 Date_____

SEND TO — Office of the State Archaeologist
S-A Ketchum Hall
University of Colorado
Boulder, Colorado 80302

(margin text, right side): Site No | County, | State | Drainage | SEC | T, | R, | Page l of..

Fig. 4–2 Printed survey form illustrating typical categories to be recorded by the archaeologist during the site survey. (Courtesy of the Office of the Colorado State Archaeologist.)

pottery, architecture, stone tools, and other surface manifestations. He records the size of the site and its depth, if that can be determined. Other pertinent factors recorded include the site situation, its location relative to local topographic features, and the location of resources such as tool stone, arable land, water, good hunting areas, or potential plant harvests. Normally the site is photographed and a sketch map is drawn. The site is also given a number for identification which is used to identify all notes or materials obtained from the site.

A final step in the survey is the collection of artifacts from the site (Fig. 4–3). This collection may be a random or statistical sample. The latter technique requires collecting all the material from the surface of selected squares (normally 1 to 5 meters in size) laid out in a systematic pattern to provide a sample from every portion of the site. Such sampling enables the archaeologist to compare the material collected from one site with that from another site.

Site surveys are variable, since they are structured in response to logistical considerations, the nature of the sites to be surveyed, and the interests of the archaeologist. Logistical factors include topography, time available, distance from sources of supply, type of field transport available, and so forth. Archaeological surveys have been carried out by foot, horseback, camel, jeep, boats, helicopters, and airplanes. Dune buggies and hovercraft would also be useful in certain situations. Whatever mode of transportation is available or

Fig. 4–3 Taking a collection of artifacts from the surface of a site. (Photograph courtesy of Philip M. Hobler.)

most reasonable is utilized. For example, while site surveying on the Nile, Phil Hobler and I chartered a freight felucca, the Egyptian sailing vessel. We spent five days on board with all cooking, eating, and sleeping being accomplished in the space between decks (some 3½ feet vertically) without any built-in facilities. When we first saw the felucca, we described the fly-filled interior as a Black Hole of Calcutta. Several days later we thought our "ship" was pretty comfortable.

Because of the distance from a source of supply, the survey may have to be limited in ways detrimental to the collection of data. Ideally, all sites in an area should be recorded. However if that is not possible, you record what you can in the time available. While site surveying in the Egyptian Desert, Bahay Issawy and I, with a crew of eight men, wished to record sites in an area near Bir Sheb and Bir Nakhlai, some 150 miles out in the desert west of Aswan. We loaded two pickup trucks with food for 10 days and water for 3 days. Our plans were for a 10-day survey; however, we had to find water at Bir Nakhlai in order to make a 10-day stay possible. None of us had ever been there, and the last previous expedition to that oasis had been in 1927, at which time they reported a water flow of about five gallons per hour. We found the water and were able to survey according to plan. It was impossible to find every site in the area in the short time available, but we located a sample of the sites present.

Site survey may also be limited by the research interests of the archaeologist. If you are interested only in sites with rock art, then those are what you look for and record. One famous example is the search that Walter Taylor made for a dry cave site in the American Southwest. He searched for a site with Pueblo Indian remains and a long continuous profile with numerous preserved ecological specimens, especially plant materials. The survey lasted all one summer, and many sites were investigated, but the ideal site was never found—primarily because the best examples of such a site had already been excavated. Most surveys are more general in nature with all sites being recorded. However, it is possible to restrict one's problem orientation. Good examples are surveys for irrigation canals or terraces, rock art sites, sites of a particular time period, or sites along the periphery of an area in an attempt to define an archaeological "boundary." With our present concern for prehistoric cultural inventories and site protection from modern construction or vandalism, it has now become the archaeologist's responsibility to record all sites found even if they do not fit his defined problem interest.

Surveys are normally conducted before an excavation project is initiated; however, it is also possible to resurvey an area once you have isolated certain problems for further study. For example, after several seasons of excavation in an area it may be possible to construct a regional chronology. This chronology building may reveal that no excavation units pertain to a certain time period or periods. At that time it would be reasonable to initiate a resurvey to locate sites to fill in the missing periods.

After the sites in an area have been surveyed the survey notes are reviewed in detail. This enables the archaeologist to determine the kinds of sites which occur in the region, with what frequency, and their size range. By studying the collections he learns which cultural periods are represented and what kinds of activities are carried out at each site. With this information in hand the archaeologist is ready to decide which sites he wishes to dig.

EXCAVATION TECHNIQUES AND EXCAVATION LAYOUT

Archaeological excavation is a complex system of techniques developed to elucidate specific types of information. These techniques also are adapted to the different kinds of sites being excavated. We will discuss some specialized techniques, but first it is appropriate to describe those techniques of almost universal applicability.

A major purpose of excavation is to provide *provenience* information on every item recovered. Provenience refers to the specific location in the site of individual objects, which is accomplished through use of horizontal and vertical controls. Horizontal control is normally provided by the setting up of a grid system which divides the surface of the site into a pattern of equal area squares. The grid system is laid out with N–S and E–W lines at equal distances (Fig. 4–4). Such grid systems are laid out in either the English or metric system of measurement. Recently there has been an emphasis on all measurements

Fig. 4–4 Laying out a grid system on a site prior to excavation. In this photograph the grid of metal stakes will also be used for a resistivity survey of the subsurface. (Photograph courtesy of Philip M. Hobler.)

being taken in the metric system (Milisaukas 1973). The intersection of these lines defines squares, usually 5 feet or 2 meters on a side. Each square is given an identifying number so that any further research in that area can be suitably labeled with the square number. Site excavation usually is a sampling process, since only rarely are entire sites excavated. The grid system thus provides a means of indicating where on the site the individual specimens were obtained. On the other hand, the grid system does not limit the excavations because any combination of squares may be selected for excavation.

A variety of sites are more suited to other types of excavation layout. For example, any sites for which there are identifiable prehistoric site divisions— such as rooms, plazas, specialized structures, and so on—can be excavated, with these aboriginal subdivisions being used as the geographic coordinants. In some cases the sites are so simple that a specialized grid system would be superfluous. In such cases any system of geographical coordinants is suitable; for example, a small cave within which the position of any object could be obtained by triangulation from two or more points established on the cave wall.

Once excavation begins, it is necessary to define the vertical provenience of each specimen within the site. Several methods are commonly utilized. It is possible to set up an arbitrary datum level, either by means of a line level on a string or with a surveying instrument, and then plot the exact depth of every object below this arbitrary datum. Another method consists of establishing a series of arbitrary levels, all of the same thickness. Provenience of specimens is then indicated by square and level; for example, square 1 East, level 4, 30 to 40 centimeters. The exact location of the item within the grid and level may or may not be identified with any greater precision. A refinement of this technique is the definition of the *natural* levels of deposition within the site and then the segregation of all specimens from each. It is possible to combine these methods, with most specimens being lumped by level and the unique items being exactly located by horizontal and depth measurements.

The provenience measuring systems are not meant to restrict site sampling but serve only as a means of data recording. Site sampling is really another consideration, inasmuch as the type of sampling to be carried out is dependent on many factors. While excavation of the entire site is often a desirable goal, it is less often practicable. Limitations of time, personnel, and funds usually require that only a portion of a site be excavated. What is desirable is the intelligent selection of the best areas of the site to provide preserved information. Occasionally it is impossible to excavate all of a site, since only part may be owned by parties willing to give their permission. In other cases the site is too large and complex. For example, excavations have been carried out on an annual basis at Monte Alban, Mexico, and Sakkara, Egypt, for over 30 years, yet much remains untouched.

Site sampling can best be provided by a series of test pits or test trenches. It is possible to dig test pits on a random basis; for example, every fifth square or some other arbitrary number. A common technique is to put in two test trenches that cross each other at right angles. The resultant wall profiles permit the examination of a cross section of the entire site stratigraphy. Other methods include the dividing of the site into quadrants and completely excavating one quadrant, which is then considered representative of the whole.

Because the archaeologist's goal is the recovery of information, he is not concerned with the removal of specific percentage of the dirt in a site. For example, in a site with architecture it is possible to excavate a trench around the interior of the room walls. Such a trench provides exact information on the height, width, composition, and abutments of the walls as well as information about the location and composition of room floors. From such a sampling it is possible to work out the sequence of room construction that occurred. The excavations may remove only 20 percent or so of the entire earth fill present, yet the information recovered may be 50 percent of that potentially available.

The broadside is another frequently utilized sampling method. A large excavation face is opened and then systematically cut back into a bank or hillside. Such an approach is most appropriate when the area to be excavated is on a slope and rigorous arbitrary levels would be unusable. Another reason for the broadside may be that the site is covered with so much overburden that no other excavation method is feasible. Olduvai Gorge is an example of such a situation.

In no way should the use of these methods be considered as restrictive or mutually exclusive. The archaeologist wants data recovery, and he will change excavation techniques at any time if he believes some other kind of sampling will better provide the information sought. Frequently he will put in test pits around the site in addition to the main excavation units just to be sure that nothing vital is being overlooked. If something important is so located, then a more complete excavation of that area will be initiated.

Since what is found buried is often not apparent from the surface, it often occurs that excavation of a small unit thought to require only a few man days may reveal time-consuming complexities. A common cause of such incidents is the finding of unexpected burials or other items requiring careful excavation.

Excavation techniques are also governed by the kinds of labor and equipment locally available. When practicable, it is often possible to use road maintainers, bulldozers, tractors with a backhoe, or other mechanized equipment. The decision to use such equipment is based on its availability, its cost, and the nature of the site. If large quantities of overburden are present, power equipment is essential. On the other hand, it may be that the site is so delicate that only hand tools may be used; otherwise valuable data might be destroyed. While I was working at the Blackwater Draw site, there was an excellent opportunity to use power equipment. The site is a commercial gravel pit, and bulldozers and payloaders were available at no charge for any use I wished. The site consisted of numerous sand and silt layers, and in some cases 12 feet of overburden overlay bone beds of ancient killsites. The available machinery provided a remarkable opportunity to cut away the overburden efficiently and quickly. Surprisingly, the bulldozers could cut within 2 or 3 inches of a bone bed without doing any damage.

Other considerations governing the use or nonuse of power equipment include cost and logistics. If local labor is very cheap, it may also be the case that large machinery is nonexistent or very expensive. Some areas are too remote, too rocky, or too marshy for heavy machinery to be imported or used. The decision of the archaeologist in such instances is always to use the most practical alternative.

In addition to measuring the depth of individual specimens, it is important to map the individual site strata. If we have sectioned the site with cross trenches, this is an easy operation, for you simply map the exposed trench walls. If the site is being excavated in sections, it is frequently necessary to map the walls of each pit separately. The construction of a site cross section then is accomplished in the laboratory after the dig is completed. Another method consists of the leaving of balks—standing remnants of original site fill—between the excavation units. Such balks can then be mapped on profile drawings. Balks are useful in the correlation of layers or other features which occur in more than one excavation pit.

Articles about archaeology in the popular press stress the exactness and care with which archaeological excavations are carried out. The archaeologist is pictured as an expert who specializes in extremely careful recovery of delicate specimens. It is my impression that this conceptualization of the archaeologist is overdone. It is true that upon occasion it is necessary to excavate with great care. However most of the time the major task at hand is to get the dirt out in an orderly fashion and record the provenience of the specimens found. The single most important task of the archaeologist is to keep accurate records of everything found.

Preservation of specimens is accomplished both in the ground prior to removal and in the laboratory. There are two major aspects of these processes: cleaning of the specimens and strengthening of them through use of preservatives. Preservatives replace the moisture that accumulated in the specimens while in the ground and cement together the various fibers or pieces of the specimen. Mechanical strengthening is also possible through binding with a wrapping of string or coating with a jacket of plaster of paris. The field treatment is often kept as simple as possible, with a primary goal being the removal of the delicate specimen so that excavation will not be delayed. Later in the lab the time is available for careful cleaning and the application of repeated coats of preservative. The processes used are complex and I will not describe them in detail here. Several of the more routine processes are: 1. Charcoal samples are soaked in a solution of gasoline and paraffin; the former evaporates leaving the paraffin as a strengthening agent. 2. Perishable wood, bark, and such may be strengthened by soaking in a solution of fish glue or polyethylene glycol. 3. Bone may be preserved by impregnating it with a thin solution of water and white glue, acetone and alvar, or shellac and alcohol. In each case the solvent evaporates after having carried the glue deep into the specimen. In some cases the specimen is soaked in the preservative for a considerable period to enable full penetration and absorption. Preservatives present problems as well as solving them. For example, if radiocarbon dating is to be performed on the specimen, it must be cleaned of all organic preservatives. A second problem is that the preservatives may also cause the specimen to shrink, thus altering its original form. This problem can be rectified by measuring the item prior to its being coated or soaked or at least before it dries, as most size changes occur in the drying process.

Excavation procedures appropriate to the recovery of delicate items are whatever methods are feasible and possible at the time. Tools are gradational in size from bulldozers to dental picks. As excavation proceeds and a delicate item is located, or suspected, the archaeologist switches to more careful techniques and more delicate tools. First the item may be cleared off from above with a shovel. If its outline can be determined it is possible to isolate the specimen on a pedestal by cutting around it. Excavation of the item then may proceed with a trowel and whiskbroom. If more care is required, finer tools are employed, including grapefruit knives, ice picks, dental picks, small paint-brushes, and small syringes. The earth is carefully dislodged with the picks and then brushed or blown away. It is usually possible to find one part of the item which is less delicate or still earth-covered, and the loose earth can be brushed away over this part without injury to the specimen. Final exposure of the item for photography can be accomplished by brushing or with water or air in a syringe. Removal of delicate items is easier if the specimen is removed encased in a block of earth. In the final analysis what is really important is the documentation of the nature of the find. If the specimen is too delicate to be removed or if the proper materials are not available for its preservation, it is still possible to uncover the specimen, photograph or draw it, and take measurements or samples for chemical analyses. After that the specimen may not be recoverable, but at least considerable information has been preserved. In Egypt, for example, we were excavating burials some 14,000 years old, the oldest ever found in that country. The skeletons were embedded in a sand dune formation cemented by groundwater activity. The result was that the bones were softer than the matrix in which they occurred. Our solution was to remove the skulls in plaster jackets and measure the length of the other bones in the ground because it was impossible to remove them in one piece. Jacketing the skulls presented problems as there was no plaster of paris available in Aswan. Instead we had to purchase ordinary commercial wall plaster which had the characteristics of quicklime. When it was mixed with water it dissolved fingernails. Nonetheless, it served well enough to permit the transportation of the specimens back to the museum laboratory.

SITE SAMPLING

Items of interest to modern archaeologists include not only actual tools or manufactured objects but all discarded food remains, waste materials discarded in the manufacturing process, and even the soil itself. Analysis of soil reveals evidence of the geologic processes in effect since the site was abandoned. We can learn much about the paleoecology of the site and area from included fossils such as pollen grains, snails, diatoms, and small animal bones. Chemical analysis of the soil is also instructive in our search for environmental and cultural data. These interests have led to the development of a variety of site sampling techniques because no single technique is applicable to all sites. There is, however, no single standard-sized soil sample. For example, samples rich in preserved pollen can provide hundreds of pollen grains in a teaspoonful of soil. On the other hand, if pollen is not preserved, the size of the sample is immaterial. If we are interested in the recovery of small mammal bones, a suitably sized sample, in the richest deposits, is perhaps 100 pounds of soil. In less rich deposits up to 1000 pounds of soil must be washed and sifted to produce one identifiable bone. Chemical samples may be of small size, from 5 to 40 grams. In any case the adequate sampling of a site for materials of this sort requires that several different sample series of differing size be collected from each level. In addition you may want close interval samples for some of these profiles, while a single bulk sample from each level is sufficient for other needs. Several things are important in such sampling. The samples must be clearly identified as to provenience on a profile drawing, and the samples must be identified as to level and sample number. As nearly as possible the individual profiles must be correlatable with each other, for it is a waste of time to collect several suites of samples if their chronological relationship to each other cannot be established. One way of coping with this problem is to collect the largest samples first and then remove the smaller samples from these, a method which provides an exact correlation. Normally such samples are processed in the laboratory, although some separation can be accomplished in the field through use of wet or dry screening. For example, in British Columbia we reduced the weight of our samples collected for their small bone content by washing them first through a quarter-inch mesh screen and then through an eighth-inch mesh. The resultant concentrate had about a quarter of the bulk of the original samples, while still retaining a statistically valid sample of the small bones we were seeking.

Sampling for artifacts is usually somewhat less complex as the standard method is to dry-screen all debris from a test pit by level, either natural or arbitrary, and bag all recovered artifacts by level. This method is fast, and it yields a statistically valid sample which provides a quick way of assessing the artifactual changes level by level.

Sampling is thus inherent in practically every kind of archaeology. It is seldom possible to excavate an entire site or collect everything from the surface. Therefore we utilize specific sampling techniques in site survey, in excavation of portions of sites, and in the collection of samples for laboratory analysis from the respective levels within the site. These techniques were developed because they provide scientifically verifiable, rather than randomly collected, information, and they also aid in the identification of site characteristics without the necessity of excavating all of the site.

LABORATORY ANALYSIS

Work in the laboratory includes washing, cleaning, and preserving specimens, and labeling them with site and level numbers so that their specific provenience can always be identified. The artifacts are measured, described, photographed, and drawn, when necessary, for purposes of illustration in reports. Broken artifacts are mended and restored when possible. All of the artifacts are then sorted into types. Even broken artifacts such as potsherds can be typed, and the frequency of occurrence of each type aids the archaeologist's description of each level and the changes in the culture at the site through time. For the most part, the kinds of laboratory analysis performed by the archaeologist are not elaborate, nor do they require expensive equipment. Laboratory work is time-consuming; therefore, much of it is carried out at the home institution rather than in the field. For example, the restoration of a pot is something that requires time for the mended piece to set before the next piece is glued on. There may also be the need for care which the field situation does not permit.

Even standard facilities such as electricity and running water may not be available in the field; thus, the general rule is that all operations which can be postponed until you are back at the home lab are carried out there. Environmental samples especially require laboratory techniques of some complexity. Pollen analysis requires the centrifuging and boiling of the samples in hydrochloric and hydrofloric acid. Radiocarbon analysis requires expensive equipment which must also be exactly calibrated by the frequent processing of radioactively dead samples. Sifting and washing of soil samples are routine laboratory tasks but time-consuming. It is often possible to collect in one day on the site enough such samples to require a month of laboratory processing.

In recent years increasing attention has been given to the study of the environmental components, the waste flakes, and the evidences of wear on artifact surfaces and edges. One versatile tool used to study such materials is a low power (10 to 50X) binocular microscope. In previous years it was thought sufficient to examine artifacts and other items with a 10 power hand lens. Today the microscope has come into widespread use as it provides greater magnification as well as a precise means of measuring details of artifacts. Another function is photomicroscopy of small objects for illustration in reports.

Numerous other techniques are of utility. Site survey can be carried out in the lab through examination of aerial photographs. For those areas with limited vegetation, such as the Peruvian coastal desert, it is even possible to make maps to scale of sites visible on the aerial photos.

Infrared photography provides a means of site location because it is highly sensitive to minute differences in vegetation. Thus the vegetal cover on a site, no matter how little different from the surrounding vegetation, will reveal the site's presence. This kind of preliminary site survey carried out in the laboratory can save days of effort in the field and much expense in the actual location of sites.

One of the greatest limitations to archaeology has been the fact that once excavated, a site is destroyed and cannot be reexcavated. Therefore the archaeologist must rely on his notes and records for all future study and interpretation. A technique recently developed consists of the taking of time-lapse movies—exposing movie film at selected intervals during the excavation of a site. This technique provides one means whereby the excavation of a particular site may be reviewed again in the laboratory on film. While such a technique is less accurate than actual examination of the site in the field, it can provide a check on the notes taken at the time of excavation.

Laboratory analysis techniques can be almost infinitely variable, since any technique developed in the physical sciences may be applicable; for example, thin sectioning of potsherds (a technique adapted from geology) and use of a sonic generator for specimen cleaning. What is standardized about archaeological laboratory analysis is that it is concerned with study of the objects recovered through excavation and includes all of the first steps in the preparation of the final archaeological report.

REFERENCES

De Laet, S. J., 1958, *The Low Countries*. London: Thames and Hudson.
Milisaukas, S., 1973, "The Need for a Common Language of Measurements," *American Antiquity* 38(1):1–2.
Piggott, Stuart, 1968, *The Dawn of Civilization*. New York: McGraw-Hill.

5

Concepts in Archaeology

Foremost among the concepts utilized in archaeology is the one we term *culture*. A brief definition is that culture is "the learned patterns of thought and behavior characteristic of a population or society" (Harris 1971:629). A more inclusive definition is that of Tylor (1871:1):

Culture or civilization, taken in its wide ethnographic sense, is that complex whole which includes knowledge, belief, art, morals, law, custom, and any other capabilities and habits acquired by man as a member of society. The condition of culture among the various societies of mankind, in so far as it is capable of being investigated on general principles, is a subject apt for the study of laws of human thought and action.

In contrast to biological evolution, the evolution of culture is less constrained by environmental factors. The reason for this is that culture provides a protective shield or buffer between man and his environment; clothing, fire, languages, and so forth, all provide means whereby man has the ability to shield himself from environmental stresses. In addition, man's technology, tools, and their associated behavioral patterns extend his capability in the food quest and other economic pursuits. One result of man's possession of culture is that it frees him to some degree from direct biological selection in the sense of the "survival of the fittest" as outlined by Darwin. Therefore human physical types have remained generalized rather than being highly adapted to specific environmental niches as are many animal species. Man's recent accomplishments in space are current proof of this continuing biological generality.

Culture is further distinct from biological evolution in its ability for quick modification. Biological inheritance is transmitted through the genetic constitution of each individual; therefore any selective change must of necessity require considerable time. In contrast, culture consists of behavioral patterns which are learned, and their transmission is dependent upon observation and communication. If certain cultural practices are seen to be more efficient or simply become popular, they may spread from individual to individual in a short span of time. Culture is also characterized by random variation or individuality. Frequently such variation is nonadaptive in a strict sense; however, since the entire matrix of culture protects the individual from environmental stresses, this nonadaptive variation is permitted to exist. This freedom is one of the greatest advantages of culture because it permits the development of attributes which later may become adaptive or at least may fulfill functions related to entertainment and the satisfaction of intellectual needs. The relevance of these observations to culture history is that there is no genetically or otherwise predetermined sequence of evolution of culture. Cultural evolution does have direction, but it can either exhibit change from simple to complex or vice versa; or it can continue for long intervals of time with little change. Culture may also influence human biological evolution through the imposition of selective pressure. In general, culture has become increasingly complex through time, but this is not true for every area at every time period in the past. Culture, because it is learned-shared behavior, can also be introduced from one culture to another. In this situation traits which have required long periods for their development in their parent cultures may be introduced to other cultures and widely disseminated in a short period of time. One only has to observe the worldwide distribution of Coca Cola to realize that future archaeologists will regard the presence of broken Coke bottles in their sites as synchronous, no matter where found. Also in contrast to biological evolution, culture traits may also be independently invented in more than one area. Convergent development can occur, with similar end results of differing evolutionary traditions—in this case a parallel with biological evolution. Another such parallel is cultural variation which in its evolutionary effect is analogous to genetic variation. In order to categorize these characteristics of culture, archaeologists have developed a series of concepts to explain the cultural processes involved in cultural change.

Archaeological concepts may be viewed as a system of building blocks, which may be recombined in various ways. It should be mentioned that there is nothing immutable about these building blocks; they are arbitrarily defined and are subject to continuing revision. The record of man's culture is a continuum; therefore any division of this continuum is arbitrary. The concepts which have been devised can be organized into a series of categories. These include descriptive units, cultural units, spatial units, chronological units, and integrative units. We will describe each of these in turn.

DESCRIPTIVE UNITS

ATTRIBUTES   Those elements which form consistent features characteristic of an artifact we term *attributes*. In a strict sense any feature may constitute an attribute even if it is unique and nonrecurring. Normally such features do occur on more than one specimen. We thus assume that their presence is an indication of cultural preference and hence, patterned behavior. Any identifiable element can be considered to be an attribute. Examples from pottery include paint type, paint color, design style, paste, temper, surface texture, thickness, porosity, weight, hardness, paste color, and so on. Stone tools are unifacially or bifacially retouched; they may be core or flake tools; they have a number of straight, convex, or concave edges, with or without serrations; and retouching may be steep or low angle. The attribute is the smallest or most detailed cultural element described by the archaeologist. Their notation, description, and statistical frequency provide the component elements of the next larger cultural concept, the artifact type.

ARTIFACT TYPE   According to Hole and Heizer (1969:167) an *artifact type* is defined as:

> By the word "type" we mean a particular kind of artifact (for example, arrow-point, house floor, metate, scraper, bone awl, and so on) in which several attributes combine or cluster with sufficient frequency or in such distinctive ways that the archaeologist can define and label the artifact and can recognize it when he sees another example.

Note that the identification of the artifact type is left up to the discretion of the archaeologist; there are no arbitrary or real limits. In fact, in dealing with a class of artifacts such as scrapers, you frequently find that in terms of form and other diagnostic attributes the scrapers constitute a continuum which, if divided into a series of "types," may be somewhat differently segregated by each archaeologist who examines them. This does not mean that types are imaginary, for they form classificatory units in the archaeologist's analysis and therefore are real to the archaeologist. In addition it is usually assumed that the "types" existed as concepts in the minds of their prehistoric makers. The archaeologist in his study and definition of types is thus reconstructing these prehistoric cultural patterns. This is the concept termed the "mental template" by Deetz (1967:45).

The idea of the proper form of an object exists in the mind of the maker, or at least a set of attributes, and when this idea is expressed in tangible form in raw material, an artifact results. The idea is the mental template from which the craftsman makes the object. The form of an artifact is a close approximation of this template, and variations in a group of similar objects reflect variation in the ideas which produce them. What gives form to the idea or mental template held by the maker of an artifact? Certainly tradition, since learning a craft entails the transmission of these templates from generation to generation, and many aspects of them have been present for so long that people simply feel that this shape for an axe or that color for a basket is inherently right. However, factors other than the purely traditional can affect the form of the mental template, and there are other factors which affect the form of the finished product which are completely unrelated to the template involved.

Deetz cites as such factors causes which are functional, technological, innovative, or the inherent result of the materials used. There is another point of view; namely, that types are "artifacts" of the archaeologist, the result of arbitrary decisions by the archaeologist which form useful descriptive categories in his analysis but should not be viewed as evidence of past cultural patterns. These two viewpoints represent the archaeologist as either "discovering" prehistoric artifactual types or "inventing" types to suit his own purposes of analysis. Both points of view have merit. It is my belief that most of the time we can come pretty close to discovering the clusters of attributes which made up the concept in the mind of the maker of an artifact. However, we may have different views from the maker as to the degree of variation around a mean that was permissible. You should also be aware that types per se in modern definitions are viewed as a description of an abstraction. Few if any artifacts are exactly like the abstract definition, and the clustering of attributes may be expressed in statistical terms. For example, in a study on Paleo-Indian materials from the Blackwater Draw site in eastern New Mexico, I described the well-known projectile type, the Folsom point, as follows:

Folsom points are presumably made from primary flakes struck from prepared cores, although evidence of this usually has been destroyed by the subsequent allover bifacial working. Major characteristics are that they are bifacially worked (100%), although a few are only retouched around the perimeter on one face, pressure chipped (94.6%), possess a slightly contracting stem (54.1%), a concave base (78.2% in whole specimens, 60.7% in fragments), are fluted (65.4%), have basal grinding (65.3% in whole specimens, 58.9% in fragments), and may have the tip reworked (7.9%). Size range: length 1.0 to 2.0 inches, average 1.42 inches; width 0.6 to 0.8 inches, average 0.71 inches; thickness 0.1 to 0.2 inches, average 0.14 inches; length of grinding on sides 0.3 to 1.3 inches, average 0.8 inches; length of flutes 0.3 to 2.0 inches, average 0.9 inches. It is apparent that while all of these attributes might appear in a "type" description, their incidence is variable by attribute. Conclusions to be drawn from this fact are that there existed a cultural norm typified by these attributes but that suitable projectile points were made and used which lacked some of these attributes. Minor attributes include: an expanding stem, parallel flaking, basal thinning after fluting, and unfluted (Hester 1972:124).

My use of this Folsom point type description is to illustrate an actual case with statistically tabulated attribute frequencies. Certainly fluting was a diagnostic and important attribute, yet almost 35 percent of the points were unfluted. However, no matter how variable are the specimens we work with, the type concept is our single most useful device in the segregation and description of individual artifacts. By means of this concept we do not have to describe every single specimen but are able to group the artifacts into types and then describe the types, a tremendous laborsaving technique which has the additional virtue of attempting to organize the data in terms of prehistoric cultural patterns.

ARTIFACT CLASSES   Artifacts may further be grouped into larger categories based on consideration of general similarities in form or function. These *classes* include examples such as scrapers, a functional category, or bifaces, a category based on form. Grouping in terms of such classes is useful to the archaeologist in several ways. In the preliminary sorting of artifacts it is easier and quicker first to sort the implements into classes from which specific artifact types may be isolated. Another major use of classes is in the descriptive report where the types are grouped by artifact class. The result is a standardization of style which makes archaeological reports easier to compare one with the other. A final use of classes may occur when the individual specimens are not readily broken down into types. An example concerns pointed bone objects. Such artifacts may have been used to perform a variety of functions, but the items are not form specific; that is, their form is generalized and does not clearly indicate which function or functions were served. In such a case rather than describe types in the report, a description of the class is sufficient.

TYPOLOGY   The next highest level of description is the *typology*. This constitutes all of the recognized and described types of artifacts characteristic of a particular industry (a term we will define later on in this chapter). The typology is a method of describing all of the artifacts representative of a particular time and place. The typology is a classification which seeks objectively to unite all artifacts into meaningful categories on the basis of form. Inasmuch as such a classification is formulated with "types" as the major constituent elements, the entire typology is viewed as an abstraction, and the size of the sample and the number of sites or levels in sites it represents are immaterial. What is significant is that the typology organizes all artifactual data with form as the primary criteria. It is also generally assumed that such developed form categories had some prehistoric reality. Possibly some of the most important aspects of a typology are what it is not or does not attempt to do. A typology is based upon variations in form which are the result of numerous processes. Form is the final shape of the item after it has been manufactured and used. (Some artifacts are solely the result of use while others were deliberately manufactured for use.) Therefore a typological description does not inform us as to the manufacturing techniques employed nor to their order. It is even possible to reach a similar final form through use of different sets of manufacturing techniques. A typology is also not necessarily culturally specific; in other words, not every prehistoric culture developed an entirely unique set of artifact forms. In fact the opposite is the case: most cultures possess numerous artifact forms similar to those in other cultures. What is distinctive about each separate culture is a few diagnostically different artifacts. This fact enables the archaeologist to describe a typology which has general applicability, which can be applied with little modification to classify the artifacts from a variety of similar or related cultures. Even cultures which are not historically related may have a number of similar artifact types if they possess a similar environmental adaptation. Probably the best example of such a general typology is that developed by François Bordes (1961). He has described 63 types which are sufficient for descriptive purposes to categorize cultural manifestations in the Lower and Middle Paleolithic.

TECHNOLOGY   Complementary to a typology is a description of the prehistoric *technology*. Here the manufacturing processes and their sequence is what is emphasized. Technological studies are of more recent development than typological ones, but today it is recognized that no archaeological study is complete without both. The technology includes the selection and preparation of stone for future use, which involves the removal of trimming flakes from cores and of primary flakes from the cores, with the flakes to be later modified into tools. Steps inherent in this preparation include the removal of cortex and the manufacture of a suitable striking platform. Overall core trimming may be practiced or may be omitted; the difference is discernible on the finished tools by the presence or absence of the original cortex. The core preparation may follow a specific pattern; for example, the Levallois technique in which many preparatory flakes are removed so that one final flake of the desired shape is struck off, the rest of the flakes and the core then being discarded. A detailed study of these preparation steps carried all the way through the final retouch and edge grinding of the finished specimen provides a history of its manufacture. The system is keyed to statistical manipulation, since the presence or absence of each of the steps can be expressed numerically as percentages of the total sample. In addition the internal relationships of the sample can be expressed in ratios or indices; for example, the frequency of tools made on Levallois flakes expressed as a percentage of all Levallois flakes identified. Such indices provide common descriptive factors which facilitate the comparison of the artifacts from a site, level, or industry with those of another such unit.

CULTURAL UNITS

Cultural units are those descriptive categories which are designed to be synonymous with prehistoric cultural entities. In actual fact, owing to the inadequate preservation of archaeological data, it is impossible for such to occur. After all, a prehistoric culture embodied a large amount of nonmaterial items which are not preserved and can only be inferred with accuracy in rare instances. When we speak of an "archaeological culture," we are normally referring to those items which have been *preserved* and recorded through use of archaeological methods. The relationships of archaeological materials to the cultural designations utilized by anthropologists studying modern societies should be explained rather than assumed. The common denominator of each archaeological unit is defined on the basis of cultural content—forms which are (according to Willey and Phillips 1958:14) physiogromic, recurrent, and internally consistent—thus the size and comprehensiveness of the sample are not major criteria. Common cultural units defined by the archaeologist are as follows:

ASSEMBLAGE   The term *assemblage* is that grouping of artifacts normally occurring in a single site or cultural level. By definition, an assemblage is considered to be an insufficient sample to be representative of a prehistoric culture. It is assumed that evidence of a prehistoric culture must be identified in more than one location or level for it to be demonstrated to possess distinctive characteristics due to cultural factors rather than to chance. The assemblage thus is a group of implements utilized by a prehistoric culture at a particular time and place. What is unique about the assemblage is the possibility that it represents only a portion of the original cultural inventory—perhaps representing a specialized economic activity but not the total life way of the prehistoric people. The term was originated by European prehistorians, and owing to the nature of most Paleolithic materials, has come to be generally associated with the stone tools and stone waste (debitage) present on a single site. There is no reason other materials such as bone cannot be included; they are normally not included because of poor preservation. The American term synonymous with assemblage is *component*. The component is also suspect in its indication of a true cultural pattern. However, any component which is unique is viewed as one which, with additional excavations, could be found in several sites and thus indicate a cultural pattern.

The assemblage or component is the smallest whole unit of a culture to be identified. Isolated finds of a few stone tools or one broken pot are considered to represent idiosyncratic behavior rather than significant portions of the cultural pattern.

INDUSTRY   The term *industry* is that cluster of artifact types which are believed to represent the remains of a prehistoric society. The usual case is that similar assemblages have been located on several sites. These assemblages can be assigned to one larger overall grouping, the industry, which because of its repetitive occurrence is indicative of a past cultural pattern. Furthermore the industry is presumed to represent the material culture remains left by a specific group of people or culture. Therefore study of an industry will reveal evidences of patterned behavior specific to that particular culture. In the European archaeological tradition, with its strong emphasis on Paleolithic remains, the industry is most often made up of stone tool types because of the lack of preservation of other material items. The American counterpart of the industry is the *focus,* made up of a number of components. The exact number of components or the total area over which they occur is of no concern; what is significant is their similar cultural content. If there is an archaeological unit which is synonymous with the term a *culture* as used by cultural anthropologists, it is the *focus* or *industry*. We recognize that a true culture includes a set of behavioral patterns; however, since archaeological findings include only objects and their associations, behavioral patterns must be inferred. In these definitions of cultural units we have refrained from applying spatial or temporal qualifications because it is possible to define such units solely in terms of their content. On the other hand some archaeologically defined concepts are based on spatial or temporal considerations, and we will discuss those next.

SPATIAL UNITS

The total amount of space in the units defined below is somewhat variable, for space is a conterminous attribute analogous to a continuum. Therefore, how much space equals one unit is arbitrarily defined. It is also true that space requirements of prehistoric cultures varied with the economy, population, and other variables. If spatial units are arbitrarily defined by archaeologists, then how do we reach agreement? One way is to follow as best as we can the definitions used by some outstanding authorities, which even if arbitrary, may be utilized in an effort to achieve consistency. One set of definitions that are widely used are those presented by Willey and Phillips in the 1958 publication *Method and Theory in American Archaeology*.

A *site* is the smallest unit of space dealt with by the archaeologist and the most difficult to define. Its physical limits, which may vary from a few square yards to as many square miles, are often impossible to fix. About the only requirement ordinarily demanded of the site is that it be fairly continuously covered by remains of former occupation, and the general idea is that these pertain to a single unit of settlement, which may be anything from a small camp to a large city. Upon excavation, of course, it rarely turns out to be that simple. The site is the basic unit for stratigraphical studies; it is an almost certain assumption that cultural changes here can only be the result of the passage of time. It is in effect the minimum operational unit of geographical space (p. 18).

A *locality* is a slightly larger spatial unit, varying in size from a single site to a district of uncertain dimensions; it is generally not larger than the space that might be occupied by a single community or local group. It is hardly necessary to add that such limits as are implied in this qualification have the variability found in the size and settlement patterns of local groups from one sort of society to another. In strictly archaeological terms, the locality is a geographical space small enough to permit the working assumption of complete cultural homogeneity at any given time (p. 18).

A *region* is a considerably larger unit of geographical space usually determined by the vagaries of archaeological history. Quite often it is simply the result of concentrated research by an individual or group. Rightly or wrongly, such a region comes to be thought of as having problems of its own that set it apart from other regions. Regional terms are those most often found in the titles of archaeological papers of wider scope than site reports. Through constant reiteration they become fixed in the literature and achieve a kind of independent existence. Regions are not altogether without reference to the facts of geography, however. In stressing the accidental factor in their information, we must not overlook the tendency for environmental considerations to assert themselves. In portions of the New World (and the Old World as well) where physical conditions of sharp diversity prevail, archaeological regions are likely to coincide with minor physiographic subdivisions (p. 19).

An *area* is a geographical unit very considerably larger than a region; it corresponds roughly to the culture area of the ethnographer. Archaeological areas like regions, have come into existence by common consent, but the element of historical accident is reduced somewhat by the fact that many individuals and institutions are likely to have been involved in their investigation. They tend to coincide with major physiographic divisions. That the North American Southwest, for example, has maintained its identity as an archaeological area through more than a half-century of intensive investigation is certainly due in large part to culture-environment correlations of a positive nature. It is hardly necessary to add that, although the area as defined here may have general physiographic integrity, its limits are not so easy to draw on a map as those of the smaller region (p. 20).

It often happens that there are territories of geographical extent intermediate between the region and the area which possess qualities and degrees of cultural unity that give them a definite usefulness in archaeological or ethnographical studies. We refer to such spatial units as *subareas* (p. 20).

Because Willey and Phillips' definitions are spatially confined and in some cases tied to physiographic provinces, they might be viewed as static configurations within which cultures had to adapt or be restricted. In actual historical fact such has not been the case. We can trace the history of a particular cultural group through time and identify whether the culture expanded or contracted its use of space at different points in its history. The exception derives from the power of new technological innovations to free cultures from prior environmental—spatial—limitations. Therefore, these spatial divisions might more properly be viewed as conveniences for the archaeologist rather than culturally binding environmental constructs.

TEMPORAL UNITS

The archaeologist is acutely aware of time, both its immensity and its regular elapsing. He thinks and organizes his data in units with both dimensions of space and time. Among the universal concepts in archaeology perhaps time is the most important. Time is a continuum which is necessary to subdivide into uniform and meaningful units. For example, our culture's concept of a century is such a unit and its meaning is arbitrarily defined. The Maya relied heavily upon time units of 20 years each and the Aztec upon a 52-year cycle.

In archaeology the exact length of time assigned each chronological unit is variable; it may vary from sequence to sequence and within a single sequence. The criteria we use to separate one cultural period from another is change in form of artifact types. When sufficient change in form in artifacts we term *diagnostic* has occurred, we designate a new cultural period. In other cases we have a series of site levels, each of which is distinctive. In either case the evaluation of what constitutes sufficient change is made by the archaeologist. In contrast then to the spatial units which are defined on the basis of spatial characteristics, the chronological units are defined not in terms of specific chronological attributes but in terms of change in cultural content. It is change in this content, rather than in the amount of elapsed time, which governs the length of our arbitrarily segmented portions of the archaeological continuum. The basic unit used in archaeological chronology we term the *phase*; however, its dimensions include not only time but space and cultural content. Therefore we will define the phase more precisely in the section on integrative units to follow.

The chronological use of the phase and other units of cultural content is their arrangement into a sequence or chronology. Willey and Phillips (1958:24–25) distinguish the following types of these sequences:

The *local sequence* in its purest form is a series of components found in vertical stratigraphic succession in a single site. It may also, however, be a composite series made by combining shorter stratigraphic 'runs' from various portions of a site or from several sites within a locality, or it may be derived from seriating components by various means without benefit of stratigraphy at all. However obtained, the local sequence has this important feature: it is local. The spatial dimension, by definition, is small enough to permit the working assumption that differences between components reflect differences in time.

We have already referred to the fact that members of a local sequence, though technically regarded as components, are often referred to as phases on the ground that they are local manifestations of the larger units and, also, that it is theoretically possible for a phase to be represented by a single component. The local sequence may, therefore, be defined as a *chronological series of components, phases, or subphases, within the geographical limits of a locality as defined in this study.*

A *regional sequence* is not merely a local sequence with larger spatial dimensions. The difference can best be approached from the operational standpoint. In the normal extension of archaeological information, components, subphases, phases, and local sequences multiply, and questions of wider relationships come to the fore. Ideally, the archaeologists of a region come together in a harmonious session where a careful matching of local sequences produces a new sequence of larger scope. Actually this happy event occurs but rarely. What more often happens is that phases and local sequences gain in scope by a sort of osmosis. They flow outward, so to speak, often propelled by their originators, uniting to themselves their weaker correlates over a widening circle. The process is necessarily accompanied by a progressive generalization of definition until much of their original usefulness to research is impaired.

Nevertheless, we will assume for the sake of argument that local sequences remain local and that regional sequences are the result of correlating them—not combining them, be it noted, because in the process the original formulations are retailored to fit the wider spatial and (sometimes) temporal dimensions. The phase now appears in its widest practicable extension and at its farthest remove from the primary data; at any rate, it is our contention that the concept of phase cannot safely be extended beyond the limits here described. With these operational conditions in mind, we may define the regional sequence as *a chronological series of phases or subphases within the geographical limits of a region as defined in this study.*

INTEGRATIVE UNITS

The integrative nature of culture is such that it has form and pattern expressed in every cultural manifestation from the attribute to the culture area. These aspects change through time in their form and in the space they occupy. We thus must view culture in its temporal and spatial dimensions as well as in terms of continuity and change, contact and isolation, independent invention or diffusion. These multivariate aspects of culture require that the archaeologist, in order to understand fully the development of culture through time, devise conceptual units which accurately reflect these configurations. These devices we term *integrative units.*

The basic integrative unit is the *phase.* We have already discussed the reasons why the component cannot serve as our basic unit: because it is unique to a site and therefore does not represent necessarily a "cultural" pattern. As our goal is to describe and understand *culture,* the phase is the smallest whole cultural unit with which we can deal.

Willey and Phillips (1958:22) define the phase as

. . . an archaeological unit possessing traits sufficiently characteristic to distinguish it from all other units similarly conceived, whether of the same or other cultures or civilizations, spatially limited to the order of magnitude of a locality or region and chronologically limited to a relatively brief interval of time.

The phase has three basic dimensions: a specific cultural content as well as temporal and spatial dimensions. In the construction of local and regional sequences, it is not, strictly speaking, a temporal unit but rather a unit representing an entire culture for a specific time and place. You have undoubtedly noticed that we have set no precise limits on any of these dimensions; there is no specific amount of culture content, time, or space mentioned in the definition. Willey and Phillips use terms like "sufficiently characteristic" and "similarly conceived." In actual practice the decision to term one cultural manifestation a phase and another a component is left entirely up to the excavating archaeologist. If he cannot make a clear decision, he may elect to term the manifestation a *subphase.* The ambiguity of the situation is more apparent than real, since the limits of phases are described in general terms and the archaeologist simply attempts to fit whatever data he recovers into the most appropriate conceptual niche.

Such imprecision is characteristic of archaeology because we are attempting to describe and understand cultural manifestations, which change at different rates through time. In addition, cultural uniqueness is important; a unique manifestation of small size is equal in cultural distinctiveness to one of large size. These variables make the most useful concepts those which are the most flexible, and this is the value of the phase concept: it is the most flexible and thus useful basic integrative unit devised to date.

HORIZON   The *horizon* is a concept which is of less than culturewide occurrence. It is limited to a cluster of culture traits or some other portion of a whole culture. The content of a horizon consists of distinctive cultural elements which may be readily identified wherever they occur, regardless of whether or not this is within the cultural matrix in which they originated. The nature of these traits is such that they may be widely transmitted in space within a brief time period. "The horizon, then, may be defined as a primarily spatial continuity represented by cultural traits and assemblages whose nature and mode of occurrence permit the assumption of a broad and rapid spread" (Willey and Phillips 1958:33). Horizons are not whole cultures, but their content may include a major segment of a culture, such as a religious cult or other discrete unit. The utility of the horizon concept as defined by the archaeologist is that horizons are *assumed* to be essentially synchronous. Therefore if a horizon is identified in a particular site, its presence can be used as a chronological indicator; that is, it can be used to establish a relative age for the site and the levels within it. Horizons are best known from Peru where they occur as distinctive styles on pottery. Their widespread occurrence geographically and the frequency with which these styles appear on the local pottery wares have greatly aided in the establishment of regional chronologies in Peru. While horizon markers and index fossils *may* be the same, typically the index fossil is a single artifact type of known age. The horizon style, on the other hand, tends to be a complex of traits occurring together. Horizons may not be precisely dated, but because of their broad geographic spread over a brief time span, they can be utilized for chronological correlations.

TRADITION   An archaeologically defined *tradition* consists of the persistence of cultural forms through time. The concept is flexible in the sense that size or complexity are not aspects of major concern; what is important is the identification of persistence. Traditions may be manifest in every aspect of culture from the individual attribute to whole cultures. Traditions vary in complexity, in their rate of change, and in the direction in which they change. A group of archaeologists studying the nature of traditions published the following set of definitions (Haury and others 1955:43–44) (Fig. 5–1).

A Direct Tradition is characterized by an essentially unchanging continuity. Those changes which take place do not effectively shift lines of development within the tradition. An example is the preference for flat-bottom vessels in the pottery shape tradition of North Coast Peru.

A Converging Tradition describes the segment in which two or more traditions come together. Convergence may result in a merger of the traditions into a single tradition. Sometimes one of the traditions is absorbed. On the other hand, convergence

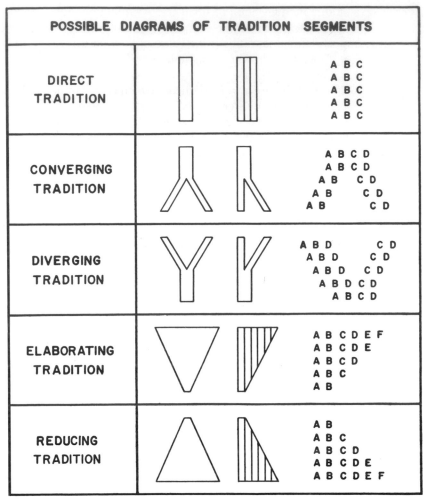

Fig. 5–1 Diagrams illustrating different forms of archaeological tradition segments. (Haury and others 1955:Fig. 1.)

may mean that the traditions impinge on one another for a time, without the submergence of either. Although contact situations between different cultures offer a ready opportunity for convergence, this process may take place between traditions within a single culture. Convergence is illustrated by the blending of the Mogollon and Anasazi cultural traditions in the Southwest.

A Diverging Tradition is in many respects the opposite of a Converging Tradition and refers to the segment in which a single tradition splits into two or more distinguishable traditions. This does not necessarily mean that the parent tradition is terminated, for it may not be appreciably affected by this process. In others, the newly formed traditions differ considerably from the original one. The development of two distinct regional variants of the Hohokam red-on-buff pottery tradition is an example of divergence.

An Elaborating Tradition is characterized by an increasing complexity resulting from the addition of traits or attributes which are integrated in a single line of development. Not only quantity and variety of traits are involved, but also their organization and embellishment. The Polychrome pottery tradition in South Coast Peru is an illustration of elaboration.

A Reducing Tradition is in some ways the opposite of an Elaborating Tradition. The Reducing Tradition is characterized by an increasing simplification through loss of traits and perhaps in terms of a less complex organization. The reduction of the Yucatecan tradition of religious architecture at Mayapan illustrates this class of tradition segments.

Disruption normally relates to the terminal phase of a tradition and describes the collapse of a tradition through the process of disorganization. Nevertheless, it is necessary to recognize the possibility of re-emergence and reconstitution of a tradition after disruption, however rare such a situation may be in reality. The revival of the decorative tradition of Sikyatki Polychrome by contemporary Hopi potters is a widely quoted example. Extinction means that the tradition has ceased to exist in a recognizable form. Stagnation might be thought of as referring to an essentially unchanging tradition which gives the appearance of lacking the capacity for further development.

An additional refinement of the concept of tradition has been the introduction of the idea of a *cotradition*. The elements of a cotradition consist of whole cultures which through time, because of overall similarities in historical factors and environment, have tended to sequentially pass through a series of similar developmental steps or stages. Cotraditions have not developed in every area; in fact their occurrence is usually an exceptional circumstance related to specific local causal or at least permissive factors. Both the American Southwest and Peru have been cited as examples of area cotraditions.

CULTURE AREA   The *culture area* concept is borrowed wholeheartedly from cultural anthropology. In its simplest form, the culture area consists of a major physiographic province, the *area* as defined by Willey and Phillips, which has had developed within it a series of similar cultural manifestations because of similar economies and historical factors. An ethnographic example would be the area inhabited by the North American Plains Indians. Archaeologically it is also possible to view cultural manifestations in terms of culture areas, as has been done for the New World by Gordon Willey in his texts, *An Introduction to American Archaeology*, Vols. I and II. Because of their environmental limits, culture areas tend to be fairly constant through time. However, it should be pointed out that climatic factors have varied through time and thus environmental boundaries have shifted. In addition, new technology may result in a culture spreading beyond its immediate environs into adjacent areas. An example is the introduction of the horse into Plains Indian culture. Before the advent of the horse, migratory bison hunting was a seasonal activity carried out near the permanent villages in the river bottoms. After the arrival of the horse, migratory bison hunting became a full-time economic activity, spreading far beyond the major river valleys. My point is that culture areas and cultures are not exactly identical through time. The archaeologist is of necessity more cognizant of this

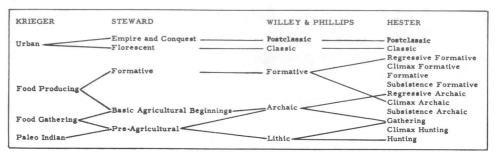

Fig. 5–2 Comparison of New World stage classifications by different authors. (Hester 1962:Fig. 4.)

factor than the ethnographer, who is primarily concerned with only one time period. The greatest utility of the culture area concept is that it provides a framework well suited for the organization of data for teaching purposes.

CULTURAL STAGE The *stage* concept is more widespread and all encompassing than is the culture area. The concern here is with the overall level of cultural development. Stages are defined in developmental terms and are not tied to any specific environment or time period. What is important is the *level* of cultural attainment. Stages are high-level abstractions, and the term may be applied to cultures with different economies or other major cultural differences. Alex Krieger (1953:247) defines stage as follows:

> For present purposes, I will consider a "stage" to be a segment of a historical sequence in a given area, characterized by a dominating pattern of economic existence. The general economic life and outlines of social structure of past peoples can often be inferred from archaeological remains and can be related to similar phenomena, whether the dates are known or not. The term "period," on the other hand, might be considered to depend upon chronology. Thus a stage may be recognized by content alone, and in the event that accurate dates can be obtained for it in a given area, it could be said that the stage *here* existed during such-and-such a *period*. Further, the same stage may be said to appear at different times or periods in different areas and also to end at different times. A stage may also include several locally distinctive culture complexes and minor time divisions.

Stages are useful for broad level synthesis. In order to illustrate their scope, it can be pointed out that Willey and Phillips have ordered all New World archaeological cultures into the following five stages: Lithic stage, Archaic stage, Formative stage, Classic stage, and Postclassic stage. Other authors have defined additional stages using similar data (Fig. 5–2). For our purposes, I believe it to be superfluous to define the individual stages that have been enumerated, as long as you understand the principles involved in their definition.

CULTURE CLIMAX Cultures fluctuate through time in ways resulting from all influences bearing on the cultural tradition. Within this broad realm of total cultural response there are some periods in the history of a culture which are more intense or highly developed than other periods in its history. The term for such a period is *cultural climax*.

The climax may be defined as *the type or types of maximum intensity and individuality of an archaeological horizon or tradition*. This is necessarily a value judgment, but only in relation to the horizon or tradition involved. In whole cultural terms the climax becomes *the phase or phases of maximum intensity and individuality of a culture or civilization* (Willey and Phillips 1958:39).

The concept of climax is useful in understanding the developments within a single cultural tradition. Comparisons of the climax in one tradition with the climax in another tradition may be nonproductive, since different causal factors may have been in effect.

Cultural Origination and Transmission

Cultures seldom are transmitted from one area to another as whole units. More frequently single traits or trait complexes are the items that are conveyed. The standard term for this transmission is *diffusion*. Traits originating in one culture are transmitted to another culture. If not threatening existing cultural patterns too seriously, they will be either adopted as they are or modified somewhat to fit existing cultural patterns. Actual traits and objects may be transmitted, or the idea of how these are to be manufactured and used may be transmitted through a procedure termed *stimulus diffusion*. The presence archaeologically in a site of an identified trait introduced from another culture is termed *trait intrusion*. The alternative, of course, to introductions is the *independent invention* of the traits by the indigenous culture.

It is occasionally the case that whole cultures or portions of them do move, and we cover this entire phenomena with the term *migration*. Migrations are difficult to establish on the basis of archaeological data because most of our evidence consists of traits which *could be* the result of diffusion. Occasionally, it is possible to identify an entire site or sites which bear a culture foreign to the area in which they are found. These sites are enclaves with a distinctive culture content which has historical antecedents elsewhere. This situation, when identified archaeologically, is evidence of migration and is termed *site unit intrusion*.

SUMMARY

Archaeological concepts have been developed to provide means of describing and understanding cultural manifestations as well as ordering them historically. The study of archaeology may be divided into three major subdivisions: observation, the collection of data in the field; description, the outlining of the formal characteristics of the data and its ordering in time and space (termed *culture-historical integration* by Willey and Phillips); and explanation, the drawing of inferences which seek to explain the cultural processes that have been in effect (*processual interpretation* according to Willey and Phillips).

Archaeology has not been shy in its eclecticism; concepts developed in other disciplines have been readily adopted if applicable. Other concepts such as the phase have been developed by archaeologists to meet their specific needs. For most of its theoretical framework, archaeology can operate easily within the conceptual structure provided by cultural anthropology. In those aspects which require description and correlation of objects, archaeology has had to forge its own methods and concepts. In one other aspect—temporal considerations—archaeology has had to be innovative. In the absence of written records tied to a calendar, archaeological data had to be examined in terms of its constituent elements, and these related to cultural change through time. The result provides us not only with dates of past events but also with information as to the rate and causal factors involved in culture change. Thus we perceive archaeology as not only a means of verification of cultural inferences and theoretical constructs derived from cultural anthropology but also having substance and merit in its own right. Archaeology is capable of providing a record of unique cultural events that have occurred in the past, as well as providing its own explanation of the processes involved in cultural development.

REFERENCES

Bordes, F., 1961, *Typologie du Paléolithique ancien et moyen,* 2 vols. Bordeaux: Publications de l'Institut de l'Université de Bordeaux.

Deetz, J., 1967, *Invitation to Archaeology,* New York: Doubleday.

Harris, M., 1971, *Culture, Man and Nature.* New York: Crowell.

Haury, E., 1955, "An Archaeological Approach to the Study of Cultural Stability," in R. Wauchope (ed.), *Seminars in Archaeology,* Society for American Archaeology, Memoir 11:31–58.

Hester, J. J., 1962, "A Comparative Typology of New World Cultures," *American Anthropologist* 64(5):1001–1015.

———, 1972, Blackwater Locality No. 1, a Stratified Early Man Site in Eastern New Mexico. Ft. Burgwin Research Center, Southern Methodist University, Publication No. 8.

Hole, F., and R. F. Heizer, 1969, *An Introduction to Prehistoric Archaeology,* 2d ed. New York: Holt, Rinehart and Winston, Inc.

Krieger, A. D., 1953, "Comment," in S. Tax and others (eds.), *An Appraisal of Anthropology Today.* Chicago: The University of Chicago Press.

Tylor, E. B., 1871, *Primitive Culture: Researches into the Development of Mythology, Philosophy, Religion, Language, Art, and Custom.* London: J. Murray.

———, *Anthropology.* London.

Willey, G. R., 1966, *An Introduction to American Archaeology,* Vol. I: *North and Middle America.* Englewood Cliffs, N.J.: Prentice-Hall.

———, 1972, *An Introduction to American Archaeology,* Vol II. *South America.* Englewood Cliffs, N.J.: Prentice-Hall.

———, and P. Phillips, 1958, *Method and Theory in American Archaeology.* Chicago: The University of Chicago Press.

CULTURAL DATA
REVEALED BY
ARCHAEOLOGY

PART

III

6

The Lower Paleolithic

Continuing research on the earliest evidences of man and his culture has pushed back the chronological horizons of our cultural ancestry to 2 million years or so at Olduvai Gorge, increasing man's known use of tools by at least 1 million years in the past two decades. Furthermore, recent research by Clark Howell and Karl Butzer indicates tool using has an even greater antiquity, on the order of 4 million years, in the Omo region of southern Ethiopia. L. S. B. Leakey has gone even further in his assertion that *Ramapithecus wickeri,* a Miocene primate some 15 million years of age, utilized stone tools.

The Lower Paleolithic, or Earliest Stone Age, was the period of time during which the primates we term *hominids* developed a system of tool using and tool manufacture which was passed on from generation to generation. The development of such a system (culture) distinguished these hominids from their primate ancestors and contemporaries because it provided a shield between them and the environmental hazards they faced. With tools they could protect themselves and secure an advantage over their prey animals. With the establishment of tool use and manufacture as a learnable cultural tradition, man had taken the most important single step in his evolution.

The last point is most important to grasp, as it is crucial to our understanding of man's prehistory. It is not tool using per se that distinguishes man, for numerous modern apes utilize a variety of implements for specified purposes and we may assume that their ancestors did likewise. Nor is it tool manufacture that distinguishes man, since modern apes prepare sticks *for* use. It is the transmission of culture, with its learned and shared behavior patterns, from one generation to the next, and the reliance on culture that distinguish man as unique.

Our investigation of man's early cultural beginnings must take into account his primate nature. Early men probably functioned like primate bands with a pattern of male dominance in social relationships, a family structure in which the strongest ties were between females and their offspring, band territoriality expressed in the food quest being conducted within a known area, group cooperation in defense and communication of danger, and a tradition of band solidarity and cohabitation. To this primate background we must add the conscious manufacture of tools and the transmission of the manufacturing techniques and knowledge of tool use to other members of the band through example and through symbolic speech (language). With respect to these innovations, it is appropriate to ask ourselves at what point in man's evolution did tool use and speech begin to qualitatively change his way of life. These are not questions that we can answer with the evidence at hand. Because modern apes are also tool users, we assume that tool using was practiced by our early hominid ancestors and through time this facility became more developed. With this view, culture, at least in tool using, was not a dramatic change at a particular time in the past but instead was a gradual development.

Speech also may have developed slowly. In addition, we have no assurance that the development of speech was synchronous with the development of other aspects of culture. However, symbolic speech would be a great asset in the transmission of cultural knowledge. On the other hand, since the archaeological record indicates that early industries were simple and changed slowly through time, we can assume that speech also was slow to change, with early men probably having a limited vocabulary.

Our assessment of the influence of culture suffers from the fact that little other than stone tools has been preserved to indicate early man's behavioral patterns. We do know that these implements were initially hand-held, and they provided man with superior skills in cutting and scraping. They were not adequate in themselves to give man much of an advantage in direct confrontations with large carnivores. They aided in the killing and butchering of animals already trapped or surrounded but did not add to man's speed or agility. It is clear that early men were at a disadvantage in the hunt because they did not possess the means to kill animals at a distance. Other disadvantages include less acuity of smell and hearing than that possessed by the prey animals. Advantages possessed by man include prehensile hands, stereoscopic vision, and superior intellectual ability.

The basic problem in our study of the beginnings of the Lower Paleolithic, this dawn age of man's development, is in the inadequacy of the archaeological record. We may find chipped flints or split and broken animal bones in an ancient strata, but they must be of patterned form in their shape or distribution for us to infer that man was responsible, rather than animals or the forces of nature. This problem greatly inhibits our search for the earliest evidences of man because the earlier and presumably less patterned these remains are, the less evidence we have to attribute them to man's activity. While the search for man's earliest remains continues, we must learn to restrain our curiosity and enthusiasm somewhat, as the earliest remains are rare and fragmentary. Therefore we must temper our judgment and insist upon scientific proof of man's influence. What is most often revealed is the later, more clearly patterned remains of man, which is the core of material we term the Lower Paleolithic. It is these stone industries, living floors, piled or scattered food debris, and such, that make up the items we collect, identify, and study in our search for knowledge of man's past. In order to comprehend the meaning inherent in these remains, we must first have a knowledge of the environments inhabited by early man. We must understand his physical capabilities, as best we can, from the incomplete fossil record, and we must learn something of the techniques of stone tool manufacture—all subjects we will cover in this chapter.

THE ENVIRONMENTAL SETTING

The entire tenure of man (Homo) on earth has coincided with one of the more unique periods in geologic history, a time marked by formation of continental glaciers. Forming in the subarctic and temperate regions, especially in Europe and North America, these glacial masses advanced outward from numerous centers, then went through a series of minor fluctuations: advances, halts, and retreats. The entire process was repeated at least four times, and these major glacial periods in Europe, from early to late, have been termed Günz, Mindel, Riss, and Würm. However such a scheme is too simplistic; there were a number of advances and retreats within each of these periods. In addition, some areas, including most of Africa, southeast Asia, and central Alaska were unglaciated. The unique aspect of this climatic regimen was that it was in strong contrast to most of the rest of geologic time, an immensely long period of approximately 2 billion years during most of which the earth's climate was warmer and unglaciated. The Pleistocene epoch, the one in which man evolved, is thus seen as climatically unique. The coincidence with mans' evolution is intriguing, although it is not possible to prove any cause-and-effect relationship.

With glaciers covering the higher latitudes and elevations, areas suitable for the evolution of man were somewhat limited. Our best evidence of early humans is from Africa, although this does not mean that Africa was the only possible hearth for human development. Early remains are also known from southern Europe and Southeast Asia, forming a zone extending from Java to Britain.

The effects of glaciation were many: 1. The total area of habitable land was greatly reduced. 2. The major vegetational zones were compressed toward the equator. 3. Rainfall and temperature patterns were altered as atmospheric circulation was similarly influenced by the glacial masses.

One way to visualize the effects of the glaciers is to plot their geographic distribution (Fig. 6–1). Another way to assess the same phenomena is to compare graphs of temperature changes, with one end of the graph reflecting present temperature. Emiliani (1966) has constructed one such temperature graph based on data from analysis of deep-sea cores. His graph, correlated with the North American and European glacial chronologies, is presented in Figure 6–2.

The deep-sea core graph presents a smoothed profile because as each layer is formed, ocean floor organisms churn up the sediments, thus blurring the record. One application of the same method (0 16/18) relies on changes in isotopic composition of glacial ice. The ice core data is the most sensitive we have to date. Unfortunately it only covers the last 110,000 years.

The glacial record is the most dramatic evidence of Pleistocene climate. However it was not man's fate to have to adjust to a periglacial climate until late in the Pleistocene. It is Africa, with its climate marked by pluvial periods rather than glaciations, which provides us with the greatest quantity of early cultural evidence. The tropical savanna zone with its warm climate, abundant rainfall, and wealth of plants and animals was most favorable for man's early development. The other major world environmental zones—the Arctic ice, tundra, temperate forest, grasslands, deserts, subtropical forests, cold dry steppe, and tropical rain forest—all provide less in the way of easily acquired foods, as well as requiring more specialized adaptations for survival. Although our record is admittedly incomplete, it seems that *after* man developed culture he began to occupy these more rigorous environmental zones.

If Africa was a major hearth of human development, what were the environmental conditions that man faced there? In a recent publication, *Atlas of African Prehistory* (J. D. Clark 1967) several hypothetical reconstructions of vegetal and rainfall patterns are presented. These maps, although hypothetical, do provide us with some idea of the environments available to our earliest ancestors (Fig. 6–3).

In an outstanding review of the evidence of Pleistocene environments and man's adaptation to them, Karl Butzer (1971) provides a framework for our understanding of man's past. Perhaps the most important facts he cites involve the carrying capacity of various environments in terms of ungulate biomass, the number of kilograms of herd-dwelling animals per square kilometer. The

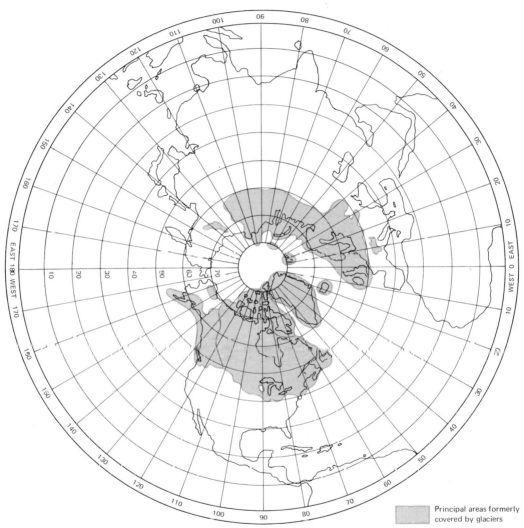

Principal areas formerly covered by glaciers

Fig. 6−1 Major areas in northern hemisphere covered with glaciers at the maximum of the last major glacial advance. Data from the southern hemisphere is too limited to permit a similar reconstruction. (After Flint 1971:Figs. 18−1, 18−5, and 25−1.)

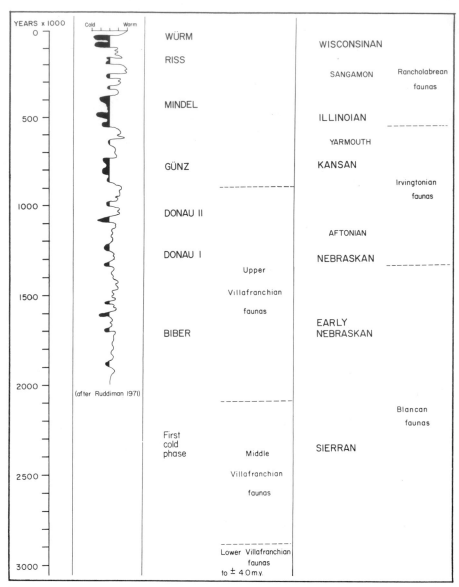

Fig. 6–2 Ancient temperatures correlated with the periods of glacial advance and retreat during the Pleistocene. (Modified from Cooke 1973:Tables 2 and 3.)

difference between the various zones is striking. There is no doubt that as man came to rely more fully on a meat diet, he would have preferred the areas of high carrying capacity (Table 6–1).

The nature of the Pleistocene fauna is truly striking, representing one of the most unique collections of species ever to inhabit the earth. The Cenozoic period is the age of mammals; the Pleistocene, its most recent portion, may be

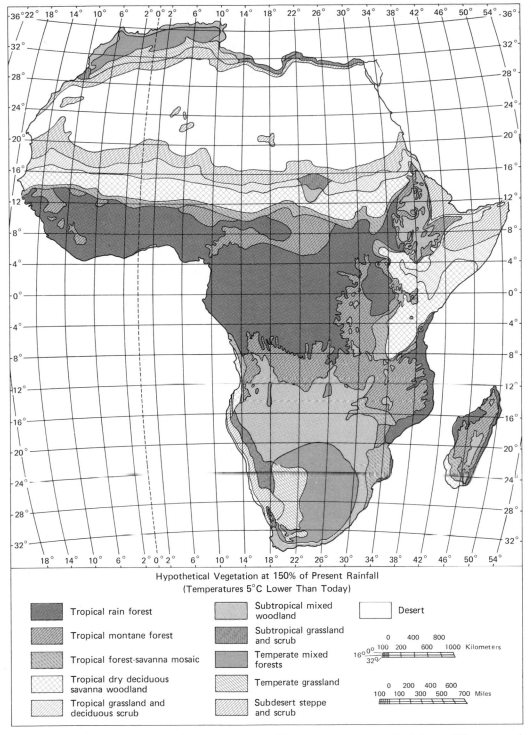

Fig. 6–3 Hypothetical reconstruction of African vegetation zones. Rainfall was 150 percent of that of today, temperature 5°C lower than at present. (J. G. D. Clark 1967:Map 11.)

101

TABLE 6–1   Ungulate Biomasses of Certain Environments*

Vegetation Type	Locality	Species Number	Biomass (kg./sq.km)
Rain Forest	Ghana	3	5.6
Thorn Forest	Southern Rhodesia	15	4900
Savanna Parkland	Congo; Uganda	5–11	5950–19,540
High Grass Savanna	Kenya; Transvaal	17–19	1760–16,560
Low Grass Savanna	Kenya; Tanganyika	over 15	5250
Semidesert Grassland	Chad	4	83
Desert Shrub	Rio de Oro; Mauretania	2	0.3–189
Temperate Grasslands	Eurasian steppe; Great Plains		350–3000
Deciduous Forest	Scotland		ca. 1000
Mixed Forest	Carpathians		ca. 500
Tundra	Northern Canada		ca. 800

*Data from overgrazed reserves omitted.
(Butzer 1971:150.)

viewed as a climactic period in mammalian evolution. There was a florescence of speciation, with an amazing wealth of diverse forms inhabiting every ecological niche. Other features of the period include tremendous concentrations of herd-dwelling species and a major emphasis on giantism. Toward the end of the Pleistocene, about 10,000 years ago, a majority of these species became extinct. Extinction of these exotic forms was an outstanding feature of the Late Pleistocene, and it has been suggested that predation by man was the cause. Whether or not man was responsible for the extinction of entire species, he was, at least by Middle Pleistocene times, an efficient predator. Man's influence was also significant in altering other aspects of the environments he inhabited. Karl Butzer has stated the nature of this influence in clear terms:

Contemporary human groups interact with their environment in many ways and at different levels, depending on their technology and organization skills. The regional environment provides a resource base that may also be relevant to the development of individual economic traits, primarily technology subsistence patterns, and even social structure. Similarly, on a more local scale, the habitat provides settlement sites and the focus for human activities. Conversely, man leaves his imprint upon the local setting and even on the regional environment. Food-gatherers modify vegetation by fire and accidental dispersal of plants; they exploit and may overexploit food resources, and they impart their mark upon the land. Food-producers leave a far more conspicuous record. Their structures are common and of some permanence. They clear or destroy forest, displace wild game with domesticated animals or mass crops, deplete or destroy the soil mantle, modify or upset the hydrological balance, and initiate the process of pollution that threatens us today (Butzer 1971:vii).

During the Lower Paleolithic man's primary influence on his environment was his predation on animal species.

THE SAVANNA ADAPTATION

If, as the evidence suggests, the savanna environment was the hearth of human evolution, what were the unique factors that made it so?

Perhaps first, in order of evolutionary priority, we should discuss the adaptations of man's primate ancestors. For many years, physical anthropologists have predicated that because man has prehensile hands and stereoscopic vision, his ancestors must have been forest dwellers adapted for brachiation, the method of locomotion by swinging from limb to limb (practiced today by gibbons). In recent years Sherwood Washburn has suggested that man's ancestors experienced a period of knuckle walking, the four-legged ground locomotion pattern of the modern gorilla. Such a pattern could eventually have led to the assumption of erect posture and true bipedalism. On the other hand, a knuckle walking stage is hypothetical rather than proved, and man may have shifted directly from brachiation and branch running to bipedalism (Jolly 1972:49–50).

If these assumptions are reasonably correct, then man's change from life in an arboreal environment to a savanna environment would have provided certain opportunities and stimuli. The greater distance between trees would have forced reliance on walking rather than on brachiation. The total vegetal productivity in a savanna is great, with a corresponding quantity and variety of animals. In contrast with a forest, the savanna would provide lesser amounts of fruits, nuts, and vegetal foods but a more than compensatory increase in animal foods. These factors would favor a species which could subsist on an omnivorous diet.

Food getting in a savanna would appear to stimulate more cooperative activity as compared with forest life. Subsistence on vegetal foods can be an individual activity inasmuch as the foods are available for the taking and are not elusive. When man was faced with the acquisition of animal foods on the savanna, he had to cope with the fact that he was weaker, slower, and less keen of ear and nose than his quarry. Probably the earliest solution to this problem was the grouping together for purposes of scavenging. The group would locate a recent animal kill and then cooperate in keeping away other scavengers. Tools could be useful in the cutting of flesh from bones (necessary to replace the function of long canine teeth), the hurling of missiles at other scavengers, and the smashing of bones to obtain the marrow.

Hunting, as a cultural practice, could have evolved rather simply from the above example. Our earliest evidence from Olduvai Gorge indicates that small and immature animals were the prey. Somewhat later is actual evidence of cooperative hunts in which the group purpose was to search intensively an area for game, to surround game to limit its escape, or to dispatch an animal trapped in a bog or at some other disadvantage. Only by cooperative effort could man overcome his inherent weaknesses and subjugate animals larger, stronger, and faster than himself. This cooperation would lead to further cultural developments, primarily in the areas of defense, territoriality, social responsibility, and specialized skills used for the common good. Once developed, these behavioral patterns would provide a selective advantage of man over his prey species. Perhaps the most important single advantage of culture, cooperation, provided man with a shield, a protection against other animals and environmental hazards. In my view this is the unique aspect of culture; with cooperative practices man is able to overcome his inherent limitations. Tool using is part of this syndrome, but it is not really tool using per se that is so important; otherwise other primates would possess culture.

NONHUMAN PRIMATE BEHAVIOR

Man's origins may be directly traced to his primate ancestry and we may utilize this basic primate background as our starting point. In a recent book Watson and Watson (1969) have summarized the major basic stages in man's evolution. Their categorization of the *nonhuman primate* can be utilized as our beginning.

All animals require protection, nourishment, and reproduction in order to survive. In the nonhuman primate these needs are met by the following anatomical and behavioral adaptations: The nonhuman primate has the head positioned so that in a sitting, standing, or walking position the head faces forward and objects may be perceived with stereoscopic vision in color. When he is sitting or standing, his arms swing freely, and the unique adaptation of the opposable thumb permits him to grasp articles with his hand. The sexes are of differing sizes with the males occasionally twice the size of females. Sexual activity may occur at any time during the year, with females in heat usually accepting the dominant male in the group, although sometimes they accept the other males as well. Infants are relatively helpless and require considerable maternal care and aid in locomotion. Compared to other animals, the brain capacity is large, resulting in greater intelligence, perception, and skill in problem solving. Such primates are adaptable to a wide range of habitats, with the primary controlling factor being extremes of temperature.

In solving problems of survival, these primates form groups occupying a specific territory. Inadequately armed in terms of strength, teeth, and speed, primates gain protection through numbers. Within the group, cooperative activity is structured in ways to minimize conflict. The primary mechanism utilized is the establishment of dominance. With this mechanism, each individual is able to establish his place in the group. He knows when he may exert dominance and when he must be subordinant. This pattern avoids conflict over sexual matters and the acquisition of food. Furthermore the pattern reduces anxiety in the individual inasmuch as he knows his rights and privileges. An additional factor is the security obtained as a result of being a member of a group. The individual is reinforced by behavior patterns, such as grooming, in which his psychological needs are clearly satisfied by others in the group.

In the food quest the individual primate primarily operates alone, consuming what he finds. While some food sharing does occur, it is relatively rare, with the individual sharing food only after he is satisfied. If there is a conflict over food, it is resolved through application of the principal of dominance. Another factor of relevance is that food is seldom carried very far or stored for future use.

Protection and food getting are further enhanced by the use of communication. Although vocalizations and gestures are interpreted by the other primates in certain ways, these responses are primarily inherited rather than learned. Thus, in no sense should primate behavior be interpreted as including a language.

A further distinction applicable to primates is their ability to learn. The young acquire behavioral skills from observing their elders. However, there is little if any attempt to *teach* the young. Tool use among primates, while present, is limited. Sticks may be prepared for use against marauders, and twigs are peeled and inserted into termite nests as a means of acquiring the termites for food. However in a strict sense primates do not *rely* upon tools to solve their problems of food acquisition, shelter, protection, and so forth. In this regard, it is perhaps important to recognize that while primates do make and use tools, this facility is not basic to their survival.

PROTOHUMANS

At this stage in our knowledge, it is inappropriate to identify with too great a precision the time and place of the development of behavioral patterns we would term *protohuman*. What we are in fact describing is a stage of evolution which, while hypothetical, is probably about what actually happened.

The protohuman has evolved to the point where he stands and walks on two legs. His posture reflects a shortening of the pelvis and a recurvature of the spine, with internal organs shifted to adjust to an upright posture. The brain has enlarged and arms are now shorter than legs. Evolution of the tongue and larynx facilitated sound production. While similar to the nonhuman primates in sexual dimorphism, size is slightly greater, and the life span was probably somewhat greater, in the vicinity of 35 years.

The diet is omnivorous and reflects a greater consumption of meat than is the case with nonhuman primates. Life in groups continues but with some major modifications; most important is the development of the nuclear family. The infant is relatively helpless for a long period of time and the mother must of necessity devote her time to child care. This need gives rise to the male's assuming greater responsibility, especially in acquiring food to be shared among the family members. A further development could have been the formation of permanently mated pairs.

Cooperation in food gathering, hunting, and child care are features of the protohuman family, reinforced with a greater dependence on an *intentional* system of communication. Such calls may not be particularly elaborate, but they are intended to facilitate sharing and cooperation. Thus the development of language is a result of the meeting of social needs.

The greater reliance on hunting among protohumans requires a larger territory and more exclusive use of such an area because of the nature of the food chain. Herbivores consume large quantities of vegetal foods; thus, reliance on the herbivores for food requires a greater area than if the same group were subsisting on vegetal foods. This expansion of exploited territory could have increased the chance for conflict with competing groups.

A major innovation relating to tool use among protohumans is that they intentionally manufactured tools for use; thus, they were capable of anticipating future needs. Cooperative hunting requires some planning, which is another feature indicative of symbolization, the intellectual quality associated with problem solving. An added requirement is that such planning refers to future events; thus there is an increasing need for language.

EARLY MAN

One definition of man we may use is based on intelligence. It is characteristic of man that he solves his problems of life through reliance on his intellectual abilities. He does not overpower, outrun, or otherwise subjugate his animal adversaries; he outwits them. Crucial to this survival technique is the use of symbolic language and reliance on the cooperation of the group to carry out planned activities for the group's benefit, with each individual carrying out his assigned task. While man is larger and somewhat more modified for erect posture than protohumans, it is his intellectual attainments that make him distinctive.

The basic structural unit in man's social organization remains the family, although the recognition of relationship has been extended to several generations and we have the development of formalized kinship systems to recognize this fact. Thus by this extension, behavioral patterns between individuals are formalized for most, if not all, of the members of a band.

CULTURE AS AN EVOLUTIONARY FILTER

Rights of inheritance, acquired status, and such are expressed in behavioral patterns keyed to the social framework of kinship. From this moment on, in the history of man's development, his behavioral patterns are influenced more by cultural needs than by his biological needs. In addition, the mass of accumulated knowledge that we know as culture is transmitted from generation to generation by means of symbolic language and intentional teaching. Thus by its nature, culture is accretional: it is forever increasing in quantity and variation. As a result, through time, man is creating a greater and greater buffer between himself and the environments he inhabits. With fire, simple and compound tools, constructed shelters, clothing, food storage, primitive medical practices, and others in the long list of cultural traits, man protected himself from the rigors of direct exposure to the natural elements. It is here that man departs from the principles of natural selection as outlined by Darwin, for man has culture—a separate system which intercedes between him and the natural environment. The survival of the fittest, in human terms, no longer refers to the quick and the strong on an individual basis, but refers instead to the ability of the group to survive and protect its individual members through cooperative activity, intellectual problem solving, and the use of tools and cultural practices not available to animal species.

With such a system at work, man is not limited in his exploitation of environments for his own needs in the way all other members of the animal kingdom are. His only limitation is cultural; with adequate cultural innovations he is able to expand into new, formerly hostile environments and survive. Thus with the growth of culture, human societies expanded over greater portions of the earth and into more and more varied environments.

THE NATURE OF THE LOWER PALEOLITHIC

In spite of the neat three-part system consisting of nonhuman primates, proto-humans, and man as explained above, we have difficulty being able to distinguish between these stages as represented by their material remains, which after all represent the remains of a continuum. What is left to be found by the archaeologist are stone tools, bone remains (either food debris or skeletal parts of the individuals), and nonmodified stones, or manuports. A concentration of these various remains in the place originally occupied is termed a *living floor*. Living floors are our best evidence of the way of life during the Lower Paleolithic because it was at these locations that the tools, waste flakes or debitage, food debris, and such were actually discarded by the former inhabitants. We analyze these materials and their relationships to each other to derive inferences as to the original life style of their users.

When making such inferences, it is most difficult to determine when these patterns of occupational debris represent the remains of man rather than those of protoman. The greatest limitation we have to face is the fact that behavior patterns are not preserved; they must be inferred from the nonperishable debris resulting from cultural activity. On the earliest time level we cannot be sure of the existence of kinship, language, or other identifying characteristics of man. It is only after a wealth of patterned occupational debris is present that we can be sure that we have evidence of true man.

CHRONOLOGY OF PLEISTOCENE EVENTS

Our understanding of man's evolution, both cultural and physical, is ordered by the presence of artifacts and fossils in specific strata. These strata are correlated one with another on the basis of stratigraphic position, faunal content, artifactual content, and age as established by independent dating techniques. These studies have enabled geologists and prehistorians to construct relative sequences of geologic events and cultural and evolutionary phenomena. All such chronologies are subject to reinterpretation, since the levels and finds that are so correlated are widely separated in time and space. Furthermore, they frequently differ in included fossils so that a true correlation is not possible. New finds continually bring about the revision of such attempts. Nonetheless this framework is the basis to which all Pleistocene studies must be referred. An example of such a correlation is presented in Figure 6–2. The introduction of early human types and cultures within this chronological framework is presented in Figure 6–4.

AN INVENTORY OF LOWER PALEOLITHIC MANIFESTATIONS

The Earliest Find

The earliest evidence of culture or presumed culture is that from Ft. Ternan in Kenya excavated by L. S. B. Leakey. At this site in a level dated to the Miocene period, approximately 15 million years of age, he has found the remains of *Ramapithecus wickeri,* a small primate. In the same deposits occur the broken bone remains of several animal species in association with a battered stone. It is Leakey's (personal communication 1970) contention that this find represents our earliest archaeological evidence of true tool using. He does not imply that this signifies culture or the presence of man. What he does suggest is that the history of tool use has an antiquity of at least 15 million years.

Early Hominids

The earliest fossil forms closely related to man are known from numerous finds in East Africa and South Africa. Dated between approximately 3.5 million and 1 million years ago by the potassium-argon method, these hominids have been termed the *Australopithecine subfamily.* They also probably occupied Southeast Asia. This group is divided into two separate lineages featuring a gracile form and a robust form. In earlier publications these groups were distinguished as separate genera, but today their relationship is viewed as at a subgeneric level. These two groups have been termed *Australopithecus,* the gracile form, and *Paranthropus,* the robust form. In reviewing the literature the reader should bear in mind that fossil finds are typically fragmentary and are seldom found in chronological order; more typically they appear as unrelated bits of a jigsaw puzzle. A final problem is that the paleoanthropologist describing the find may exaggerate the differences between his find and some found previously, in order to justify a new species or generic name. As time passes the known forms are restudied and the inappropriate names dropped; however, it makes an understanding of the subject difficult for the nonspecialized student. The

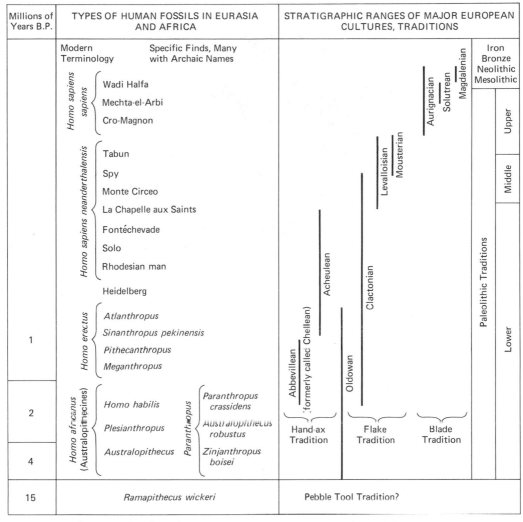

Fig. 6–4 The chronological range of early humans and cultural traditions.

Paranthropus forms have been assigned to two species, termed *Australopithecus (Paranthropus) boisei* and *Australopithecus (Paranthropus) robustus*. Features in common between these species are heavy brow ridges, a saggital crest, no forehead, small incisors and canines, and large molars and premolars. The major difference between the two is that the molars and premolars of the *boisei* form are especially large. It is presumed the large molar development of both forms was an adaptation for the crushing and chewing of tough vegetal foods. Some authorities view both *boisei* and *robustus* as within the same species.

The gracile form, *Australopithecus africanus,* is smaller in size, possessed something of a forehead, and lacked a saggital crest (Fig. 6–5). The contrast in size between the cutting and grinding teeth was less marked than in

Fig. 6–5 Restoration of the head of *Australopithecus* by A. Forestier. (Copyright; The Illustrated London News.)

the *robustus* forms. Presumably this feature reflects an omnivorous diet. Both subgenera possessed a cranial capacity of about 500 cc. and habitually walked erect. The robust form possessed a body weight of 120 to 150 pounds, with the gracile form somewhat smaller, probably in the 50- to 100-pound range. Differences between the various *Australopithecus* forms may be attributed to differing ecological adaptations, variation between populations, differences in age (these finds cover some 2.5 million years), and sexual dimorphism.

Sites with Australopithecines are known only from East and South Africa from environments which today are either semiarid or semihumid. Chronology of the finds suggests that *A. africanus* occurs earlier than *A. robustus*. Somewhat after 2 million years ago, a further gracile form evolved in East Africa. Known from Bed I at Olduvai Gorge, this early hominid, termed *Homo habilis,* appears to be the connecting link between the Australopithecines and true man. Sites with *H. habilis* remains contain tools and food debris and will be described in further detail later in this chapter.

In summary we currently view the Australopithecines as in part ancestral to man and in part a related but evolutionary dead end. Butzer (1971:417–419) has provided an up-to-date list of the Australopithecine finds which is reproduced in Figure 6–6.

The ecology of the sites in which these Australopithecines have been found is of two principal types. In East Africa sites are typically located along the edges of streams or lakes. The occupation sites were selected for their

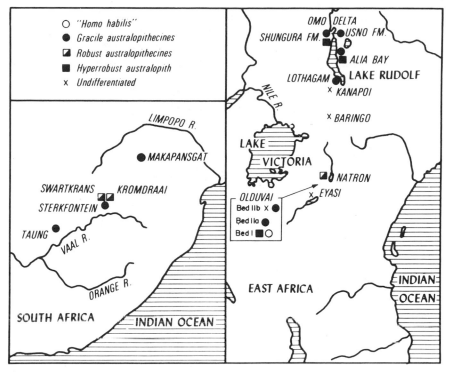

Fig. 6–6   Australopithecine sites of East and South Africa. (Butzer 1971:Fig. 4.)

proximity to watering places frequented by ungulates, or at least those areas in the environment which were best watered. The fauna preserved in the sites suggests that nearby were open uplands as well as fringes of trees along the water courses. The sites represented camping spots located in the open, frequently in places that show evidence of seasonal inundation.

The South African remains are primarily located in cave fills. After deposition the sediments within the caves were impregnated with carbonates, resulting in the formation of breccia, a soft rock including large quantities of bone cemented together with the carbonate matrix.

Although differences in the geological content of the cave deposits have been interpreted as indicative of climatic changes, Butzer (1971:424) contends these interpretations are improbable, in that materials of different ages were swept into the caves with the breccia formation being carried out under one specific climatic regimen. He thus infers that the climate at the time was drier than today or at least featured a less well-distributed rainfall. Paleoclimatic interpretations based on the habitat requirements of the included fauna suggest the presence of an open grassland. Perhaps most important is the fact that both robust and gracile Australopithecines are known from the same sites and their geographic ranges overlapped to a considerable degree. Another consideration suggested by the coassociation of the Australopithecines is the possibility that the gracile forms may have preyed upon their vegetarian relatives. The possibilities afforded the *A. africanus* and *H. habilis* forms by their omnivorous diet may have permitted them to exploit a wider range of habitats than the *robustus* forms and therefore insured them a greater chance of survival.

Tool Making by the Australopithecines

Evidence for the manufacture and use of tools by the Australopithecines is primarily limited to two sites, Sterkfontein in South Africa and Bed I at Olduvai Gorge in East Africa. An additional few possible stone implements are known from the Omo beds in Ethiopia, but their scarcity makes their evaluation difficult.

Sterkfontein today is a small hill in which are the remains of small caves and sinkholes formed by solution of the local dolomite bedrock. The breccia fill within these chambers was derived in part from slope wash and thus does not represent an in situ association between all of the materials within the fill. The deposits also contain accumulations by carnivores, including owls. The general impression is that while the cave entrances were suitable for camping by Australopithecines, the site was more commonly used as a leopard's lair.

In the youngest breccia at the site there has been recovered a total of 286 stone objects of which 97.5 percent are foreign to the site, although they could have been introduced by floodwaters of the nearby Blaauwbank River when its bed was some 30 meters higher than present. If such a natural cause can be ruled out, then the only other supposition is that these rocks were carried to the site by hominids. The stones themselves have been studied by several archaeologists. R. J. Mason termed 98 of these as actual manufactured artifacts, with the rest as natural pebbles or naturally fractured rocks. M. D. Leakey, restudying the same collection, identified only 73 as artifacts. R. G. Klein in an unpublished study was only able to accept 35 as artifacts. It should be apparent to the reader that the study of the earliest tools poses serious problems in analysis. An attribute of the collection is that the stones were randomly scattered through the upper layers and thus do not indicate a living floor. The tools themselves exhibit numerous flake scars, with the detached flakes not common in the site. Most of the implements are irregular rock lumps which have had a few flakes removed or oval pebbles with flaked rough cutting edges. Three crude so-called "hand" axes are known as well as one split bone point.

Who made the Sterkfontein tools? The beds contain remains of *A. africanus* but not in association with the artifacts. In association with the implements are only three adult teeth and a juvenile palate, fossils not diagnostic as to species; they could represent remains of *A. africanus, Homo habilis,* or even *Homo erectus.*

Our best evidence for early tool making comes from Bed I at Olduvai Gorge. Younger than at least some portions of the Sterkfontein deposits, Bed I has been dated by the potassium-argon method as covering the period from approximately 1.75 to 1 million years ago. At several locations within Bed I (Fig. 6–7), we have evidence of actual in situ living floors. Furthermore these

	Beds	Hominid remains	Living sites	Industries	K/A dates
					(millions of years)
UPPER PLEISTOCENE	Bed IV	Homo˙ cf. Broken Hill (?)	VEK˙	UPPER ACHEULEAN	
MIDDLE PLEISTOCENE	Bed III			OLD TO UPPER ACHEULEAN	
MIDDLE PLEISTOCENE	Upper Bed II	Paranthropus˙	TK. BK II˙ FLK II SHK II	OLD TO UPPER ACHEULEAN	
MIDDLE PLEISTOCENE	Upper Bed II		CK	OLD TO UPPER ACHEULEAN	
MIDDLE PLEISTOCENE	Upper Bed II	Homo erectus˙	FLK S II LLK II˙	OLD TO UPPER ACHEULEAN	0 49
MIDDLE PLEISTOCENE	Aeolian		6 SURFACES		
FINAL AND UPPER VILLAFRANCHIAN	Lower Bed II	Homo erectus˙ Paranthropus˙	MNK II˙˙	OLDOWAN	1 1
FINAL AND UPPER VILLAFRANCHIAN	Lower Bed II		FLK II.N1	OLDOWAN	
FINAL AND UPPER VILLAFRANCHIAN	Lower Bed II	Homo (Pithecanthropus) erectus?˙	FLK Maiko Gully˙	OLDOWAN	
FINAL AND UPPER VILLAFRANCHIAN	Bed I		FLK N1	OLDOWAN	
FINAL AND UPPER VILLAFRANCHIAN	Bed I	Paranthropus (Zinjanthropus)˙ Australopithecus˙ Australopithecus (Pre-Zinjanthropus)˙	FLK Main˙˙ FLK N.N.1˙	OLDOWAN	1 75
FINAL AND UPPER VILLAFRANCHIAN	Bed I	Australopithecus (Homo) habilis˙	WK. DK. MK˙	OLDOWAN	1 85
FINAL AND UPPER VILLAFRANCHIAN	Basalt				

Fig. 6–7 Finds made at Olduvai Gorge; the living floors, cultures, and remains of fossil men are listed according to the specific site at which they were found. (Bordes 1968:Fig. 12 [after F. Clark Howell].)

floors have been sealed in by subsequent volcanic ash falls so that the chance of postdepositional alteration or introduction is minimal. The floors contain specific use areas for stone tool manufacture and food butchery and even one ring of small boulders about 30 feet in diameter and 3 feet in width. The latter structure has been termed a "house," although a more probable explanation is that the stones formed a ring of missiles ready for use against carnivores. Bone fragments indicate the economy featured reliance on birds, fish, snakes, small mammals, tortoise, gazelle, antelopes, pigs, and even carnivores. A final equivocal specimen consists of remains of *A. boisei,* the famous 1959 find, initially termed a new genera, *Zinjanthropus.* With the more recent finding of *H. habilis* remains in Bed I in the same sites, the Leakeys now regard *H. habilis,* the smaller gracile form, as the tool maker and site occupant with the robust *A. boisei* as a possible prey species.

The sites are of incalculable importance, for they represent our earliest unequivocal evidence of true cultural living floors. The sites contain the camp debris of tool-manufacturing man with a varied and omnivorous diet. Further, the species was capable of taking prey much larger than itself through reliance on cultural means. Also of importance is the fact that for the first time in the ancestry of man's culture, we have evidence of a true stone industry, a collection of stone implements and chipping debris indicative of a pattern of tool manufacture, and an inventory of specialized tools, including tools of differing form with presumably differing functions. Termed the Oldowan industry, this collection of stone implements has been described by M. D. Leakey (1967). The sites from which the implements have been recovered occur from the very base of Bed I, throughout Bed I, and into the lower portion of Bed II— representing more than 1 million years (Fig. 6–8). According to Mary Leakey,

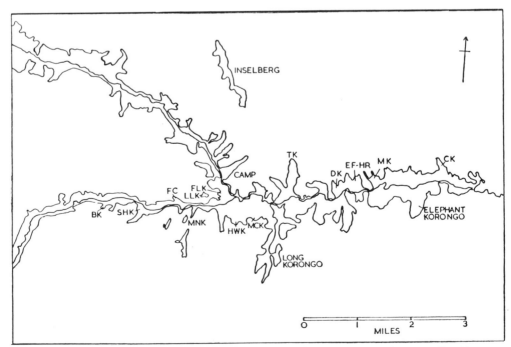

Fig. 6–8 Location of major excavation localities, Olduvai Gorge. (Leakey 1967:Fig. 4.)

this entire sequence demonstrates little change in an evolutionary sense over this enormously long period. What is evident is that the implements from the different sites differ in their frequency by type, suggesting that there was some specialization in function at these sites. The most important fact is that these early pebble tools are not just crude lumps of rock but may be subdivided into a wide variety of categories based on form. According to Mary Leakey the following types are distinguishable:

1. *Tools* Artifacts manufactured to conform to recognizable types:
   Choppers, side
   Choppers, side and hammerstones
   Choppers, end
   Choppers, end and hammerstones
   Choppers, two-edged
   Polyhedrons
   Discoids
   Spheroids
   Proto-bifaces
   Scrapers, heavy duty
   Scrapers, light duty
   Burins
   Sundry tools
2. *Utilized Material*
   "Anvils"
   Hammerstones
   Cobblestones and nodules with a minimum of flaking or else evidence of battering and percussion
   Light-duty flakes and other small fragments with fine chipping on straight, concave or convex edges
3. *Debitage*
   Whole or broken flakes and core fragments without retouch or evidence of utilization
4. *Manuports*
   Natural unmodified cobblestones and nodules artificially introduced to the sites

By far the greatest number of tools are made on "cores," that is, cobblestones, nodules, or blocks (M. D. Leakey 1967:420).

In summary, the finds from Bed I are extremely important in our understanding of man's past, for they represent our earliest substantial evidence of early man's cultural inventory and their makers, *Homo habilis* (Fig. 6–9). The evidence is further augmented by abundant examples of the local fauna.

In the lower portion of Bed II we have evidence of the appearance of a new culture, the Acheulean. This industry is widespread in the world and represents the culture of the next stage in human evolution, *Homo erectus*. At Olduvai Bed II the unique feature is that Acheulean materials overlap stratigraphically with the Oldowan culture, suggesting that at least for a time two different human species *(H. habilis* and *H. erectus)* with different cultures occupied the same area at the same time.

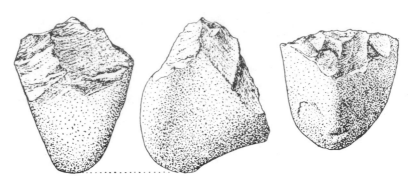

Fig. 6– 9   Pebble choppers used by *Homo habilis,* Bed I, Olduvai Gorge.   (J. G. D. Clark 1967:Fig. 7 [after Oakley].)

The Acheulean Tradition

The Acheulean culture covers a major unit of human prehistory. It extends over the remainder of the time interval which archaeologists term the Lower Paleolithic, lasting from approximately 500,000 years ago until as late as 50,000 years ago. The geographic distribution of Acheulean remains is widespread, covering much of Africa, the southern portion of Europe, and east to India. There seems to have been a northern limit to occupation by men during this period—probably evidence of man's cultural inability at this time to adequately cope with cold climates.

The first finds of Paleolithic materials were those made in France by Boucher de Perthes and others of bifacially flaked implements termed fist axes or *coup-de-poing.* The earliest of these tools featured bifacial flaking only along the sides and at one end of a flat core. This resulted in a crude tool, pointed on the one end, and of a size to be conveniently held in one hand (Fig. 6–10). These tools were termed Abbevillian because they were first found near Abbeville in France. Since those initial findings, similar tools have been recovered from numerous sites from England to Africa. The stage of cultural evolution so represented has been known by a number of terms including Pre-Chellean, Chellean, Abbevillian, and Lower Acheulean. According to Francois Bordes, one possible development from the Oldowan pebble tools to the true handaxe was as follows:

. . . first, a development of retouching all around the pebble, except at the butt, giving proto-handaxes; then the extension of this retouching to the whole upper and lower surface of the pebble; and finally a total retouching doing away with the butt altogether. Incidentally, this last feature is by no means constant, and right into the Mousterian period some handaxes keep their unchipped butt. For a long time the handaxe remains asymmetrical, trihedral in section, with one face flatter than the other; then it becomes symmetrical in section. But those that are asymmetrical in section persist right up to the end (Bordes 1968:51).

Abbevillian type implements are fairly common, but sites in which they occur in stratigraphic position are rare. As a result, little is known about the

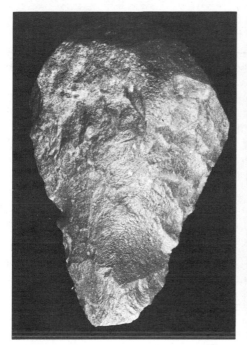

Fig. 6–10 Typical Acheulean implements. (Photographs courtesy of James Grady.)

transition to the later main period of handaxe use termed the Acheulean. In the absence of remains from living floors, we are forced to define the transition from the Abbevillian to the Acheulean period in terms of the nature of the stone tools recovered. The major distinction is that the handaxes, or bifaces as they are frequently termed, are better made in the Acheulean period. They tend to be flaked all over, and most importantly, there seems to have been a shift in manufacturing technique from the use of hammerstones as the flaker to the use of cylinder hammers. The latter are objects, rounded in cross-section, of a material softer than the stone being flaked. Typical cylinder hammers are portions of mammal long bones or wood of a similar size and shape. The use of a cylinder hammer produces flakes that are flatter and thinner than those produced with a hammerstone, giving greater control over the end product. Handaxes may have been utilized as weapons, although they were probably more often used as skinning knives. The handaxe is the hallmark of the Acheulean tradition. For many years it was believed that these core tools represented a distinct tradition, with another tradition relying on flake tools existing simultaneously in Europe. In recent years, more complete excavations of in situ living floors have clearly indicated that the Acheulean peoples had a substantial inventory of flake tools. In his monumental studies of the Lower and Middle Paleolithic tools, Bordes has identified a total of 63 separate implement types, most of which are present in the Acheulean. The most important core tools are the handaxe and bifacially flaked cleavers, with flake tools made to perform a variety of cutting and scraping functions. Specific types include scrapers, borers, backed knives, notched tools, and denticulates.

At the site of Cagny, near Amiens, in deposits attributed to the Riss glaciation, we have the earliest documented presence of a new stone tool manufacturing technique. Termed the Levallois technique, after the French site where these particular tools were first discovered, this procedure resulted in the manufacture of flakes that were trimmed to a predetermined form before being detached from the core. These prepared flakes were then further modified by edge chipping to form a wide variety of flake tools. The Levallois technique became the dominant tool tradition in the Middle Paleolithic and will be discussed more in detail in that section.

Throughout the Acheulean period the bifaces changed in form. Through time they became better made, flatter, thinner, and smaller. Differences in their form—for example, elliptical, ovoid, tear-drop shape—seem to bear little relationship to differences in time or spatial distribution.

The Nature of Acheulean Hunter-Gatherers

A striking feature of Acheulean industries is that they are similar in general characteristics, in spite of the fact that they cover at least 500,000 years and are distributed over much of three continents. We explain this continuity of tradition in a number of ways: 1. The lack of evolutionary change in Acheulean implements has been linked to the rate of evolution of the human brain. It is conceivable that such a simple culture was all that man could develop at that time. 2. Because Acheulean implements are not specific as to function, adaptations to different environments could be effected through modifications in the social structure rather than in the form of the tools used. 3. Where careful excavation of Acheulean sites has been carried out, artifacts of wood and bone have occasionally been recovered. Thus it is possible that artifacts of differing form have not been preserved. What is clear is that most of our studies of the stone tools provide information as to the form of the implements rather than their function.

In addition to the stone tools, we have evidence of a number of structures and the use of wooden spears, wooden digging implements, wooden clubs or throwing sticks, and fire. The structures are marked by crude circles of stones, linear arrangements of stones and elephant bones, and post impressions backed with bracing stones. These huts or windbreaks range from 4 to 6 meters wide by 8 to 15 meters long. As found, their floors were covered with ash, bones, and artifacts. The presence of waste flakes suggests that tool manufacture was actually carried out at these locations. These structures are not common, although they are known from Spain, Italy, Nubia, Syria, and Zambia. This suggests that Acheulean man frequently camped without building any type of permanent shelter.

Major food resources were the large mammals, including elephants, hippopotamuses, horses, cattle, baboons, pigs, rhinoceroses, as well as an occasional carnivore. Small animals were also common, with rodents, birds, and reptiles being represented in Acheulean sites. The bulk of our evidence suggests that by this time man was a successful hunter, although our knowledge of specific hunting techniques is vague. Large animals were driven into bogs or swamps, there to be dispatched with spears, clubs, and handaxes. The use of the bolas, fire drive, or vegetable poison, while possible, is very difficult to establish with the archaeological data at hand.

With only stone tools and bones as our major data, it is extremely difficult to interpret Acheulean social structure and subsistence patterns. We are forced to rely on analogies with modern hunter-gatherers (Lee and DeVore 1968) which suggest that most such groups are made up of bands of 20 to 30 individuals with a population density seldom exceeding 100 persons per 1000 square kilometers. Such a population stabilizes at only 20 to 30 percent of the carrying capacity of the environment. The fact that modern group size is so constant even in differing environments suggests that the band size of 20 to 30 may be conditioned more by human social factors than by environmental limitations.

The Acheulean economic pattern probably included seasonal movement in search of food, with some favorable sites functioning as central loci to which the band returned periodically. Much of the food must have been of vegetable nature, for modern hunter-gatherers only rely on meat for 20 to 40 percent of their diet. Unfortunately the archaeological record provides little evidence of these vegetal foods.

Sites in both Europe and Africa suggest that open savanna or grasslands were preferred, with sites being located near streams, lakes, and other sources of water. Acheulean man did not modify his environment appreciably, and even his use of fire, at least in terms of the frequency with which we find evidence of it, was somewhat restricted. Presumably Acheulean man expanded to the geographic and climatic limits permitted by his culture, and was not then able to expand beyond those limits. Acheulean living floors are relatively common and an example of the one from Ambrona, Spain, is illustrated to demonstrate the type of evidence which we have to work with (Fig. 6–11).

The Diet of Acheulean Man

The inference of Lower Paleolithic diet is of course limited by the nature of the materials preserved. Since plant parts have not been preserved, our evidence is limited to food bones and their patterning within the butchery site. Clark and Haynes (1970:407–409) have summarized those bone occurrences as follows:

1. Finds of semi-articulated skeletons where there is minimal evidence of disturbance by either man or animals.
2. Partly broken up skeletons of a single animal with only a small degree of bone dispersal and associated with comparatively few stone artifacts.
3. Extensive disarticulation and dispersal of the bones of one, sometimes more than one large animal.

Fig. 6–11 Distribution of bones and artifacts in the Acheulean site at Ambrona, Spain, excavated by Clark Howell of the University of Chicago. The bones are those of the extinct, straight tusked elephant, deer, horse, and auroch. (de Sonneville-Bordes 1967:Fig. 45.)

4. Multiple kill or "occupation" sites at which diverse activities were carried on as reflected by the overall area covered by the concentration, the considerable quantities of Large Cutting, Heavy Duty and Light Duty tools and waste which occur in very varying proportions on sites of this kind.

One further category, or subcategory, may, perhaps, be included, at least in regard to the Acheulean:

5. "Occupation" sites with numerous Large Cutting tools together with some Heavy and Light Duty equipment, but very little bone.

The evidence from Mwanganda and the other sites mentioned here, where a single or a minimal number of carcases are present, slight as it is, suggests first, that human butchering practices generally resulted in the disarticulation, dispersal and differential fracture of the bones of the large food animals. It would seem also that they were butchered at the place where they were killed or where the carcase was found.

Secondly, the evidence suggests that Palaeolithic butchering and meat processing equipment consisted predominantly of small numbers of Light Duty tools and cutting flakes and small scraping tools with a few only of larger elements. This large tool element appears to be supplementary rather than primary to the main purpose of the equipment.

Thirdly, it would seem also that little change can be observed in the basic pattern of these occurrences from the Lower Pleistocene right through to Holocene times.

Reviewing much the same evidence Isaac (1971) has formulated a series of observations concerning the diet of Lower Paleolithic man. His conclusions are that throughout the Pleistocene, back at least 2 million years, the hominid diet has been omnivorous and specifically included meat. Further, the utilization of large animals is attested by the finding of their bones in refuse of Lower Pleistocene age. The exact age of the origin of cooperative hunting is as yet unknown, although positive evidence dates back to the Middle Pleistocene. More important, according to Isaac, was the division of labor between male hunters and female gatherers which he believes is basic to the hominid pattern of adaptation over the past 2 million years. He stresses the fact that an omnivorous diet was of greater importance to the survival and evolution of early man than was the mere fact of predation.

Acheulean Man

The human species most commonly associated with Acheulean remains is *Homo erectus* (Fig. 6–12). However it is not intended to imply that there is a precise correlation between a human physical type and the cultural tradition, at least with a tradition as long-lived as the Acheulean. Our latest Acheulean sites are in the vicinity of 50,000–100,000 years of age, which is within the time span of *Homo neanderthalensis*. According to some authors, this time span could even include *Homo sapiens*.

Major finds of materials now referred to as *Homo erectus* are those from the Trinil beds in Java (*Pithecanthropus erectus,* as originally termed by Dubois the discoverer) and the finds from Choukoutien near Peking, China, originally termed *Sinanthropus pekinensis*. A modern list of the more important localities featuring *H. erectus* is reproduced below (Butzer 1971:443):

A. **Early Lower Pleistocene**
   a.   Olduvai; upper Bed II. *Homo* cf. *erectus* ("Chellean Man") and one or more Australopithecines.
   b.   Swartkrans. *Homo erectus* ("Telanthropus") and *Australopithecus robustus*.
   c.   Sangiran and Modjokerto, Java; Djetis fauna. *Homo* cf. *erectus* ("Meganthropus palaeojavanicus") and *Homo erectus* ("Pithecanthropus").

B. **Late Lower Pleistocene**
   a.   Heidelberg-Mauer, Germany. *Homo* cf. *erectus* ("Palaeanthropus"), of post-Cromerian but pre-Elster age.
   b.   Verteszöllös, Hungary. *Homo* cf. *sapiens* of Elster age.

Fig. 6–12 Reconstruction of *Homo erectus*. (Drawing by Maurice Wilson. Courtesy of the Trustees of the British Museum (Natural History).)

  c. Ternifine, Algeria. *Homo erectus* ("Atlanthropus").

  d. Koro Toro, Chad. *Homo* cf. *erectus* ("Tchadanthropus"), a poorly preserved fossil of uncertain age.

  e. Sangiran and Trinil, Java; Trinil fauna. *Homo erectus* ("Pithecanthropus").

C. Uncertain, Early to Mid-Pleistocene

  a. Olduvai; Bed IV. *Homo erectus*.

  b. Choukoutien I, near Peking, China. *Homo erectus* ("Sinanthropus pekinensis") of Holstein age or from an earlier interglacial or interstadial.

  c. Lantian, China. *Homo erectus* ("Sinanthropus lantianensis"), of Holstein age or more probably from an earlier interglacial.

The above list verifies the confusion in the literature caused by the proclivity of human paleontologists to coin new generic and specific names at the finding of a new bone or even a single tooth. In this introductory work we will not review each *H. erectus* find in detail. General characteristics of the species include large canine teeth, remarkably primitive teeth for man, and with large roots, sharp backward slope to the forehead, very thick cranial vault (1 centimeter), heavy brow ridges, post orbital constriction, a cranial

TABLE 6–2   Measurements of Some *Homo erectus* **Skulls**

	Maximum Length	Maximum Breadth	Cephalic Index	Distance from Basion to Bregma	Cranial Capacity (in cc.)
Pithecanthropus I	183(e)* (153)**	135	—	105(e)	935
Pithecanthropus II	176 (148)	129	76.5	105	775
Sinanthropus III	188 (156)	141	72.3	—	915
Sinanthropus XI	192 (167)	143	72.4	115(e)	1015
Sinanthropus X	195.5 (173)	147	71.0	—	1225

*(e) = *estimate*
**The figures in parentheses refer to the maximum length of the interior of the skull; the differences from outside lengths are considerable because of the thickness of the bones. The brain capacity is small. Measurements are in mm.

(Von Koenigswald 1962:89 [after Weidenreich 1943].)

capacity ranging from 775 to 1225 cubic centimeters, and marked sexual dimorphism. Measurements of *H. erectus* skulls are presented in Table 6–2.

The original type site was found by Eugene Dubois, a Dutch physician, on the banks of the Solo River near Trinil in Central Java (Fig. 6–13). In 1891 he located a skull cap and in 1892 a femur which led to his terming the find *Pithecanthropus erectus,* the ape man that walked erect. After the finds at Choukoutien by Davidson Black in 1927 and 1928, the true nature of the species became clear, the Trinil finds being too fragmentary to permit accurate reconstruction. Finds at Choukoutien include portions of 14 skulls, 14 lower jaws including 148 teeth, plus fragments of the post cranial skeleton. During

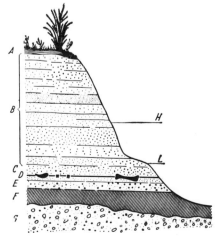

Fig. 6–13 Profile of the site on the Solo River, Java, location of the original finds of *Pithecanthropus erectus* (in layer *D*). *H* is the high water mark; *L* the low water mark. (Von Koenigswald 1962:Fig. 47 [after E. Dubois].)

World War II the original Peking finds were lost, but fortunately for science, casts of the originals were preserved. A surprising fact is that Dubois failed to accept the *Sinanthropus* finds as similar to those at Trinil. He regarded the former as a degenerate Neanderthal type.

The site of Choukoutien, which is a hill today (Fig. 6–14), was formerly a narrow gorge which has partially collapsed and is filled with rubble. *Sinanthropus* camped here in small caves and under projecting rocks (Fig. 6–15). He possessed fire and manufactured chopping tools of quartz. Unfortunately quartz is a poor material and the implements are difficult to compare with those of other industries. Bones within the cave include deer, pig, antelope, bison, horse, water buffalo, elephant, monkey, and rhinoceros. Hyenas were also common, suggesting that when man was not present the caves were used as lairs. Most importantly, all of the human skulls had the foramen magnum enlarged—evidence that *Sinanthropus* was cannibalistic, also evidenced by femurs cracked for the marrow (Fig. 6–16). He may even have been a head-hunter.

The implements made by *Sinanthropus* feature the bipolar technique, with the core being placed on an anvil prior to the removal of flakes (Fig. 6–17). As the flakes were struck off, the rebounding force of the blow from the anvil produced a secondary bulb of percussion; thus the flakes are "bipolar" with a bulb at each end. Major tool types are choppers, chopping tools, scrapers, and a few bifacial leaf-shaped tools.

An Acheulean Hunt

One of our best examples of a reconstruction of a Lower Paleolithic hunt is that of F. C. Howell, based on his excavations in the Ambrona Valley of Spain (Howell and others 1965:91–100). Such a reconstruction is hypothetical at best, owing to the variables affecting preservation of site data. For example, we have no human remains from the site so we must infer that the hunters were *Homo erectus* from the presence of their Acheulean type implements. The actual tools found were made of imported stone; thus they were carried there in preparation for the hunt. A linked inference is that since the hunt was planned in advance it took place at a specific time in the year, such as autumn when the migratory mammoth would have been moving South to warmer locations. The valley itself would have formed a natural funnel which the hunters were able to use for their ambush. The hunters would have normally consisted of bands of a few adult males and females plus their offspring; no more than 30 people at the most, at least that is the typical group size of modern primitive hunting bands and we believe the Acheulean bands were similar. If such was the case, then more than one band grouped together to provide the manpower for the Ambrona mammoth drive. The actual drive itself was conducted through use of fire by means of which the prey were driven into boggy ground where they were killed with wooden spears and rocks. The elephants would have been hemmed in by the steep sides of the valley as well as by fires set by the hunters

Fig. 6–14 The site at Choukoutien, near Peking, China; the home of *Sinanthropus* for thousands of years. (Courtesy of American Museum of Natural History.)

Fig. 6–15 Reconstruction drawing of *Sinanthropus pekinensis* at home. (Photograph courtesy of the Trustees of the British Museum (Natural History).)

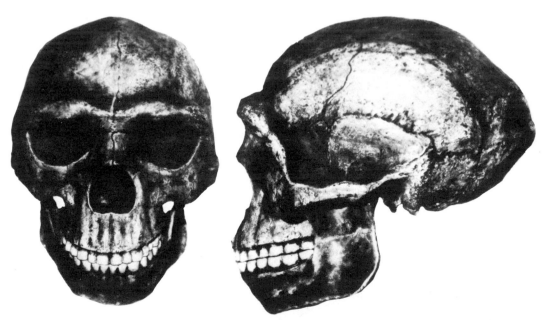

Fig. 6–16 Skull of *Sinanthropus pekinensis*. (Restoration by F. Weidenreich. Courtesy of British Museum (Natural History).)

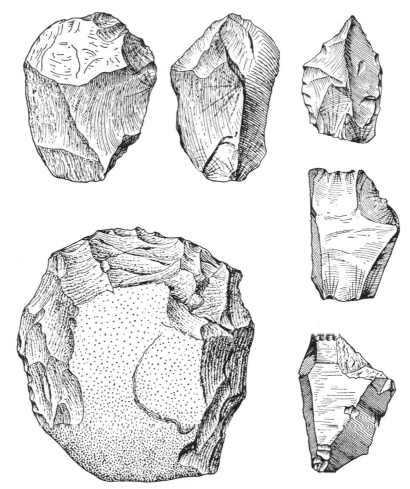

Fig. 6–17 Choppers and flakes from Locality I, Choukoutien—the implements used by *Sinanthropus*. (J. G. D. Clark 1967:Fig. 8 [after Pei and Black].)

to cut off their escape. Howell found the charcoal and stones used in the kill as well as the bones of the mammoths in the spot where they were killed, still mired in the bog. Other specific evidence found consisted of a smashed elephant skull from which the brains were taken and a line of bones—a tusk, two femurs, and two tibias, all from the same animal but dismembered. Howell infers that these bones formed a causeway across the bog providing a means for the hunters to carry the butchered meat to dry ground (see Fig. 6–11). After the hunt there was undoubtedly a feast. Probably some of the meat and internal organs were eaten raw immediately after the kill to be followed later by more leisurely gorging around the campfires. Other activities inferred are of a social nature. We cannot prove that there was boasting about the day's successful hunt or its reenactment, but such seems probable. Likewise, with a number of people gathered together, larger than the normal group, there must have been much social interaction which could have included courtship and the learning by the young of the skills and traditions of the adults. After all, even though we cannot prove that they did these things, these were early humans and such cultural practices had to begin at some time in the distant past.

Non-Acheulean Traditions

The Acheulean remains are not indicative of all Lower Paleolithic remains; in fact there are a number which do not possess handaxes. Examples in Europe have been termed the Clactonian, Tayacian, and Levalloisian. While we cannot as yet assess the geographical extent of the Clactonian industry, it is a valid industry featuring the removal of large flakes from cores by striking the hand-held core against an anvil resting on the ground. The resultant flakes have a broad striking platform at a wide angle to the flake face, a well marked percussion cone, and marked ripple marks on the flake surface. Cores are globular and handaxes are absent. According to Bordes, the Tayacian, which has been described as a flake industry featuring a specific type of primitive point—the Tayac point—should be redefined because it contains materials probably referable to several industries. The concept of the Levalloisian as a separate flake industry is no longer tenable. Originally defined on the basis of collections from the Somme Valley terraces, it has subsequently been demonstrated not to exist independently of true Acheulean implements. Further, the Levallois technique is now known to persist in time to characterize a number of later stone tool industries including the Mousterian and even the Khargan of North Africa. Thus the Levalloisian is a flaking tradition rather than a specific culture.

The industries of Southeast Asia, extending from northern India to Java and north to Peking, China, are referred to a major tradition termed *Chopper-Chopping tool*. Tools are made on pebbles and flakes, with bifacially flaked core tools rare to absent. Tool types include pebble choppers, chopping tools made on flakes, and edge retouched flakes made into cleavers and scrapers. Similarities with the Oldowan industry may be perceived, although exact relationships are yet to be established. The entire region clearly features a cultural evolution contemporaneous with much of the Acheulean traditions but essentially different in its component elements. Regional variants of named industries include the Soan in northwestern India, the implements associated with the *Sinanthropus* fossils at Choukoutien, the Fenho complex in Shansi and Honan provinces, the Anyathian from the Irrawaddy Valley terraces of Burma, and the Tampanian in northern Malaysia. The simplicity of these implements and the use of poor stone sources inhibit detailed typological comparisons. These industries are referable to the general Chopper-Chopping tool tradition, but their interrelationships are not yet clear.

Other pebble tool industries without handaxes are known from eastern

Europe, including sites at Verteszöllos, Hungary, in Poland, some layers in the cave of Pech de l'aze II, France, and at Sainte Anne-d' Evenos, France. Pebble tools are also known from Ain Hanech, Algeria. Thus we know that humans of the *H. erectus* type were utilizing implements of two major cultural traditions, the Acheulean and the Chopper-Chopping tool tradition, throughout the Lower Paleolithic.

The pebble tool tradition appears to have been the first developed, with the later Acheulean tradition sweeping over most of the habitable Paleolithic world. Possibly remnants of pebble tool users hung on for long periods of time in Europe and Africa, with their preference continuing to be dominant in Southeast Asia. Both traditions overlap in India. Reasons for this distribution of Paleolithic traditions are not clearly understood. One hypothesis is that the Acheulean industry was superior as a tool kit for hunters specializing in the hunting of herd-dwelling mammals of Europe and Africa.

SUMMARY

The Lower Paleolithic is an immensely long period of human cultural history. During this interval man survived several glacial and interglacial periods, learned to control fire, developed cultural techniques for hunting, butchering, and such, and even began to diversify his tool inventory. Major tool innovations include the Levalloisian technique which came to dominate later periods of tool manufacture. Also during the Lower Paleolithic man evolved physically from one of the more capable Australopithecines into true man. His cranial capacity increased and concomitantly his abilities to communicate, organize, and symbolize. However at this time we have no evidence that man had developed elaborations of social organization nor any religious beliefs. At this level, man became a capable predator but was only on the threshold of his role as a major influence on his environment. Presumably during this interval, man lived in small bands of 25 to 30 individuals, hunted and gathered, and followed a migratory way of life, accumulating few permanent possessions. Having evolved this far man was ready to take a new cultural step into the Middle Paleolithic.

REFERENCES

Bordes, F., 1968, *The Old Stone Age.* New York: McGraw-Hill.
Butzer, K., 1971, *Environment and Archaeology,* 2d ed. Chicago: Aldine-Atherton.
Clark, J. D., 1967, *Atlas of African Prehistory.* Chicago: The University of Chicago Press.
———, and C. V. Haynes, Jr., 1970, "An Elephant Butchery Site at Mwanganda's Village, Karonga, Malawi, and Its Relevance for Paleolithic Archaeology," *World Archaeology* 1(3):390–411.
Clark, J. G. D., 1967, *The Stone Age Hunters.* New York: McGraw-Hill.

Cooke, H. B. S., 1973, "Pleistocene Chronology: Long or Short?" *Quaternary Research* 3(2):206–220.

Dansgaard, W., and others, 1969, "One Thousand Centuries of Climatic Record from Camp Century on the Greenland Ice Sheet," *Science* 166:377–381.

Dart, R. A., 1926, "Taungs and Its Significance," *Natural History* 26(3):315–327.

de Sonneville-Bordes, D., 1967, *La Prehistoire Moderne*. Perigeux: Pierre Fanlac.

Emiliani, C., 1966, "Paleotemperature Analysis of Caribbean Cores p6304-8 and p6304-9 and a Generalized Temperature Curve for the Past 425,000 Years," *Journal of Geology* 74:109–126.

Flint, R. F., 1971, *Glacial and Quaternary Geology*. New York: Wiley.

Howell, F. C., and others, 1965, *Early Man*. New York: Time/Life Books.

Isaac, G. L., 1971, "The Diet of Early Man: Aspects of Archaeological Evidence from Lower and Middle Pleistocene Sites in Africa," *World Archaeology* 2(3):278–299.

Jolly, A., 1972, *The Evolution of Primate Behavior*. New York: Macmillan.

Leakey, L. S. B., 1970, Personal communication.

Leakey, M. D., 1967, "Preliminary Survey of the Cultural Material from Beds I and II, Olduvai Gorge, Tanzania," in W. W. Bishop and J. D. Clark (eds.), *Background to Evolution in Africa*. Chicago: The University of Chicago Press.

Lee, R. B., and I. deVore, eds., 1968, *Man the Hunter*. Chicago: Aldine.

Von Koenigswald, G. H. R., 1962, *The Evolution of Man*. Ann Arbor: University of Michigan Press.

Watson, R. A., and P. J. Watson, 1969, *Man and Nature*. New York: Harcourt.

7

The Middle Paleolithic

The Middle Paleolithic includes those cultures which flourished during the early and middle stages of the Würm glaciation. With cultural roots extending back in time to the preceding interglacial period, these industries are for the most part a direct outgrowth of the late Acheulean. Our dating of these cultures ranges from approximations, where their relative stratigraphic position and correlation with glacial fluctuations is known, to precise dates obtained with the radiocarbon method. Whereas the earliest cultures termed Middle Paleolithic may date as early as 75,000 to 100,000 years B.P., we have radiocarbon dates only back to 55,000 B.C., because of the limitations of the radiocarbon method. Securely dated Middle Paleolithic sites thus extend from 55,000 B.C. to 30,000 B.C. On the other hand, late Acheulean sites are as recent as 55,000 B.C., as in Kalambo Falls, Rhodesia; thus there was regional variation in cultural evolution, with some areas evolving more rapidly than

TABLE 7–1 Table of Radiocarbon Determinations for the Mousterian and Allied Cultures

Europe		B.C.
1. Les Cottés, Vienne, France	GrN 4334	30,350 ± 400
	GrN 4421	35,650 ± 700
2. Grotte du Renne, Arcy-sur-Cure, Yonne, France	GrN 4217	32,650 ± 850
3. La Quina, Charente, France	GrN 4494	32,150 ± 700
	GrN 2526	33,300 ± 530
4. Radošina, Czechoslovakia	GrN 2438	36,450 + 2800
		− 2100
5. Nietoperzowa, Poland	GrN 2181	36,550 ± 1240
6. Broion Cave, nr. Vicenza, Italy	GrN 4638	38,650 ± 1200
7. Érd, Hungary	GrN 4711	37,400 ± 830
	GrN 4444	42,350 ± 1400
8. Regourdou, Dordogne, France	GrN 4308	43,550 ± 1800
9. La Cotte de St. Brelade, Jersey	GrN 2649	45,050 ± 1500
10. Gibraltar (Gorham's Cave G)	GrN 1473	45,750 ± 1500
11. Lebenstedt, Germany	GrN 2083	53,290 ± 1010
12. Mussolini Canal, Italy	GrN 2572	55,950 ± 500
North Africa		
13. Haua Fteah, Cyrenaica (level xxviii)	GrN 2564	41,450 ± 1300
14. Haua Fteah, Cyrenaica (level xxxiii)	GrN 2023	45,050 ± 3200
Southwest Asia		
15. Tabun B, Israel	GrN 2534	37,750 ± 800
16. el Kebarah, Israel	GrN 2561	39,050 ± 1000
17. Geulah Cave A, Israel	GrN 4121	40,050 ± 1700
18. Jerf Ajla, Syria	NZ 76	41,050 ± 2000
19. Ksar 'Akil, Lebanon	GrN 2579	41,800 ± 1500
20. Shanidar, Iraq (level D, top)	GrN 2527	41,950 ± 1500
	GrN 1495	48,650 ± 3000
21. Ras el-Kelb, Lebanon	GrN 2556	> 52,000
22. Al Ghab, Syria	GrN 2640	> 53,000

(Clark 1971:46–47.)

others. After all this is what we should expect in a situation marked by small local groups frequently evolving in isolation without any widespread network of communication.

The major cultural tradition of the period is that termed Mousterian, first identified in the rock shelter at Le Moustier, France. Mousterian industries were widespread throughout the ancient world, being found in most of the region characterized by the earlier Acheulean (Table 7–1). In fact there seems to have been little Middle Paleolithic expansion into regions not populated by Acheulean peoples. Meanwhile, the Chopper-Chopping tool tradition continued in existence forming a cultural isolate in Asia. Mousterian sites are widespread in Europe, the Middle East, and North Africa (see Table 7–1). South of the Sahara the period is characterized by another tradition of stone tool manufacture with cultures termed Sangoan and Lupemban. The period is thus not marked by the expansion of peoples into new geographic regions. What

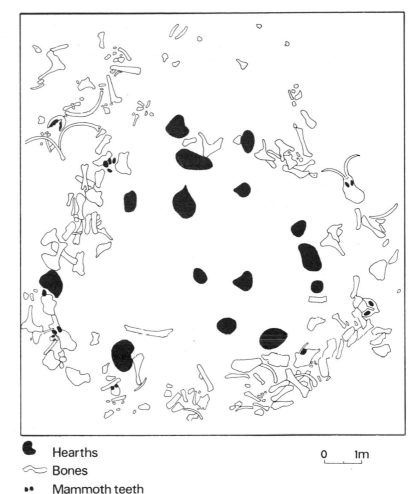

🔥 **Hearths**

〰 **Bones**

•• **Mammoth teeth**

0   1m

Fig. 7–1 Ground level plan of the Mousterian hut at Molodova I (western Russia). (Bordes 1968:Fig. 51.)

happened was that the environment changed with the onset of the Würm glaciation, and some Mousterian cultures became adapted to life in a cold climate. Major cultural innovations included the development of varieties of tool complexes ("tool kits"), presumed to represent increasing adaptations to local environments. Thus the Middle Paleolithic is marked by an increasing diversification and specialization of tool inventories. There was a major emphasis on the use of caves and rock shelters as occupation sites, while sites in the open featured constructed shelters (Fig. 7–1). The economy included heavy reliance on the hunting of herd-dwelling animals. Site remains indicate that the Mousterian hunters were highly proficient, for some sites have bones of thousands of animals. The species hunted were highly selected. Other innovations, such as intentional burial, reflect the development of a system of beliefs which may be termed magicoreligious.

The human variety present during the period is predominantly of the type we know as Neanderthal man, a heavy browed, large brained descendent of *Homo erectus*. We again do not have identity between culture and physical type, although the typical Middle Paleolithic human was of Neanderthal type.

In our consideration of the Middle Paleolithic we will review the nature of the stone industries and their distribution, Neanderthal man, the Würm environments, the growth of cultural elaboration, and finally the disappearance of Neanderthal man and the rise of his replacement, *Homo sapiens*.

MOUSTERIAN INDUSTRIES

Mousterian industries are characterized by tools made on flakes, with the predominant flake blanks being of the Levallois type. Though handaxes are present, they tend to occur in limited frequency. The flake tools are usually retouched on only one face—termed unifacial retouch by the archaeologist—with such retouch normally limited to the edges of the flake rather than extending over the entire flake surface. Additional tools consisted of unmodified Levallois flakes, blades, or points, which were shaped to their intended form on the core and, once struck off the core, were ready for use. The variety of implements, as contrasted with the earlier Acheulean industries, increased. Tool types of high frequency in the Mousterian include backed knives, a variety of end and side scrapers, burins, borers, and points. The increase in tool variety suggests new functions were performed, such as the scraping of hides, the manufacture of clothing, and the working of wood and bone into a variety of useful objects. In summary, there is a dramatic increase in the number of tools used to make tools.

The Mousterian culture is widespread geographically and possesses distinct cultural variants. For example, the Mousterian of the Levant is somewhat different from those of North Africa and Europe. It is in the Mousterian of Europe where we have had the greatest amount of study, with four major subtraditions being defined. These have been termed the Typical Mousterian, Mousterian of Acheulean Tradition, Quina Mousterian, and Denticulate Mousterian (Figs. 7–2 to 7–6). These are not geographical variants, for they occur in the same region and even in the same sites. Furthermore they are not entirely chronological variants, as several of them existed contemporaneously. At one well-known site, Combe Grenal in Southern France, there are 68 layers of Mousterian culture. Within these layers the Mousterian variants occur and reoccur without chronological segregation. Francois Bordes, the excavator, suggests that these different varieties of Mousterian industries should be viewed as different tool kits to be employed as the occasion required, perhaps because of environmental changes. A brief description of the salient features of each of these variants is presented below (Bordes 1968, 1972).

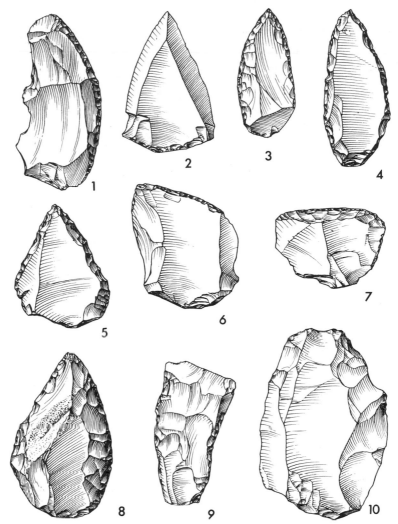

Fig. 7–2 Flint implements of the typical Mousterian: *1*. convex sidescraper; *2*. Levallois point; *3, 4, 5.*, Mousterian points; *6*. canted scraper; *7*. transversal scraper; *8*. convergent scraper; *9*. double scraper; *10*. Levallois flake. (Bordes 1968:Fig. 33.)

Typical Mousterian Group

The Levallois technique is present with handaxes being rare to not present. Scrapers make up 25 to 55 percent of the tools. Points are well made, and backed knives are rare. The limace, a double-pointed scraper, is rare. Notched flakes and denticulates are also rare. The typical Mousterian is present from the beginning of Würm I to the end of Würm II.

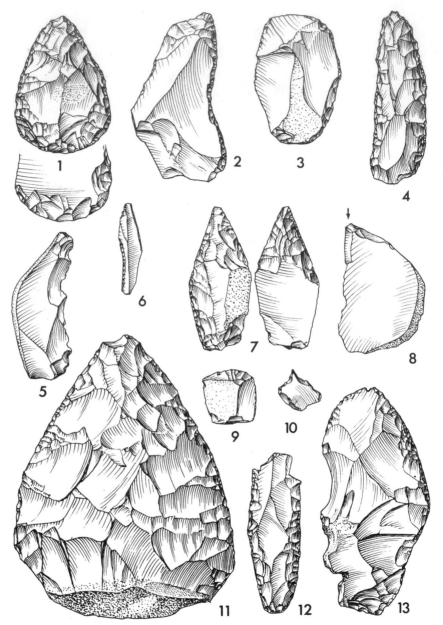

Fig. 7–3 Mousterian of Acheulean tradition, Type A: *1.* point with a thinned butt; *2.* concave scraper; *3.* backed knife; *4, 12.* double scrapers on blades; *5.* denticulated tool; *6.* bladelet with a small retouch; *7.* bifacial point; *8.* burin; *9.* short end scraper; *10.* small border; *11.* cordiform handaxe; *13.* convex side scraper. (Bordes 1968:Fig. 36.)

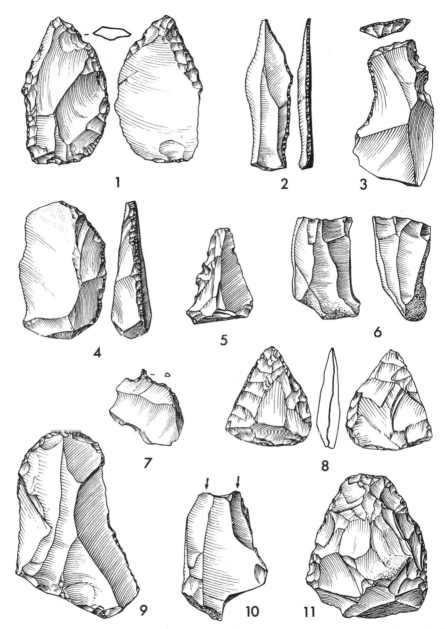

Fig. 7–4 Mousterian of Acheulean tradition, Type B: *1.* bad point, more or less bifacially worked; *2.* backed knife on a blade, foreshadowing the Chatelperron knives of the early Upper Paleolithic; *3.* denticulated and truncated flake; *4.* backed knife on a flake; *5.* denticulated tool; *6.* core for the production of bladelets; *7.* borer; *8, 11.* small handaxes; *9.* end scraper; *10.* double burin. (Bordes 1968:Fig. 37.)

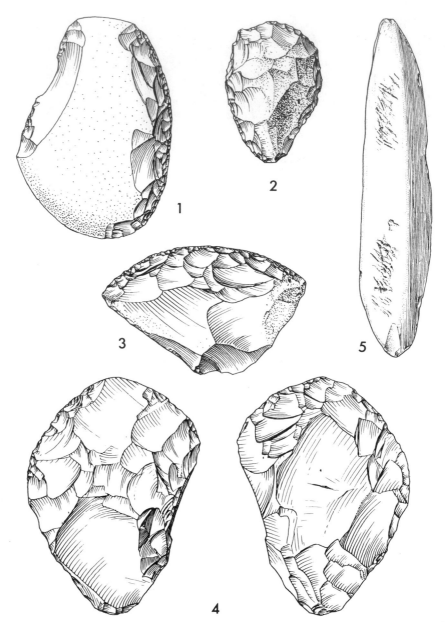

Fig. 7–5 Tools from the Quina-type Mousterian: *1.* convex side scraper; *2.* thick end and side scraper; *3.* transversal scraper, Quina-type; *4.* bifacial scraper, Quina-type; *5.* bone retoucher. (Bordes 1968:Fig. 34.)

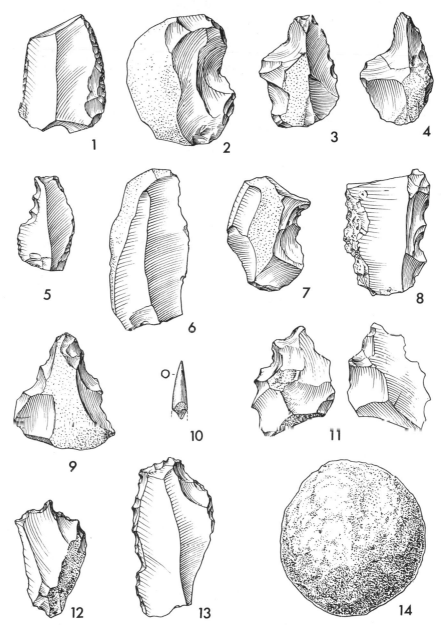

Fig. 7–6 Denticulated Mousterian tools: *1.* side scraper; *2, 3, 4.* Clactonian notches; *5, 7, 8, 11, 13.* denticulate tools; *6.* knife with natural back; *9.* Tayac point; *10.* broken tip of a point made of reindeer antler; *12.* borer; *14.* bola stone. (Bordes 1968:Fig. 35.)

Mousterian of Acheulean Tradition Group

This variant has been divided by Bordes into two phases, termed Type A and Type B. The difference in this case is chronological, for Type A always precedes Type B. The Type A variant is present from the beginning of the Würm glaciation. Distinctive tools are handaxes, present in frequencies up to 40 percent but averaging 10 to 15 percent. Typical handaxe forms are triangular, cordiform (see Fig. 7–5), or subcordiform. Flake tools are varied but feature 20 to 40 percent scrapers. Points are common, having thinned butts and some bifacial flaking. Denticulates are also common. Burins, endscrapers, borers, flakes, and truncated blades are more common than in the other types of the Mousterian. Backed knives are rare. Type B features fewer handaxes, only 2 to 8 percent, and few side scrapers. Most common are denticulates and backed knives, the latter made on elongated flakes or blades. A rare occurrence is double burins. Type B seems to date from the beginning of Würm II to the Würm II/III transition.

Denticulate Mousterian Group

This variant includes a large frequency (35 to 55 percent) of denticulated implements; these are flake tools of varying form featuring serrated edges. Other characteristics are primarily negative. There are no typical handaxes, no backed knives, few points, and few scrapers. Clearly the functions of many of the typical implements were performed by the denticulate tools. No skeletal remains have been found with the denticulate variant. The Denticulate Mousterian lasts from the beginning of Würm I through Würm II.

Charentian Group

The Quina variant is represented by a very high percentage of scrapers, from 50 to 58 percent. Many special scraper forms not present in the other Mousterian industries occur, including transverse scrapers, scrapers with bifacial retouch over the entire surface, simple thick scrapers, and limaces. The Quina index is high (14 to 30) which represents the percentage of total scrapers that are of the Quina type. There are a few end scrapers, very few handaxes, no backed knives, few denticulates, and numerous notched flakes. The flakes are short and thick. Levallois flakes occur in limited frequency but the industry is primarily non-Levallois in character. Most of the Neanderthal specimens from western Europe are associated with Quina implements.

The Ferrasie variant features a high scraper index comparable to that of Quina, with a low frequency of transverse scrapers. The Quina index is moderate (6 to 14). Handaxes and backed knives are rare to absent. The Levallois index is high (14 to 30).

Dating of the Mousterian variants has been summarized by Laville (1973). He states that the Quina, Ferrasie, and Mousterian of Acheulean

Tradition industries were manufactured throughout the entire Würm I and Würm II periods and therefore are not chronologically distinct as have been suggested by other authors (Fig. 7–7).

NEANDERTHAL MAN

Most of you have heard of Neanderthal man and have some idea of his general characteristics. He is the archetype of the beetle browed caveman portrayed in cartoons and comic strips. In scientific fact, the Neanderthals are something of an enigma, for they form a varied group from the standpoint of their physical characteristics. Most interestingly, those specimens which are the most different from modern man are among the most recent. We will review the sequence of Neanderthal discoveries in order to clarify how we came to know about these early men. First we will describe their general physical appearance in somewhat greater detail. Simultaneously, the reader should know that internal variation within the Neanderthal physical type was substantial. Our description is in fact an abstraction.

The classic Neanderthal possessed massive brow ridges, a lower and flatter skull as compared with modern man, a large cranial capacity (1350 to 1723 cubic centimeters), which exceeds slightly that of modern man (1350 to 1500 cubic centimeters). The large cranial size is achieved by a bulging out of the sides and rear of the skull rather than through an increase in skull height, as is the case with modern man. The nasal bones are prominent and the nasal aperture is large. The chin is weak to absent. The cheek bones are prominent. The molars are large with strong cusp development and have deep pulp cavities. The premolars and canines are similar in size to those of modern man. The remainder of the skeleton indicates that Neanderthals were short, 5 feet to 5 feet 4 inches in height, but very powerfully built. Their limbs were short and slightly bowed, and the hands and fingers were short. The muscle attachments on the long bones are massive, indicating that great strength was a Neanderthal trait. One author has suggested that these muscle attachments were necessary to support an increased fat layer, up to 60 pounds, built up to sustain them over the winter—a human hibernation theory. Most authorities believe this concept stretches the available data beyond the level of reasonable inference.

The first find of a fossil specimen was by workmen quarrying a cave deposit, Feldhofer Grotto, in the Neander Valley 7 miles east of Düsseldorf, Germany, in 1856. A local teacher, J. C. Von Fuhlrott, recognized the importance of the find and it was preserved. The portions of the recovered skeleton included a skull cap, one clavicle, one scapula, five ribs, two humeri, one radius, two ulnae, two femora, and part of the pelvis. The scientific classification of the find as that of a new fossil species termed *Homo neanderthalensis* was carried out by an Englishman named King in 1864. This find antedated any other finds of fossil man, and thus investigators began to form impressions of man's ancestry with only limited evidence—a situation in part responsible for

Stratigraphic and climatic correlation chart for Würm sites (Combe-Grenal, Caminade, Pech de l'Azé II, Le Moustier).

Chronology	Climatic Phases	Climate	Combe-Grenal Layers	Combe-Grenal Industries	Caminade Layers	Caminade Industries	Pech de l'Azé II Layers	Pech de l'Azé II Industries	Le Moustier Layers	Le Moustier Industries
Würm II – Würm III Interstadial	VIII	Temperate Very wet / Very cold - Very dry	1	Mousterian of Ach Trad.						
			2	Mousterian						
			3	Mousterian of Ach Trad						
			4	Mousterian						
			5	Typical Moust (Levall)						
			6	Typical Moust (Levall)						
Würm II	VII	Mild and wet	7	Mousterian					? J	Typical Moust
			8	Mousterian						
	VI	Cold and dry	9	Typical Mousterian	M3 Sommet	Quina Mousterian / FERRASSIE MOUST				
			10	Denticulate Moust (Levall)						
	V	Mild and wet	11	Denticulate Moust	M3				? I	Denticulate Moust
			12	Denticulate Moust						
			13							
	IV	Very cold - Very dry	16 15 14	Denticulate Moust	M3 base	FERRASSIE MOUST			H9 to H2	Moust. of Ach Trad."B"
			19 18 17	Quina Mousterian						
	III	Mild and wet	20	Denticulate Moust.	M2	FERRASSIE MOUST				
			21	Quina Mousterian						
			22							
	II	Very cold - Very dry	23	Quina Mousterian	M1 Sommet	Typical Moust ?			H1	Moust. of Ach Trad."B"
			24							
			25							
	I	Cold and wet	26	Quina Mousterian	M1 base	Typical Moust ?				
			27	FERRASSIE MOUST						
			28							
			29	Typical Moust						
			30							
			31							
			32 to 35	FERRASSIE MOUST						
Würm I – Würm II Interstadial		Temperate Very wet		Weathering of the underlying deposits					G4 G3	Weathering of the underlying deposits
Würm I	VII	Very cold - Very dry	36	Typical Moust			?		G2	Moust. of Ach Trad."A"
			37							
	VI	Mild and wet	38	Denticulate Moust. (Levall)			?		G1	Moust. of Ach Trad."A"
	V	Cold and dry	39	Mousterian			2D	Mousterian		Moust. of Ach Trad."A"
			40	Typical Moust			2E	Quina Mousterian		
							2F	Mousterian		
	IV	Temperate-wet	41	Typical Mousterian (Levallois)			2G	Mousterian	F	Denticulate Moust
			42				2G'	Mousterian	E	
			43							
	III	Cold and dry	46 45 44	Mousterian			3	Typical Moust	D	Typical Moust
			47	Typical Moust						
			49 48	Mousterian						
	II	Temperate-wet	50A	Typical Moust			4A	Mousterian	C	Typical Moust
			50	Mousterian			4B	Denticulate Moust	B	
			51	Typical Moust			4C1	Typical Moust	A	
			52				4C2	Typical Moust		
	I	Cold and dry	53	Mousterian			4D	Typical Moust		
			54	Typical Moust			5			
			55	Mousterian						

the "caveman" impression of man's ancestors held by the uninformed today. Subsequent finds of similar specimens were made at Spy, Belgium, in 1886, including two skulls and some skeletal remains; La Chapelle aux Saints, France, 1908, a complete adult skeleton; Le Moustier, France, 1908, a complete adolescent skeleton; La Quina, France, 1908–1921, several skulls; and La Ferrassie, France, 1909–1921, several skulls. Subsequent to these initial finds, Neanderthal remains were found in numerous other parts of the world: Broken Hill, Rhodesia, 1921, a skull without mandible with some skeletal fragments; Saldanha Bay, South Africa, 1953, a skull cap and lower jaw fragment; Ngandong, Java, 1931–1933, 11 skull caps and two tibias; Sidi-Abderrahman, Morocco, 1955, lower jaw; Mugharet-es-Skhul, Palestine, 1931–1932, parts of 10 individuals; Mugharet et-Tabun, 1931–1932, a female skeleton, a male lower jaw, other skeletal remains, and teeth; and Shanidar Cave, Iran, 1951–1960, nine skeletons, including those of two infants. These are only some of the most important finds. Today, remains of at least 155 Neanderthal individuals are known from 68 sites in Europe, Africa, the Middle East, and Southeast Asia. Several of these finds have been reconstructed (Fig. 7–8).

Today these finds are given subspecific rank by physical anthropologists *(Homo sapiens neanderthalensis)* because as more complete skeletons were found and as other early man fossils were discovered (*Homo erectus, Australopithecus,* and so on), it became apparent that the Neanderthals were anatomically closer to modern man than had been originally believed. Another major result of the increasing number of recent finds, especially those from the Middle East, was a reassessment of the evolutionary position of the various Neanderthal groups. The Middle Eastern specimens exhibit a variety of physical features from those of classic type to some quite modern in appearance, with reduced brow ridges and higher cranial vaults approximating those of modern man; other specimens are intermediate in form. The Middle Eastern population consisted of an extremely varied gene pool which was capable of producing individuals both of the classic form and others which probably were directly ancestral to true *Homo sapiens sapiens*. How then do we explain the extreme primitive character of the classic Neanderthals of Western Europe? Probably they represent a population living under the stress of severe environmental conditions and thus were subjected to considerable genetic selection. Other significant factors would be isolation caused by the ice masses during the height of the Wurm and consequent inbreeding. Isolation would also lead to the formation of small distinct groups—the variability we mentioned previously. These are all factors different from those present in the Middle East at the same time. It has been suggested that these classic Neanderthals became extinct as their environment became too cold and severe for their continued existence. Such explanation is too simplistic, for they had already survived

Fig. 7–7 The correlation of climatic fluctuations with the variants of Mousterian industries in several major sites in France. (Laville 1973:325.)

Fig. 7–8   Reconstruction of early men by the sculptor Maurice P. Coon. From Left to right: Combe Capelle; La Chapelle aux Saints; Upper Cave Male; Skhul 5; the sculptor; Wadjak; Cro-Magnon, Circeo 1; Steinheim. (Courtesy of Maurice P. Coon and the photographer Wayland Minot.)

previous glacial maxima and their culture was highly adaptive as we have already discussed. More likely a combination of factors was responsible in a way which is not yet clear to us because of the lack of suitable evidence. Meanwhile the other Neanderthals throughout the world provided a gene pool which has most likely been incorporated into that of modern man. Von Koenigswald (1962) views the Mt. Carmel finds in Palestine as representing an intermediate group which resulted from actual interbreeding between classic Neanderthals and modern men. The controversy continues and we await new discoveries to give rise to new explanations in the future. Differing views as to man's physical evolution are expressed in Figure 7–9.

CULTURAL ELABORATION IN THE MIDDLE PALEOLITHIC

For the first time in the course of cultural evolution, we find evidence that men were concerned with more than mere subsistence. Culture is a cumulative process; it consists of learned shared behavior which, once developed, can then be transmitted to future generations. Thus we perceive that Middle Paleolithic man, having a legacy of hunting and other food-getting techniques developed in the Lower Paleolithic, could elaborate upon those as well as develop new interests not related to the economy. A major shift in human habits in the Middle Paleolithic was the reliance on caves and rock shelters as habitations. Neanderthal men also were home builders. Several deliberately constructed houses have been found such as that at Molodova, Russia, made of stones, tusks, bones, and presumably wood (see Fig. 7–2). At Combe Grenal, France, the cave deposits had preserved within them the outline of a posthole dug by Neanderthal man. This is one of the oldest postholes yet discovered by archaeologists. The change in human culture resulting from life in permanent

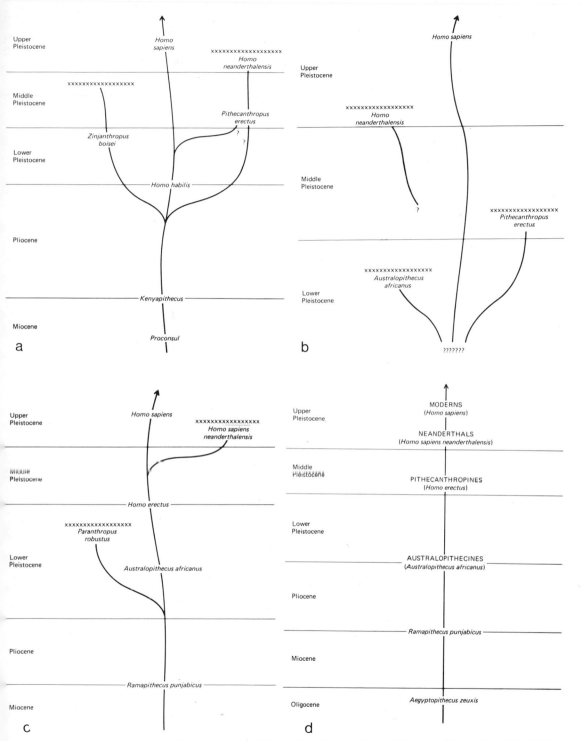

Fig. 7–9 Alternative views of hominid evolution. (Brace, Nelson, and Korn 1971:144–147.)

dwellings was subtle but significant. For the first time in culture history, large numbers of humans were living together in a situation which isolated them and gave protection from the natural environment. Thus men became adjusted to living more closely with each other; their universe became more completely cultural and thus more separate from the natural environment. One of the first possible results of this contact would be the intensification of social relationships. Families were more closely united, a fact verified by archaeological evidence, for actual family burial plots have been found. At least there have been found Neanderthal burial groups with members of differing age and sex, identical to those we would expect in the nuclear family. In addition, the mere fact of intentional burial implies that the living felt sufficient concern for the recently deceased that disposal of their body was a matter of group planning and execution. Intentional burial further implies that there existed beliefs concerned with an afterlife. Thus we have the beginnings of what may be termed religion. Specific archaeological findings demonstrating these practices are numerous. A few of the most interesting of these are described below.

At La Ferrassie, France, the cemetery contained the skeletons of two adults and four children. The two adults were buried head to head with two of the children being buried at their "mother's" feet. The graves of the other two children are unique. One, possibly a stillborn baby, was buried in the top of one of nine small mounds of earth, the remainder of which were empty. With the bones were three beautifully worked flint implements. The other child was buried covered with a triangular slab of stone hollowed out on the bottom. Artifacts with this burial included two scrapers and a point. The inclusion of implements with burials is clear evidence of some belief in an afterlife. The La Ferrassie examples are not isolated finds. For example, in the cave at Teshik-Tash, Uzbekistan, a child was buried with the horns of six mountain goats placed to form a circle around the head. The cemetery at Mugharet-es-Skhul, Palestine, contained 10 graves, with the individuals ranging in age from 3 to 50 years. In Shanidar Cave, Iran, one group, found within a single grave, was made up of four individuals, one of whom was a child. Some of the nine burials present in the cave were the result of accidental death due to a roof cave in; nonetheless, such recently dead were then interred with stones placed over the bones. Also present were small rodent bones—possibly the remains of a funeral feast—and even an offering of flowers. The latter is proved by the recovery of flower pollen from the burial soil. A fire had been built over the grave, and within the ashes were found more animal bones and several stone points.

Another proclivity of Neanderthal man was his liking for human flesh. A Neanderthal skull from Monte Circeo, Italy, had the base broken open to permit removal of the brain. A mass of bones found at Krapina, Yugoslavia, includes wild animal bones as well as the partial remains of a dozen Neanderthals, all treated in the same fashion. The long bones were broken open for marrow, and all were charred by fire—rather clear evidence of a cannibalistic feast.

For the first time in human culture we also have the appearance of nonutilitarian objects. These are items of presumed ceremonial or decorative use, for they could have performed little of functional importance. From the site of Tata, Hungary, has been recovered a polished piece of mammoth tooth cut to an oval form. Another find at the same site is a marine invertebrate fossil, a nummulite, which has an X or cross scratched upon it. Perhaps it was worn as an amulet.

Evidence from the Neanderthal bones themselves also bear witness to cultural practices. At La Ferrassie the Neanderthal man possessed unusual tooth wear on his incisors. The closest similarities to a modern example is found in the Eskimo where such wear is the result of years of chewing to soften skins. Thus we may infer that skin clothing was probably a Mousterian culture trait. The Broken Hill skull from Rhodesia possesses a small hole cut in the left side. The edges of the hole show evidences of healing, suggesting the hole was cut during life and was not presumably the cause of death. One explanation would be that this hole represents a prehistoric medical operation; if so, it is the earliest for which we have evidence. More likely, this hole was punched with a wooden spear.

In addition to burial customs, Neanderthal man possessed a system of ritualistic beliefs connected with the cave bear, *Ursus spelaeus*. We cannot define such beliefs as a religion, yet they must have been ritualistic in nature. At Drachenloch, Switzerland, there has been found a stone-lined pit in which were stacked several skulls of the cave bear. Another find at Drachenloch was a bear skull which had leg bones of a younger bear placed through the arches formed by the cheek bones; this arrangement was then placed on top of two bones from two other bears. Such an arrangement could not be the result of chance; it represents deliberate human placement, although we cannot interpret why. Hunting the cave bear may have been a demonstration of prowess similar to the modern Masai's hunting of lions with spears. The arrangements of bear bones could be trophies of such hunts. In another cave, the Drachenhöhle or Dragon's Cave near Mixnitz, Austria, is a similar trophy of a cave bear skull with an ulna thrust through the cheek arch. Also present in the cave were more than 30 bear skulls as well as the remains of Mousterian age campfires with charred bear bones. In this cave the bears were hunted as they tried to escape through a narrow passageway. The killing was accomplished by hitting the bears on the muzzle or forehead with a sharp pointed club. Numerous skulls show the marks of such blows (Able 1926).

CLIMATE AND ENVIRONMENT

Our knowledge of the climate and environments inhabited by Middle Paleolithic man is more complete for Europe, less complete for Africa, and nearly nonexistent for most other areas of the world. Consequently we will discuss the European data in greatest detail.

The major environmental zones occupied by European Middle Paleolithic man were the forest-tundra and the cold loess steppes. Farther south in the Mediterranean region, including the North African coast, there was a warmer temperate woodland, but this environment was less intensively occupied by man. Most likely man's preference for the colder environments at this time was the result of several factors: his control of fire permitting him greater comfort, his skill at hunting, his skin clothing, and most importantly the carrying capacity of the low latitude tundra. Middle Paleolithic man was primarily a hunter, and the tundra was an optimum environment for the cold-adapted, herd dwelling mammals of the period.

A summary of the chronology of the last glacial fluctuations is presented in Table 7–2. In addition, reconstructions of the actual geographic limits of the various environmental zones are plotted (Figs. 7–10 and 7–11).

Temperature depressions during the Würm glaciation varied according to region and of course time. For example, southwestern England during the coldest phase had forest-tundra with July temperatures averaging 10°C, whereas today the range is 10°C to 14°C. In southern France the Würm snowline was at 1200 meters, about 100 meters lower than at present.

The presence of permafrost evidence in the Alps suggests a temperature

---

TABLE 7–2 Chronology of Glacial Fluctuations in Midlatitude Europe during the Late Pleistocene

Middle Paleolithic Culture	a.	ca. 75,000 B.P. End of Eem Interglacial and onset of Early Würm. Inception of Scandinavian glacier. Cold climate.
	b.	ca. 65,000 B.P. and ca. 60,000 B.P. Temperate phases of the Early Würm, designated as the Amersfoort and Brörup, respectively. Almost total deglaciation in Scandinavia (?).
	c.	ca. 58,000–40,000 B.P. First cold maximum of the Würm with full glacial conditions (*Lower* Pleniglacial). Ice front south of the Baltic Sea (?).
	d.	ca. 40,000–29,000 B.P. Complex interval of cool-temperate climate, the Würm *Inter-Pleniglacial*. Once incorrectly called the Gottweig, now generally designated as Paudorf Interstadial. Two brief temperature maxima ca. 37,000 and ca. 30,000 B.P. (Hengelo and Denekamp phases), interruped by a longer, cold interval. Partial deglaciation.
Upper Paleolithic Culture	e.	ca. 29,000–13,000 B.P. Second cold maximum of Würm *(Upper Pleniglacial)*. Maximum glaciation during Brandenburg interval, ca. 20,000 B.P., followed by recessional halts at the Frankfurt (ca. 18,000 B.P.) and Pommeranian (ca. 15,000 B.P.) moraines.
	f.	ca. 13,000–12,100 B.P. Rapid glacier retreat initiated at beginning of *Late Glacial;* relatively warm oscillation ca. 12,500 B.P. (Bölling interval). Palynologically the Upper Pleniglacial is known as the Oldest Dryas, while the cold oscillation between the Bölling and the Alleröd is called the Older Dryas.
	g.	ca. 12,100–11,300 B.P. Important oscillation of temperate climate, the Alleröd. Ice retreat into central Sweden and south-central Finland.
	h.	ca. 11,300–10,200 B.P. Last phase of the Late Glacial, the Younger Dryas interval. Very cold but only minor glacial readvance.

(Modified from Butzer 1971:274–275.)

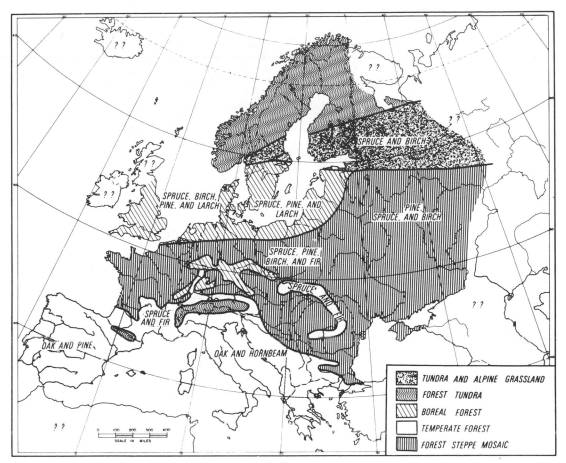

Fig. 7–10 Reconstruction of European environmental zones for the Brörup Interstadial (60,000 B.P.). (Butzer 1971:Fig. 54 [after Frenzel 1968].)

some 11°C lower during the Würm. Farther east the arctic tree line was probably as far south as Vienna; thus Würm summer temperatures were 7° to 9°C lower than today. A further change in the landscape would have been vegetationless, arctic barrens immediately adjacent to the glacial masses and large melt-water streams crossing the loessal plains in summer. There is evidence that the Mousterian hunters moved north onto these plains, camping in the open along streams to take advantage of the summer hunting. On the other hand, the evidence from other Mousterian sites, especially caves, is that they were occupied year round, as indicated by the ages of the game killed. Thus Mousterian man was not universally nomadic but where possible was apt to be semisedentary.

The game hunted was part of one of the most varied faunas of which we know. It was further divided into an interglacial fauna and a glacial fauna. Representative species of each are listed below. Of significance is the value of

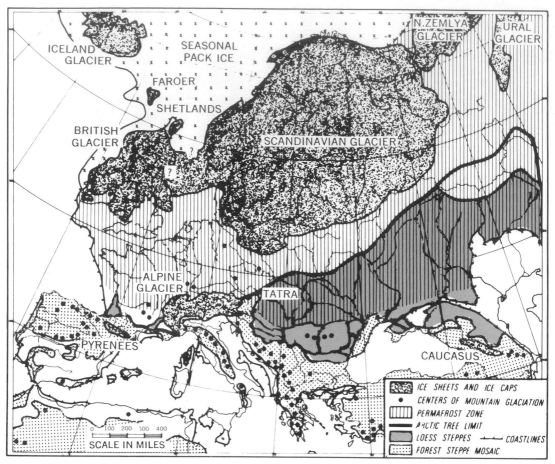

Fig. 7–11 Reconstruction of European environmental zones for the Würm maximum (20,000 B.P.). (Butzer 1971:Fig. 51.)

these genera for habitat reconstructions, since only three of the genera are now extinct, and of these, the woolly mammoth and the rhinoceros have been found reasonably intact frozen in tundra soil. We have even preserved stomach contents with identified pollen grains and plant species. Thus we have excellent evidence of the tundra plant environment and species preference in diet.

The interglacial (Eem) fauna (Butzer 1971:258) includes the extinct straight-tusked woodland elephant *(Elephas antiquus),* the extinct woodland rhino, the African hippo *(H. amphibius major),* the boar *(Sus scrofa),* the fallow deer *(Dama dama),* and the roe deer *(Capreolus capreolus).* These were characteristic of midlatitude Europe during interglacial periods. During colder glacial epochs they were present only in southern Europe and Africa.

The glacial fauna (Würm) was made up of several components. In southern France it contained temperate and boreal woodland forms. Other species were clearly tundra dwelling. There were alpine forms, a cool midlatitude steppe fauna, plus special cave forms. A list of each is provided in Table 7–3 plus an illustration of the most important forms (Fig. 7–12).

An impression of how Mousterian hunters utilized these beasts is provided by a graph illustrating faunal remains from the 68 levels of Combe Grenal. This graph illustrates man's changing reliance on different species through time (Fig. 7–13). Bear in mind that these data represent bone count frequencies which are difficult to translate into animal units. Furthermore these animal units are of varying size, for example, a mammoth is equal to numerous reindeer. Nonetheless, such a graph tells us something about Mousterian food preferences.

TABLE 7–3   Würm Glacial Faunas

Temperate and Boreal Woodland	Tundra	Cool Steppe	Alpine	Cave
Elk *(Alces alces)*	Reindeer	Saiga Antelope	Ibex	Cave Bear
Red Deer	Musk Ox	Steppe Horse	Chamois	Cave Hyena
Auroch *(Bos primigenius)*	Snowshoe Hare	Steppe Fox	Marmot	Cave Lion
Woodland Horse	Lemming	Steppe Polecat	Alpine Vole	
Lynx	Arctic Fox	Steppe Marmot		
Wildcat	*Woolly Mammoth	Hamster		
Fox	*Woolly Rhino	Gerbil		
Wolf	*Steppe Bison			
Wolverine	*Giant Elk			
Sable				
Brown Bear				

*Also found in Cool Steppe.
(Compiled from Butzer 1971.)

African Environments

In recent years research scientists have come to realize that little firm evidence exists concerning the nature of past African environments. Initial research on the problem was carried out by E. J. Wayland between 1922 and 1934. He studied the terraces of the Kagera River in Uganda and on this basis defined a series of pluvials and interpluvials. In 1947 at the first Pan-African Congress of Prehistory held in Nairobi, this basic concept was expanded to a series of four named pluvials, the Kageran, Kamasian, Kanjeran, and Gamblian, separated by three interpluvials. The impetus for such a fourfold sequence was the European sequence of glaciations. The African pluvials, with little solid evidence to support such a view, were thought to be synchronous with the European glaciations. In other words, glacial advances in Europe were thought to produce colder, wetter intervals in Africa. A second portion of the scheme was the assumption that climatic fluctuations were essentially synchronous throughout Africa; that is, that the pluvials were characteristic of the entire continent. The basic data supporting the pluvial concept had been gathered primarily from two regions, the East African Rift Valley and the Vaal River terraces of South

Fig. 7–12 The Upper Pleistocene megafauna of central Europe. (Butzer 1971:Fig. 49 [after Thenius 1962].)

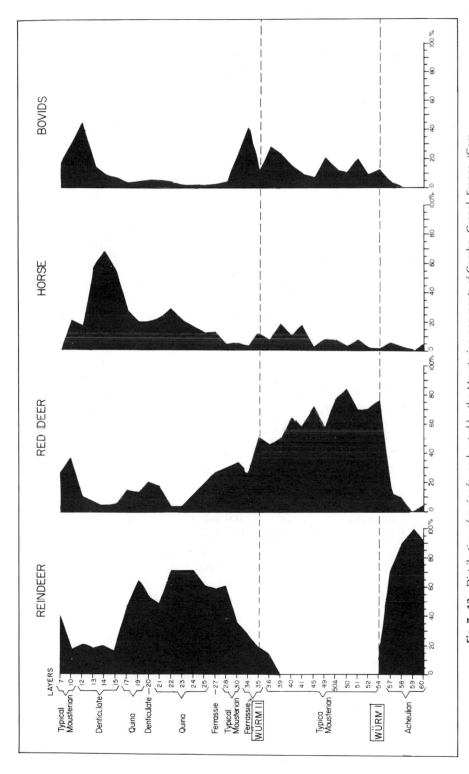

Fig. 7–13 Distribution of major fauna hunted by the Mousterian occupants of Combe, Grenal, France. (Compiled by James Grady, from Bordes and Prat, 966.)

Africa. At present, some 25 years after the first Pan-African Congress, these views seem naive and simplistic. We now know, after the collection of much geological, paleontological, and palynological data, that those views were premature.

Current impressions based on African data are that the assumption of Pan-African fluctuations in climate is not supportable. Instead the changes in climate were regional in character. For example, movement of European climatic zones influenced North Africa, while the equatorial region was directly affected by the southeast trade winds and the Indian monsoon. South Africa received influences from the west wind drift and the Antarctic currents. The desert regions, the Sahara and the Kalahari, because of their continental positions, typically received little moisture from the northeast trade winds and the dry westerly winds. We may thus briefly describe Late Pleistocene African environments as follows: During glacial maxima there was a southward displacement of the Mediterranean flora and fauna to North Africa including the Sahara. The higher and typically more moist regions of East Africa and equatorial Africa may have experienced increased moisture (pluvial conditions), some mountain glaciation (snowline depression of 1000 to 1200 meters), and temperatures 5° to 9°C lower than today. During periods of glacial retreat in Europe (interstadials), the major shifts in sub-Saharan climate were controlled by the Indian monsoon. Climates featuring warmer, drier conditions were accompanied by savanna-woodland invasion of the Congo (former tropical forest) and upslope retreat of vegetal zones in East Africa. Simultaneously there seems to have been an expansion of the sub-Saharan savanna and thorn scrub zones northward into the southern Sahara. These interpretations of African climatic fluctuations are tentative because the area concerned is enormous and for much of it we have no paleoecological data whatsoever.

Human and faunal migrations were keyed closely to these climatic fluctuations. One result of the monsoonal expansion into the Sahara, for example, was the expansion of the Ethiopian fauna: giraffe, elephant, hippo, white rhino, antelopes, gazelle, and even a species of crocodile into the higher mountain ranges of the central Sahara. The Hoggar range, for example, is more than 10,000 feet in elevation and attracted considerable rainfall, possibly as much as 150 millimeters per year. On the other hand, most of the evidence from the Sahara suggests that through time the typical climatic regimen there has been arid and that the wetter intervals have been of brief duration.

Cultural distributions in Africa may be understood through reference to these climatic factors. The North African and Saharan Middle Paleolithic features Mousterian industries. Although these are best known from sites along the North African coast, that fact is related to the difficulty of carrying out research in the modern Sahara rather than to the distribution of Mousterian man. On the other hand, Sub-Saharan Africa during the Middle Paleolithic was characterized by non-Mousterian, non-Levallois industries termed the Sangoan, Fauresmith, and Lupemban.

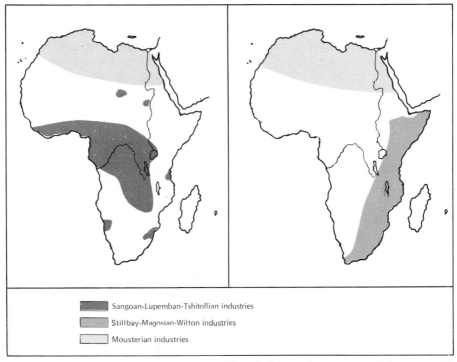

Fig. 7–14 Map of distributions of African Middle Paleolithic industries. (After Cole 1963:196.)

Sangoan

The Sangoan culture was a forest and woodland adaptation found within the region which today has more than 40 inches annual rainfall (Fig. 7–14). The distribution suggests a dry period occupation of the equatorial forest region. At Kalambo Falls, the Sangoan levels are dated 41,000 to 38,000 B.C. with the subsequent Lupemban industry dated 27,000 to 25,000 B.C. At Mufo, Angola, radiocarbon dates indicate that the upper Lupemban lasted as late as 12,550 B.C. The basic implements are presumed to have been utilized for woodworking and digging. The basic Sangoan implement, the pick is described as

> . . . an elongated, steep-sided, double-ended implement with small, flat dorsal and large ventral faces, rhomboidal in cross-section at the centre, segmental in cross-section near the blunter end and triangular or subtriangular towards and near what appears to be the "business" end. The most finely finished product is somewhat canoe-like in shape— sharp prow, blunt stem. Some of these picks are a foot long; others are short and stubby, about six inches long (Cole 1963:186).

Other implements include rough handaxes, prepared cores, points, and several kinds of scrapers made from flakes. While the Lupemban seems to be a direct outgrowth of the Sangoan, featuring somewhat finer and better made implements, its distinctive element consists of well-made, laurel-leaf-shaped, bifacially-flaked points. In general, the flaking technologies of both the Sangoan and Lupemban feature heavy, crude implements, less well made than those of the preceding Late Acheulean. This shift is believed to be related to the change in function of the implements from cutting and skinning in Acheulean times to chopping and digging in the Middle Paleolithic.

The Fauresmith culture is an East African variant derived from the Acheulean. The culture is geographically distinct from the Acheulean in that it records an upslope movement of peoples during a dry period to altitudes of 7000 to 8000 feet. Typical implements include small handaxes and cleavers, stone balls (possibly used as bolas), and numerous tools made from flakes with faceted platforms such as scrapers and chisels. One descriptive statement is that the Fauresmith is a kind of crude miniature version of an Acheulean industry. Geographically the industry is known from Gondar in northern Ethiopia to South Africa. Not present in the industry are picks, the Sangoan standby, thus suggesting that contact between East Africa and the equatorial region at this time was limited.

MIDDLE PALEOLITHIC INDUSTRIES OF ASIA

The Mousterian industry is widespread in northern Asia with sites extending from Syria, Lebanon, Turkey, and Iran eastward to northern China (the Ordos region near the Great Wall). In between, Mousterian cultures are known from the Asiatic part of the U.S.S.R. south of the Caucasus Mountains at Akhchtyr-skaya Cave, Koudaron Cave, open sites on the east shore of the Caspian Sea, and in Central Asia in Uzbekistan. South of Samarkand, the Aman Kutan Cave has Mousterian implements in addition to a Neanderthal femur. Northern India features an industry termed Upper Soan which some authors believe shows Mousterian affinities. South of the above areas in Southeast Asia, the Middle Paleolithic is marked by a continuation of the Chopper-Chopping tool tradition. One of the best known such industry is the Sangeran flake culture of Java. The implements are flake tools of Clacton type made on chalcedony. The Ngandongian culture, also from Java, includes antler picks, stingray points, bola stones, and small flakes. These and other insular paleolithic industries are related to those of the Southeast Asian mainland, for during low water phases of the Pleistocene all those East Indian islands west of Wallace's Line were connected to the mainland by the Sunda Shelf. The Sino-Asiatic fauna was also continuous in this region at the time. To the east, man's distribution was blocked by the Macassar Strait between Borneo and Celebes, 900 fathoms in depth, and thus never bridged by land during the Pleistocene. Another industry includes finds at Niah Cave in Borneo where the implements are bone points, stone flakes, some flake blades, and chopping tools made on river pebbles.

Industries of similar type are also found in the Philippines, in spite of the fact that land connections during the Pleistocene were to the mainland to the west rather than to the East Indies to the south.

REFERENCES

Able, O., 1926, "How Neanderthal Man Hunted Cave Bears," *Natural History* 26(3):252–256.

Bordes, F., 1968, *The Old Stone Age*. New York: McGraw-Hill.

———, and F. Prat, 1966, "Observations sur les faunes du Riss et du Würm I," *L'Anthropologie* 69:31–46.

Brace, C. L., H, Nelson, and N. Korn, 1971, *Atlas of Fossil Man*. New York: Holt, Rinehart and Winston, Inc.

Butzer, K., 1971, *Environment and Archaeology*, 2d ed. Chicago: Aldine-Atherton.

Clark, J. G. D., 1971, *World Prehistory: A New Outline*, 2d ed. London: Cambridge University Press.

Cole, S., 1963, *The Prehistory of East Africa*. New York: Mentor.

Coon, C. S., 1966, *The Origins of Races*. New York: Knopf.

Laville, M., 1973, "The Relative Position of Mousterian Industries in the Climatic Chronology of the Early Würm in the Perigord," *World Archaeology* 4(3):321–338.

Von Koenigswald, G. H. R., 1962, *The Evolution of Man*. Ann Arbor: University of Michigan Press.

Wayland, E. J., 1926, *Ecology and Paleontology of the Kaiso Bone Bed*. Geological Survey of Uganda, Occasional Paper, No. 2.

———, 1931, *Report on a Geological Reconnaissance of Southern Kavirondo, Colony and Protectorate of Kenya*. Nairobi.

8

The Upper Paleolithic

The Upper Paleolithic is the first period marked by the dominance of anatomically modern man, *Homo sapiens sapiens*. As we discussed previously, there were populations living during the Middle Paleolithic, especially in the Middle East, which had evolved in the direction of modern man. Thus the appearance of *H. s. sapiens* was not a precipitous affair but was instead contemporaneous with the later stages of Neanderthal *(H. s. neanderthalensis)* evolution. At least that is the view held by many researchers. On the other hand there are much older fossil finds, usually fragmentary, which have been tentatively assigned to *H. s. sapiens*. Three such finds are those at Swanscombe, England; Steinheim, Germany; and Fontechevade, France. The age of the specimens is Middle Pleistocene, second interglacial. Only the Steinheim specimen is a reasonably complete skull, the others are skull caps without the diagnostic brow ridges. According to Brace, Nelson, and Korn (1971), these specimens show affinities closer to the Neanderthals than to modern man. A recent find by Richard Leakey on the northeast shore of Lake Rudolf in East Africa consists of three skulls and some other skeletal parts of anatomically modern individuals *(Homo sapiens)*. These finds are believed by Leakey to be some 250,000 years of age (Middle Pleistocene); however other researchers (Butzer 1969) believe the geology of the site to be confused, with the result that the true age of the finds predates 30,500 years and may be as old as late Middle Pleistocene. The argument continues as to the earliest appearance of *H. s. sapiens*. Suffice it to say that *H. s. sapiens* became widespread in the interval between 30,000 and 20,000 B.P., with well-dated specimens becoming abundant after about 25,000 B.P. Some C-14-dated early specimens are Dolni Vestonice, Moravia, 25,820 ± 180 B.P.; Pavlov, Czechoslovakia, 26,620 ± 260 B.P.; Predmost, Czechoslovakia, 26,000 B.P.; and Isturits Cave, France, 27,000 to 22,000 B.P. By contrast, few Neanderthal specimens are assigned ages more recent than 35,000 B.P. From this date until the present, *H. s. sapiens* has been the human species on earth. During the Upper Paleolithic and more recent cultural periods, man has become increasingly divergent in his culture and more adapted to specific climatic regimes and environments. One response to differing environmental conditions has been the selection for those traits diagnostic of the differing human races. The amount of elapsed time necessary for such modifications is probably variable. We know, for example, that skeletons 14,000 years of age in Egypt and Sudan are dramatically primitive in form, while skeletons only 1000 to 6000 years old in the same region were remarkably gracile. Thus change in human physical type can occur rapidly, the result of not only climatic factors but also diet; thus man's culture was a cause in his continuing physical evolution.

It is probably appropriate at this point briefly to place in context the find termed Cro-Magnon. Our reason for doing so is because of the historical importance of the Cro-Magnon find—the earliest find of an ancient example of modern man. The specimen, also termed the Old Man from Cro-Magnon, from Les Eyzies, France, was found by L. Lartet, a geologist, in 1868 (Fig. 8–1). A railroad cut revealed a filled rock shelter within which were found the remains of five adults and some fragmentary infant bones. The best preserved skull, that of a male aged about 50, is the one termed the Old Man. Associated with the skeletons were artifacts of the Aurignacian culture, an Upper Paleolithic manifestation. Today, on the basis of the relative age of the associated culture, the remains are estimated to be approximately 20,000 years of age. Thus the skeletons are not now the earliest known *H. s. sapiens,* and their importance has probably lessened as more and earlier specimens have come to light. Nonetheless Cro-Magnon has earned a definite place in the history of Human Evolution.

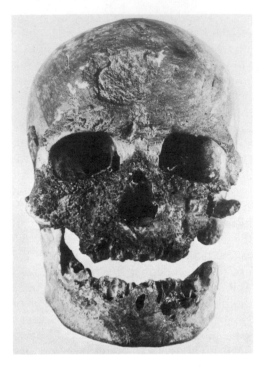

Fig. 8–1 Cranium of Cro-Magnon man, Les Eyzies, France. (Photograph courtesy of Musée de l'Homme.)

CLIMATE AND FAUNA

Upper Paleolithic culture was initiated in the cool temperate phase in the Würm II/III interstadial ca. 35,000 B.C. and continued throughout the entire Würm III cold maximum (Fig. 8–2); similar environmental conditions as were present in the earlier Middle Paleolithic. In Europe during the cool temperate interstadial there occurred some northward movement of all the environmental zones. In the south there was Mediterranean deciduous woodland with oak, pine, and hornbeam; a zone of spruce, pine, birch, and fir (the forest steppe) covered most of central Europe. Surrounding the Baltic Sea was a spruce, pine, and larch forest. Farther north there was a zone of spruce and birch, and north of that there was forest-tundra in northern Scandanavia. In terms of faunal adjustments, there would have been an expansion of the steppe-dwelling forms—the bison, steppe horse, woolly mammoth, and ass—with the red deer, elk, auroch, and woodland horse as the primary food species in the expanded temperate woodland. Species of the forest tundra—the reindeer, musk ox, woolly mammoth, and woolly rhino—would have had their range restricted except where they could adapt to cool steppe conditions.

After 29,000 B.P. there was a resurgence of glacial advance with the Würm III cold maximum lasting until 13,000 B.P. During this interval there was

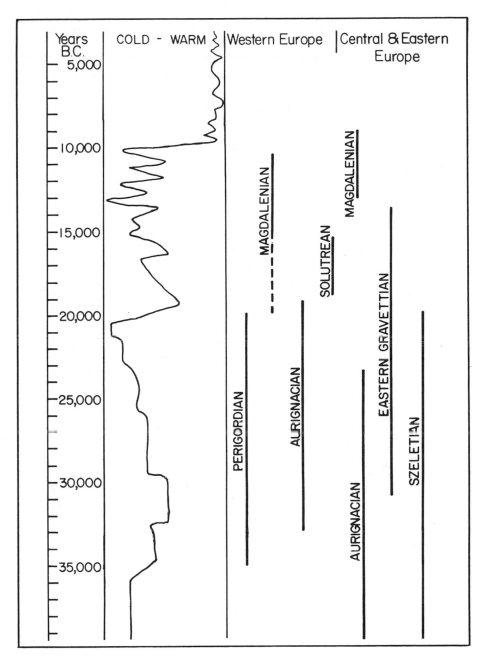

Fig. 8-2 Chronological chart of Upper Paleolithic cultures. (After Oakley 1968:171.)

southward movement of the environmental zones with a major expansion of the glaciers and tundra zone and a reduction of all other zones. Between 13,000 and 12,100 B.P. there was a warming trend accompanied by rapid glacial retreat. Upper Paleolithic cultures in Europe do not seem to persist beyond this point in time. The European Upper Paleolithic consisted of a series of cultures adapted to the hunting of cool steppe and tundra species. With the advent of post-Würm warming, the fauna became either reduced in numbers or extinct, and the Upper Paleolithic cultures were forced to modify their economy.

UPPER PALEOLITHIC INDUSTRIES

Industries of the Upper Paleolithic are numerous and varied. There are regional traditions within which are a series of evolutionary forms with specific industry names. Thus we have developed by archaeologists, for the first time in human prehistory, regional sequences or chronologies (see Fig. 8–2). Such sequences are based upon two major characteristics: the presence of deep stratified occupation layers in caves and distinctive tool types characteristic of specific areas and chronological periods. The tools themselves are primarily variants of knives, scrapers, points, and burins, made on core struck blades. The sequences of industries, one after another, are preserved for our study in the cave deposits, just as they were left as occupation layers by Upper Paleolithic men. Thus we have considerable data with which to construct the regional chronologies. In addition, these levels are well dated by radiocarbon.

In this introductory text it is impossible to describe each Upper Paleolithic industry in detail; such treatment should be reserved for an advanced course in European prehistory. Here we will describe the major features of the period. Cultures termed Upper Paleolithic are widely distributed geographically. They occur throughout most of Europe including Russia, Siberia, and eastward into Japan. To the south, similar industries are present in the Middle East and North Africa. The earliest migrants to the New World crossed the Bering Strait during this period, and their tool inventories show strong Upper Paleolithic affinities. Although we stress the importance of this cultural continuity between the Siberian Upper Paleolithic and the New World Paleo-Indian tradition, we will reserve discussion of the New World remains until a later chapter. It was also during this period that we have the earliest known migrants to the continent of Australia, peoples presumably using tools related to the Chopper-Chopping tool tradition of Southeast Asia rather than to the European Upper Paleolithic. South of the Sahara, African cultures evolved separately, not evincing relationships with the European blade industries. Other areas of great size including most of Arabia, Pakistan, India, China, and Southeast Asia have been little studied by archaeologists searching for remains of this period; thus our knowledge is limited. Major known sites are plotted in Figure 8–3.

Fig. 8–3 Map of Europe with the location of the major Upper Paleolithic and Mesolithic sites. (Clark 1967:Fig. 26 [drawn by Charles Hasler].)

Industries of the Upper Paleolithic are marked by the introduction of numerous technologies based on the working of materials other than stone. Although the stone tools tend to be those most frequently used by archaeologists as their type specimens or index fossils, the tools of other materials are common and well made. The new materials include bone, ivory, and antler worked by grooving and splitting, then ground, polished, and frequently carved. Ornaments were made from these materials, as well as utilitarian objects such as spear points, harpoons, throwing sticks, and clubs. Also prepared were carved ornamental staffs or batons, termed *bâtons de comandement,* which are thought to represent symbols of authority. The implements used for bone splitting and carving are presumed to be the stone burins which occur in enormous quantity and variety at this time. Another major innovation was the manufacture of composite tools, which are made by hafting a blade or point to a shaft of some type. We thus have the haft, a wrapping of thong or cordage; possibly a separate peice of wood or bone which fits between the haft and the point, termed a foreshaft; and lastly the point or harpoon to which a separate line may have been tied. Numerous specimens exhibit realistic carving and incising—the first evidence of Paleolithic art.

The hallmark of the Upper Paleolithic industries is of course the core struck blade. These are symmetrical flint blades struck from trimmed and specially prepared cores. As each blade is struck off, it bears upon its upper face the scars of the blades struck off previously. The blades are long and slim, rectangular to triangular in form, with a triangular or trapezoidal cross section. They are exceptionally sharp without retouch, although a variety of implements such as end scrapers, side scrapers, backed blades, and points were made on blades by retouching the edges. Burins differ in that they are not the product of retouch but instead were made by striking off spalls from the blades in much the same fashion as the original blades were struck.

Figures 8–4 to 8–7 illustrate a variety of blade tools characteristic of several of the best known Upper Paleolithic industries. Following Bordes (1968), definitions of some of these industries are offered.

The Perigordian has strong features of the Mousterian of Acheulean tradition, including scrapers, Mousterian points, Levallois flakes, and denticulates. Perigordian diagnostic tools include pointed blades with curved backs blunted by steep retouch (the Chatelperron knife), end scrapers on flakes, and mediocre burins on a retouched truncation or dihedral butt. Bone implements are few, but awls occur as well as pendants and teeth and bones notched for suspension. Later in the Perigordian sequence the Mousterian type tools disappear and burin types multiply. Small implements become more common, especially backed bladelets, La Gravette points, and small foliate points. By Perigordian V we have the introduction of a tanged point, called Font-Robert (Fig. 8–4.13).

The Aurignacian industry, in contrast to the Perigordian, may represent an intrusion into western Europe. The tools are considerably different from those of the Perigordian culture, featuring fine blades with strong retouch forming a scraper edge on the blade end. Burins increase through time but are never as frequent as in the Perigordian. Other tools are thick end scrapers similar to the Quina Mousterian style, strangled blades, *bâtons de commandement,* awls, and split-base bone points. Through time the fine blades are abandoned, burins are developed, and scrapers increase in variety. Later bone points lack the split base, being either rounded or beveled at the base. Another feature is the presence of small bladelets. Bordes suggests that the Aurignacian and Perigordian peoples lived side by side in the same region without much influence on each other.

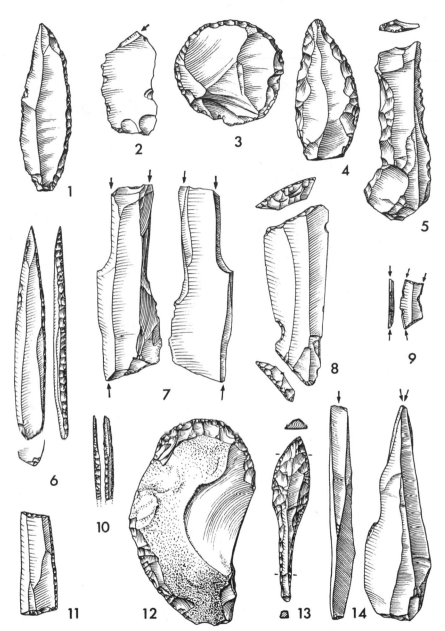

Fig. 8–4 Flint tools from the Perigordian. Lower Perigordian: *1*. Chatelperron knife; *2*. burin; *3*. scraper on a flake; *4*. Mousterian point; *5*. denticulated and truncated blade. Upper Perigordian: *6*. Gravette point; *7*. multiple burin or truncation; *8*. bitruncated blade; *9*. Noailles burin; *10*. backed bladelet; *11*. truncated element; *12*. flake scraper; *13*. Font-Robert point; *14*. dihedral burin. (Bordes 1968:Fig. 54.)

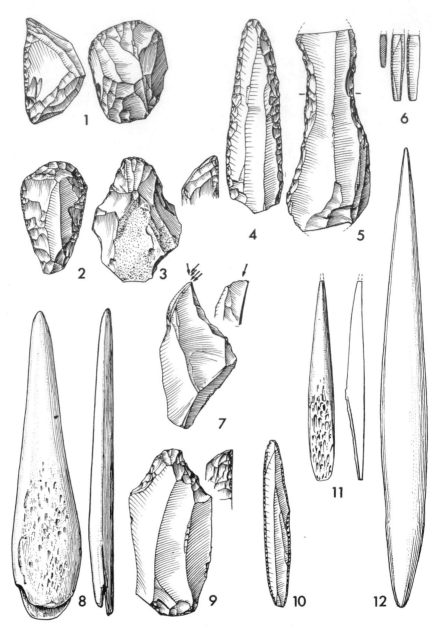

Fig. 8–5 Aurignacian I: *1*. carinate scraper; *2*. scraper on retouched blade; *3*. nosed scraper; *4*. Aurignacian blade; *5*. strangled blade; *8*. split base bone point; *9*. flat nosed scraper. Aurignacian II: *6*. Dufour bladelet; *7*. busked burin; *12*. lozenge-shaped bone point. Lower Aurignacian: *10*. Font-Yves bladelet. Aurignacian V; *11*. bone point with a single bevel. (Bordes 1968:Fig. 56.)

The Gravettian industry represents a culture of central and eastern Europe similar in time to the Aurignacian and Perigordian. Its primary index fossil is the La Gravette point, a small point with a convex blunted back, possibly hafted in composite tools. Other tool types include triangular points with shallow bifacial flaking, perforated needles, shaft straighteners, awls, reindeer antler clubs, handled scoops, heavy chisels of mammoth ivory, carved human figurines of ivory, and flat bracelets. The Gravettians were adapted to life on the steppe, camping in the open in tents, and specializing in mammoth hunting—thus the wide range of implements and ornaments of ivory.

Later cultures of western Europe include the Solutrean and Magdalenian. Early Solutrean projectile points are unifacial, but by Middle Solutrean times they become bifacially worked, laurel leaf shaped in form, and very well flaked. Presumably they also served as knives in addition to use as points. Some of the points are extremely large and beautifully worked, suggesting that they may have been works of art rather than utilitarian. Pressure flaking was introduced as a means of producing finer specimens. In the Upper Solutrean we have the introduction of shouldered points and stemmed points, presumably innovations for hafting. A new form, the willow leaf also appears, and unifacial points persist. Other implements include end scrapers, borers, rare burins, some Mousterian-type tools, as well as bone implements such as eyed needles.

The Solutrean industry, which may have originally been intrusive into western Europe, suddenly disappears to be succeeded by the later but seemingly unrelated Magdalenian culture. The early Magdalenian levels feature small, simple, unifacially retouched flake tools, including tanged points, star-shaped multiple borers, and little steeply retouched scrapers called raclettes.

In Magdalenian I, bone tools include needles, pierced batons, and smoothing tools. By the Magdalenian III period, bone tools are quite common and include bone points with a beveled base and decorated wands. After Magdalenian III the major tool changes occur in the bone industry with the flint tools changing little. Bone harpoons appear and proliferate into a variety of single-barbed and double-barbed varieties (Fig. 8–8). Other tools are awls, javelin bone points, needles, spear throwers, decorated wands, and works of art. In some of the latest levels, geometric flints appear in the form of triangles, trapezoids, and semilunates.

In eastern Europe (Czechoslovakia) the Szeletian industry is partially contemporaneous with the Aurignacian. Tool types include leaf-shaped points (some bifacial), Levallois flakes, side scrapers, end scrapers, burins, borers, and some backed tools.

Upper Paleolithic sites of mammoth hunters are common throughout Siberia. Sites such as Molodova, Kostienki, and Ust Kanskaiya provide evidence of the Russian Upper Paleolithic. These cultures feature some Mousterian type tools, flake and blade tools retouched unifacially, plus rare bifacial points. These cultures should be the antecedents of the American Paleolithic,

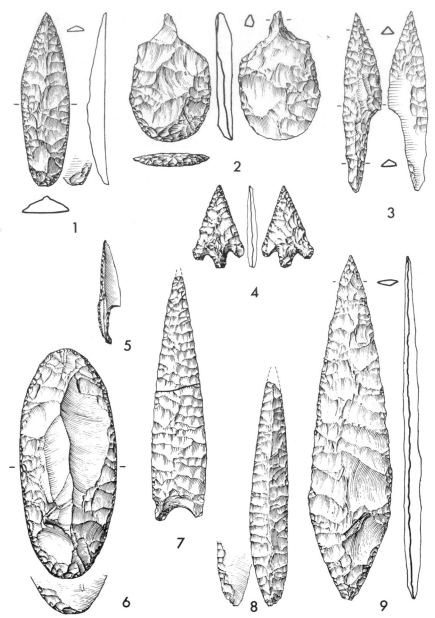

Fig. 8–6 Lower Solutrean: *1.* leaf-shaped point with one flat face; *6.* finely retouched end scraper. Middle Solutrean: *2.* borer end scraper on a broken laurel leaf. Upper Solutrean: *3.* shouldered point; *9.* laurel leaf; *8.* willow leaf; *7.* point with a concave base. Spanish Solutrean: *4.* tanged and barbed point; *5.* shouldered point. (Bordes 1968:Fig. 57.)

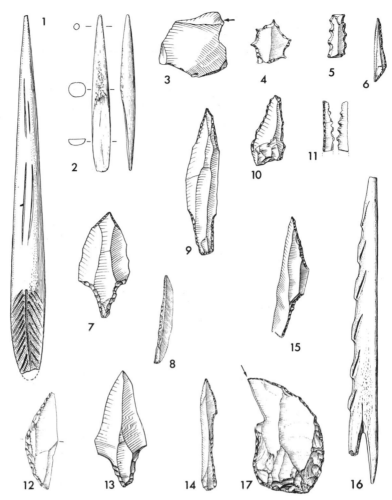

Fig. 8–7 Magdalenian I: *1*. bone point with single beveled base; *3*. transversal burin; *4*. star-shaped multiple borer; *10*. "raclette." Magdalenia II: *6*. triangle. Magdalenian III: *5*. denticulated bladelet; *11*. denticulated backed bladelet; *2*. bone point. Upper Magdalenian: *7*. Teyjat point; *8*. backed bladelet; *12*. Azilian point; *14*. Magdalenian shouldered point; *17*. parrot-beak burin; *16*. harpoon prototype from the Magdalenian IV. Hamburgian: *15*. shouldered point. Ahrensburgian: *9*. tanged point. Bromme culture: *13*. tanged point. (Bordes 1968:Fig. 58.)

although the details of cultural evolution in Siberia are not as well known as those of western Europe.

The Upper Paleolithic of North Africa is closely related to the traditions of Europe with a complicating factor being the possibility of east-to-west movements from the Middle East. Excavations by McBurney at Hagfet et Dabba (cave of the Hyena) on the coast of Libya have revealed a sequence of occupations extending from Mousterian through a series of levels with Upper

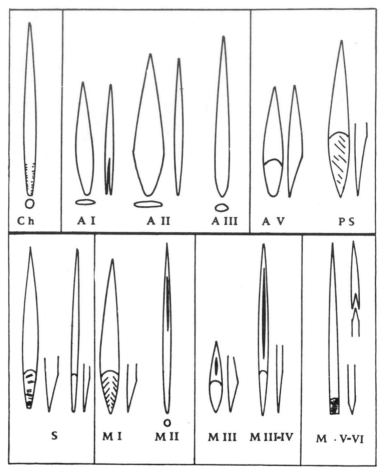

Fig. 8–8　Upper Paleolithic harpoon types and decorative engraving. Ch—Chatelperronian; A—Aurignacian; PS—Proto-Solutrean; S—Solutrean; M—Magdalenian. (Leroi-Gourhan 1967:Chart 8.)

Paleolithic-style blade tools. Termed the Dabban, this industry is dated between ca. 38,000 and 31,150 B.C. Tool types include backed blades, gravers, end scrapers, and transverse burins. McBurney cites the presence of Middle Eastern fauna as evidence that the Dabban origins should be found in that region.

A later industry in North Africa, more widespread than the Dabban, is that termed Aterian from Bir el Ater, Tunisia, the type site. The Aterian is a blade industry with a strong Levallois tradition. Major tools feature unifacial retouch with some bifacial working at the base. Typical forms are a whole series of stemmed or pedunculate tools. The stemmed forms are the hallmark of the industry, and more than 30 forms of pedunculate points, scrapers, knives, and such have been identified (Fig. 8–9). Other implements include some flake tools, scrapers, piercers, as well as bifacially worked points, bifacially worked

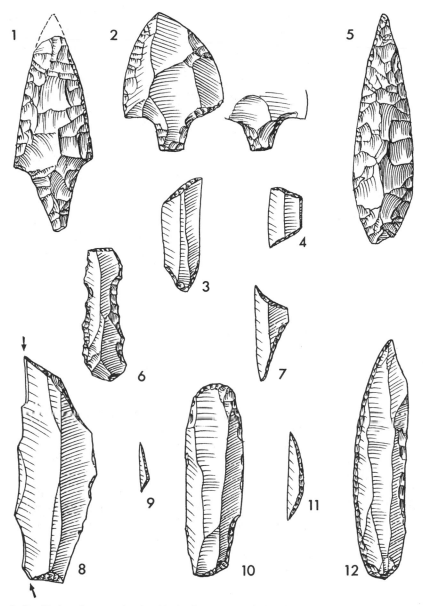

Fig. 8–9 Aterian: *2.* tanged point. Evolved Aterian: *1.* bifacial tanged point; *5.* bifacial point, Capsian: *3, 4, 7.* trapezes; *6.* denticulated blade; *8.* burin; *9.* small triangle; *10.* end scraper; *11.* lunate; *12.* backed blade. (Bordes 1968:Fig. 71.)

blades, and true Mousterian points. The Aterian is only peripherally related to the European Upper Paleolithic industries, being primarily an outgrowth of the local North African Mousterian. The Aterian extends along the entire North African coast and south across the Sahara to Lake Chad. Presumably this culture, which is guess dated at 15,000–20,000 years of age, flourished during a brief wetter interval.

Another related North African industry, the Khargan, features numerous multiple-use tools made on short truncated flakes. The Khargan industry also appears to be a local derivitive of the Mousterian without much reliance on blades. The Levallois component of the technology is quite high. Age relationships between the Khargan and the Aterian are not clear, although the Khargan is presumed to be slightly older. The Khargan is regionally restricted having been identified only from the western desert of Egypt.

A series of later industries found along the North African coast, such as the Capsian and Ibero-Maurusian, feature a highly specialized blade technology. These are Upper Paleolithic industries in form, but their age is late, contemporaneous with the Mesolithic or even Neolithic periods.

Cultures in Sub-Saharan Africa from this time period are not assigned to the Upper Paleolithic. These industries are derived from the Sangoan, Lupemban, and Fauresmith cultures described previously, and they pertain to a non-Levallois, nonblade-making tool tradition. Presumably there was little contact between North Africa and Sub-Saharan Africa, and the evolution of cultures in those regions remained independent of each other. This period in East and South Africa consists of the later portion of the Middle Stone Age. Cultural traditions extant during this interval are two: the Sangoan-Lupemban-Tshitolian tradition of heavy woodworking and digging implements, characteristic of the wetter portions of central Africa, and the East African Stillbay-Magosian-Wilton industrial tradition. The terms refer to a historically related cultural tradition, with names given to the various individual recognized chronological variants. These cultures are poorly known and have few described cultural diagnostics. We do not have available detailed descriptions of excavated sites to aid our understanding. The Stillbay-Magosian-Wilton peoples were hunting groups who inhabited the eastern side of Africa from Uganda to South Africa. The Stillbay is characterized by pressure chipped bifacial points made on flakes of the prepared faceted-platform type. The points were leaf shaped or subtriangular and were probably used on lances or spears. Other implements include backed blades, lunates, and burins. One date on Stillbay materials is 33,000 years B.P. (obsidian). The Magosian industry which follows has been dated at 7550 B.C. and has elements indicative of a Mesolithic way of life which we will describe in our next chapter. It is appropriate to state that so far we know very little about these African industries of the Middle and Late Stone Age.

UPPER PALEOLITHIC ART

The art of the Upper Paleolithic period in Europe is justly well known, for it not only embodies the earliest major development of art by man but also is frequently sensitive and of high quality (Fig. 8–10). The art that first became known to the scientific world consisted of a number of finds of carved objects

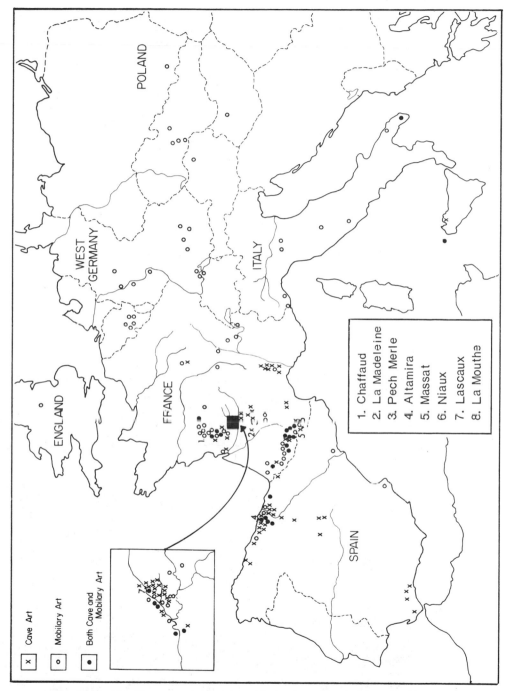

Fig. 8–10 Map illustrating the location of finds of Upper Paleolithic art. (After Leroi-Gourhan 1967:Chart 3.)

termed *chattel* or *mobilary art*. These finds were first made in France, the earliest being a bone engraved with figures of deer, found by a notary, Brouillet, in Chaffaud Cave near Savigne about 1834. The find was not recognized as Paleolithic in origin but was given to the Cluny Museum. Edouard Lartet perhaps was the first man to document the Paleolithic age of such finds. In 1860 he found a *baton de commandement* (a type of presumed ceremonial staff) carved with a bear figure in the Massat Cave. In 1864 he recovered from a Paleolithic layer in the cave of La Madeleine, in the Vezere Valley, a piece of mammoth tusk engraved with the figure of a mammoth. Two features supported the age of the specimen. Because it had clean cut edges, the carving was done when the specimen was fresh, not fossilized. The engraving was of an animal now extinct, the mammoth; thus the artist must have been contemporary with and familiar with such an animal. Such proof was conclusive evidence that the art was made by Paleolithic man. Numerous other carvings were later found in the region, and the Vezere Valley became recognized as a center for such art (Fig. 8–11).

Throughout the last half of the nineteenth century, finds of art became common as Paleolithic archaeology became widespread. In the summer of 1879, a Spanish nobleman, Marcelino de Sautuola, was excavating in the cave of Altamira in Santander province. One day he took his daughter, Maria, with him and she noticed, for the first time in modern history, the Paleolithic

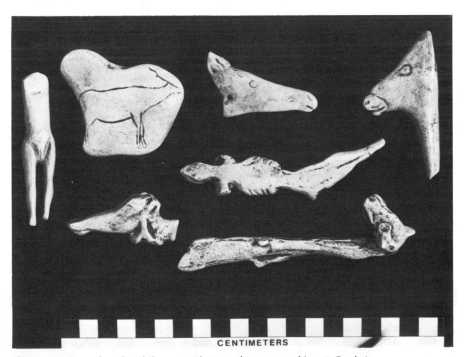

Fig. 8–11   Examples of Mobilary art. (Photograph courtesy of James Grady.)

Fig. 8–12 Plan of Altamira, Spain, showing the distribution of paintings and the details of the great painted ceiling. (Leroi-Gourhan 1967:Figs. 132 and 133 [animal figures after H. Breuil].)

paintings of bison on the cave ceiling (Fig. 8–12). De Sautuola was convinced the paintings were those of Paleolithic man, and he published a monograph in 1880 describing the paintings and estimating their age. The world remained unconvinced of the authenticity of the finds, but for 15 years De Sautuola persisted in his beliefs. Finally in 1895, Emile Riviére, a French prehistorian, decided to examine Altamira in person. What he saw there led him to search caves in the Dordogne region of France where he found similar paintings. What provided the final proof was his find of paintings in the cave of La Mouthe which had until that time been sealed, thus validating the Paleolithic origin of the cave paintings. From that date (1895) until the present, interest in Paleolithic cave art has reigned rampant in European prehistory, with the result that today 110 caves and rock shelters with paintings, engravings, or sculpture are known (see Fig. 8–10). One of the best preserved galleries of art ever found is that of the Cave of Lascaux, not discovered until 1940 when it was accidentally found by two boys. It is conceivable that other concealed caves will be found in the future, for frequently they have collapsed or been filled since their use by Paleolithic man.

Cave Art

Cave art, or *parietal art* as it is sometimes called, features the painting and engraving on cave walls or ceilings of animals, primarily the herd-dwelling forms that were hunted by Paleolithic man (Fig. 8–13). Some animals were engraved, some painted, and many exhibit a combination of both techniques.

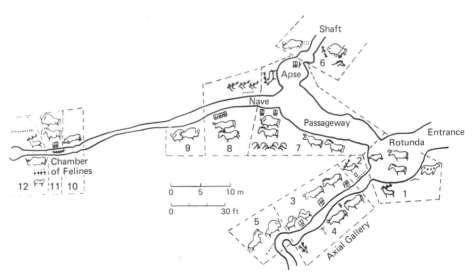

Fig. 8–13   Schematic plan of Lascaux. The numbers indicate the specific designs. Note the positions of the rows of dots (*1, 2, 5, 6, 8*), the cervids (*1, 2, 7, 12*), the bison (*5, 7, 9, 11*), the ibexes (*3, 7*), the rhinoceroses (*6, 12*), the felines (*10*), and a headless animal (*12*). (Leroi-Gourhan 1967:Fig. 125 [after a diagram by the Service de l'Architecture].)

The animals were illustrated singly, in pairs, and in larger groups. Occasionally they are portrayed in conjunction with lines or stakes which could represent traps. In addition there are bas-relief carvings, occasionally featuring the use of rock protuberances in the caves for added dramatic effect. Also present within the caves are animal figures, primarily bear and bison, sculptured in clay and resting on the cave floor. Such figures are sizable, up to several feet in length. Clay deposits within the caves were also decorated by engraving. A final evidence of Paleolithic man is his own footprints in the soft clay of the cave floors.

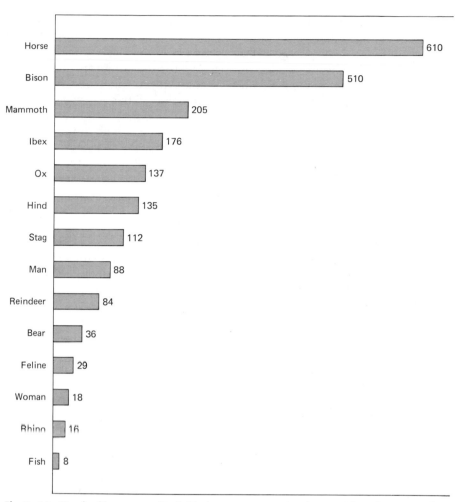

Fig. 8–14   Graph of frequency of individual cave representations by type. These frequencies bear little relationship to the bone frequencies by species from the occupation levels, suggesting their occurrence is not a record of animals killed. They could indicate the species desired. (Compiled from Leroi-Gourhan 1967:502.)

In addition to the numerous and skillful renditions of reindeer, mammoth, stag, rhino, bison, wolf, boar, ibex, bear, felines, cattle, and other animals, the cave art features other symbols (Fig. 8–14). There are infrequent examples of men and women with bodies accurately portrayed but with strangely awkward and crude faces. Another major category includes geometric designs, many of which are interpreted as male or female symbols, abstract geometric forms, and lines of dots or trailing lines. The so-called tectiform designs look like plank houses although there is no proof that such was their intended representation. The painting was done by the light of burning torches, and the paints consisted of ochre, manganese, and charcoal mixed with animal fat. The paint was smeared on, possibly with pieces of cancellous bone being used as brushes; there was direct application of sticks of charcoal, and paint may have been blown on the cave wall as a dry powder. Some finger painting was also done. Engraving was done on hard surfaces with sharp stones and burins; in wet clay the fingers were used. There are numerous small flat pebbles which have been found with engravings on their surfaces. The engravings are difficult to decipher, as up to 10 animals of different species may be engraved one on top of the other. It has been suggested that such pebbles represent practice by the artists, since the designs are identical with those on the cave walls. There are also chronological and regional styles, suggesting that the art was taught from one generation to the next. Natural accidents in the caves were frequently incorporated into the art. At Niaux, a bison sculptured in clay features natural depressions in the clay resulting from water dripping. These depressions were used to represent wounds in the bison. At Pech Merle a stalagmite has been modified into a mammoth.

A major feature of the art is its organization within the caves. Leroi-Gourhan, in his exhaustive coverage of the subject, has identified what he terms sanctuaries—main caves which are painted in a specific order. The cave will have a sequence of short strokes painted at each end; in between, the pattern features bison next to horses, stags and ibex in the deeper parts of the cave, and women associated with bison. In addition, some combinations are repeated within the same cave. The conclusion reached is that the decoration of an entire cave was conceived as a unit. Of course over time there came to be superposition of forms which made the architectural unity of the compositions difficult to decipher. Nonetheless Leroi-Gourhan believes he can identify the composition of the ideal sanctuary. His illustration (Fig. 8–15) is reproduced on page 179.

Chronology

The art has been divided into a series of periods as follows:

Period I, 30,000–23,000 B.C. Early Perigordian and Aurignacian scrawls; only mobilary art was present, at least no cave art dating from this period has been identified. Major themes are the same as later but are represented only by fragments of design—animal heads, forequarters, dorsal lines, vulvar figures, dots and strokes.

Period II, 23,000–17,000 B.C. This period, associated with Upper Perigordian and Gravettian cultures, witnessed the first development of the great sanctuaries. A major feature is the animal silhouettes on the cave walls embodying a flattened S-curve for the dorsal line. Engravings are common.

Period III, 17,000–13,000 B.C. This is the period marked by mastery of the painting techniques, relief sculpture, and the depiction of movement. Chronologically this was the period of Solutrean and early Magdalenian cultures.

Period IV, 13,000–8000 B.C. Late Magdalenian period. The style features finer modeling, an increase in mobilary art, and use of more conventional symbolism. (Leroi-Gourhan 1967:).

Cave art has been commonly thought to be indicative of sympathetic magic: the painting of animals that the hunters wished to possess. However not

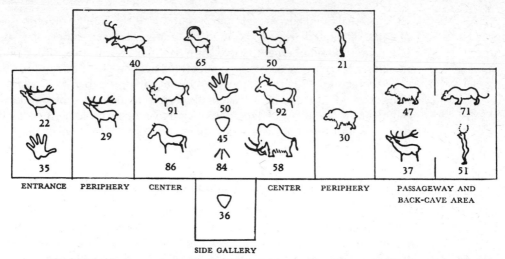

Fig. 8–15   Ideal arrangement of a Paleolithic sanctuary. The percentages have been based on 865 subjects located in 62 caves of which a complete topographical analysis was made. A subject is counted once each time it is represented, regardless of the number of times it is repeated in the same panel (for example, a composition containing 12 bison, 3 horses, 4 ibexes has been counted as bison 1, horse 1, ibex 1). (Leroi-Gourhan 1967:501.)

all of the art can be so viewed; for example, the hands outlined in red, the geometric figures, and the rows of dots are difficult to interpret as part of hunting magic. A further hypothesis is based on the prevalence of paired animals and male and female sexual symbols. This view holds that much of the cave art is based on the maker's concept of sexuality and its role in nature. In any event we concede that Upper Paleolithic cave art is among the grandest expressions of art known to man from any time period.

Mobilary Art

Art carved on small objects which are either utilitarian or decorative is equally indicative of the skill of their makers. Perhaps the most famous such objects are the so-called venuses, figures of human females carved in the round, with exaggerated hips, thighs, and breasts. These presumed fertility figures have no known utilitarian function and are widespread in Europe. They are especially common in the Gravettian culture sites of central and eastern Europe. They are typically of mammoth ivory or bone. According to Leroi-Gourhan, they feature a consistent set of proportions. Thus they were made according to a specific mental concept. While to our eyes, they appear to be lumpy and poorly proportioned, we assume they fit the standard of beauty of their makers.

Mobilary art includes engraving on bone, antler, ivory, or stone; carving in the round, primarily on bone or ivory; and the manufacture of cutout profiles further elaborated with relief carving and engraving, again in ivory and bone. The elements portrayed include the full range of animals known from the cave art plus seals, snakes or eels, rabbits, birds, fish, and geometric symbols. Objects decorated include bone staffs, antler shaft wrenches, the so-called *bâtons de commandement,* spear throwers, half-round rods, disks, pendants, pebbles, and venuses. Most of the decorated items were utilitarian. Some of the other objects such as the batons and bone staffs probably had specific functions, but we do not know what they were. Much of the mobilary art is fragmentary, as many of the specimens have been broken since they were originally in use. Other examples such as cutout profiles never portrayed an entire animal.

Paleolithic Notation: A Search into the Mind of Primitive Man

As we have mentioned previously much of the mobilary art in the Upper Paleolithic period features enigmatic rows of lines or dots. For years scientists have pondered the meaning of these notations without making much progress. This situation was dramatically reversed during the 1960s by a single man, Alexander Marshack. Not an archaeologist by training, Marshack has had a long career in scientific journalism. In connection with his responsibilities in the U.S. space program and the International Geophysical Year, he became interested in the history of man's development of science, mathematics, and astronomy. These inquiries led him to contact Ralph Solecki of Columbia University who suggested that the authority on Upper Paleolithic art, Leroi-Gourhan, might provide further information concerning the mentality of Paleolithic man.

On June 13, 1962, Marshack (1972:15) wrote Dr. Leroi-Gourhan asking if there was any indication that the time of the painting or drawing was seasonal or periodic in nature. Dr. Leroi-Gourhan responded by stating that the painting and use of the Upper Paleolithic caves could have been on a seasonal basis. However, proof was lacking. The best evidence that Leroi-Gourhan could offer was that the cave paintings repeated the same theme which was mythical. He cited the fact that seasonal calebrations of myths is a widespread human trait. Such proof was more conjectural than positive and thus Marshack searched farther.

The next step in Marshack's search led him to the undeciphered bone from Ishango in the Congo, a Mesolithic site. The bone tool, probably a knife handle, bore on its exterior a number of scratches or grooves in distinct groups as follows: 7, 5, 5, 10, 8, 4, 6, 3, and on the opposite side two sets, 8, 19, 21, 11, and 19, 17, 13, 11. The excavator, Jean de Heinzelin, asserted these grooves were not mere decoration but in fact must have a meaning, which he interpreted as "an arithmetical game of some sort, devised by a people who had a number system based on 10 as well as a knowledge of duplication and of prime numbers" (de Heinzelin 1962).

Marshack was not convinced, and he tried thinking from the evidence:

Since the cranial capacity of *Homo sapiens* had not varied greatly since his first appearance in Europe, I made the assumption that the basic function of the brain was the same then and now, and that man before history and in the Ice Age was not much different from what he is now. What differed primarily were the facts, ideas, and relationships with which the brain was educated and with which it worked, not the manner of its functioning, its ability, or its capacity and intelligence (Marshack 1972:24).

Marshack was convinced the Ishango bone represented some form of notation rather than an arithmetic game, and he sought further clarification. His first step was to assume that the markings represented some sort of count of time, possibly a lunar count, since this is a common concern of primitive peoples. Having made this assumption, he proceeded to attempt to verify it. Adding the numbers together he found the two columns each totaled 60, a possible count for two months. Following this lead, he aligned the sequence of grooves with a lunar sequence of the same length and found the sequence of marks (days?) matched the waxing and waning of the moon. Marshack now had a hypothesis but so far no proof. To broaden his base of evidence he decided to go to Europe and consult original specimens of Upper Paleolithic mobilary art.

In his research at the Musee de Antiquités Nationales near Paris Marshack realized that his inquiry, in order to be successful, had to incorporate a scientific methodology. He states:

I realized that if I began my search by seeking only those pieces that seemed to be notational or lunar I might find a piece, or a few such pieces among the mass of materials here or elsewhere in Europe. But this would be a search by default, directed to prove a hypothetical point. If I were right, I would have to prove my point in a single cabinet, with the limited random sampling offered by a small collection of bones and stones. If I failed in this random sampling, there would be no point in performing the agonizing search through the other cabinets or through the rest of Europe for some chance piece that might give the proof. Either notation was common in the Upper Paleolithic or there was no notation (Marshack 1972:44).

One of the first specimens he studied was the engraved bone from the Abri Lartet. His search was seemingly a success, for within that first cabinet he found a strong correlation of the bone records with the lunar sequence. Not only the bone from Abri Lartet but numerous others could be so interpreted.

It is not my intention here to cite all of the specific steps in Marshack's approach, nor will I attempt to verify his results. The attempt he makes at interpreting the mental patterns of prehistoric man is sufficient in itself. He provides strong evidence that Upper Paleolithic men possessed a system of notation, that these records were made at different times and in different ways and media, and very possibly that they record lunar counts. He has come as close as any archaeologist ever has to reading the mind of ancient man.

THE LIFE OF UPPER PALEOLITHIC MAN

We have given considerable coverage to the art of this period, for the art was one of the triumphant achievements of Paleolithic man. In addition, we have much archaeological evidence of the daily life of these peoples. They were hunters, specializing in the hunting of the large herd-dwelling mammals of the time. Their reliance depended on the availability of the various species; with changes in climate the fauna changed accordingly. In areas, such as the steppes of Russia and Siberia, the mammoth and woolly rhino were most common. Hunting techniques were varied and successful. Traps and pitfalls are portrayed in the cave art, and the evidence from actual killsites indicates that the ambush and stampede were commonly utilized. At Predmost, bones of at least 1000 mammoth are present. The cliff drive site at Solutre has the bones of 100,000 horses at its base. The Magdalenian peoples were specialized reindeer hunters, living in a close symbiotic relationship with the reindeer herds. They obtained almost their entire subsistence from the reindeer as well as skins for clothing and tents, bone and antler for tools, sinew for thread, teeth for ornaments, and so forth. In some Magdalenian levels reindeer make up more than 90 percent of all bone remains. The Magdalenians moved north with the herds in summer and south in the winter.

Shelter in the period was provided by the abundant caves and rock shelters of western Europe or the skin tents common to the steppe and tundra dwellers of eastern and northern Europe. Examples of such tent villages have been excavated in several localities (Fig. 8–16). Typical villages consisted of three or more tents, some of which were quite spacious, up to 40 by 12 feet. Associated with the tents were hearths, both inside and outside, with large piles of discarded food bones between the tents. The tents had a supporting structure, probably of poles, set in postholes in the ground, in holes cut in large bones, or propped together with large stones and bones wedged against their bases. Over this framework skins were stretched and further secured by weighting with bones and mammoth tusks. Pits dug in the ground were used for food storage.

Other traits evidenced by the artifacts are sewn skin clothing and the wearing of ornaments. We know little about the form of clothing worn. The venuses were portrayed as nearly nude but wearing a type of fringed belt around the waist as well as a long apron extending down the back of the legs. Presumably for cold weather there was an entire inventory of full body covering of which we have little specific knowledge. Beads were especially common and were made of amber, brown coal, fish vertebrae, fired clay, and shells. Other ornaments included pendants, pins, bracelets, and anklets. The presence of amber and shells indicates that some trade was carried out, since these items are found beyond their natural areas of origin.

Burials indicate that specific ceremonies were carried out at death. The dead were interred fully clothed with all of their ornaments being worn. Also

Fig. 8–16 Reconstruction of a mammoth hunter's dwelling based on finds at Pushkari, near Novgorod-Seversky, South Russia. The dwelling was nearly 40 feet long and 12 feet wide, and was placed in a shallow pit. (Clark 1967:Fig. 31 [reconstruction after Mongait].)

included were everyday tools and trophies of the hunt, such as tusks. Over the entire burial would then be sprinkled a coating of powered red ochre, possibly to restore color to the body. Whatever the reason, the placing of red ochre in burials became a widespread trait which occurs in the earliest levels of New World cultures as well.

Spiritualism and religious practices include the major complex of the painting of the cave sanctuaries. In addition, within the caves there was a continuation of the bear cult practiced by Neanderthal men. Bears were hunted in the caves as evidenced by their bones with associated skull wounds. One of the sculptured bear figures shows signs of having been utilized in rites where it was attacked, possibly by novices being initiated into the cult—at least that is one theory. Human remains were also mutilated, possibly for ceremonial reasons. Several human skulls were cut off and utilized as cups. When found they were all arranged side by side on a rock deep within a French cave. Their use is problematical but ceremonial purposes seems the best answer.

The Upper Paleolithic was a time of increasing expansion by man—the modern species, *Homo sapiens*—into previously unpopulated regions of the world including the New World and Australia. Furthermore he clearly had mastered life in the extremely cold portions of Europe. His control of the environment permitted him leisure time to paint and carve, and his use of these techniques in magic suggests that he was striving to further exert his will on his surroundings. The period was a time of major adaptation to the late glacial environment, achieving a period of cultural climax for peoples existing as specialized hunters. With the major retreat of the glaciers beginning approximately 13,000 years ago, major species of the fauna, such as the woolly mammoth, woolly rhino, bison, and cave bear, became extinct. The climatic warming brought about a northward movement of environment zones which reduced the amount of cool steppe and tundra and increased the area of temperate woodland. The environment had changed to new conditions typical of the Postglacial period. The nature of these changes and man's response to them forms the subject of our next chapter, the Mesolithic.

REFERENCES

Bordes, F., 1968, *The Old Stone Age*. New York: McGraw-Hill.

Brace, C. L., H. Nelson, and N. Korn, 1971, *Atlas of Fossil Man*. New York: Holt, Rinehart and Winston, Inc.

Butzer, K. W., 1969, "Geological Interpretation of Two Pleistocene Hominid Sites in the Lower Omo Basin," *Nature* 222(5199):1138–1140.

Clark, J. G. D., 1967, *The Stone Age Hunters*. New York: McGraw-Hill.

deHeinzelin, J., 1962, Ishango. *Scientific American* 206(6):105–116.

deSonneville-Bordes, D., 1967, *La Prehistoric Moderne*. Perigeux: Pierre Fanlac.

Graziozi, P., 1960, *Paleolithic Art*. New York: McGraw-Hill.

Howell, F. C., and others, 1965, *Early Man*. New York: Time/Life Books.

Leroi-Gourhan, A., 1967, *Treasures of Prehistoric Art*. New York: Abrams.

Marshack, A., 1972, *The Roots of Civilization*. New York: McGraw-Hill.

Oakley, K., 1968, *Frameworks for Dating Fossil Man*. Chicago: Aldine.

The Mesolithic

The Mesolithic period may be characterized as a time of environmental adjustment by prehistoric men. The adjustments were necessary as a result of the change from Late Glacial conditions with the associated tundra fauna to Postglacial conditions similar to those of the present, associated with a modern fauna. The adjustments necessary were not primarily climatic, since prehistoric hunters of the Upper Paleolithic had adjusted to a more severe climate and the warming trend must have been favorable to man. The changes that were required pertain to acquiring a living. Man's food resources had changed; gone were the large herds of tundra and steppe-dwelling forms, the bison, mammoth, horse, and rhino. In their place most of Europe became forested, and the red deer, roe deer, and other solitary dwelling species became prevalent. These changes in environment required that man change his hunting techniques and implements and begin to develop skills in food collecting. During this interval,

185

vegetal foods became more important, shellfish were gathered, fishing was important, and sea mammals such as whales and seals were hunted or utilized when they washed ashore. Most of the evidence we have for the Mesolithic comes from northern and western Europe, although this stage of environmental adjustment is known from other areas of the world including Africa, the Middle East, and North America. Archaeologically speaking, the best known sites are from Europe, and we will confine most of our discussion to those data.

THE POSTGLACIAL ENVIRONMENT

The Postglacial period is marked by warm or temperate climatic oscillations interspersed with brief colder, wetter intervals. The entire trend is one of warming continuing to the present. Major features are the northward movement of biotic zones, the melting of ice, and the rise in sea level accompanied by isostatic rebound of the land formerly weighted down by ice.

These climatic oscillations are well known because we have numerous pollen profiles covering the entire period, mostly from peat bogs, the optimum environment for pollen preservation. In addition, the anaerobic environment of bogs inhibits decay of organic remains. Thus we have preserved within them numerous plant parts including whole trees. As a result we know the composition of the forests of the period quite well. The Postglacial of northwestern Europe has been divided into a series of pollen zones summarized in Table 9–1.

Vegetation zones during the Alleröd are typical of the Mesolithic environment of northern Europe and these are illustrated on the map on p.188 (Fig. 9–1). The sites of Mesolithic man are best known from the zones featuring birch parkland and birch with pine. During much of this period England was connected to continental Europe by a land bridge. A second geographic feature of major importance was the presence of a freshwater lake, the Ancyclus Lake, in the region that today is the eastern half of the Baltic Sea. The Ancyclus Lake at times was frozen over and at times not; in any event it formed a major resource of fresh water.

During the colder intervals the snowline depression was 500 to 800 meters below modern limits, and temperatures were depressed $2°$ to $7°$ C. The sudden temperature reversals of the warmer periods resulted in rapid colonization by forest of the zones formerly occupied by ice and tundra. Johannes Iverson, the Danish palynologist who has devoted his life to the study of Postglacial floras of Europe, views the pollen record for this period as indicating a succession of species normal to forest colonization. This succession progresses from early colonization of "pioneer" species followed by "climax" species. Pioneer species reproduce rapidly and have a quick rate of dispersion. These species, which include willow, aspen, and birch, have a high need level for light and thus are successful in newly vacated ground. Soon competition from the climax species is telling, for the pioneer species have a short life span

TABLE 9–1 Correlation of Habitat, Biome, and Economy in the Mesolithic of Denmark.

	CLIMATE		VEGETATION	FAUNA	POLLEN	ECONOMY		LAND/SEA
POSTGLACIAL	Sub-Atlantic Wetter, Colder	VIII	Pine Revertence	Red and Roe Deer, Wild Pig, etc.;	Forest	Herding, Agriculture, Marine and Inland Hunting, and Fishing	Iron / Bronze / Neolithic	Baltic Sea
	— ca. 800 B.C. —		Beech					
	Sub-Boreal Drier, Continental	VII	Spread of Grasses Oak Forest Introduction of Cereals and Weeds	Domesticated Ox, Pig, Sheep, Dog, Horse		← Forest Clearance Shifting Agriculture, Pastoral Activities, Marine and Inland Hunting, and Fishing		Littorina Sea
	— ca. 3000 B.C. —							
	Atlantic Warm max.; Moist, Oceanic	VI	Mixed-oak Forest and Alder	Auroch, Red and Roe Deer, Wild Pig, etc.; Dog		Hunting, Gathering, Fowling, Fishing, and Strand-Looping	Mesolithic	
	— ca. 5600 B.C. —		Pine Hazel; Mixed-Oak Forest	Auroch, Elk, Red and Roe Deer, Wild Pig, Beaver, Bear; Dog				
	Boreal Rising Temperature Continental	V	Pine/Birch Forest					Ancylus Lake
	— ca. 7500 B.C. —							
	Pre-Boreal Slow Rise of Temperature	IV	Birch Forest	Auroch, Elk Reindeer, Bison		Hunting, Gathering, Fowling, and Fishing		Yoldia Sea
	— ca. 8300 B.C. —			Wild Horse				
LATE GLACIAL	Younger Dryas Subarctic	III	Tundra / Park Tundra	Reindeer, Bison, Alpine Hare	Open Vegetation		Upper Paleolithic	Baltic Ice-Dammed Lake
	— ca. 8850 B.C. —							
	Allerød Osc. Warmer	II	Park Tundra / Birch Forest	Giant Irish Deer, Elk, Beaver, Bear				
	— ca. 10,000 B.C. —							
	Older Dryas Subarctic	I c	Tundra	Reindeer				
	— ca. 10,500 B.C. —							
	Bölling Osc. Warmer	I b	Park Tundra					
	— ca. 11,500 B.C. —							
	Oldest Dryas Arctic	I a	Tundra	Reindeer				

(J. G. D. Clark 1952:12.)

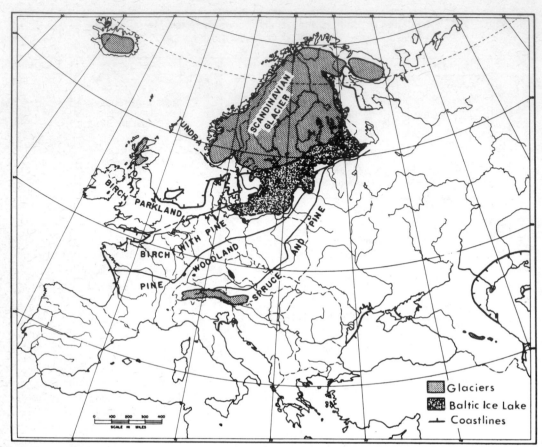

Fig. 9–1 Reconstruction of vegetational zones of northwestern Europe during the Alleröd climatic period. (Butzer 1971:Fig. 72.)

and their seedlings compete with the climax species which are hardy and long-lived and have a reduced need for light. Thus the pioneer species are crowded out by elm, oak, beech, and other deciduous hardwoods. The changes in the pollen diagrams record successions such as juniper followed by aspen, then birch and pine. These changes are successional rather than climatic. Thus the Postglacial experienced both a true climatic change—the shift to a modern climate—and local successional changes in flora.

Faunal changes are linked to both the worldwide end of the glacial epoch and the local fluctuations in floras. The tundra and steppe faunas of mammoth, rhino, reindeer, bison, horse, musk ox, and such were common in Europe until 11,000 B.C. Between that date and 9000 B.C., most of these species became locally extinct in western and nothern Europe. The time of greatest stress would appear to have been the Alleröd warmer interval dated

10,000–8850 B.C. Only the reindeer survived in quantity and provided a continuing supply of animal protein for Mesolithic man. Local pockets of forest species, the woodland horse and forest bison, existed until recently in Europe, but the herd-dwelling steppe forms became extinct much earlier. The entire period of 11,000 to 7500 B.C. was one of transition from tundra to forest with consequent extinction pressure on the tundra and steppe species. Within this changing environmental scene, man adapted; most of the large Pleistocene animal species did not.

THE MESOLITHIC ADAPTATION

Man during the Mesolithic became a forest dweller. He developed tools suitable for woodworking, axes and adzes, and became skilled at forest clearance. The results of his skill are even visible in the pollen diagrams which show reduction in tree species and an increase in shrubs and herbs, indicating for the first time a pronounced effect of man on the environment. With the trees felled, Mesolithic man filled in bogs and swamps or stabilized their surfaces with logs, stones and clay so that he might then build residences. His houses consisted of rectangular huts with floors of bark. The walls were of branches tied at the top. Other uses of wood included the manufacture of implements, especially a variety of hafts. For the first time, man became interested in various means of transportation. We have preserved remains of dugout canoes, paddles, skis, and skin boats. Man was no longer a terrestrial animal but could travel on snow or water with ease. Sledges were also made, and since the dog was domesticated, it is possible they were drawn by dog power. The development of boats may well have been an Upper Paleolithic feat, since early C-14 dates from Australia place the earliest occupation of that continent between 20,000–30,000 years B.P. The spread of microblade industries from Japan to the mainland after 11,000 B.P. can also best be explained through reliance on water transport.

The economy featured adjustments to the new forest environment. It was no longer possible to utilize the old Upper Paleolithic hunting techniques developed for use on herd-dwelling species. The new environment required the stalking or trapping in dense cover of individual animals such as the red deer, elk, roe deer, and auroch. A new implement was developed for their hunting: the bow and arrow. The bow was of elm or yew wood and was of simple one-piece construction, the self bow. The new hunting conditions undoubtedly reduced the success of the hunter, and even on those days when he was successful, his bag would be one animal instead of many.

Percentages of food provided by the various species hunted may be ascertained from bone remains at the sites. At Star Carr, England, one of the most meticulously excavated sites from the period (Table 9–2), the food remains were distributed as follows:

TABLE 9–2 The Distribution of Food Remains at Star Carr

	Dead Weight	Clean Carcass Weight	
160 Red Deer	4800 stone	67,200 lb.	30,545 kg.
66 Roe Deer	240 stone	3360 lb.	1527 kg.
22 Elk	700 stone	9800 lb.	4454 kg.
18 Ox	1980 stone	27,720 lb.	12,600 kg.
10 Pig	140 stone	1960 lb.	890 kg.
TOTAL	7860 stone	Approx. 110,000 lb.	Approx. 50,000 kg.

(J. G. D. Clark 1971:15.)

The reduction in large animals available meant that everything else edible in the environment had to be exploited. New devices were developed for the taking of game—which in many cases did not require the actual presence of the hunter. Snare traps became common, the wooden tread trap was developed, and a variety of fishing techniques were employed. Fish were taken with hook and line, fish spears, harpoons, net, and traps. Late in the period this economy was extended to the sea fauna, with seal and other marine species being taken. Stranded whales were also utilized. With the necessity of adapting to a varied economy, each element of which provided limited amounts of food, it is probable that Mesolithic men spent more time in the food quest than did his Paleolithic forebears; thus less leisure time was available. One result of this fact was a reduction in art. We find that Mesolithic art is confined to pebbles and bone and antler implements decorated with incised geometric designs of lines and dots. Most naturalistic art is no longer present, although a few animals are portrayed as simple stick figures. Among the more unique objects are the Azilian painted pebbles. These are named from the French site of Mas d' Azil where they were found in quantity. They consist of smooth river pebbles painted in red ochre with designs of stripes, spots, and zigzags. Some may represent degenerate efforts at portraying the human figure. Some of the pebbles have also been broken—perhaps as part of a ceremony. Their use is unknown, with their closest known counterpart being the sacred *churinga* of the modern Australian aborigines.

Another element of the times is the appearance of trade. Items such as amber and polished stone axes were traded long distances over specific trade routes from known source areas. Although true craft specialists probably did not exist at the time, trade does indicate specialized development of regional resources. Whereas this trade began in the Mesolithic, it continued for a long time as recorded by the exchange of Mycenaean items (Fig. 9–2) in the second millennium B.C. We assume that trade brought about considerable knowledge of adjacent regions, a trend in contrast to the earlier Paleolithic tendencies toward localization.

Mesolithic man was a colonizer, inasmuch as many of the areas he inhabited had formerly been covered with ice, water, or tundra. His economic

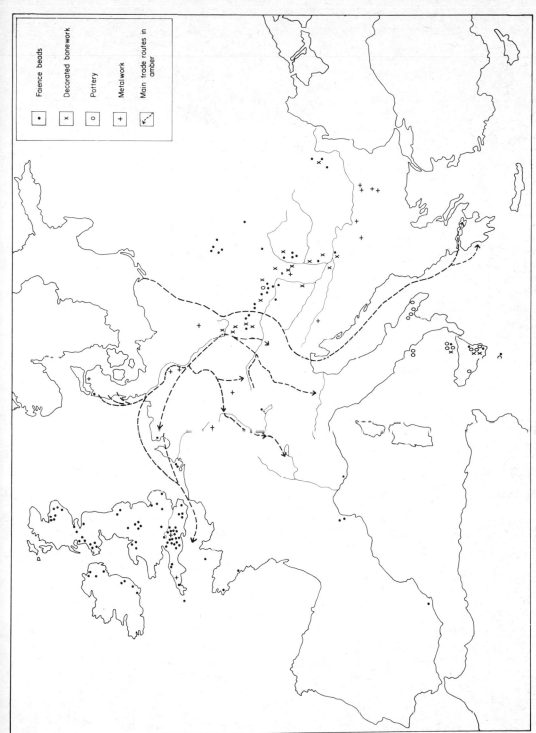

Fig. 9–2 Mesolithic trade routes, mid second millennium B.C., showing distribution of Mycenaean objects and influences beyond the Aegean. (After Piggott 1965:Figs. 73 and 75.)

Faience beads

Decorated bonework

Pottery

Metalwork

Main trade routes in amber

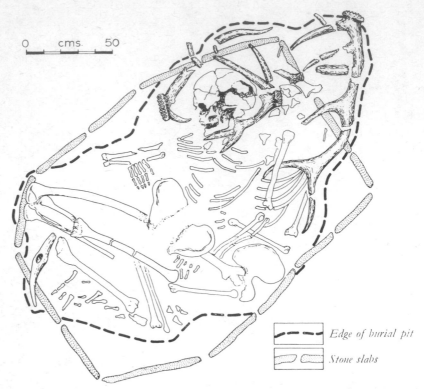

0   cms.   50

Edge of burial pit

Stone slabs

Fig. 9–3 Mesolithic burial surrounded by stone slabs and covered with stag antlers; from the coastal site at Téviec, Morbihan. (J. G. D. Clark 1967:Fig. 106 [drawn by Philip Ward after Péquart].)

practice of multiple resource use led to semisedentary occupation of a series of sites over a region. At Star Carr, for example, analysis of the stage of growth of the deer antlers in the site clearly pinpointed the time of year the site was occupied—during the late winter and early spring. The size of the group was probably somewhat dependent upon the food resources locally available. The average site was some 12 by 20 meters, suggesting that the local group was not large, probably less than 50 and perhaps no more than 15 or 20 persons. Grahame Clark, in his analysis of the remains at Star Carr, believes that the site size is similar to the area within caves occupied by Paleolithic man; thus he estimates that group size did not increase during the Mesolithic. On the other hand, early Neolithic sites featuring food production may be as much as 100 times larger.

Mesolithic burials indicate concern for the welfare of the individual after death; at least some burials feature individual interment on the back with legs flexed. The burials frequently were placed within an excavated pit surrounded by stone slabs set on edge (Fig. 9–3). The burial was then covered with several stag antlers. The body was dressed in a skin cloak fastened by bone pins. Another form of burial, termed head burial, had several skulls placed together in a pit. The skulls and attached neck bones were coated with

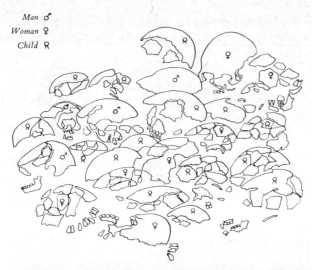

Man ♂
Woman ♀
Child ♀

Fig. 9–4 Arrangement of skulls in the mass head burial from Ofnet, South Germany. (J. G. D. Clark 1967:Figs. 126 and 128 [photo after R. R. Schmidt; drawing by Diana Holmes].)

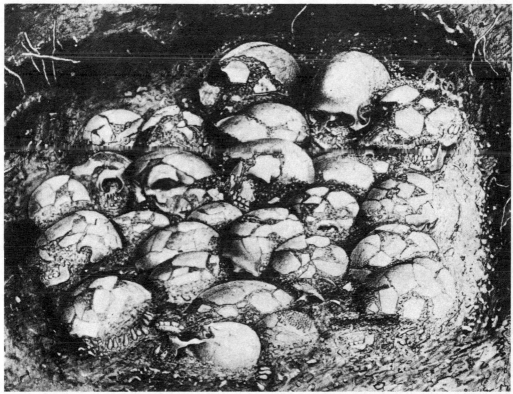

red ochre. Associated with the bones were personal ornaments and a few microliths. The best known such burial (Fig. 9–4), from Ofnet, in South Germany, featured 27 skulls in one burial. It seems clear that the burial pattern was ceremonial in nature. In the modern aboriginal societies of Melanesia the skulls of ancestors are kept within the house as objects of veneration. Whether a similar form of ancestor worship is indicated by the Mesolithic head burials cannot be determined from the evidence at hand.

In many of the sites the anaerobic environment of bogs and swamps has preserved items of wood and other organic materials. We thus have evidence of a wide variety of implements not found in Paleolithic levels. It is possible to view these finds as evidence of the *sudden* appearance of boats, skis, and sleds. In fact, the transition to the Mesolithic way of life undoubtedly continued many traditions originating earlier, for which we have little preserved evidence. We do know that harpoons were elaborately developed in the prior Magdalenian culture, thus the adaptation to fishing and sealing does not represent such a dramatic shift.

AN INVENTORY OF MESOLITHIC INDUSTRIES

Major industries of Mesolithic type in Europe are placed in geographic and chronological perspective in Table 9–3. The geographic distribution of major sites is presented in Figure 8–3.

TABLE 9–3   Mesolithic Chronology in Europe

Years B.P.	N.W.	Europe		S.E.
7000	Campignian			
8000	Maglemosian			
		Tardenoisian		
9000	Star Carr			
		Sauveterrian	Crvena	
10,000			Stijena	Asprochaliko
	Ahrensburgian			
11,000				
	Federmesser			
12,000		Azilian		
	Hamburgian			
13,000		Magdalenian		

(Braidwood 1967:101.)

Mesolithic implements continued and elaborated upon several traditions established in the Upper Paleolithic. Probably the most important of these was a bone industry, featuring hafted, barbed spears and harpoons. These implements are composite tools, for they feature several parts of different materials socketed and glued or wrapped together to form one implement. These composite tools are the hallmark of the Mesolithic.

A major innovation at this time was the invention of the *microlith*. These are small geometric shaped portions of core struck blades—triangular,

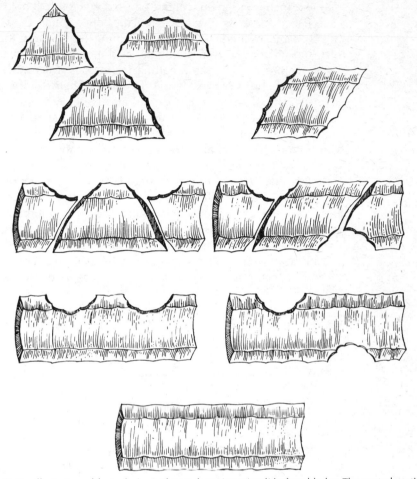

Fig. 9–5 Illustration of the technique of manufacturing microliths from blades. The central portions became the geometric shaped microliths. The notched ends, termed microburins, were probably discarded as waste fragments. (Bordaz 1970:Fig. 42.)

crescentic, or trapezoidal in form. The method of their manufacture is illustrated in Figure 9–5. The development of the microlith represents the culmination of a long trend of increasing the quantity of cutting edges prepared from a specified amount of raw material. Leroi-Gourhan has calculated that Acheulean bifaces tripled the usable edge as contrasted with the earlier and thicker Abbevillian bifaces. The Levallois technique increased this ratio four times over that of the Clacton flake technique. The introduction of core struck blades produced up to five times more length of cutting edge than the Levallois technique. Finally the development of microliths enabled prehistoric men to produce up to 300 feet of cutting edge from two pounds of flint, roughly the weight of one Abbevillian biface. The microliths themselves, being from a half inch to 2 inches in length, cannot be used efficiently if held in the hand. They were hafted in series in grooves cut in bone, antler, or wood. So mounted, they became exceedingly efficient cutting tools. Thus the development of microliths depended on not only the evolution of flint knapping but also upon the development of suitable hafting techniques. Microliths are the most distinctive stone tools of the Mesolithic period. Their distribution is widespread, covering not only most of Europe but also North Africa, East and South Africa, the Middle East, India, and Australia. The spread of microliths from early centers of development was slow, with the result that in some areas they were introduced long after food production had developed in the more advanced cultures. For example, microliths do not appear in Australia until 3000 B.C. and in South Africa not until 1000 B.C. In other regions, for example, the Nubian Nile, microliths continued in use after the introduction of agriculture. Thus the presence of microliths does not automatically signify that a particular site is of Mesolithic age; it could also be of Neolithic age.

Other implements of chipped stone include backed and tanged flakes and blades, serrated blades or saws, awls or borers, core scrapers, flake and blade scrapers, burins, flaked adzes and axes, and a variety of flaked utility tools.

The earliest axes and adzes in both northwestern Europe and southwestern Asia appear about 9000 B.P. They feature an initial flaking to shape, then edge grinding of the bit. Later forms feature all-over grinding and smoothing. One typical form, the celt, consists of a straight blade, somewhat triangular in form with the bit at the widest end. The narrow tapering butt was hafted in a sleeve of antler which had a socket for the insertion of a wooden handle. It was with the development of the ground and polished cutting tools, celts and adzes, that Mesolithic man was able to become proficient in tree cutting and woodworking.

The antler industry may be considered in part a result of the economic shift to deer. For example, at Star Carr three types of antler were available: roe deer, red deer, and elk. Roe deer antler was not used, although the bones were. Red deer antler was commonly used, but the bones were not. Both shed and unshed antlers were used as a source of material. Typical manufacturing techniques were that the crown and tines were initially removed. Then longitudinal splinters were removed from the beam by a grooving and splitting technique. The grooving was done with use of burins. The splinters were then further modified by grinding and polishing into barbed points. The points were unilaterally barbed, with the barbs ranging in number from two to about thirty. When hafted in groups of three, these formed the leister type of point, the elements of which spring apart slightly on contact then contract to hold the game securely. Modern aboriginal peoples use similar spears or arrows for the taking of birds and fish. Tines were also converted into tools by grinding their tips to a beveled point. Elk antler was used for mattock heads. These feature a flat beveled point at one end and a hafting hole cut through the rear portion of the blade. Small bone pins (bodkins), presumably to secure clothing, were made of elk bone. Other large sections of bone and antler were prepared by grinding a flat beveled edge which was then used for scraping. The most distinctive antler artifacts were the worked stag frontlets, which are portions of the frontal bone with antlers attached. Two to four holes for attachment were drilled in the frontal bone. It is assumed these frontlets were worn in ceremonies, perhaps by the religious practitioner, the shaman. Such a costume is known to have been worn in recent times by tribal shamans among the Tungu. Evidence that the Star Carr frontlets were to be worn is suggested by the fact that they were lightened by hollowing out the back of the beams.

Other typical objects include crude beads with holes drilled for suspension. Beads were made of amber, shale, hematite, and animal teeth. The presence of iron pyrites is interesting; they may have been used as strike-a-lights.

Special mention should also be made of transverse arrowheads called tranchets (Fig. 9–6). These were arrow points with a straight sharp edge at right angles to the arrow shaft. These points were microliths of triangular or trapezoidal form, hafted with one of the long axes as the leading edge.

THE MESOLITHIC IN AFRICA

Mesolithic cultures are widespread in Africa where they represent adaptations to environmental conditions different from those of Europe. Africa possesses several major environmental situations: the North African coast with its Mediterranean climate, the Sahara, the equatorial rain forest, and the South African veld. Between the rain forest and the Sahara there is a series of zones grading from savanna to thorn scrub. East and South Africa feature grassland to wooded savanna, primarily influenced by elevation. An added feature is the Rift Valley lakes. With such a varied set of environmental conditions it is obvious that the archaeology of the period must be equally varied. Several items exist as constants characteristic of the period. The inhabitants were locally adapted food collectors; therefore whatever resources were available were utilized. In North Africa this included the African land snail, available in great quantity on the scrub vegetation. In the Sahara native grasses were collected for seeds. Along the Nile a variety of fish, freshwater mollusks, gazelle, hippo, and water birds were available. The savannas were rich in tree and root foods. Another sign of the times was the presence of microliths. They occur over most of the continent with the possible exception of the equatorial forest region. There is a large area extending across North Africa, south along the Nile Valley, and reaching into the East African horn and Kenya, which may have had strong internal cultural connections. These include the Capsian culture of North Africa, the Natufian culture of Palestine, the Sebilian and related industries along the Nile, and the Kenya Capsian, Magosian, and Doian cultures of East Africa. Characteristics in common include core struck blades and bladelets, microliths (especially the crescent shaped lunate forms), backed blades, and burins.

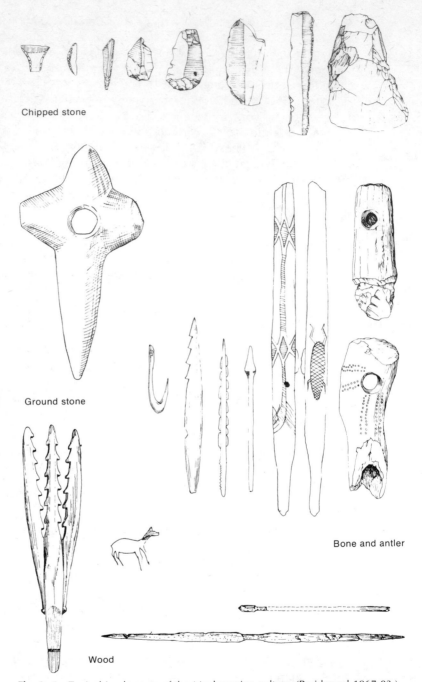

Chipped stone

Ground stone

Wood

Bone and antler

Fig. 9–6 Typical implements of the Maglemosian culture. (Braidwood 1967:83.)

As yet there is insufficient archaeological evidence to arrange specifically these various cultures into a comparative chronology. While they have culture traits in common, we do not know that they are of equivalent age. Their similarities may in fact be more apparent than real, the result of convergent evolution.

In sites along the Nubian Nile there was also the use of grinding stones for food preparation. The cultural levels containing these have been dated at 12,000 to 14,000 years of age. These represent the world's oldest known grinding stones. An unique aspect of the region is that this early use of food grinding, perhaps of wild seeds, did not lead to agriculture. Agriculture seems to have been introduced to the Nile Valley from the Middle East several thousand years after its first appearance in that region. One explanation could be that food collectors living along the Nile had such an easy time getting food and were so well adapted to their way of life that they were not stimulated to develop food production.

Another tradition is represented in parts of East Africa, the Congo, and Sudan. In this well-watered region we have the widespread taking of fish using barbed bone points. The wide geographic separation between this region and Europe, with the arid Sahara in between, suggests that a fishing economy in central Africa represents an independent development. Some authors disagree and claim that harpoons were actually diffused from Africa to Europe. We need more archaeological research in the Sahara to resolve questions of this type.

Some stone industries of South Africa and portions of East Africa are clearly derived from prior traditions in the region. These include the cultures assigned to what has been termed the African Late Stone Age. Such industries include the Stillbay, Magosian, and Wilton cultures. Chronologically and culturally these are transitional groups with both a late hunting economy and a Mesolithic type of omnivorous food collecting. One variant, the so-called South African Strand Looper culture, had a littoral economy featuring the gathering of crabs and shellfish as well as fishing. The stone tool traditions possess small core tools and flake tools, with disk cores, small thumbnail scrapers, backed blades, burins, hollow based arrowheads, lunates, and even pottery. Dates on these industries are quite late, as recent as 186 $\pm$ 150 B.C., therefore the African Late Stone Age should be viewed as a cultural backwater far behind contemporaneous developments in other parts of the world.

In the following summary taken from J. Desmond Clark (1959), we have a reconstruction of life in the Late Stone Age of Africa. His reconstruction is based on not only the archaeological remains from settlements but perishable materials preserved in rock shelters and paintings on the shelter walls. Further confirmation is provided by the cultural practices of the modern Bushmen who lead a similar life. The social unit was the band, 20–30 people, who had no permanent dwellings; their possessions were limited to what they could carry. In the rainy season the band size could increase to 200. They probably hunted over an area of 2000 to 3000 square miles. Regions were claimed by specific bands and were seasonally occupied to utilize food resources currently available. Caves or rock shelters were favored for occupation, with reed windbreaks also constructed. Rock paintings illustrate band activities such as warfare, marriage, rain ceremonies, burial, abduction of women, sexual intercourse, homicide, and theft. Trade by barter was conducted with salt, sea shells, and red and yellow ochre. Some groups may have had chiefs, for the burial scenes show individuals of unique status. Men did the hunting and made the hunting implements. Women did the food collecting and made the tools they needed. The one-piece bow was used with composite arrows (probably poisoned). Throwing sticks and stabbing spears were used. Hunting disguises included the use of ostrich skins. Pit traps with or without stakes were employed as well as spring traps and nets. Fishing was done with barbed harpoons and arrows and through the use of tidal traps made of reed basketry. Women used the digging stick weighted with a bored stone. Bone adzes were used for skin scraping. Stone scrapers were used for woodworking and removing meat from bones. Ostrich egg shells were used for containers. Containers also were made of bark, animal bladders, turtle shells, and late in the period, pottery. Foods included meat, ants, eggs, locusts, grass seeds, berries, honey, tree caterpillars, snakes, and the abdominal juices of freshly killed animals. Cooking was done by baking, stone boiling, and roasting; meat was also eaten raw. Clothing was not worn, although there was much use of body painting and the wearing of ornaments. These people wore grass bracelets; pendants of shell, bone, and stone; beads of bone, ivory, and stone; and necklaces of seeds and berries. Burial was in a grass bed with objects of personal ornamentation. Sometimes a windbreak was burned and thrown over the burial. After burial there was a feast. The mythical animals portrayed in the scenes of rain ceremonies suggest that a cosmology was present. The ceremonies also had music provided by reed flutes and musical bows.

The economy of the Late Stone Age was of Mesolithic type—a mixture of hunting and food collecting. After the invention of food production, about 8000 years ago in the Middle East, and its subsequent spread to other regions during the period 5000–2000 B.C., we may view all subsequent Mesolithic peoples, such as those of the Late Stone Age, as peoples in marginal areas practicing a marginal economy. They were no longer in the mainstream of man's cultural evolution. Another point of view is to recognize that some Mesolithic cultures were so well adapted to their environment that change to food production offered few advantages.

PRECONDITIONS FOR FOOD PRODUCTION

Mankind at this time was about to begin a series of cultural developments among the most significant in his long history. The change to production of food, from hunting and collecting, was so significant that it has been termed a "revolution" (Childe 1953). When man could produce food and was no longer dependent upon the availability of wild game, his hunting ability, or the presence of wild plant foods in a seasonal harvest, he made a giant step forward. His new found independence had widespread ramifications, for he could begin to make permanent settlements, increase in population density, begin to specialize in crafts, and in a multitude of ways increase and diversify his cultural practices.

Food production did not simply appear without stages of prior development. In fact R. J. Braidwood, the world's leading authority on the subject, believes that we may discern a series of periods of development. He considers these to be: 1. the terminal level of food collection, 2. the level of incipient cultivation and domestication, and 3. the level of primary village farming communities— the full-fledged Neolithic period (Braidwood 1967:92–94). At the end of the Mesolithic, man was concerned with the terminal level of food collecting. What conditions were present at this time in the environment, and what cultural adaptations of the Mesolithic peoples living then made up the necessary preconditions for the development of food production? Perhaps the most important single factor was the change in climate. Postglacial warming with consequent glacial retreat brought about major shifts in the distribution of plant and animal communities. These changes led to the extinction of large herd-dwelling animals and increasing reliance on the solitary living forms. With hunting becoming less reliable as a major source of food, man became increasingly reliant on plant resources. He thus became more aware of where the plant foods occurred and when they might be harvested, and he began to develop specialized techniques for their harvest. One of these techniques consisted of setting a series of crescent-shaped microliths in a curved blade to form a sickle. Such implements have been interpreted as having been used for cutting of wild grain, for the silica content of grain stalks produces a lustrous polish on the sickle flints which remains to this day (Wendorf 1968:865). Such sickle flints are common in terminal food-collecting sites from North Africa eastward to the Zagros Mountain foothills of Iran. Before man began planting crops, he must have gone through a long period of concern with wild grain crops, camping near them, and harvesting them.

The antecedents of animal domestication are not quite as well known. We assume that a prior condition was the hunting of certain species, perhaps even selection of individuals within a certain age group in order to maintain a local herd size. Gradually through time the relationship became more symbiotic, with man finally managing the herd.

A final major consideration is that with Postglacial changes in the distribution of wild plant and animal species, certain areas would have been more productive of species suitable for domestication. Such an area, termed by Braidwood a *nuclear area,* is defined as a region with a natural environment which included a variety of wild plants and animals, both possible and ready for domestication. Several such nuclear areas are known where domestication did occur. They include the Middle East, Mesoamerica, the Andean Highlands, subtropical Africa, and Southeast Asia. The earliest development of food production anywhere in the world occurred in the Middle East.

In the Middle East there is a crescent-shaped region of foothills that extends from the Zagros Mountains of Iran northwestward to Lebanon and southern Turkey. This region, popularly termed the "hilly flanks," is the region from which we have the earliest evidence of food production. H. E. Wright, Jr., (1970) has explained the climatic reasons for this development as follows: During the Late Glacial period (pre-11,000 B.P.), this region featured a cool steppe environment with sagebrush as the dominant plant cover. With the warming trend, beginning about 11,000 B.P. and lasting until 5500 B.P., there was a major expansion of oak woodland with associated grasses including wheat and barley. After 5000 B.P. the climate became as today with semidesert steppe below 700 meters, oak woodland between 700 and 2000 meters, and cool steppe above 2000 meters. Wright suggests that at the time man was adjusting to Postglacial conditions, between 11,000 and 9000 B.P., the natural habitats of wild grains were increasing. The associations between these wild grains and oak woodland today is shown in Wright (1970:Fig. 3).

Details of the development of food production revealed by archaeological excavations in the Middle East will be presented in the chapter to follow.

REFERENCES

Bordaz, J., 1970, *Tools of the Old and New Stone Age*. New York: Natural History Press.

Braidwood, R. J., 1967, *Prehistoric Men,* 7th ed. Glenview, Ill.: Scott, Foresman.

Butzer, K., 1971, *Environment and Archaeology,* 2d ed. Chicago: Aldine-Atherton.

Childe, V. G., 1953, *Man Makes Himself*. New York: Mentor.

Clark, J. D., 1959, *The Prehistory of Southern Africa*. London: Pelican.

Clark, J. G. D., 1952, *Prehistoric Europe: The Economic Basis*. London: Methuen.

———, 1967, *The Stone Age Hunters*. New York: McGraw-Hill.

———, 1971, *Excavations at Star Carr, an Early Mesolithic Site at Seamer near Scarborough Yorkshire*. London: Cambridge University Press.

Piggott, S., 1965, *Ancient Europe*. Edinburgh: Edinburgh University Press.

———, 1968, ed., *The Dawn of Civilization*. New York: McGraw-Hill.

Wendorf, D. F., 1968, *The Prehistory of Nubia,* Vol. II. Dallas: Southern Methodist University Press.

Wright, H. E., Jr., 1970, "Environmental Changes and the Origin of Agriculture in the Near East," *Bioscience* 20(4)210–212.

The Neolithic

THE NEOLITHIC AS A REVOLUTION

Initially, as a result of the three age classification of prehistoric implements developed by Thomsen, Worsaae, and their predecessors, the Neolithic (New Stone Age) was perceived as a time when man shifted from chipped and flaked stone implements to those manufactured by grinding and polishing. With subsequent research, it has become clear that this change in tool manufacturing was not the important factor. We now know that ground and polished implements were first used in the Mesolithic period and were not in themselves a significant factor in the Neolithic adaptation.

We view the Neolithic change in economy as a significant change in the human condition. For the first time, through *production* of food, man was able to restructure his relationship with his environment. No longer was he simply improving techniques used to obtain naturally occurring foods. Man no longer viewed himself as part of the environment or at least directly responsive to

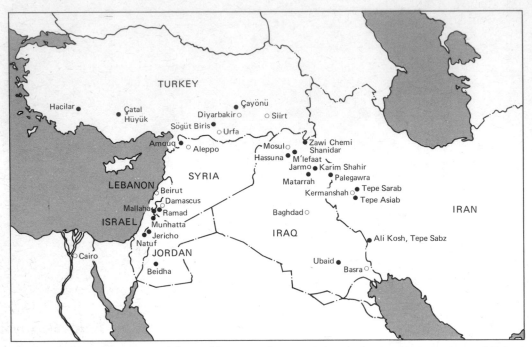

Fig. 10–1 Map of the Middle East with excavated early farming sites. (Harlan and Zohary 1966:Fig. 2.)

environmental factors. For the first time, man was able to modify his environment on a substantial scale and therefore stood apart. Food production was responsible for numerous changes in man's culture. While he was still subject to the deleterious effects of drought, floods, blight, and such, he was able to nourish the food-producing plants and animals and protect them to some degree from adverse natural influences. He was able to live in larger groups because of the availability of stable food resources. Individual sites increased in area from the Mesolithic average of 20 by 12 meters to an average of 200 by 50 meters; an increase in area of 40 times. Probably the population increase was of similar magnitude. While archaeologists cannot precisely correlate site area with population, at least formulas to compute site population have been attempted (Naroll 1962). Food production also resulted in the establishment of stable permanent villages (Fig. 10–1). Once man began to live in one place on a permanent basis, he began to take more interest in his rights of ownership. He could afford to construct more elaborate dwellings and furnishings, for they no longer had to be moved or abandoned during the seasonal food harvests as was the case with occupational sites of hunter-gatherers. With food production there occurred concomitant developments in architecture, systems of ownership rights, and crafts. Food production also led to the generation of food storage and food surpluses. We have the widespread development of pottery, the result of alteration of malleable clay into a hard permanent form through the mechanism of firing. Pottery is brittle and friable as well as heavy, all unsatisfactory traits to the mobile hunter or food collector. However, with a settled way of life, pottery became extremely important, for it could be made into almost any form and if broken, could be easily replaced. From the archaeologist's standpoint, pottery is extremely important, for once broken, the remnant sherds are nearly indestructible and provide a wealth of information about past culture. Throughout the Neolithic, pottery became increasingly important in food preparation and food storage.

With the accumulation of food surpluses, societies could afford the luxury of nonfood producers—specialists such as potters, priests, and warriors—those individuals whose value lay in their contributions in areas outside the basic economy. With the rise of craft specialists we perceive the beginnings of the complex society that we have today. The Neolithic is thus the foundation of modern society. At this time many activities which are still practiced, such as agriculture, animal husbandry, brewing, wine making, bee keeping, irrigation, use of fertilizer, were established. Only recently, in many parts of the world, has man shifted out of a Neolithic economy. Many modern societies still persist in a Neolithic way of life; these are the societies we term peasant, where reliance is on agriculture performed with hand tools and frequently draft animals.

THE ORIGINS OF DOMESTICATION

The development of agriculture and animal domestication was dependent on two major interacting factors: the availability of suitable native species for domestication and the cultural incentive and technology to enable such domestication. As Braidwood (1967) has pointed out, these factors were confined to specific regions, the nuclear areas. The primary area of initial domestication seems to have been the "hilly flanks" region of the Middle East. The 15 to 20 inches of rainfall per year in this region is ample to support wild grassland. These grasses include two kinds of wild wheat and a wild barley (Fig. 10–2). Also occurring in the wild state were sheep, goat, pig, and cattle (Fig. 10–3). An example of the way in which these wild plants and animals were locally available or restricted is illustrated in Figure 10–4.

Three recent hypotheses have been proposed to explain the development of agriculture. After all, why should man shift from hunting and gathering if those techniques provided an adequate food supply? We have little evidence that hunting and gathering societies suffer from lack of food. More typically they acquire their food with much less than full-time effort. It is obvious then that other factors led to food production. The hypotheses we will consider are those proposed by Braidwood, Binford, and Flannery. Each of these men rejects the earlier propinquity hypothesis of V. Gordon Childe, which stated that owing to environmental change—for example, drought—men and animals were forced into closer relationships around water holes which then led to domestication.

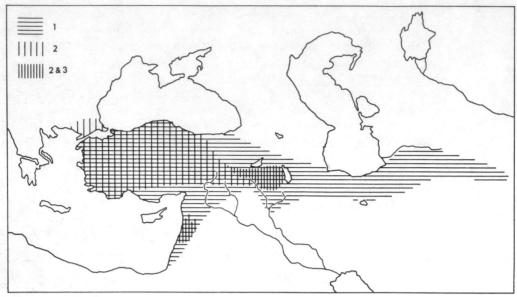

Fig. 10–2   Generalized distribution of *1*. wild barley *(Hordeum spontaneum); 2*. wheat *(Triticum aegilopodes); 3*. wheat *(Triticum dicoccoides)*. (Piggott 1965:Fig. 9.)

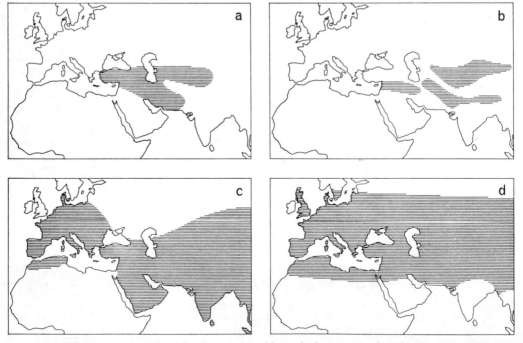

Fig. 10–3   Generalized distribution of *a*. wild goat; *b*. sheep; *c*. pig; *d*. cattle. (Piggott 1965:Fig. 8.)

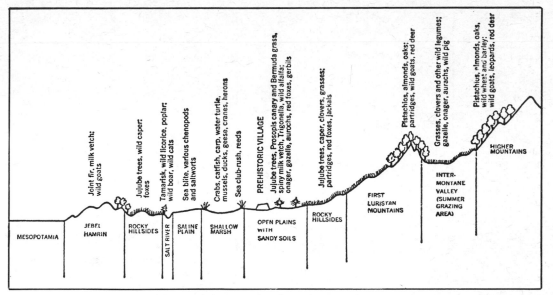

Fig. 10–4 Idealized cross section of northern Khuzistan, showing "microenvironments" with some of their characteristic flora and fauna. (Hole, Flannery, and Neely 1969:Fig. 2.)

Braidwood's explanation relies on cultural rather than environmental factors. He contends that the development of agriculture was the logical result of the evolution of groups living in the right environment at the right time. In other words, the time and place were ripe, and culture developed in that direction simply because of inherent human nature.

Lewis Binford (1968) has taken strong exception to Braidwood's approach. He is critical because he believes the causes were more concrete than "human nature"; furthermore, there is little in the Braidwood explanation that may be tested through standard archaeological techniques. Although Binford proposes an environmental cause as one of only two possible testable factors which could have brought about the development of agriculture, he then goes on to reject the environmental explanation as not feasible, owing to the minor nature of the Post-Pleistocene environmental changes. His other explanation relies on demographic factors:

Change in the demographic structure of a region which brings about the impingement of one group on the territory of another would also upset an established equilibrium system, and might serve to increase the population density of a region beyond the carrying capacity of the natural environment. Under these conditions manipulation of the natural environment in order to increase its productivity would be highly advantageous (Binford 1968:328).

The demographic factors he cites include internal population growth as well as external pressure and the emigration of peoples into a region. Binford goes

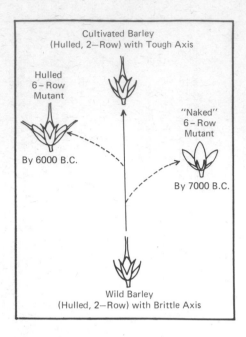

Cultivated Barley
(Hulled, 2—Row) with Tough Axis

Hulled
6 – Row
Mutant

"Naked"
6 – Row
Mutant

By 6000 B.C.

By 7000 B.C.

Wild Barley
(Hulled, 2—Row) with Brittle Axis

Fig. 10–5 Simplified diagram of barley spike-lets, showing some of the changes which took place after domestication. (Flannery 1965:Fig. 3.)

further to state that the influx of peoples was from the seacoasts to the less populated inland regions.

Flannery (1968) views the entire process within the framework of specific relationships between man and his plant and animal resources. He believes the shift from nomadic hunting and gathering to settled village life based on agriculture was a process of gradual change over a long period of time. The regulating mechanisms he terms negative feedback and positive feedback. Negative feedback encouraged the status quo and inhibited change. Food resources collected seasonally, without conflicts in the scheduling of harvests, led to long-term, balanced use of these environmental resources; thus nonchange—negative feedback. On the other hand, those resources which increased their productivity as a result of man's exploitation tended to become more important to man through time or, in Flannery's terms, exhibited positive feedback. An example is the wild grasses which, after man began to utilize them, experienced a series of genetic changes making them more productive and they were used to the neglect of other species (Fig. 10–5). Man had embarked on a course of greater and greater reliance on specific plants. Thus the positive feedback loop intensified, leading to the development of agriculture.

J. Thomas Meyers (1971), in an article evaluating the above hypotheses, proposes that agriculture developed as a result of demographic stress, the proper environment, and the proper type of exploitative technology.

Whatever the causes of the development of agriculture, several other points should be kept in mind concerning Neolithic origins. One is that considerable time was required for these changes with the new crops, at least for some time, being little more productive than wild resources. Some peoples, perhaps because of the high productivity of wild resources in their region, were reluctant to change to food production. The long-term results of food production were many; two of these—population increase and reduction of land area suitable for the new exploitive techniques—are graphed below (Fig. 10–6).

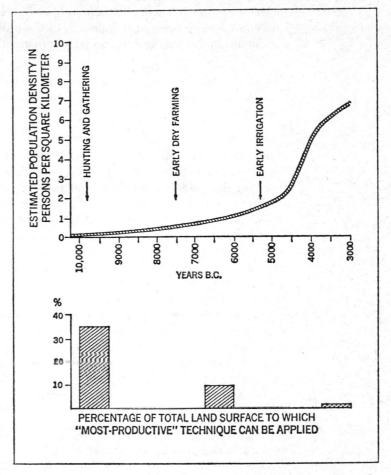

Fig. 10–6 Inverse ratio between population growth and percentage of total land surface to which "most productive" techniques (hunting and gathering, early dry farming, and early irrigation) could be applied at various stages of Iranian prehistory. (Flannery 1971:76.)

According to Harlan and Zohary (1966), the specific cereal grains that were domesticated in the Middle East are found today in a wild state in somewhat differing environments. For example, wild barley does not tolerate extreme cold and is only occasionally found above 1500-meters in elevation. However wild barley has a wide ecological range with a number of distinct varieties. One type is specifically adapted to the wadis of the Negev and Sinai where it occurs in elevations from 350 meters below sea level to 600 meters above sea level. On the other hand, wild einkorn wheat is more tolerant of cold than wild barley and occurs to 2000 meters in southeastern Turkey. Wild emmer wheat is adapted to a warmer climate, and extensive stands are found today around the Sea of Galilee. Thus early agriculturalists had a range of suitable plants to choose from.

THE RECORD OF DOMESTICATION

We will review the Middle Eastern data because it represents a suitable model for the way in which agriculture could have developed in nearby ecologically similar areas. The ecological approach to the problem of the development of agriculture in the Middle East can be summarized as follows:

The food producing revolution is viewed as the result of a long process of changing ecological relationships between men living in different environments and the locally available plants and animals being exploited on a shifting seasonal basis (Flannery 1965:1255).

The initial phase would have included cultivation of the locally available plants. Only after plants had been cultivated in their native habitats would these new domesticates be introduced into other areas.

In the Middle East the actual proof of agriculture as evidenced by preserved plant parts is still somewhat rare, with new findings continuing to modify prior views. The presence of agriculture is verified as much as anything by the subsequent developments of sedentism and urbanism. As Flannery suggests, the local economic mix was probably quite variable depending upon what was available and the practice of seasonal movements (Fig. 10–7). Only after a lengthy developmental period would systematic planting and harvesting of a few cultigens become the pattern.

These processes are described in greater detail by Flannery (1965). He states that "collecting patterns were keyed to seasonal aspects of the wild resources of each environmental zone, with perhaps a certain amount of seasonal migration from zone to zone." The evidence from Ali Kosh suggests that intensive collecting of wild plants may have been the predominant pattern everywhere in Asia Minor—not just where wild wheat occurred (Flannery 1965:1250).

. . . from an ecological standpoint the important point is not that man planted wheat but that he (i) moved it to niches to which it was not adapted, (ii) removed certain pressures of natural selection, which allowed more deviants from the normal phenotype to survive, and (iii) eventually selected for characters not beneficial under conditions of natural selection (Flannery 1965:1250).

He also asks, "Was 'incipient cultivation' a fumbling attempt at cultivation or only the intensification of an already existing system of interregional exchange?" (Flannery 1965:1251).

The role of climatic change in the development of Middle Eastern agriculture is less clear. Flannery states:

The facts we have are too few to permit us to say dogmatically that climatic change played no role, but it appears that the problem is cultural rather than climatic; the inescapable conclusion is that agriculture began in an area where, then as now, only about 10 percent of the land surface is suitable for dry farming (Flannery 1965:1249).

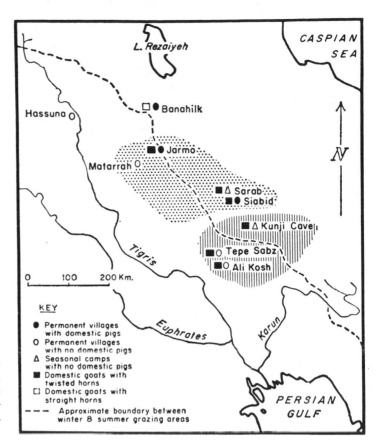

Fig. 10-7 Map of Greater Mesopotamia, showing areas where seasonal movements were practised to permit utilization of native resources. (Flannery 1965:1247.)

On the other hand, Wright (1970), utilizing pollen data from Lake Zeribar, Iran, suggests that climatic change recorded ca. 10,000 B.C. set the stage for the later agricultural developments.

BIOLOGICAL ASPECTS

Flannery (1965) has reviewed the nature of biological obstacles to early food production. These problems had to be removed by selection of existing varieties or mutants before the plant species could be successfully cultivated on a large scale. There is no doubt that the necessary selection process took considerable time, probably on the order of several thousand years. Identified problems are as follows:

1. Wild grains have a brittle rachis which holds the seeds together in the head. Harvesting of such plants is difficult, since the seeds are adapted for easy dispersal; thus the harvester recovers only a percentage of the grain.

2. Primitive grains are enclosed in a tough husk which is difficult to remove, even with severe thrashing.
3. The wild grains are native to hilly slopes which are not the best locations for extensive farming from the standpoint of soil type and moisture.

According to modern botanists, a single gene controls the differences between hulled and naked barley grains; therefore, mutation followed by selection would have produced thrashed grains easily. Another mutant was the six row type of barley, a variety adapted to dry spring weather, which became the successful irrigated form grown in the Mesopotamian alluvial floodplain.

Early farmers probably overcame these biological problems (either consciously or unconsciously) by:

1. Selecting for tough rachis grains—selection had to be important here, since the tough rachis grains would naturally have less dispersion than the brittle rachis varieties.
2. Roasting of grain and grinding were both techniques that could be utilized to remove the grains from their husks.
3. Genetic change was also encouraged with man selecting those varieties which had a less tough husk.
4. Finally, for farming to become most productive, the grains had to be introduced into the alluvial flood plains outside their native habitat.

According to Flannery, most of these changes had occurred by 7000 B.C., with the six row form of barley first appearing about 6000 B.C. The age of appearance of free-threshing wheat is about the same as that of barley, 6000 B.C.

THE ARCHAEOLOGICAL RECORD OF PLANT DOMESTICATION

Since plant parts are perishable, they probably have not been found in archaeological contexts as early as they were domesticated. The grains and husks may be recovered, sometimes in charred form, or their impressions may be preserved on pottery. However, the wild plants had to undergo genetic change before we can positively identify the grains as domesticated (Table 10–1). In any event, the early evidence of actual grains is sparse; thus we must estimate the earliest date of domestication. For leads as to how agriculture can be demonstrated from archaeological evidence, we turn to the writings of Braidwood and Reed (1957:21). In their view the process is described as a sequence of three stages (Fig. 10–8):

1. The Terminal Era of the Food Gathering Stage—specialized food collectors with a population of 12.5 persons per 100 square miles. Modern analogies might be the Ojibwa wild rice gatherers or the Great Basin seed gatherers.

TABLE 10–1 Archaeological Evidence of Early Cereal Cultivation and Animal Herding in the Near East

Sites and Stratigraphy	Approximate Dates B.C.	Barley	Einkorn	Emmer	Bread Wheat	Sheep	Goat	Cattle	Pig	Dog
Aegean Area										
Argissa (Thessaly), Aceramic	6500	X	X	X		X	X	X	X	?
Nea Nikomedeia (Macedonia)	6200	X		X		X	X	X	X	?
Knossos (Crete), stratum X	6100	X		X	X					
Khirokitia (Cyprus), Aceramic	6000						X			
Sesklo (Thessaly), Aceramic	6000–5000	X	X	X						
Ghediki (Thessaly), Aceramic	6000–5000	X	X	X						
Anatolia										
Hacilar, Aceramic	7000			X						?
Hacilar, Ceramic	5800–5000	X	X	X	X					?
Çayönü	7000		X	X		X	X	?	X	X
Catal Hüyük, VI–II	7000	X	X	X	X	X	X			
Levant										
Tel Ramad (Syria)	7000	X	X	X	X					
Jericho, Prepottery Neol. A.	7000–6500	X		X						
Jericho, Prepottery Neol. B.	6500–5500	X	X	X						
Beidha (Jordan), Prepottery	5850–5600			X		X	X			
Amoug (Antioch), A.	5750	X		X		X	X			
Mesopotamia–Khuzistan										
Ali Kosh, Bus Mordeh	7500–6750		X	X		X	X			
Ali Kosh, Ali Kosh	6750–6000	X		X		X	X			
Ali Kosh, M. Jaffar	6000–5600	X		X		X	X			
Tepe Sabz, Sabz	5500–5000	X			X	X	X	X		X
Tell es-Sawwan (Samarra)	5800–5600	X	X	X	X					
Hassuna	5800	X					X			
Kurdistan–Luristan										
Zawi Chemi, Karim Shahir	8900					X	X			X
Jarmo	6750–6500		X	X		X	X		X	
	?6500									
Tepe Sarab	6200–5500	X				X				
Tepe Guran	6200–5500	X		X						
Matarrah	5800	X							X	

(Butzer 1971:224–225.)

B.P.

5000

6000

7000

8000

9000

10,000

11,000

12,000

13,000

B.C.

3000

4000

5000

6000

7000

8000

9000

10,000

11,000

N.W.–EUROPE–S.E. | N.E. AFRICA EGYPT | NUCLEAR SOUTHWEST ASIA | E. IRAN, TURKESTAN–INDUS

"CIVILIZATION"

LITERACY, URBAN LIFE, MONUMENTAL ART AND ARCHITECTURE ... ETC.

IN LOWER MESOPOTAMIA THE BEGINNINGS OF LARGER TOWN-SIZED COMMUNITIES, SMALL TEMPLES, A DEGREE OF CRAFT SPECIALIZATION

AS TIME GOES ON AND THE NEW WAYS OF LIFE BECOME CONSOLIDATED IN ITS ALLUVIAL SOUTH, MESOPOTAMIA BECOMES THE CENTER OF THE GREATEST CULTURAL ACTIVITY

THE VILLAGE-FARMING COMMUNITY WAY OF LIFE

HERE, CULTIVATED CEREALS AND HERDED ANIMALS BECOME THE BASIS FOR A NEW AND SETTLED LIFE

THE BEGINNINGS OF EFFECTIVE FOOD-PRODUCTION IN THE UPLANDS OF SOUTHWESTERN ASIA

SOME HIGHLY INTENSIVE AND SETTLED—FOOD COLLECTORS PERSIST

INCIPIENT CULTIVATION AND DOMESTICATION

?

THIS LEVEL IS (AND WILL NO DOUBT REMAIN) VERY DIFFICULT TO IDENTIFY ARCHEOLOGICALLY

THE POTENTIALLY DOMESTICABLE WILD PLANTS AND ANIMALS WERE ALREADY AT HOME IN THE INTER-MONTANE VALLEYS AND ALONG THE PIEDMONTS OF THE LEBANON, TAUROS AND ZAGROS MOUNTAINS

TERMINAL LEVEL OF FOOD COLLECTION

VAST STRETCHES OF EASTERN IRAN AND TURKESTAN ARE DRY AND COLD, AND HAVE NEVER BECOME "FULLY AGRICULTURAL

THE QUESTION WHETHER EARLY EXPERIMENTS IN THE DOMESTICATION OF SEMI-TROPICAL PLANTS AND ANIMALS WERE ATTEMPTED IN SOUTHERN ASIA HAS NOT YET RECEIVED ADEQUATE ARCHEOLOGICAL ATTENTION

DID END OF GLACIATION IN NORTHWEST EUROPE HAVE EFFECT IN TROPICS?

THESE REGIONS ARE VERY POORLY KNOWN ARCHEOLOGICALLY FOR THIS GENERAL TIME RANGE

TERMINAL LEVEL OF FOOD COLLECTION

IT IS PROBABLE THAT THE NEW WAY OF LIFE HAD—AT FIRST—SOME DIFFICULTY IN ADAPTING ITSELF TO THE EGYPTIAN ENVIRONMENT

THE SPREAD OF THE NEW WAY OF LIFE INTO EUROPE TOOK TIME AND MANY ADJUSTMENTS, AS SOME OF THE FOOD ANIMALS AND ESPECIALLY THE PLANTS WERE NOT AT FIRST ADAPTED TO THE EUROPEAN ENVIRONMENTS

IN NORTHWESTERN EUROPE, THIS IS THE TIME OF THE INTENSIFIED HUNTING, FISHING AND COLLECTING CULTURES WHICH SHOW HOW MEN READAPTED THEIR WAY OF LIFE TO THE SUCCESSION OF NEW ENVIRONMENTS WHICH FOLLOWED THE END OF THE LAST GLACIATION

INCREASING ATTENTION TO THE COASTAL AND RIVER REGIONS

FOLLOWING THE END OF THE LAST GLACI-ATION, THERE APPEARS TO HAVE BEEN A DEPOPULATION OF THE PLAINS OF CENTRAL AND SOUTHEAST EUROPE

APPROXIMATE END LAST GLACIATION NORTHWESTERN EUROPE

TERMINAL LEVEL OF FOOD COLLECTION

FOOD COLLECTORS OF THE LAST PHASES OF THE LAST GLACIATION

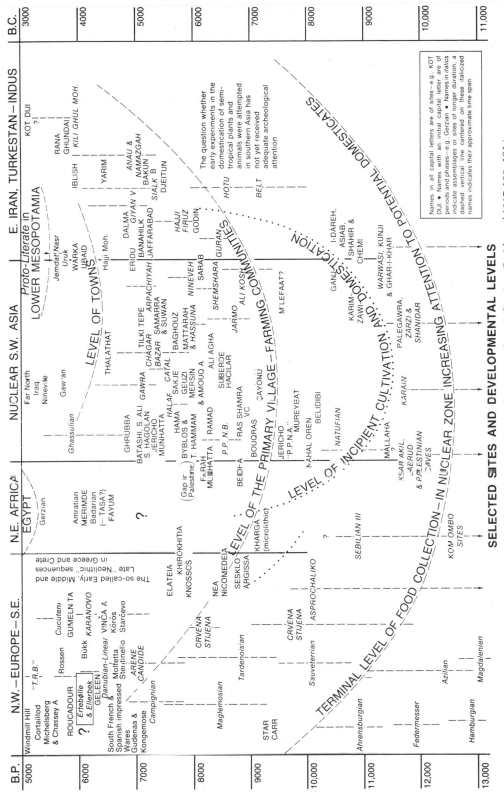

Fig. 10-8 Eras or levels of development from food collection to urban civilization. (Braidwood 1967:100-101.)

2. The Era of Incipient Agriculture and Animal Domestication. No modern analogies exist.
3. The Era of Village Farming Efficiency—2500 persons per 100 square miles, although some areas are unsuitable for such density. A modern analogy would be the modern settlement near Jarmo.

Braidwood and Reed also suggest that southwestern Asia was the single instance of the independent appearance of effective village farming in the Old World.

ANIMAL DOMESTICATION

The evidence for animal domestication is also unclear. Basic problems relative to identification of domestication are several. The species are the same as wild species; thus, domestication must bring about recognizable phenotypic differences before the domesticates may be identified. Butchering patterns influence the distribution of unwanted bony parts which may or may not be preserved for the archaeologist to find. Frequently the most diagnostic elements are the ones that are not recovered. One major clue is the ratio of bones found. With domestication, the frequency of young animals being butchered increases, with older animals being kept for breeding purposes; also reliance is concentrated on a few species (Fig. 10–9). Hunters, on the other hand, take what they can get; thus the age/sex ratio is similar to that of the wild population. Some traits represent changes due to domestication, even though the changes had no utilitarian value. For example, as goats were domesticated there was a change in horn form from the scimitar shape of the wild form to the twisted form of the domestic variety (present by 6000 B.C.). Other changes were of obvious value such as the change from hairy to wooly sheep (Fig. 10–10).

According to Reed (1971), several preconditions governed man's early domestication of animals. The earliest domesticates were the dog, pig, sheep, goat, and cattle (see Table 10–1). Of these species the dog and pig were food competitors with man, requiring an omnivorous diet. In Reed's view, man had first to begin living in settled communities with a food surplus available before dogs and pigs could be kept in any quantity. On the other hand, the ruminants, sheep, goats, and cattle all subsist on roughage—grass stems, leaves, and such—not utilizable by man for food. Man would have been able to increase greatly the food available for these species as agriculture developed, making available the plant by-products as forage.

Dogs were probably the earliest domesticates. They aided in hunting and were domesticated by Mesolithic times. The earliest date for dog remains in the Middle East is ca. 9000 B.P. from the site of Cayönii in southwestern Anatolia. Other early occurrences of dog are from Star Carr, England, 9500 B.P. and surprisingly, Jaguar Cave, Idaho, 10,400 B.P. Remains of dogs in early sites in the Middle East are rare; however, they were not used for food, and their remains may have been buried rather than being scattered within the

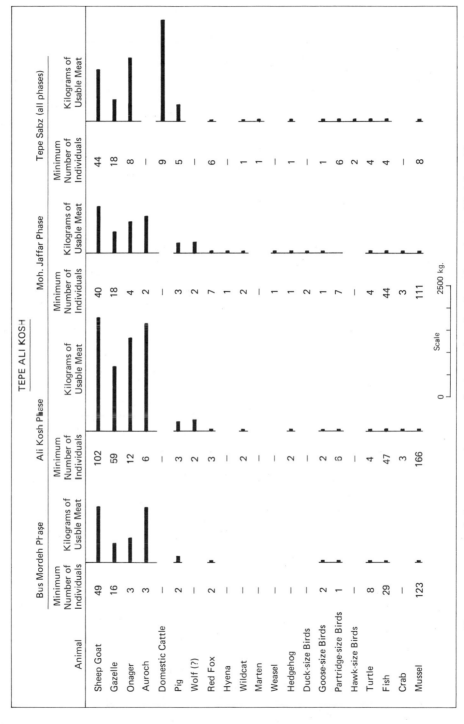

Fig. 10—9 Record of change in preference of food animals utilized at Ali Kosh. (Modified from Flannery 1971:Table 2.)

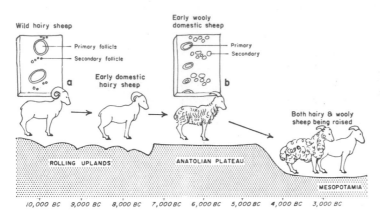

Fig. 10–10 Diagram illustrating steps in the evolution of domestic sheep: a. Section, as seen through a microscope, of skin of wool sheep, showing the arrangement of primary (hair) and secondary (wool) follicles b. Section similarly enlarged of skin of domestic sheep, showing the changed relationship and the change in the size of follicles that accompanied the development of wool. (Flannery 1965:Fig. 4 [after Ryder].)

village. The dog was domesticated from either the wolf or a common dog ancestor. Dog lovers notwithstanding, it is most probable that the ancestor was the wolf, with puppies less than six weeks of age being the initial domesticates. Modern experiments support such a hypothesis.

The pig is clearly descended from the wild pig, but in the absence of organized pig lovers, few question this relationship. The earliest known domestic pigs occur at Cayönii where they form a minor portion of the bone remains. While pigs were domesticated at least as early as 9000 B.P., they rarely occur in village remains in frequencies greater than 5 percent prior to Sumerian times (after 2900 B.C.). Early domestic pigs have been recovered from levels at Jarmo dated 8000 B.P. The distribution of early domestic pigs is irregular, with some areas having them much earlier than others (see Table 10–1). Flannery suggests this is due to the ecological requirements of pigs in that they are not adapted to a pastoral herding economy. Therefore in those regions with a steppe ecology and a practice of seasonal transhumance pigs were not favored.

Sheep as domesticates are early, having been found at Zawi Chemi in levels dated 10,000 B.P. They also occur at Cayönii and probably at Jarmo. The domestication of sheep included selection for the woolly variety. Goats were common at Jarmo. At Ali Kosh in Iranian Khuzistan, goats, especially yearlings, are common in levels dated 9000 B.P. In this site goats are especially important as domesticates, since they: 1. occur outside their native range and 2. occur earlier than the domestic sheep.

Cattle were not domesticated as early as other species, at least according to present knowledge. The earliest evidence of domestic cattle is from the site of Argissa-Maghula in Greece dated ca. 8500 B.P. Whether cattle were first domesticated in southeastern Europe rather than southwestern Asia is as yet unknown. Inasmuch as cattle were domesticated later than sheep and goats, their domestication may have been intentional, perhaps with an interest in their use as draft animals. The earliest evidence we have of the plow is from Warka IV (Mesopotamia) dated ca 5200 B.P. The earliest cattle remains from southwest Asia, from Tepe Sabz in Iranian Khuzistan, are dated 7450 B.P. Further study is required to understand cattle domestication, since the early evidence is widespread and identifies no single center for their domestication.

Erich Isaac (1971:453) proposes a series of arguments supporting an agricultural origin for cattle domestication: 1. Nomadic herders use harnesses modified after those of nearby farmers. 2. No wild bovines, whose range was primarily in the area of nomadic hunters, have been domesticated. Those bovines domesticated lived in the same area as agricultural peoples. 3. No deer or elk species was domesticated, except reindeer, and they were not domesticated early. 4. The feeding of captured animals was dependent upon the plant food surpluses of an agricultural people.

THE ERA OF INCIPIENT CULTIVATION AND DOMESTICATION

Braidwood and Reed (1957) define *incipient agriculture,* with or without animal domestication, as a mixed food-getting activity with specialized food collecting. They conceptualize incipient agriculture as having been primarily concerned with small grains, in open field and seasonbound situations, in temperate parkland, or in open woodland.

Incipient agriculture does not seem to have survived to the present: either it developed in antiquity into the succeeding full-fledged village farming community level, or it became extinct or was subsequently "captured" by an intrusive village-farming community level (Braidwood and Reed 1957:22).

Unfortunately there is a further qualification to this scheme; incipient agriculture is difficult to isolate archaeologically. They state:

The really weak link in the chain is the second "era" that of incipient agriculture and animal domestication. This phase is so weakly represented archaeologically that there is not yet truly conclusive evidence of either "incipient agriculture" or of "incipient animal domestication" (Braidwood and Reed 1957:21).

Archaeological evidence of this era is difficult to produce. In part this is a semantic problem, since once true domestication can be proved to have occurred, it is no longer "incipient." Further, the remains from incipient sites are not particularly different from those sites occupied by specialized food collectors. Since no such cultures exist today, we are left without recourse to the study of modern analogous societies. We may not even rely on the presence of specific artifact types, for the tools developed by food collectors for food collecting could as well have been used by early cultivators. Our best candidates for cultures of the incipient era are the Natufian culture of Palestine (Fig. 10–11) and the peoples of Karim Shahir (Fig. 10–12).

Natufian remains are found in numerous caves as well as a few open sites. Most of the findings are of stone tools. The major implements suggestive of incipient cultivators are geometric sickle flints (microliths), showing the

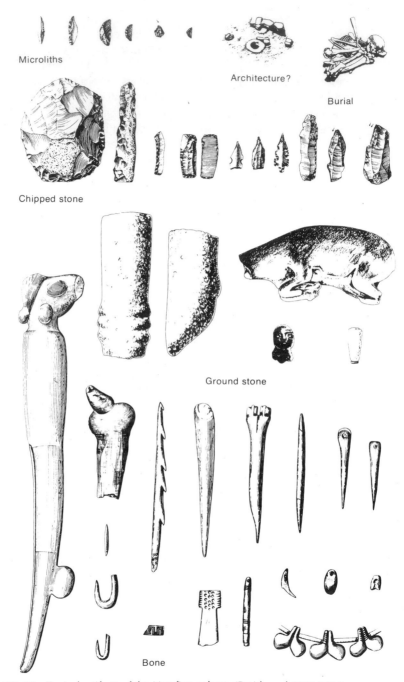

Microliths

Architecture?

Burial

Chipped stone

Ground stone

Bone

Fig. 10–11   Typical artifacts of the Natufian culture. (Braidwood 1967:105.)

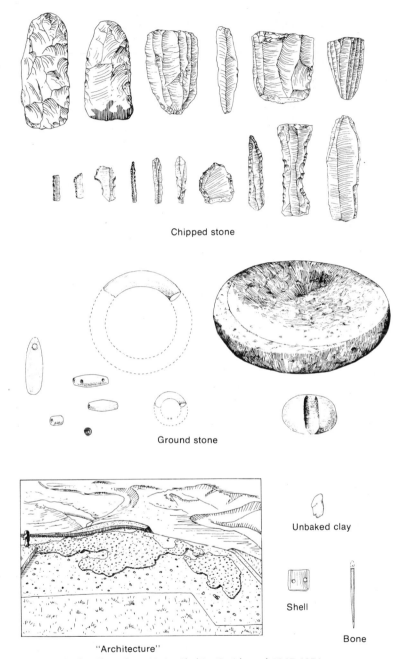

Chipped stone

Ground stone

"Architecture"

Unbaked clay

Shell

Bone

Fig. 10–12 Typical artifacts from Karim Shahir. (Braidwood 1967:107.)

characteristic sheen or polish from the cutting of grain. Other tools include mortars and pestles, possibly used for seed grinding. Bone tools include sickle shafts, points, harpoons, fishhooks, awls, pins, needles, beads, and pendants. Food bones from the sites are typical of those associated with hunters: deer, gazelle, bear, boar, and even leopard and hyena. The domestic dog is reported but has not been verified. Architecture is confined to low stone walls built in the caves. Flexed burials are present, often with beads or other grave offerings. The Natufian dates from about 8000 B.C. which would be an acceptable date for people at the incipient level.

The assemblage from Karim Shahir is best known from open-air semi-permanent encampments, although one cave site is known. Two of the excavated sites, Zawi Chemi Shanidar and Ganj-i-Dareh have been dated 8900 ± 300 B.C. and 8450 ± 150 B.C., respectively. The earliest levels at Ali Kosh, while related in artifact content, are probably not quite so early. Another related site, M'lefaat, has yet to be excavated in detail. These sites are related and provide additional evidence of the incipient level. The finds at Karim Shahir (Fig. 10–12) possess numerous geometric flints but few sickle bladelets. Grinding stones are present. Other artifacts include stone ornaments—beads, pendants, rings, and bracelets. Bone tools feature simple points and needles. Two unfired, possible animal effigies of clay were also found. The kinds of plants consumed are not known, as no vegetal remains were recovered. The bones most common are those of the species that were later domesticated—sheep, goat, cattle, horse, and wolf—but proof that domestication had already occurred at Karim Shahir or Zawi Chemi is lacking. At Ali Kosh the earliest levels contain evidence of domesticated wheat and barley, with wild goats possibly having been herded.

We have not answered our question regarding the validity of the assignment of these sites to the incipient level. The evidence is suggestive but most of the diet probably was supplied by specialized food collecting. Perhaps the one diagnostic of the incipient level was the fact that these peoples had yet to realize or conceptualize the significance of true food production and how it could modify their lives. Perhaps a few individuals could glimpse the changes to come, but the majority were unaware that they were embarking on a "revolution" in human culture.

THE ERA OF PRIMARY VILLAGE FARMING COMMUNITIES

Our next latest evidence from the Middle East is a clear-cut example of a primary farming village. Jarmo, in the Kurdish hills of Iraq, has some 27 feet of village deposits with a dozen layers indicative of architectural renovation. Jarmo is a one period site not covering an extended length of time. It has been dated at 6750 ± 200 B.C. Thus there is a time gap between Karim Shahir and the full-fledged village era represented by Jarmo. What lies within this 2000-year gap has yet to be determined by archaeologists. At Jarmo we have evidence of barley, two kinds of wheat, domestic goats, sheep, dogs, and in the latest levels, pigs. The site itself covers some four acres, which is indicative of how the economy influenced population. One new trait (Fig. 10–13) was that houses of several rooms were made of puddled adobe walls built on stone foundations. Stone bowls were used for food and ovens of clay were used for baking. Pottery appears in the upper one third of the site. In the earlier levels the appearance of pottery was presaged by clay figurines of both humans and animals. Braidwood suggests the village looked much like modern villages in the same region. Using this modern analogy, the 20 or so houses occupied at any one time in prehistoric Jarmo probably housed about 150 people.

By no means were all the new cultural developments universal or contemporaneous. For example, a similar village in Iran, Sarab, has sheep, goats, wheat, stone bowls, clay figurines, and so forth, but the houses were no more than reed huts.

Somewhat later than Jarmo is the Hassuna assemblage dated 5100 and 5600 B.C. ± 250 years. The Hassuna materials are well known, having been fully excavated (Fig. 10–14). A major development was the increase in architectural skill, although walls were still made of puddled mud. Pottery was by now made in several different styles, and decorative pottery painting had been introduced. In contrast to Jarmo, where the tradition of excellent stone tool manufacture persisted from earlier times, the Hassuna stone tools are poorly made. We assume that with increased reliance on produced foods, the old stone tool types became less functional, and new forms, in ground stone and pottery, fulfilled the necessary functions.

Other sites, not to be described here in detail, fill out our knowledge of the village farming era. We can identify as an important site Jericho near the Dead Sea, which is dated 9700–7450 B.P. and has mud-walled houses. Also of importance at Jericho was a large building which has been termed a shrine, a storage structure, or even a possible watchtower. Specialized architecture signals the rise of organized religion, featuring priest specialists and a formalized set of beliefs. At Cayönii, in southeastern Turkey, an assemblage similar to that at Jarmo, but without pottery, has been discovered. Houses with stone foundations and stone paved floors are dated about 7000 B.C. The economy at Cayönii featured reliance on sheep, goat, and pig, and a primitive, possibly not cultivated, wheat. Two sites in southwestern Anatolia, Hacilar and Suberde, have early levels dated 8700–8450 B.P. The sites feature mud brick walls, plastered floors, and cultivated wheat and barley. Another major site in the same general region, Catal Hüyük, features outstanding preservation. The most unusual feature is architectural decoration consisting of murals and sculptured reliefs. Other items of importance are pottery, clay and stone figurines, stone tools of flint and obsidian, and some traces of weaving. The C-14 dates from Catal Hüyük average 8700 B.P. Cultivated plants include three types of wheat, naked barley, and a variety of legumes.

By 8000 B.P. the village farming level had expanded to include most of the Middle East. There was still in progress the domestication of individual

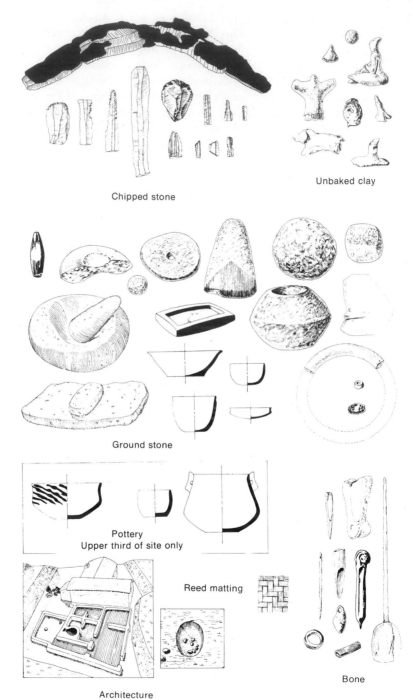

Chipped stone

Unbaked clay

Ground stone

Pottery
Upper third of site only

Reed matting

Bone

Architecture

Fig. 10–13 Typical artifacts from Jarmo. (Braidwood 1967:119.)

Fig. 10–14 Artifacts from Hassuna. (Braidwood 1967:123.)

species with concurrent genetic change and mutation. Although we may now attribute true food production to these peoples, they were practicing regional adaptations rather than a single integrated economy. Other traits, such as architecture and pottery, were developing at differential rates in the different regions.

SETTLEMENT TYPES

The Neolithic as a cultural stage embodies three major attributes: food production (which we have already discussed), sedentary life, and villages. These three variables have been proved not to be necessarily interdependent (Flannery 1973). In contrast to Braidwood's simplistic scheme of three eras, we now know that in the Middle East, sedentary communities dating as early as 8000 B.C. existed without any evidence of domesticated plants or animals. As we have also mentioned, the transition to full food production was a gradual process encompassing many patterns of use of different species. Flannery (1973) suggests that a similar pattern may have led to the development of the village; villages are the result of not one but more than one sequences in the evolution of social systems. He cites the fact that food collectors and hunters utilize at least two different systems, a base camp of 15–40 persons from which small hunting parties of 3–8 males foray, and macrobands of 15–20 persons occupied alternatively with microbands of 2–5 persons—here the groups' size is seasonally adjusted to food availability.

In his analysis Flannery suggests that the causal factors for sedentary life are not agriculture but the building of permanent facilities and the establishment of heriditary ownership of critical core areas of high resource potential (Flannery 1973:R1–6). He further sets up ideal village types: 1. A compound or homestead of small circular houses and 2. a true village of somewhat larger rectangular houses (Flannery 1973:R1–7). These types are further characterized:

a. On the average, roughly 10m² of house floor space are available per individual in societies of Neolithic type.
b. Circular dwellings tend to correlate (at a statistically significant level) with nomadic or semi-nomadic societies; rectangular dwellings tend to correlate with fully sedentary societies (although numerous exceptions occur).
c. Rectangular structures replace circular ones through time in many archaeological areas around the world (although reversals of this trend occur).
d. While circular structures may be easier to construct (and often portable), it is much easier to add units to rectangular structures (Flannery 1973:R1–7, 8).

The social correlates of the compound or homestead are several. The huts are primarily designed to house only one or two persons; for example, a man and wife, a wife, a man and one or two cows, and so on. The huts have further specialized use, for some are not residences but have storage, cooking, or other functions. Other typical features are that the total population may be less than the number of huts; the huts are arranged in a circular pattern with a central joint-use work area; and the food storage units are for the joint use of compound members. All of these features tend to deemphasize the nuclear family as the central social unit, replacing it with other residence or work groups.

The village of rectangular houses ranges from what have been termed "hamlets" with less than 100 persons to larger communities up to 1000 in population. Hamlets are said to lack public or ceremonial structures, but that distinction is tenous at best. Distinctive characteristics of villages are that the units are designed for families, each unit has its own storage facilities, and growth was through simple accretion of contiguous rooms—therefore room clusters are indicative of family structure. Of greatest importance are the communal strengths of the village as contrasted with the compound. The village is made up of nucleated households, with crosscutting ties based on work parties, social exchange relationships, and ceremonial responsibilities. The result is a socially integrated society much stronger than that of the compound. Advantages of the village in comparison with the compound are several: the ability to intensify food production through cooperative labor, the ability to grow to larger population size through the availability of cohesive social institutions, and the increased defensibility of the nucleated households. The differential accumulation of surplus food by certain households leads to social stratification, and nucleated houses lead to urbanism—both features emphasized later in the archaeological record.

THE SPREAD OF VILLAGE FARMING

Although the cultural pattern we have described was not fully integrated, these ideas were of compelling importance. After 8000 B.P. they began to be diffused beyond the limits of the Middle East. The isochronic lines in Figure 10–15 documenting this spread are based on current radiocarbon dates. With the acquisition of new radiocarbon dates, the precise location of a specific isochronic line may well be modified. Such plots help orient our thinking concerning the major events happening at the time. The spread of Neolithic life was differential in rate. It moved more rapidly up the major river valleys such as the Danube. Other areas with less to offer agriculturalists, such as the cold dry steppes and deserts, were actual barriers. If we plot the isochronic lines on a graph (Fig. 10–16), we are able to more clearly perceive this differential rate of spread. According to Braidwood (1967), the colonization of Europe by farmers was made up of a combination of several processes, including: 1. The actual movement of farming peoples from the Middle East outward; 2. the spread of objects and ideas from the Middle East beyond the actual migration routes of immigrant farmers; and 3. modifications of these objects and ideas by the indigenous European Mesolithic peoples. The earliest farming communities in England and the Scandinavian countries date some 3000 years after farming appears in Greece. We thus know the transition to a farming way of life in Europe was gradual; therefore the change should not be termed due to "migration." The population movement we refer to most likely consisted of small villages of farmer folk moving a few miles at a time, settling down and building a new village. Perhaps such a movement occurred only once or twice

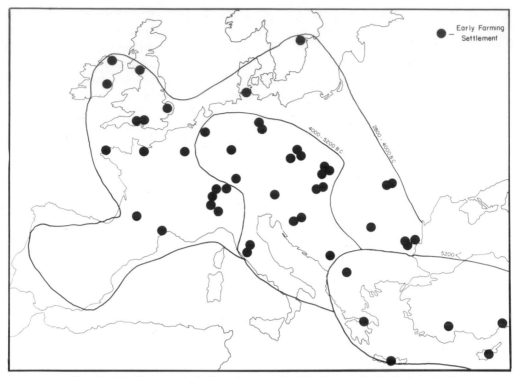

Fig. 10–15   The spread of village farming. (Modified from J. G. D. Clark 1969:Fig. 4.)

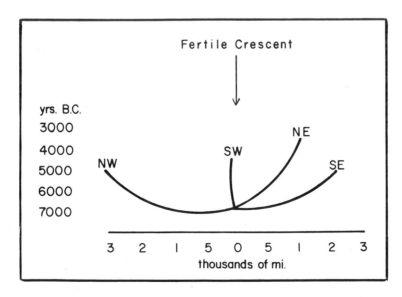

Fig. 10–16 The spread of Neolithic culture in time and space.

in an individual's lifetime. If we assume a generation interval of 20 years, then 150 generations (3000 years) were required to move the 1500 miles from Greece to Britain. This represents 10 miles per generation, or only a half mile per year. One of the factors inhibiting a more rapid spread of farming throughout Europe was the presence of forest. We have ample evidence from pollen diagrams that Neolithic man carried out major forest clearing (Fig. 10–17).

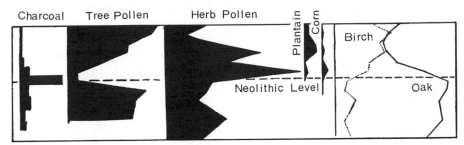

Fig. 10–17 Fluctuations in charcoal and fossil pollen resulting from Neolithic colonization; Ordrup Mose, Denmark. (J. G. D. Clark 1952:Fig. 44 [after Iverson].)

While the spread of farming and domestication across Europe was occurring, the peoples of the Middle East continued to make further progress. Although domestication first occurred in the Middle East, we do not imply that domestication occurred only once in the history of man. Such developments took place in numerous nuclear areas at different times in the past. The Middle Eastern developments are significant from two major standpoints. Domestication occurred there early, and the particular complex of plants, animals, and their associated care patterns form the tradition ancestral to Western Civilization. Other nuclear areas of importance include southeastern Asia, with the most important species being rice, chicken, water buffalo, and elephant. Africa has a whole complex of root and grain crops that were probably independently domesticated in the savannaland south of the Sahara. Domesticates include millet, kaffir corn, and sorghum. The New World has a completely independent line of development, with corn, beans, and squash being domesticated in Mexico. Peru was another major hearth, adding the potato, various fruits, quinoa, oca, llama, alpaca, vicuna, and guinea pig. Tropical South America added manioc, the tapioca plant. Other major plants such as breadfruit, coconut, pineapple, various nuts, and bananas began to be cultivated for food in different places at different times. For purposes of classification perhaps rather than through any inherent logic, we archaeologists term *Neolithic* those cultures which are historically related to the Middle Eastern Revolution. We are well aware that there was a New World "Neolithic" period, but we call it by another name—the *Formative*. A similar situation exists in sub-Saharan Africa and in other regions. In a broad definition we would state that the Neolithic is a way of life featuring food production through agriculture and animal husbandry, with the people living a sedentary life in small permanent villages located near their fields. Further characteristics include handcrafts and the initiation of craft specialties.

NEOLITHIC MANIFESTATIONS IN EUROPE

The earliest agriculturalists in Europe, according to Piggott (1965:44), practiced a cultural pattern diffused from the Middle East. By 5000 B.C. these patterns had spread westward to southeastern Europe. A basic feature of the cultural pattern was villages or small towns made up of mud-brick dwellings—a permanent settlement pattern supported by a stable agricultural base. The social system included a headman, an assembly of elders, and a body of citizenry. This pattern endured in eastern Europe for the next 3000 years, and according to Piggott (1965:44), this was in essence a western province of Middle Eastern culture. Simultaneously, however, there emerged unique "European" patterns. One of these was the long-term trait of individual houses rather than the Mesopotamian style of contiguous units. Added to the introduced construction mode of mud walls were wattle and daub construction. Roofs were also different in being pitched instead of flat. We are not merely speculating here, for preserved models of house types clearly illustrate the pitched roofs. The causes of these changes included environment, since housing developed in the arid Middle East had to be adapted to the colder, wetter European climate. One characteristic in common between the eastern European and Mesopotamian settlements was the formation of tells, the layered sequence of prior settlements forming a mound. Through time there was a change in house form from square to the later oblong house with a porch—the megaron type. Typical villages were of 50 to 60 such houses with a population in the vicinity of 300. Piggott (1965:47–49) estimates the amount of grain consumed by such a group would require a total cropland of about 430 acres or 7 acres per family.

Settlements of these Starčevo peoples (Fig. 10–18) occurred throughout the peninsula of Greece and north into Bulgaria as far as the Danube. North of the Danube, they extended up the valleys of several tributary rivers—the Tisza, Maros, Olta, Seret, and Prut. The economy was mixed, with shifting cultivation combined with the keeping of cattle, sheep, goats, and pigs. Hunting and fishing were also important. They raised one-corn wheat and millet, both plants indigenous to the region. The agricultural system was probably of the slash and burn type—the clearing and planting of small plots within a forest for several years, followed by several years of fallowing before replanting. Crops were stored in small clay-lined silos. Hunting was done with slings and fishing with nets. Agricultural implements included an adaptation of the Middle Eastern type of sickle. Grains were processed with grinding stones, and ovens were used for baking. Adzes were used for woodworking. Pottery, both undecorated and painted, was abundant. Trade indicates the existence of an intervillage and

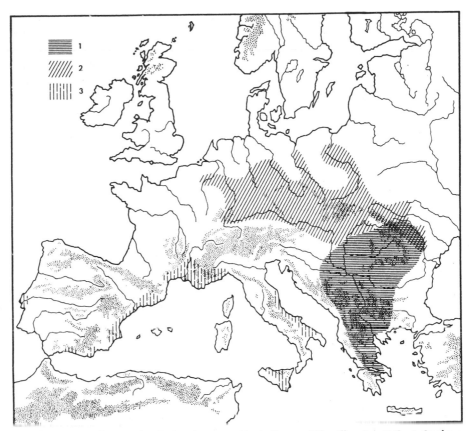

Fig. 10–18 Distribution of agricultural communities in Europe, fifth millennium B.C.: *1.* Starĉevo and allied cultures; *2.* Linear Pottery culture; *3.* Impressed Pottery cultures. (Piggott 1965:Fig. 26.)

regional communication system. Major items traded were ornaments of *Spondylus* shell from the Mediterranean and obsidian from Hungary and Transylvania. Religion is suggested by the female statuettes and so-called cult rooms found in the farmhouses. Clay stamps similar to the Mesopotamian stone seals are known, but their use was probably for body painting.

The distribution of farming spread up the Danube into central Europe then to the north and west. A major attraction was the deep loess soils so favorable to agriculture. We may view this spread of agricultural peoples as a *colonization*. It was marked with forest clearance and the spread of a distinctive pottery style termed *Linear Pottery* (Fig. 10–18).

Pigs, goats, sheep, and cattle were kept but do not seem to have been major sources of food. Also neglected were the hunting resources of the region. These peoples practiced slash and burn agriculture with barley, beans, lentils, peas, flax, and three kinds of wheat—one-corn, emmer, and hexaploid. The major agricultural tool was the hoe.

Another innovation was the introduction of the longhouse. Villages included up to 20 such houses. They were large, with gabled halls, and walls of wattle and daub construction. The houses were 18 to 22 feet wide and from 30 to 130 feet in length. Villages had from 200 persons to perhaps 600. The occupants of the longhouses were probably some form of extended family. No matter what the exact social form, it must have differed considerably from the small-house settlements of the Starčevo peoples.

Adzes were used for woodworking. Pottery was in simple gourdlike forms. Decoration was in spirals, meanders, and linear patterns. Trade was carried on between villages, with major trade items being *Spondylus* shells and stone adze blades. The absence of fortifications suggests that warfare was not common. Other cultural absences include the lack of status and rank, funeral ritual, and religious elaboration.

The longhouse structure was not only common to central Europe but is also known from the forest-steppe region of the Ukraine where about 3000 B.C. we have the Tripolye culture (Fig. 10–19). The settlements have from 30 to 50 houses, each capable of housing up to 20 people. The culture is more eastern in its associations rather than being affiliated with the Linear Pottery culture. Unique aspects of the settlement pattern are baked clay foundations for the houses and occasionally the arrangement of houses into a circular plan. In this region the settlements were built on promontories surrounded by defensive earthworks. Most importantly the longhouse plan again signifies that the Middle Eastern village plan and social structure were limited to southeastern Europe.

We have mentioned the early dichotomy of the longhouse and tell settlements. To the south along the Mediterranean coast there was an east-to-west spread of a separate cultural tradition—the Impressed Pottery culture. This culture is known by its distinctive pottery decorated with impressions made with the serrated edge of a cardium shell. The distribution of the culture is almost exclusively coastal, with sites located within 50 miles of the coast (see Fig. 10–18). The sites are found along the Mediterranean from Italy west to Spain. Most sites consist of caves rather than constructed villages. Since numerous sites occur on offshore islands, we assume these people possessed boats.

Their economy featured herding of sheep, goats, and cattle, and they also cultivated barley, hunted, and fished. The bow and arrow was their principal hunting weapon. Trading by sea, especially of obsidian from the Lipari Islands, was another important economic pursuit. The initial Neolithic immigrants to the region probably amalgamated with the indigenous Mesolithic peoples to produce this distinctive regionally oriented culture.

According to Piggott (1965:57), after 3000 B.C. Neolithic culture spread inland to France, Switzerland, and the Italian lake district. In this region the settlement type is termed *lake dwellings*. When initially discovered, such pile dwellings built along lake shores were thought to represent villages built over water. Subsequent research indicates that most were originally built on boggy ground along lake shores; for example, Aichbühl, Württemburg (Fig. 10–20). Subsequent peat growth has frequently covered the village remains so that

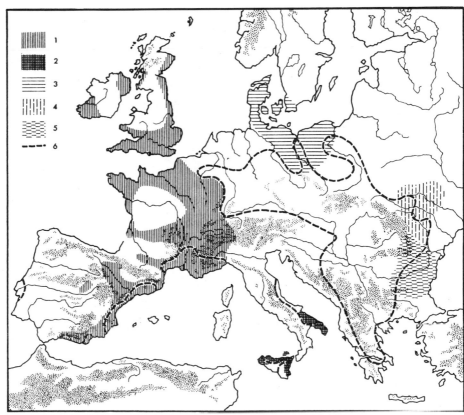

Fig. 10–19 Distribution of agricultural communities in Europe, late fourth–early third millennium B.C. *1.* "Western" cultures; *2.* South Italian-Sicilian cultures; *3.* TRB cultures; *4.* Tripolye culture; *5.* Boian cultures; *6.* area of settlement from fifth millennium B.C. (Piggott 1965:Fig. 28.)

today they are found within bogs. A major feature of such sites is their excellent preservation of materials including perishable artifacts. The houses probably housed a nuclear family, for they were about 10 by 20 feet and included two rooms and a porch. Up to 75 houses are known from such villages, with a population estimated at from 120 to 370 (Piggott 1965:58).

Fig. 10–20 Reconstruction of a Neolithic lakeside village, Aichbühl, Württemburg. (J. G. D. Clark 1952: Fig. 74 [after Schmidt].)

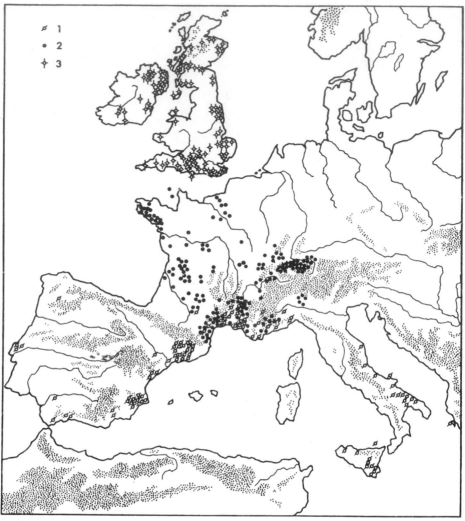

Fig. 10–21 Distribution of main sites of *1*. Impressed Ware cultures, from fifth millenium B.C. onward; *2*. Chassey-Cortaillod cultures, fourth–third millenium B.C.; *3*. Windmill Hill and allied cultures, late fourth–early second millennium B.C. (Piggott 1965:Fig. 27.)

The Western Neolithic Tradition

Cultural manifestations assigned to this tradition extend from Spain to Britain. They include the Spanish Almeria culture, the Dolmen culture of Portugal, the Chassey culture of France, the Cortaillod culture of Switzerland, and the Windmill Hill culture of England (see Figs. 10–19 and 10–21). One hypothesis proposes that Neolithic peoples forced out of North Africa by increasing dessication influenced the above groups and thus led to a distinctive Western culture pattern. An opposing fact is that the Neolithic peoples of Western

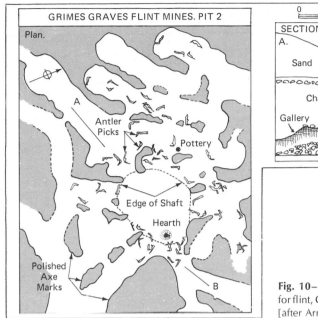

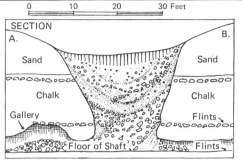

Fig. 10–22 Mines exploited by Neolithic peoples for flint, Grimes Graves, England. (Piggott 1954:Fig. 7 [after Armstrong].)

Europe continued using, to a great extent, cultural traits derived from the prior Mesolithic inhabitants of the region.

Basic traits in this Western Neolithic tradition include leathery pots, lake-side villages, considerable hunting and stock breeding, the mining of flint (Fig. 10–22), and the use of axes rather than adzes. Wheat was grown and the domestic animals were cattle and pigs with a few goats and sheep. Axes were manufactured in what amounts to actual factories. Burials were important, with the typical pattern being simultaneous collective burials under earthen mounds as long as 300 feet (Fig. 10–23). The bones or cremated bones of the dead were heaped together at the wider end of the mound on top of a low platform of chalk or within a pile of flint nodules. The total number of burials is small, 25 being the maximum number buried in one mound. These burials, because of their associated mounds, probably represent the interments of chiefs and their families.

The settlement of northern Europe by farmers was late; for example, 2650 B.C. in Denmark. The region was cold and damp and was not particularly favorable for agriculture; therefore farming was not introduced until after all of central and southern Europe had been occupied. The initial farmers in the north tried the same agricultural practices that had been perfected farther south, with little success. The subsequent farmers of the region went through several periods of economic adjustment before suitable crops such as barley and rye and the techniques for their cultivation were adopted. Meanwhile at the same time cultural developments in the Middle East had progressed to the level of true urbanism.

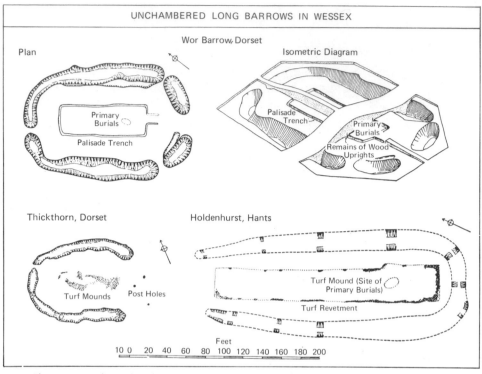

Fig. 10–23 Plans of English long barrows. (Piggott 1954:Fig. 8 [after Pitt-Rivers].)

We have not reviewed in detail the cultural attributes of a number of named European cultures, such as TRB, Boian, and South Italian-Sicilian. We have attempted to portray an impression of early agriculturalists in Europe, a peasant society marked with some similarities but simultaneously indicative of several major sets of influences or cultural patterns. In other words, the spread of agricultural life in Europe was diffused in several different directions and according to several basic patterns. The details of each cultural variant form the subject matter of a course in European prehistory.

By the third millennium B.C. the European agriculturalists were subsisting through the cultivation of wheat, barley, peas, lentils, beans, apples, and flax; the seeds were used for food and the fiber used in textiles and basketry. Cattle were kept and fed leaves of the elm tree, among other foods. A further development at this time was the building of monumental stone-lined, chambered tombs indicative of a major religion, one we will discuss in Chapter 12.

By 2500 B.C. we have reached the end of an era in European prehistory; the agricultural colonization had ended and peasant farmers were established all over Europe. Simultaneously in northern and western Europe there continued in existence nonagricultural hunters and fishers, a tradition which persisted for several millennia. Meanwhile we have had in the Middle East the development of civilization, the first harbingers of which, copper implements, appear in the Mediterranean by 2500 B.C.

THE NEOLITHIC IN OTHER REGIONS

We will not be able here to review the Neolithic developments in other regions in detail. Like every other chapter in this book, our study of the Neolithic could be expanded to an entire semester course. It should be adequate to point out that many other early Neolithic cultures are well known from archaeological evidence. Such cultures include the Japanese Jomon culture; the Ordos region of north China, home of the Yang Shao peasants; the Neolithic peoples of the Indus Valley; the Badarian culture of the Nile Valley of Egypt; the Shaheinab culture of the Nilotic Sudan, and others (see Fig. 10–17). Generally such outlying Neolithic cultures were belated; their cultural development lagged behind that in the Middle Eastern heartland. A further complication is that by the time such peoples adopted a Neolithic economy, they were simultaneously offered traits such as metalworking which developed later and also diffused from the Middle East. We will review these subsequent developments: towns, organized religion, metalworking, and so on in the next chapter.

REFERENCES

Binford, L. R., 1968, "Post-Pleistocene Adaptations," in S. R. Binford and L. R. Binford (eds.), *New Perspectives in Archaeology*, pp. 313–341. Chicago: Aldine.

Braidwood, R. J., 1967, *Prehistoric Men*, 7th ed. Glenview, Ill.: Scott, Foresman.

———, and C. A. Reed, 1957, "The Achievement and Early Consequences of Food Production: A Consideration of the Archaeological and Natural-Historical Evidence," *Cold Springs Harbor Symposium on Quantitative Biology* 22.19–32.

Butzer, K. W., 1971, "Agricultural Origins in the Near East as a Geographical Problem," in Struever, pp. 209–235.

Clark, J. G. D., 1952, *Prehistoric Europe: The Economic Basis*. London: Methuen.

———, 1969, *World Prehistory: A New Outline*. London: Cambridge University Press.

Daniel, G., 1965a, "The Ecology of Early Food Production in Mesopotamia," *Science* 147:1247–1256.

———, 1965b, *The First Civilizations*. New York: Crowell.

Flannery, K. V., 1965, "The Ecology of Early Food Production in Mesopotamia," *Science* 147:1247–1256.

———, 1968, "Archaeological Systems Theory and Early Mesoamerica," in B.J. Meggers (ed.), *Anthropological Archaeology in the Americas*. Washington, D.C.: Anthropological Society of Washington.

———, 1971, "Origins and Ecological Effects of Early Domestication in Iran and the Near East," in Struever, pp. 50–79.

———, 1973, "The Origins of the Village as a Settlement Type in Mesoamerica and the Near East: A Comparative Study," in Ruth Tringham (ed.), *Ecology and Agricultural Settlements*, Book 3. Andover, Mass.: Warner Modular Publications, pp. R1-1–R1-31.

Harlan, J. R., and D. Zohary, 1966, Distribution of Wild Wheats and Barleys. *Science* 153:1074–1080.

Hole, F., K. V. Flannery, and J. Neely, 1969, "Prehistory and Human Ecology of the Deh Luran Plain." Ann Arbor: Museum of Anthropology, University of Michigan, Memoir No. 1.

Isaac, E., 1971, "On the Domestication of Cattle," in Struever, pp. 101–121.

Meyers, J. T., 1971, "The Origins of Agriculture: An Evaluation of Three Hypotheses," in Struever, pp. 101–121.

Naroll, R., 1962, "Floor Area and Settlement Population," *American Antiquity* 27:587–589.

Piggott, S., 1954, *The Neolithic Cultures of the British Isles*. London: Cambridge University Press.

———, 1965, *Ancient Europe*. Chicago: Aldine.

Reed, C. A., 1971, "Animal Domestication in the Prehistoric Near East," in Struever, pp. 423–450.

Struever, S., (ed.), 1971, *Prehistoric Agriculture*. New York: Natural History Press.

Wright, H. E., Jr., 1970, "Environmental Changes and the Origin of Agriculture in the Near East," *Bioscience* 20(4):210–212.

The Development of Civilization

WHAT IS CIVILIZATION?—SOME DEFINITIONS

Through time most societies grow in complexity. Superimposed upon this long-term trend are subdivisions arbitrarily defined by archaeologists. These classifications are based upon trends in major societal characteristics, a higher level of abstraction than the day-to-day activities of prehistoric peoples or the artifacts they produced. Civilization may thus be viewed as a level of cultural attainment. In several major regions of the world, including Mesopotamia, coastal Peru, Mesoamerica, and China, cultures progressed through a similar set of levels. Thus civilization would appear to be an evolutionary result of a certain set of enabling or permissive conditions. Julian Steward (1971) has identified these evolutionary levels. In Steward's scheme the era of Incipient Agriculture is followed by a Formative era, a Florescent era, and finally by the era of Militarism, Fusion or Conquest, and Cyclical Empires.

In examining the usage of these terms, Robert M. Adams (1971:574) defines the Formative as referring to assemblages which possess neither full-time craft specialists nor substantial concentrations of wealth.

Adams also presents a formal definition (1971:589):

Formative. Adoption and spread of typical upland village subsistence pattern, and perhaps also of its corresponding forms of social organization. Sedentary agriculture with digging-stick and hoe cultivation of wheat and barley, domestication of sheep, goats, and probably cattle, ceramics. Communities remained small and relatively uniform in size and composition but increased in number, spreading into the alluvium with the introduction of irrigation techniques. "Fertility cult," small shrines.

Relying on New World data, Willey and Phillips (1958:146) define the Formative:

. . . by the presence of agriculture, or any other subsistence economy of comparable effectiveness, and by the successful integration of such an economy into well-established, sedentary village life. . . . Pottery-making, weaving, stone-carving, and a specialized ceremonial architecture are usually associated with these American Formative cultures.

The Florescent era, according to Adams (1971:574) is characterized by the coherence of several periods of growth during which a distinctively civilized pattern of living emerged out of a folk village substratum. His formal definition, based on Mesopotamian data, follows:

Florescent. Emphasis shifted to the lowlands with the development of plow-irrigation agriculture. Expansion of technology and appearance of full-time craft specialization; introduction of potter's wheel, cart and chariot, sail, copper metallurgy, early phases in the development of writing. Rapid growth in concentration of surpluses, largely in hands of priestly heirarchies, with consequest building of monumental religious structures in town-urban centers. Beginnings of warfare (Adams 1971:590).

The New World counterpart of the Florescent era is the Classic stage defined by Willey and Phillips (1958:182):

. . . the criteria of the Classic stage are, to a large extent, qualitative and relative rather than quantitative and absolute. We listed such qualities as excellence in the great arts, climax in religious architecture, and general florescence in material culture. We adhere to these definitions, but we wish to add one more, which overrides them in importance. The Classic stage in New World native cultures marks the beginning of urbanism.

The Dynastic or Militaristic era features little change in subsistence patterns with some elaboration in crafts. The major changes lay in the rise of militarism and the assumption of political power by secular authorities. Major characteristics of the era include increased control over the supply and production of goods and the growing importance and privilege of the ruling class. The latter are marked by the construction of palaces, special tombs, and the accumulation and conspicuous consumption of luxury goods. Population increase led in part to the wars of conquest and the rise of empires.

Adams' (1971:590) definition of the Dynastic era includes:

Separation and institutionalization of secular-political and religious-economic controls in true urban centers—the appearance of kingship and the city-state. Emphasis on fortifications and growing importance of warfare, culminating in Sargonic conquests. Slow growth of private capital in trading and manufacturing, but at the end of the era temples probably still dominated the economic life. Rationalization and expansion of handicraft production; bronze metallurgy, refinement of cuneiform script.

The New World counterpart of the Dynastic is the Postclassic defined by Willey and Phillips (1958:193) as "marked by the breakdown of the old regional styles of the Classic stage, by a continuing or increased emphasis upon urban living, and inferentially , by tendencies toward militarism and secularism." This is the period of the city and city-state, with pyramids, temples, and palaces making up a political and religious center.

Although we have referred to the sequence of these eras as being similar in both the Old World and New World, we should stress that there is nothing automatic about the sequence of development. Perhaps the best way to illustrate this fact is to reproduce here a chart prepared by Julian Steward which documents the times of appearance of some of the major aspects of civilization in various regions (Table 11–1). Having reviewed these definitions of civilization we will now proceed to review the specific history of development of several such civilizations.

CHRONOLOGY

Dating of the sequences established for the various civilizations is based upon a variety of techniques. There is the sequence of ceramic types established through cemetery excavations in Egypt by Sir Flinders Petrie (1904); the relative sequences established through detailed excavations of stratified sites, especially the Mesopotamian tells; radiocarbon dates; the Egyptian king lists tied to historically recorded dates; calendrical dates established by correlation of ancient calendars with modern ones; archaeomagnetic dates in Mesoamerica; and even a few tree ring dates for Mesoamerica and Turkey. The dating methods continue to be improved and revisions are continually in preparation. A recent discovery was the fluctuations in C-14 content of the atmosphere through time, resulting in revision of published dates (Table 11–2). Chronology is thus a continuing field of research. In our review of civilizations the important feature is that we are able to develop a sequence for a region and that such a sequence can be correlated with those of other civilizations. This chronology provides us with a tool to infer the direction and timing of cultural traits that were diffused from one region to another. A version of such a chronological chart is presented in Figure 11–1.

Ancient civilizations in the Old World are numerous and range from the famous to the obscure. The earliest developments were in the major river

TABLE 11–1   Stage of First Appearance of Some Aspects of Civilization

	Coastal Peru	Mesoamerica	Mesopotamia	China
Canal Irrigation	Late Formative	Militaristic; possibly Florescent	Formative	Formative
Irrigation Maximum	Florescent (Militaristic in Highland)	Late Militaristic	Militaristic	Late Florescent to Early Militaristic
Population Maximum	Florescent (Militaristic in Highland)	Late Militaristic	Militaristic	Militaristic?
Urbanization	Militaristic	Militaristic; began in Florescent?	Militaristic	Florescent
Fortifications	Late Formative	End of Florescent	Late Florescent or Early Militaristic	Florescent
Raiding	Late Formative	Florescent	Florescent	Florescent
Wars of Conquest	End of Florescent	Militaristic	Militaristic	End of Florescent
Private Enterprise (land, production, commerce)	Negligible	Militaristic Merchants in Florescent?	Militaristic	Late Florescent to Early Militaristic
Bronze Tools	Militaristic	Militaristic	Militaristic	Florescent

(Stewart 1971:619.)

TABLE 11–2 Approximate Mesopotamian Chronology (C-14 dates in parentheses).

B.C.	ERA	SOUTH—ALLUVIUM	NORTH—UPLANDS
		KINGLISTS STRATIGRAPHIC SEQUENCES	STRATIGRAPHIC SEQUENCES
2000	Cyclical Conquests	Ur III (1993±106) Agade	Akkadian
	Dynastic	Proto-Imperial Early Dynastic III, II, I	Early Dynastic
3000	Florescent	Protoliterate d, c, b, a Warka Developed Ubaid (Eridu VII, VI)	Ninevite Gawran Developed Ubaid (Tepe Gawra XII, XIII)
4000	Formative	Early Ubaid Eridu	Early Ubaid (3447±325) Halaf Samarran painted pottery style Hassuna Jarmo (4750±320)
5000	Incipient Agriculture		Karim Shahir
6000	Terminal Food-Gathering		Pale Gawra Zarzi
7000			

(Adams 1971:571.)

valleys such as the Tigris, Euphrates, Indus, Nile, Yangtze, and Yellow (Fig. 11–2). Later civilizations developed in Anatolia, Greece, Italy, Tunisia, Sudan, Ethiopia, and Arabia. We do not have the opportunity here to describe each of these civilizations in detail. We will summarize the Mesopotamian sequence, as well as those of Egypt, the Indus Valley, and North China.

THE MESOPOTAMIAN SEQUENCE

The initial steps in the Mesopotamian development are the Jarmo and Hassuna assemblages. These initiate the Formative era which is terminated by the Early

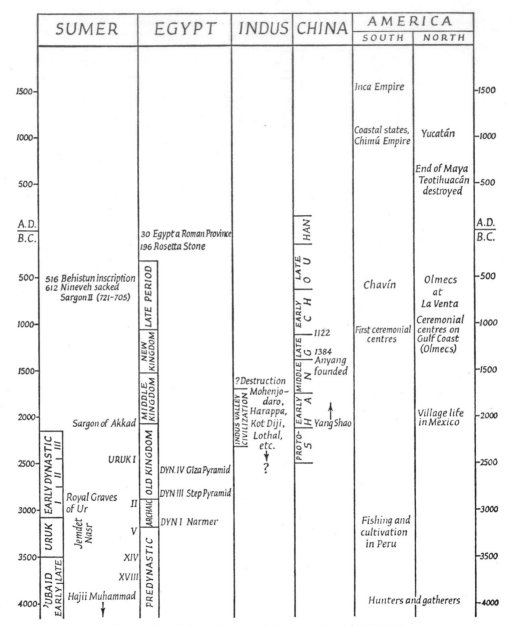

Fig. 11–1 Chronologies of the major early civilizations. (Daniel 1968:11.)

Ubaid period (Fig. 11–1). The Ubaid developments lead into the next major era, the Florescent. Perhaps the most important single event was the shift to irrigation agriculture. The agricultural system in the southern alluvial plains requires planting in September or October, with the major growth period awaiting the melt-water runoff the following April and May. During planting, the streams were at a low level which required that the ditches be dug deeply to permit irrigation. Because the threat of silting of the canals was constant, large forces of organized labor were required to maintain the irrigation system. With irrigation came greater reliance on vegetables, dates, fish, and centralized herds.

At this point we should clarify the nature of the archaeological data available. The Florescent era witnessed the rise of major permanent urban settlements with structures of mud brick. These towns featured continuous occupation over a long period of time, with later settlements built on the remains of earlier ones. The result was a typical Mesopotamian feature: the tell, a hill made up of layer upon layer of stratified urban remains (Fig. 11–3). With the tells being up to 63 feet in height (for example, Ras Shamra) and containing up to 30 distinct cultural layers, it is possible for the archaeologist to reconstruct a nearly continuous record of Mesopotamian culture history.

Advances in social organization in the Florescent era included increasing numbers of craft specialists. For example, the manufacture of copper into simple implements by casting is known from an Early Ubaid level at Tepe Gawra. During the subsequent Warka and Protoliterate periods we have the introduction of smelting and the use of closed molds. From this time on, copper weapons and ornaments increase in frequency and the smith is increasingly a craft specialist. The potter's wheel was introduced in the Warka period. We can doubt the exclusive devotion of these specialists to nonagricultural pursuits, but the tendency was toward increasing specialization through time.

A major feature of the period was the erection of temples (Fig. 11–4). Through time the temples grew in size and complexity, therefore stone masons, setters of mosaic, architects, and so forth were needed as full-time specialists. It has been estimated that the A Ziggurat at Warka required 1500 men five years to build. The size of settlements is not too well known; one estimate of the population of Jemdet Nasr is 2800. During this period population increased more rapidly and to a greater size in the southern alluvial plains than in the uplands of the north. Extensive trade was carried on between the two regions, but by this time the major developments were originating in the south.

The temples are the most impressive features of the time, and a correspondingly great amount of archaeological attention has been devoted to their study. The temples were built of mud brick set occasionally on stone foundations. Part of the underlying foundation consisted of filled-in remains of earlier buildings. These mound foundations gave the temples their commanding setting overlooking the entire community. A flight of steps led up to the long central room which had an offering table at one end and a broad platform at the other. Flanking the central room were smaller rooms. From the latter, ladders led to a higher story and the roof. The exterior was ornamented with projections and recesses.

Although the temples were of obvious importance, there is some doubt as to their functioning in the society. The temple buildings were used to store

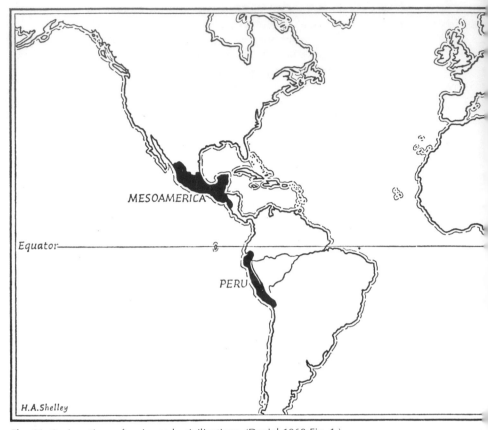

Fig. 11–2 Locations of major early civilizations. (Daniel 1968:Fig. 1.)

the communities' surplus crops. Further, the priests were probably the only centralized authority capable of directing the large-scale irrigation projects. We cannot even determine when the role of the priesthood became a full-time specialty, but almost certainly it was within the Florescent era.

Writing appeared during the Protoliterate period. Initially there were accounts of quantities of goods, but before long the method was expanded to include lists of gods and other esoteric matters. The story of the Mesopotamian system of writing on clay with a stylus, with the clay tablets then providing a permanent record, is a fascinating study in itself.

We should also remark here the development of the cylinder seal (Fig. 11–5). Small cylinders of stone or pottery were decorated with recessed figures which, when the cylinder was rolled upon damp clay, left a permanent impression. Seals were used as indications of ownership, either the property of individuals or that of the temples. Another possible function was their representation of the owner in a religious sense, bearing a type of magical relationship to their owner's personality.

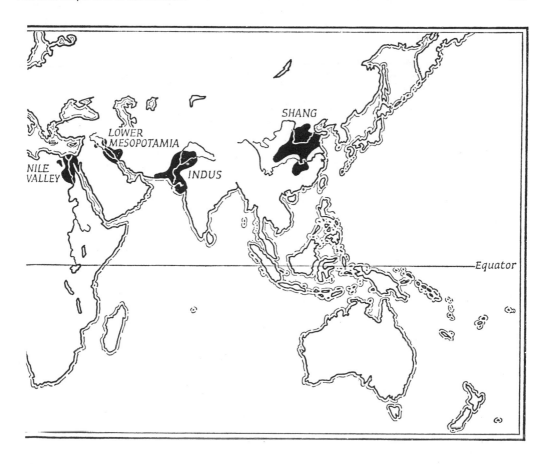

In summary, the Mesopotamian Florescent era possessed a society with strong economic controls, probably exercised by a theocracy, with developing urbanism and external trade relationships. The degree of private ownership is debatable. The most obvious candidate for political authority and ownership of surplus property would be the temple and its associated priesthood.

THE DYNASTIC ERA

The Dynastic era reflects numerous developments which are more tied to social and political influences than to changes in the economic base. The economy was not the important cause of events that it was in prior eras. Instead we may hold the economy as a constant. The important changes reflect a shift from theocratic rule to the secular rule of kings. The shift was accompanied by the appearance of palaces and royal tombs. The concept of royal privilege carried with it elaborate tombs, some with use of the true arch, containing

Fig. 11-3 The tell at Eridu, Mesopotamia, a stratified mound made up of layers of house foundations and occupational debris. On top (see photograph below) is the ziggurat built about 2000 B.C. by Ur-Nammur. (Beek 1962:33.)

valuable offerings. The latter included costly statuary, metal vessels, and even chariots. The concept of the intentional burial of wealth reveals that status was related to conspicuous consumption. The afterlife needs of the ruler took precedence over the daily needs of his constituents.

Crafts continued to be elaborated but the emphasis was on increased production rather than the acquisition of new manufacturing techniques or materials. One exception was the development of bronze in the Early Dynastic II period. In addition there was segregation of craft products, with metal and stone being used for the royal vessels, while pottery was increasingly limited to the use of the common people.

Perhaps as important as any other single element was the increase in population to the level of true urbanism. Sites covered up to 700 acres and the population of individual cities reached 20,000 to 30,000. The increase in size of cities was the result of both actual population increase and population concentration for purposes of defense. Warfare was, after all, a major feature of the period. The combination of factors leading to warfare included population increase, possibly to the limit of available resources, plus the demands for

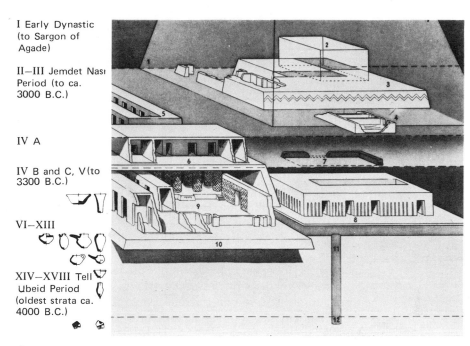

I Early Dynastic
(to Sargon of
Agade)

II—III Jemdet Nasr
Period (to ca.
3000 B.C.)

IV A

IV B and C, V (to
3300 B.C.)

VI—XIII

XIV—XVIII Tell
Ubeid Period
(oldest strata ca.
4000 B.C.)

Fig. 11–4   Reconstruction of the layers beneath the tell at Eridu. These layers date back to 4000 B.C. and contain the remains of sixteen temples (Beek 1962:33.)

greater and greater amounts of forced labor to build the palaces and temples, and maintain the irrigation system. Early conflicts were fought by armies made up of craft guilds directed by their foremen who were responsible to palace officials. This lack of concern for permanent conquest of adjacent territories came to an end with the accession of the Akkadian Dynasty. Under the leadership of Sargon, the prior kingdoms of Akkad and Sumer were united and new emphases emerged. Among these was the awarding of spoils to one's victorious followers as well as a concern for the capture of slaves.

Fig. 11–5 An example of a cylinder seal impression. (Trustees of the British Museum (Natural History).)

So far we have discussed the development of civilization as a series of stages, each with its major characteristics. While this method has merit from a classificatory standpoint, it tends to omit the human element. Civilization did not develop in any sort of preordained manner dictated by any superorganic nature of culture. Civilization was the result of innovations by people made to solve their intimate problems of daily life. We owe it to these people to give credit for their accomplishments by describing them in greater detail. The earliest of the civilizations was that of the Sumerians, peoples of the alluvial southern plains of Mesopotamia (Fig. 11–6).

The early development of Sumer, represented archaeologically by period IV at Uruk and at Jemdet Nasr, begins about 3200 B.C. These remains represent true civilization for they include cities, writing, large irrigation projects, and other criteria we accept as evidence of civilization. The Early Dynastic period extended from 2800 to 2400 B.C. and was followed by the Akkadian conquest from the north under Sargon I. After 2120 B.C. Sumer was again an independent nation until the fall of Ur about 2000 B.C.

The Sumerians possessed city-states with each city at its center. The cities themselves were constructed of mud brick with surrounding city walls. Within the city the dominant structures were the temples and ziggurats (actually artificial mountains of brick, the basis of the concept of the Tower of Babel). The city limits enclosed several square miles and populations are estimated at from 100,000 to 500,000, with Ur possibly the largest city. There were 15 to 20 of these city-states, each trying to extend its control over intervening lands. The cities were economically interdependent but politically autonomous; thus the conflicts between cities while common were not serious.

URBANISM

Urbanism is a process which is intimately linked with the rise of civilization.

Truly urban agglomerations depend upon the institution of the state as a political form, and the emergence of the latter is but an aspect in turn of the formation of stratified class societies. Also linked to the emergence of cities are increased levels of specialization in labour; innovations like writing that facilitate administration and assure the pre-eminence of a few of the many strands of unrecorded tradition; and symbolic affirmations of the newly achieved status of kings and cults in the form of monumental art and architecture (Adams 1973:16–17).

In Mesopotamia we have evidence of the growth of urbanization which has been analyzed as to the processes at work. Several major features are cited by Adams (1973) as relevant:

1. The growth of urbanism in Mesopotamia was differential both in the time of its appearance and its duration. Several patterns of development are evidenced.
2. The preurban settlement pattern was less varied. Settlements were of types labeled small towns, villages, and hamlets and were evenly distributed over the landscape.

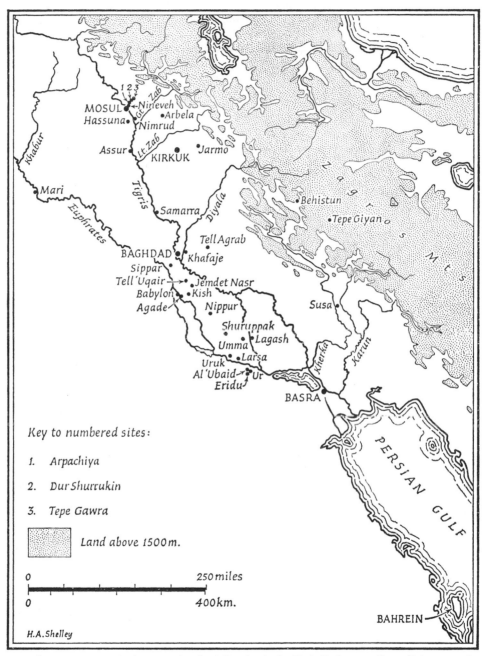

Fig. 11–6   Major settlements of early civilization in the Tigris-Euphrates valleys of Mesopotamia. (Daniel 1968:Fig. 4.)

3. The next step was the depopulation of much of the alluvial plain, with people shifting to residence in the cities. The emphasis was on forced or persuaded resettlement. The settlements did not nucleate because of population growth; what occurred was a politically motivated restructuring of the existing society. In Adams' view this restructuring was artificial and was carried out for the benefit of a small oligarchy with a strong political consciousness. The actual size of the cities may reflect the political organization rather than any inherent environmental facts.
4. Life in the city had disadvantages for the common citizen, specifically since he was subject to demands for communal labor in agriculture and the construction of public buildings. He also paid taxes and was subject to military service. A final detrimental factor was the increase in opportunity for epidemic disease.
5. A result of the negative effects of urbanism was that the individual citizen remained in the city under at least partial duress and further did not truly participate in many of the social institutions associated with urban life.
6. Nonetheless the trend toward urbanism was very strong with the result that by the Dynastic period nearly one fourth of all settlements in Mesopotamia were cities.

   The economy was based upon intensive irrigation agriculture of grain crops with barley most common, followed by wheat, millet, and sesame. Other crops included fruits, vegetables, and dates, as well as cattle and sheep. This was the time of maximum agricultural potential of the region. Subsequently it has deteriorated from the increase in evaporated salts in the soil. Probably the major feature of the economy was the degree of organization and control of the irrigation system that was employed. Such control was essential to the development of urbanism. Crafts were highly specialized. There were masons, metal smiths, glaziers (as glass had been developed), jewelers, potters, carpenters, and seal cutters.

   We have in this chapter ignored the earlier archaeological subdivision termed the "Bronze Age." While bronze was an important commodity and its appearance provides a useful archaeological index fossil, the major developments of the times were in the social and political realm. We should therefore emphasize that while bronze containers, weapons, and other implements were functionally useful, they do not in themselves bring about the important characteristics of civilization; that is, urbanism, political autonomy, and such. The Sumerians were capable craftsmen in metal, having learned to alloy tin and copper to produce bronze about the beginning of the Dynastic period. They are credited with the invention of the closed mold and the lost wax technique of casting, which appeared about 2500 B.C. They were also working gold, silver, and lead, and after 3000 B.C. they were manufacturing a few objects in iron. Since metal ores do not occur in Mesopotamia, an elaborate system of trade relations was established with Asia Minor, Syria, Cappadocia, Oman, and Afghanistan. Besides metals, items of trade included lapis lazuli, shells, cedar, pine, and stone for statuary.

   We must also credit the Sumerians with the invention of the wheel. First used for the potter's wheel, the wheel was adapted to use on carts by 3000 B.C. The earliest writing dates to Uruk IV (3200–3100 B.C.) documented by the finding of 500 to 600 clay tablets. Largely pictographic, these early tablets functioned as inventories or receipts of products.

Other Sumerian accomplishments are almost too numerous to mention. They were outstanding in their ability to produce sculpture in the round. They had calendars and a system of mathematics. They possessed a system of dividing a circle. They wove garments, built boats, brewed beer, made music on harps, raced chariots, and maintained an elaborate religion. The religious centers were the temples and the ziggurats. Each city probably had a patron deity as well as a pantheon of gods, to whom the temples were dedicated. Built of plano-convex-shaped adobe bricks, the temples were large structures as much as 245 by 100 feet, with the associated ziggurat standing even taller. The Sumerians produced the world's first civilization. We will find evidence of the spreading influence of cultural ideas from Sumer as we review developments in other early civilizations.

ANCIENT EGYPT

Egypt has been termed the "Gift of the Nile," which is both accurate and redundant, for in most respects the Nile Valley and Egypt are identical. The situation is little different today from the time of pharaohs; approximately 97 percent of the modern nation is made up of uninhabited desert. Thus the desert functioned to isolate the Nile Valley from nearby regions. Our concepts of the life of Ancient Egypt are based on the world-famous ancient remains consisting primarily of tombs and temples dedicated to the gods or the royal family. The way of life of the common people is still inadequately known. We also know less than we would like of the origins of Ancient Egyptian civilization. It is standard archaeological opinion that plant and animal domestication were introduced from the Fertile Crescent. These introductions first appear in cultures termed *Predynastic:* the Badarian, Amratian, and Nagadan which date about 4000 B.C. or even earlier. These cultures were the antecedents of the *Dynastic* civilization. They were village dwellers with a mixed economy featuring hunting and fishing as well as farming and animal husbandry. Sir Flinders Petrie was able to demonstrate through studies of the pottery that these Predynastic peoples were in fact the direct ancestors of the First Dynasty. Archaeologically there are still omissions in the record, for the appearance of the Dynastic manifestations seems abrupt, with little advance notice that a major civilization was developing. Narmer, the first pharaoh of the First Dynasty, unified Egypt into one nation (Fig. 11–7), a land which traditionally had been divided into Upper and Lower Egypt. The First Dynasty, which began about 3200 B.C., introduced royal tombs of great size, writing, stone vessels, and artifacts of both copper and bronze. Such manifestations imply a long period of development, but here the archaeological record is inadequate. One explanation is that the development of Egyptian civilization occurred in the Nile Delta and has subsequently been covered by thick layers of alluvium.

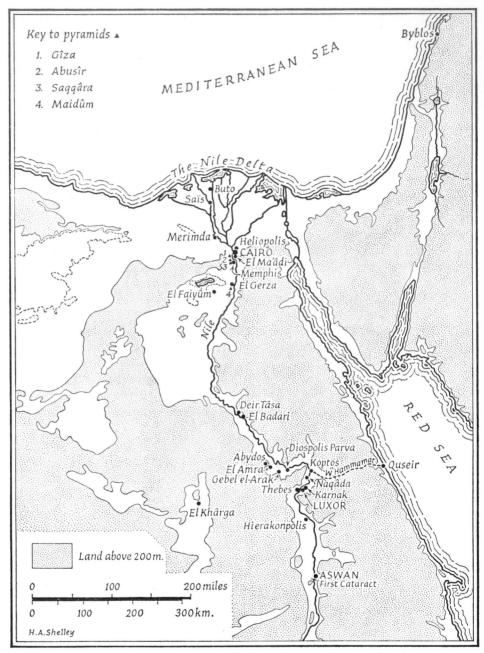

Fig. 11-7 The Nile Valley, location of one of the world's most impressive early civilizations. (Daniel 1968:Fig. 6.)

Another explanation is that the ideas leading to civilization radiated outward from Sumer and influenced such indigenous cultures as the Egyptian Predynastic. Probably both explanations have a basis in fact. With respect to the Delta theory one line of evidence cites the fact that in hieroglyphics the symbols for right and left are the same as those for west and east. This suggests an origin of Egyptian writing in the Delta, with a cultural orientation facing upstream. Archaeological evidence of Sumerian influence includes three cylinder seals from the Uruk period. Subsequently the Egyptians engraved their own seals. Some engravings feature Mesopotamian art styles; for example, a Gilgamesh type of culture hero is shown on an ivory knife handle from Gebel el-Arak. Writing is the other major trait with Sumerian priority. Finally the introduction of mud brick dramatically changed Egyptian architecture.

The Early Dynastic period is subdivided into the Archaic period—Dynasties I and II (3200–2700 B.C.)—and the Old Kingdom—Dynasties III–VIII (2700–2160 B.C.). The archaeology gives little evidence that this was a *developing* civilization. The largest pyramids date from this period, and we have ample evidence that the pharaoh had assumed supreme power. The pharaoh exercised divine rule, for he was considered a deity on earth. Furthermore his power from the First Dynasty on was supreme, since there does not seem to have been a period featuring the rise of individual city-states. The entire Nile Valley from the first cataract at Aswan north to the Mediterranean was under one ruler.

The Egyptians varied in other respects from the Sumerians. The Egyptian population lived in villages rather than cities, and although Egypt was densely populated, it was not in a strict sense urban—at least we have limited evidence of true cities. The populace was well organized, as enormous quantities of labor were required to build the pyramids and other public works; for example, thousands of men must have been necessary to build the Pyramid of Cheops (the largest), which contains 2 million blocks weighing up to 15 tons apiece.

Evidence of life in Ancient Egypt is derived from several sources. There are the buildings themselves, the pyramids, other tombs, temples, forts, and domestic dwellings. There are paintings on tomb walls, bas-relief carvings (Fig. 11–8), and small models of details of everyday life in wood or clay which made up part of the tomb offerings.

The towns evolved from small walled units which were circular in early times and later rectangular (Fig. 11–9). Within the town wall were rectangular house blocks with segregated uses. A few sites approach urbanism. For example, at Tell el Amarna (see Fig. 11–11) we have rows of three-room house blocks with streets between them. Near the pyramid complexes rows of small uniform houses were built for the occupancy of the workers. At Giza these were of brick and were of identical size, 164 square meters per unit. The lack of interior furnishings and trash suggests that these units were kept clean in response to a royal decree.

A pylon or massive city gate, carved in bas relief illustrating the deeds of the Pharoah who had it built.

Remnants of a hypostyle hall with one massive papyrus column standing to its original height, Temple of Karnak, Luxor.

Bas relief carving from the wall of a tomb.

Facade of the temple of Nefertari cut into the bedrock sandstone at Abu Simbel.

Fig. 11–8 Details of Pharonic civilization. (Photographs courtesy of Philip M. Hobler.)
(*Left*) Subterranean crypt which contained a solar boat at the pyramid complex of Giza, near Cairo.
(*Right*) Nubian slaves with ropes tied around their necks. Bas relief carving from the main temple built by Ramses II at Abu Simbel.

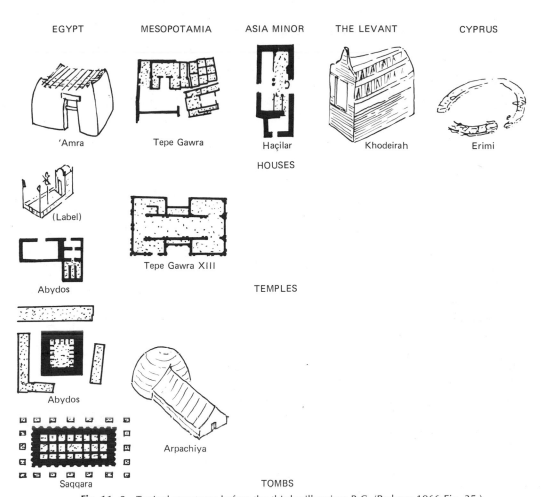

EGYPT MESOPOTAMIA ASIA MINOR THE LEVANT CYPRUS

'Amra Tepe Gawra Haçilar Khodeirah Erimi

HOUSES

(Label)

Abydos Tepe Gawra XIII

TEMPLES

Abydos

Arpachiya

Saqqara TOMBS

Fig. 11-9 Typical structures before the third millennium B.C. (Badawy 1966:Fig. 35.)

Middle class houses from the Third Dynasty (Fig. 11–10) feature a vestibule, a small closet, a hall, living room, and a bedroom. The models from the tombs feature several house types. The simplest is a rectangular enclosure of several rooms with an awning at the rear. Another type is of two stories with terraces in front. There is an associated courtyard with a water basin, an oven, and grain bins. The roofs were of vaulted brick, windows were small and high, and at the top of the roof were small ventilation cupolas. There were granaries formed by rows of domed mud bins. The bins were filled at the top and had a small trapdoor at the bottom for the removal of the grain. Rows of pottery jars were set in racks for food and water storage. Another feature built within the houses were latrines. Houses of the Middle Kingdom (Fig. 11–11) consisted of large rectangular units with many rooms facing on a street; also associated were enclosed courtyards. Analysis of the change in house type through time

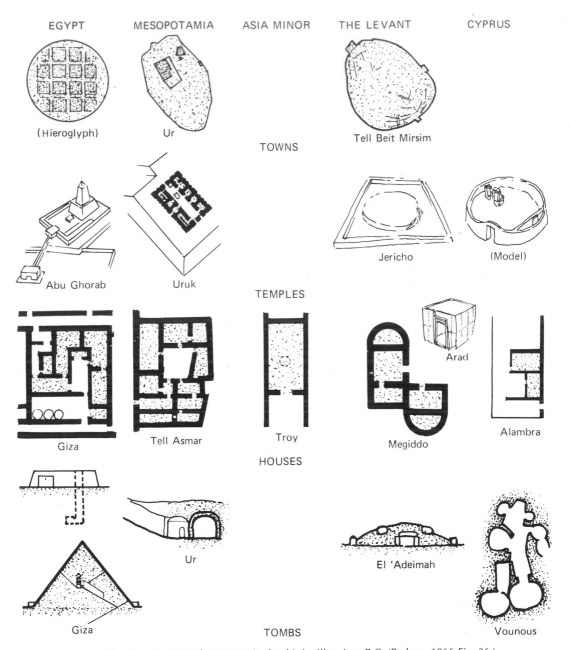

EGYPT   MESOPOTAMIA   ASIA MINOR   THE LEVANT   CYPRUS

(Hieroglyph)   Ur   Tell Beit Mirsim

TOWNS

Abu Ghorab   Uruk   Jericho   (Model)

TEMPLES

Giza   Tell Asmar   Troy   Megiddo   Arad   Alambra

HOUSES

Ur   El 'Adeimah

Giza   TOMBS   Vounous

Fig. 11–10   Typical structures in the third millennium B.C. (Badawy 1966:Fig. 36.)

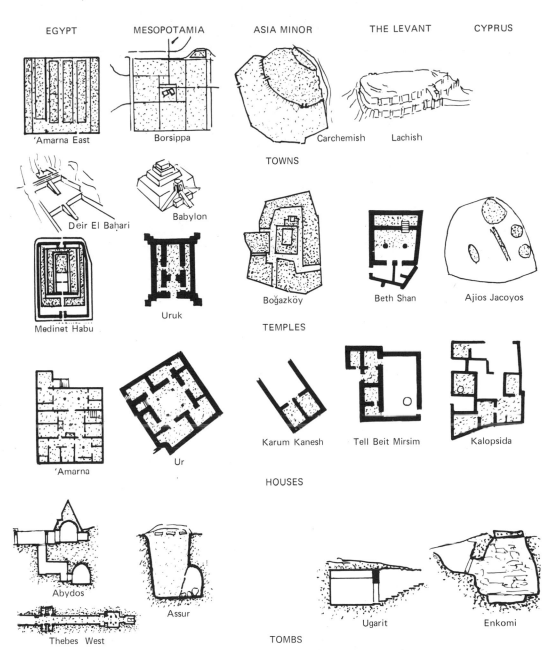

EGYPT MESOPOTAMIA ASIA MINOR THE LEVANT CYPRUS

'Amarna East Borsippa Carchemish Lachish

TOWNS

Deir El Bahari Babylon

Medinet Habu Uruk Boğazköy Beth Shan Ajios Jacoyos

TEMPLES

'Amarna Ur Karum Kanesh Tell Beit Mirsim Kalopsida

HOUSES

Abydos Assur

Thebes West Ugarit Enkomi

TOMBS

Fig. 11–11 Typical structures in the second millennium B.C. (Badawy 1966:Fig. 37.)

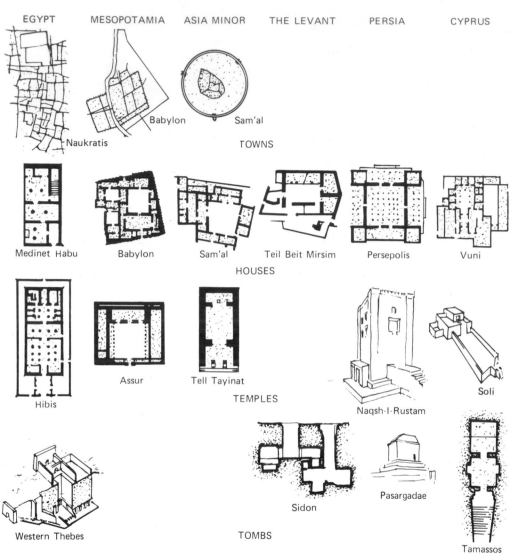

EGYPT MESOPOTAMIA ASIA MINOR THE LEVANT PERSIA CYPRUS

Babylon Sam'al

Naukratis

TOWNS

Medinet Habu Babylon Sam'al Teil Beit Mirsim Persepolis Vuni

HOUSES

Assur Tell Tayinat

Hibis TEMPLES

Naqsh-I-Rustam

Soli

Western Thebes TOMBS

Sidon Pasargadae

Tamassos

Fig. 11–12 Typical structures in the first millennium B.C. (Badawy 1966:Fig. 38.)

would provide one means of studying changes in family composition in Ancient Egypt (Fig. 11–12).

The temples held a core position in the religious life. Because of the concern of each pharaoh to dedicate new temples during his reign, they came to dominate the daily life of the common people as well. Several forms of temples were built, each with a specialized function. These included cult temples, sun temples, and mortuary temples. The cult temples were dedicated to a specific god represented by a statue of gilded wood or stone placed at the rear of the temple. The building plan was rectangular, symmetrical, and divided into three parts. Major associated features included courtyards with rows of support columns (the hypostyle hall), an inner sanctuary with only one door that was manned by a priest, and pylon-type gateways (see Fig. 11–8). Another feature was a crypt for valuable offerings. A solar boat (see Fig. 11–8) was also a common addition.

Sun temples were rectangular walled structures open to the sky. There was no cult statue and therefore no need for a sanctuary. There was an altar and frequently an obelisk—a stone monument symbolic of the sun's rays.

Mortuary temples were the scene of mortuary services. The typical arrangement consisted of a building termed a valley portal located at the edge of the Nile. Leading from this portal was a causeway to the mortuary temple several hundred meters distant. The mortuary temple was adjacent to the pyramid tomb (Fig. 11–13). The features of the mortuary temple included a false door facing east and an offering table behind it for the food needed in the afterlife. Facing the table was a statue of the deceased. More elaborate decorations within the temple included wall murals illustrating the daily life of the deceased.

Tombs were of three types. In general order of appearance from early to late, they are mastabas, pyramids, and rock cut tombs. Mastabas were rectangular superstructures built of massive brickwork and surrounded by an enclosing wall. The burial chamber was initially inside but was later expanded into an underground substructure with a central chamber surrounded by storage compartments. The early mastabas were designed with a single burial chamber; later two chambers were common. By the Fourth Dynasty the mastabas were situated at the western desert edge of the Nile and arranged in orderly rows.

Pyramids are the most impressive tombs built in ancient Egypt. They are also the best known; thus there is less need to describe them in great detail. The pyramids, massive structures with a variety of internal features, have led to Edwards' (1952) specialized text on the subject. The pyramids were built of massive blocks set closely together. Sir Flinders Petrie measured the gap between blocks as averaging 1/50th of an inch. The typical incline is 52°. Within each pyramid was a tunnel leading to a burial chamber. Other features include false tunnels and chambers to distract tomb robbers (Fig. 11–14). The actual construction relied on masses of labor using simple tools. According to Badawy (1966:52):

The technical excellence of the masonry owes more to the ability of the craftsmen than to the use of mechanical devices more elaborate than sledges hauled up ramps, windlasses and pulleys for lifting and transporting, adzes, chisels, saws, drills, and polishing stones for dressing and finishing the stone blocks.

The dimensions of the larger pyramids are enormous (Fig. 11–14) and are truly ranked among the wonders of the world. The development of the pyramids can be traced from the early stepped form, such as Saqqara, to a unique specimen

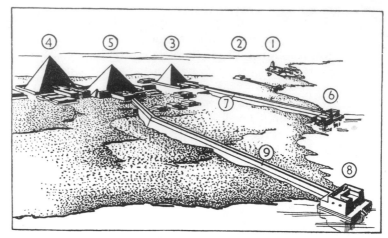

Fig. 11–13 The pyramids and other fifth dynasty structures of Abu Sir: *1.* Sun temple of Niuserra; *2.* Sun Temple of Userkof; *3.* Pyramid of Sahura; *4.* Pyramid of Neferirkara; *5.* Pyramid of Niuserra; *6.* Valley Building of Sahura; *7.* Causeway of Sahura; *8.* Valley Building of Niuserra; *9.* Causeway of Niuserra. (Edwards 1952:Fig. 18.)

at Dashur, the Bent Pyramid, with its two separate angles of incline, and finally the true pyramidal form first exemplified at Meidum (Fig. 11–14). By the Fifth and Sixth Dynasties, pyramids were smaller and less well built. Although pyramids continued to be built during the New Kingdom, they were no longer a royal prerogative and the pharaohs were buried in rock cut tombs.

Rock cut tombs were developed at the end of the Old Kingdom and were first used by the nobles. They feature greater security than mastabas and even more than pyramids, since the entrance may be more easily concealed. During the New Kingdom the royal tombs as well as those of the nobles were cut into the living rock. The necropolis at Thebes, on the west bank of the Nile, is the best known burial area, with the pharaohs buried in the Valley of the Kings, their families in a nearby valley, and between the two an area reserved for tombs of the nobles.

Badawy (1966:55) describes a New Kingdom royal tomb as follows:

It consists of a slightly slanting corridor with three offset stretches flanked by niches; passing through an antechamber, the corridor is intercepted by shafts and ends in a sarcophagus chamber.

Badawy's (1966:31) description of the palaces of Amenhotep III provide a glimpse of the nature of these structures.

The ruins at 'Amarna and Thebes give some idea about the splendor of royal palaces, even though they are always built of brick and wood with some stone elements and lining in the bathrooms. The palace complex of Amenhotep III at Malgata in Western Thebes, . . . which is about 350 by 270 meters, consists of four palaces with subsidiary buildings and a huge lake, probably T-shaped and connected to the Nile. In the so-called palace of the king the official quarters feature a few columned audience halls,

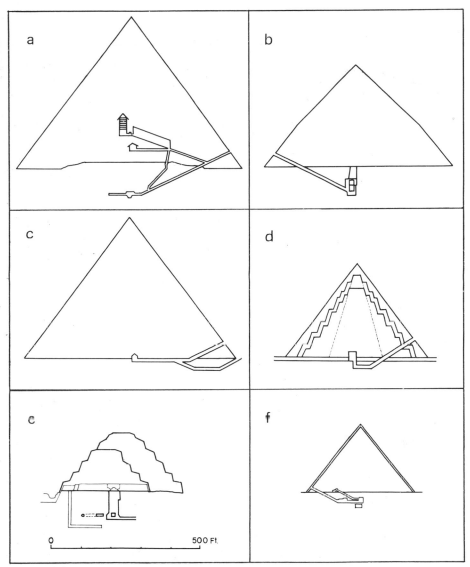

Fig. 11–14 The best known and largest pyramids of Ancient Egypt illustrated on the same scale to show relative size: *a.* Great Pyramid of Cheops; *b.* Bent Pyramid at Dashur; *c.* Pyramid of Chephren; *d.* Pyramid of Meidum; *e.* Step Pyramid at Saggara; *f.* Pyramid of Mycerinus.

each with a throne on a dais along the east wall, a staircase to the upper floor or terrace, a large central hall with two rows of columns arranged symmetrically with four separate suites for *harim* ladies on each side and a royal suite at the rear (south). The kitchens are in a separate block between this palace and another one to the south. Paintings and decorative moldings in applique lavishly cover the walls with scenes from official life or with images of the household genius Bes; floors are decorated with the representation of pools, plants, and birds, and ceilings have rows of flying vultures and geometric patterns. Each suite in itself forms a complete dwelling based on the tripartite plan and featuring a front columned vestibule, a central hypostyle hall with a canopied throne, a closet, a bedroom, and a robing room.

A final type of public structure was the fort. Constructed of mud brick, the walls followed the natural contours of a defensive location. Within the walls were public buildings, granaries, barracks, and a temple. A further refinement was the inclusion of bastians in the walls.

We have confined our description to the major features of Egyptian civilization, especially the monumental remains. Much has been omitted, for example, we have not described the burial ceremonies or the mummification process. The elaborate crafts include the carved painted wooden sarcophagi, the tomb furniture, jewelry, and monumental stone statuary. All attest to the height of cultural attainment. For details of these findings numerous well illustrated popular works on the subject are available.

ANCIENT INDIA

We have the rise of another major civilization in the Indus River Valley region (within the modern nations of India and Pakistan) after 2500 B.C. (Fig. 11–15). The two major centers were at Mohenjodaro and Harrapa. The origins of the Indus civilization are not clearly revealed through reference to local earlier manifestations. We infer that cultural ideas spreading outward from Sumer gave rise to the Indus developments.

Although relatively unknown archaeologically until after 1920, there is no question that we are dealing with true civilization. The major cities are urban (Fig. 11–16), with large rectangular house blocks joined into larger contiguous units separated by streets. The public buildings such as the communal granaries, baths, assembly halls, and religious structures were frequently segregated into a separate area termed a citadel. We perceive many cultural elements here which, while not identitical to Sumerian traits, are similar. These include seals, mud brick architecture, wheeled carts, stone statuary, and casting in bronze. Even the division of cities into residential areas and ceremonial centers has Sumerian counterparts. Unique features in the Indus sites are the grid pattern of the streets, the use of built-in garbage containers, and brick-lined drains in the streets. There were bathrooms in the homes. The houses themselves were somewhat monotonous in their regularity. Another major difference concerns the geographic spread of Indus civilization. The cities were not restricted to a small area as were Sumer and ancient Egypt. Instead the 70 or so major Indus cities extended over an area 1000 miles north to south (see Fig. 11–15). This is an area of a half million square miles, which easily makes it the largest in area of the ancient civilizations.

The economy featured the familiar Middle Eastern crops plus some interesting Asian additions. They grew wheat, six-rowed barley, sesame, dates,

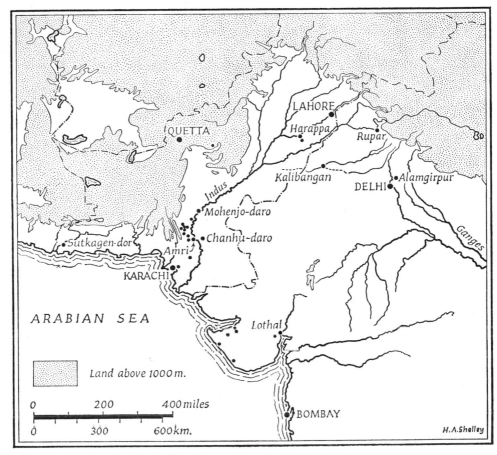

Fig. 11–15   The Indus Valley, showing sites. (Daniel 1968:Fig. 8.)

melons, cotton, and peas. Domestic animals included cattle, ass, horse, buffalo, and camel. We might point out here that the camel, today considered one of the diagnostic characteristics of Egypt, was actually domesticated in western Asia and was not introduced into the Nile Valley until about 500 B.C. by the Persians.

The archaeological importance of the Indus civilization may be assessed in several ways. The ruins themselves are massive (Fig. 11–17) and are a clear indication of a major urban population. Within the centers, craft specialists were at work producing seals, pottery, and bronzes, as well as continuing the production of a well-made stone blade industry (Fig. 11–18). The copper and bronze implements included tanged knives, ax and chisel blades, mirrors, fishhooks, spear and arrow points, as well as a range of jars, vases, bowls, and even a handled pan of skillet form. The bronze vessels were of similar form to the pottery vessels.

Fig. 11 −16 Plan of part of the residential quarter of Mohenjo-daro, Indus Valley, illustrating its urban character. (Piggot 1968:Fig. 5.)

The major concerns of the Indus civilization seem to have been internal rather than being focused on external conquest and expansion. According to Daniel (1968:114, Fig. 9), evidence of trade, although widespread, was limited to small objects, including pottery, seals, beads, and other small artifacts. While these items have been found as far away as northern Iraq, they are all indicative of limited trade and thus technological independence. We will close our consideration of the Indus civilization by quoting a summary statement concerning its origins (Allchin and Allchin 1968:126–127):

The present evidence, either of archaeological sequence or of absolute dating, does not permit any certain conclusion of the rate at which the Harappan culture expanded nor of where the new culture traits first evolved, apart from the pre-Harappan cultures of the Indus valley. There is some evidence both at Mohenjo-daro and Harappa of a general cultural evolution, but the earlier excavations of Marshall and Vats are not helpful on this point. We feel that the expansion was something of an 'explosion' and that it represented among other things an outcome of the successful control of the tremendous

Fig. 11–17 A typical street in Mohenjo-daro. The walls in many instances still stand today to their first-floor height. Windows are few and generally the only large openings are the refuse chutes. (Photograph courtesy of Roger Viollet in Daniel 1968:Fig. 28.)

agriculturally productive potentialities of the Indus plains. The refinement of the archaeological evidence concerning the development of the civilization and of its regional variants, and the consequent possibilities of discovering the first centres of the culture and of tracing its diffusion, are thus desiderata of the research programme of the coming decades.

Unique features cited by the Allchins (1968) as important to the development of the Indus civilization were little evidence of significant climatic change and the use of burnt brick as a defense against floods. Within the time span of the Indus civilization, the level of the flood plain rose by 30 feet, which has placed the earliest village levels inaccessibly below the present water table. Another characteristic of the culture is that while it developed suddenly, once established, there was little further cultural change. We are impressed with cultural uniformity over a long period of time including the standardization of

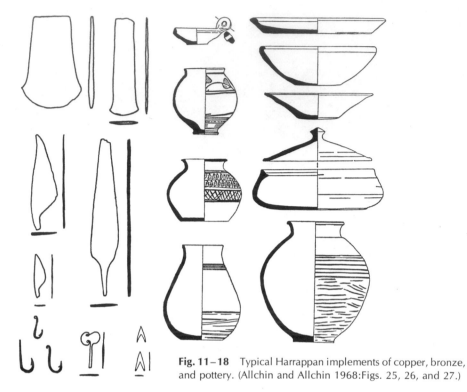

Fig. 11–18 Typical Harrappan implements of copper, bronze, and pottery. (Allchin and Allchin 1968:Figs. 25, 26, and 27.)

brick form and size. The sites themselves possess little individuality, and we are not even sure that the major sites functioned as true capitals or city-states. Uniformity and conservatism are also evident in the crafts.

After a period of decline marked by reuse of bricks and less city planning, the culture disintegrated about 1750 B.C. Causes cited for the collapse include repeated flooding by the Indus, course alterations in the river, and finally an invasion of Indo-European-speaking peoples from the west—the Aryans (Allchin and Allchin 1968:143). Further archaeological research is required before these causal factors can be properly evaluated.

ANCIENT CHINA

The earliest civilization in China is confined to the valley of the Hwang Ho or Yellow River and dates from 2100 to 1200 B.C. The culture, termed the Shang Dynasty, is derived from the previous Yang Shao culture of Neolithic peasant village farming. The introductions or innovations marked by the appearance of urbanism, bronze casting, writing, and other civilized traits cannot be easily traced outward to other cultures or back in time in the Hwang Ho Valley.

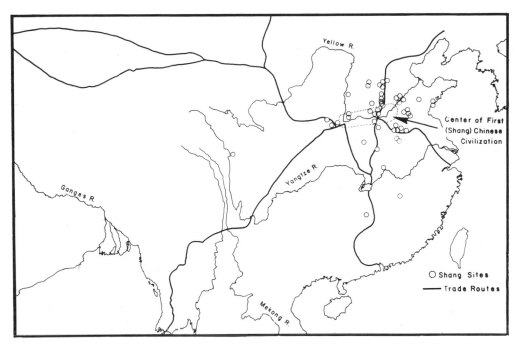

Fig. 11-19 Location of the Shang civilization with trade routes to the west. (After Daniel 1968:Figs. 10 and 11.)

Nonetheless these traits—the bronzes and the writing are two excellent examples—are clearly of Chinese type. In fact the writing, which is ideographic, can be partially translated, for 1500 of the 5000 characters used have been deciphered. On the other hand, there is no prior developmental phase for the bronze industry, suggesting that it at least was the result of outside influences. Perhaps the most reasonable explanation would be to couple increased population, resulting from increased exploitation of the fertile loess lowlands of the Hwang Ho Valley, with a simultaneous introduction through stimulus diffusion of traits from the already advanced civilizations to the west (Fig. 11-19). A major reason for trade could have been the export of silk from the Shang cities to the west.

The economy was agricultural, exploiting the rich valley floor. Major crops were millet, and Chinese cabbage dated 4115 B.C., rice dated 3395 B.C., and a variety of other crops dated 2750 B.C.—broad bean, water chestnut, peanut, sesame, melon, peach, and sour date (Chang 1973:527). Domestic animals were cattle, pig, sheep, dog, chicken, and horse. In addition, silk worms were kept and clothing was woven of silk as well as hemp.

We can cite numerous general parallels with the other early civilizations of the Old World. The Shang peoples lived in walled cities and were ruled by kings who possessed chariots, bronze vessels (Fig. 11-20), and slaves, and were buried in elaborate tombs (Fig. 11–21). Furthermore we have clear evidence that these developments occurred later than they did in Sumer and the Indus valley. What is of even greater concern to us here are those traits which were unique to the Shang period. These unique features are mainly artistic, and they mark one aspect of civilization—the ability to create—one result of the rise of craft specialties.

Fig. 11–20 Bronze ritual wine vessels of the late Shang dynasty, eleventh century B.C. (Photographs courtesy of The Metropolitan Museum of Art, Rogers Fund, 1943.)

A truly unique item, of which at least 100,000 examples have been recovered, are inscribed bones and shells covered with writing ideographs. These specimens were used in the ancient art of scapulimancy or fortune-telling. A hot pointed piece of metal was applied to a pit that had been specially cut on the inscribed side of the bones. As a result, cracks appeared on the back of the object. The cracks so generated were interpreted by fortune-tellers. It has been suggested that the shape of the prepared pit might have governed to some degree the form of the cracks and thus the predications. Most of the answers requested could be in terms of yes or no. In any event the oracle bones were used for predicting weather, the fate of crops, other agricultural matters, and military concerns. The bones were also consulted to resolve all of the private matters of the king, including questions concerning his health, the health of his family, the future, and so on. Daniel (1968:130) relates the example of Kin Wu-ting who even consulted the oracle to determine which of his ancestors was responsible for his toothache.

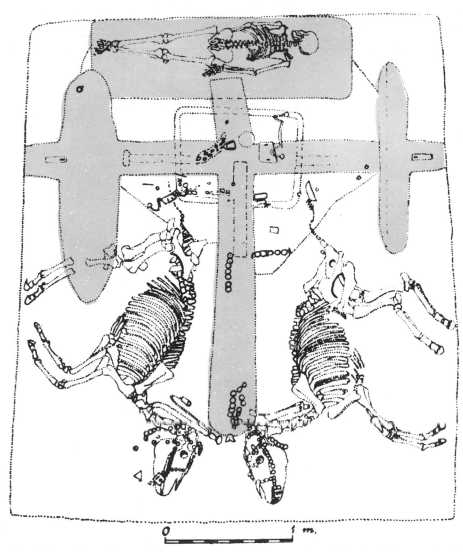

Fig. 11–21 Plan of Shang civilization tomb which shows outline of chariot (darker area) and miscellaneous artifacts. (Piggott 1961:273.)

REFERENCES

Adams, R. M., 1971, "Developmental Stages in Ancient Mesopotamia," in S. Struever (ed.), *Prehistoric Agriculture*. New York: Natural History Press, pp. 572–590.
———, 1973, "Patterns of Urbanization in Early Southern Mesopotamia," in R. Tringham (ed.), *Urban Settlements*. Andover, Mass.: Warner Modular Publications.
Allchin, B., and R. Allchin, 1968, *The Birth of Indian Civilization*. Suffolk: Pelican.

Badawy, A., 1966, *Architecture in Ancient Egypt and the Near East.* Cambridge, Mass.: M.I.T. Press.

Beek, M. A., 1962, *Atlas of Mesopotamia.* London: Thomas Nelson.

Chang, K. C., 1973, "Radiocarbon Dates from China: Some Initial Interpretations," *Current Anthropology* 14(5):525–528.

Daniel, G., 1968. *The First Civilizations,* Apollo ed. New York: Crowell.

Edwards, I. E. S., 1952, *The Pyramids of Egypt.* Harmondsworth, Middlesex: Pelican.

Lloyd, S., 1963, *Mounds of the Near East.* Edinburgh: Edinburgh University Press.

Petrie, W. N. F., 1904, *Methods and Aims in Archaeology.* London.

Piggott, S., ed., 1968, *The Dawn of Civilization.* New York: McGraw-Hill.

Steward, J. H., 1971, "Some Implications of the Symposium," in S. Struever (ed.), *Prehistoric Agriculture.* New York: Natural History Press.

Willey, G. R., and P. Phillips, 1958, *Method and Theory in American Archaeology.* Chicago: The University of Chicago Press.

12

The Transition to History*

At this point in our narrative we need to pick up the leftover pieces of prehistory to fit them into an orderly scheme. As we have mentioned previously, the later we are in time the more varied and complex are the cultures extant. There have also been differential rates of cultural development. Cultural innovations were rapid in the Middle East, while other areas like northern and western Europe changed more slowly. In part, cultural lag reflects the limited and slow acceptance of traits introduced from other regions. On the other hand, these developments should be viewed not as necessarily indicating resistance to change but as cultural adaptations which had to adjust to local

*In this chapter we have converted all dates to agree with the radiocarbon recalibration. This revision was necessary, for the new dates have clearly indicated that previously held views of cultural diffusion were in error (Renfrew 1971). This is the only chapter with recalibrated dates.

conditions. In Europe there were long-established hunting and fishing economies which were successful. Therefore, the introduction of cultivated plants and animals during the Neolithic was a slow process, marked by intermittent acceptance by the indigenous hunting and gathering peoples and crop failure due to environmental limitations. This pattern has been termed Secondary Neolithic by Piggott (1965). Similar adaptive trends may be perceived with the introduction of bronze implements and later those of iron. Throughout this period, beginning as early as 4500 B.C. (Renfrew 1971:68–69) and lasting until the Roman conquest of Gaul and Britain, we perceive much continuity in European society. We have mentioned the continuties in economy. Other long-standing traditions included trade in flint axes and amber, burial in barrows, Megalithic religion, the building of religious monuments—menhirs, dolmen, trilithons, and henges (Fig. 12–1)—and late in the period the construction of hill forts. These facts of continuity document the presence of a unique European adaptation—a continuing peasant society which, while exposed to numerous influences from the centers of civilization, went its own way, a fact which led V. Gordon Childe to summarize these events in a separate volume, *The Prehistory of European Society* (1958). The narrative he presents—and that of most other authors on the subject (Hawkes and Hawkes 1949; Braidwood 1967; Piggott 1965; Clark 1952)—outlines a pattern of sequential movements of peoples across the European continent and the British Isles, each bringing a distinctive set of culture traits: bell beakers, battle axes, food vessels, hero burials, cremations, urnfield burials, bronze, iron, and hill forts.

Originally these events were summarized under two major rubrics: the Late Bronze Age and the Iron Age. While such categorizations have merit in terms of the types of artifacts recovered from sites, they are not very informative with respect to the cultural processes that were shaping European society.

We must bear in mind that during this same interval of time there developed the major civilizations of southern Europe: Cretan, Mycenaen, Etruscan, Phoenecian, Greek, and finally Roman. The wealth of cultural complexity of these civilizations is staggering. They featured codified laws, state religions, monumental sculpture and architecture, standing armies, political institutions still in effect today, fine arts, and the writing of history and poetry—an almost unending list of accomplishments. It is not our goal here to review these civilizations, for their study lies within the field of classics rather than prehistory. The presence of these civilizations on the southern fringe of Europe provided constant input of cultural ideas to the north. The unique quality of the cultures of northern and central Europe is evidence of the strength of the indigenous peasant society. These "crude barbarians," at least so-termed by their civilized neighbors, had the cultural integrity to lead their lives in their own fashion.

The North European economy featured a mixed reliance on hunting and gathering of wild foods with the addition of cereal agriculture. Originally this featured the clearing and planting of the forested loesslands for growing wheat and barley. Later these cultigens spread northward, with the result that environmental selection favored the former weeds, rye and oats, which were better

Fig. 12–1 A Megalithic monument—West Kennet Long Barrow, Wiltshire, England. (Courtesy of Ministry of Works. Crown copyright.)

adapted to damp and cold. Millet was also an early European cultigen as were flax and apples. The fields were cultivated by means of a two-field system with fallowing between crops. Another part of the system involved the rotation of cereal crops, which exhaust the soil of nitrogen, with legumes, peas, beans, vetches, and lentils, all of which enrich the soil. The thin scatter of potsherds found on the old fields suggests that village debris and manure were spread on the fields for fertilizer. The fields were small and cultivation was by the individual family.

The earliest domesticated animal was the dog, first used by Mesolithic man in the hunt. As the hunt continued in importance, the dog retained his position. The addition of domesticated food animals and crops did not replace hunting and gathering, but instead the economy featured a greater variety of resources. The economy relied on stable domesticated food resources, with the secondary availability of wild foods during poor crop years. The result was a balanced economy without the specialization in and reliance on a few crops, development of large food surpluses, and other features characteristic of the Middle East. The economy thus encouraged cultural stability in the form of continuing peasanthood, rather than change leading toward population increase, urbanism, and ultimately civilization.

According to Clark (1952:117), we do not have reliable information concerning the relative frequency of the various domestic animals kept. The domesticates included cattle, sheep, pig, horse, and in the north, reindeer. Clark does state that through time in temperate Europe there was a decline in the frequency of pig and cattle with a corresponding increase in sheep and horses. He correlates this change with an increase in forest clearance.

Agricultural techniques employed slash-and-burn forest clearing, then the cultivation of small fields with hoes and digging sticks. The presence of linear scars on ancient fields indicates plowing, sometimes in crisscross patterns. Such plowing dates back to the Middle to Late Bronze Age (first half of the second millennium B.C.) but is more typical of the later Iron Age peoples. The dating of plow furrows is not easy, but in some instances dated barrows (burial mounds) have preserved beneath them such furrows (Piggott 1965:150). The plow was of wood with a single foot or sole and a long beam attached to the yoke of oxen. There is still controversy as to whether metal shares were used; replaceable wooden shares have been found, but evidence of iron shares dates after the Roman conquest. A major invention now attributed to these peasant peoples was the rotary grinding mill or quern which spread from northern Europe to the Classical world.

The practice of forest clearing, planting, and fallowing was further modified by the frequent shifting of villages. The existing houses were abandoned and the people moved elsewhere to clear new fields and build new houses. Estimating the population at 5 per house and from 50 to 60 houses per village, we derive an average village population of 300 (Piggott 1965:47).

POLITICAL STRUCTURE

The structure of the society of barbarian Europe is known to us from archaeology as evidenced by the chariot burials of heroes or chieftains (Fig. 12–2), as well as the historical writings of Julius Caesar, Tacitus, and others. The basic unit was the tribe or tuath. This was a small group ruled by a local chieftain below whom was a level of nobility made up of warriors. A third class was the craftsmen, priests, and poets. Basic features of the society were its barbarism and love of warfare. It was a rural society given to idleness, boasting, and feasting, when not engaged in endemic intertribal warfare. It was a tradition which, in the more remote locations, was long to endure. It characterized the medieval Norsemen and even the Irish of the eighteenth century.

RELIGION

Our earliest evidence of religion within this period, beginning about 4300 B.C. (Renfrew 1971:69), consists of enormous stone-lined chambered tombs (Fig. 12–3). These are evidences of a religious cult termed *Megalithic,* which featured the construction of numerous monuments built of large individual stones. We have little besides the stone monuments to document the nature of this cult which was in vogue for 1000 to 2000 years over most of western Europe (Fig. 12–4). The monuments include a variety of forms, not all of which are tombs. There are large areas covered with parallel rows of individual stones

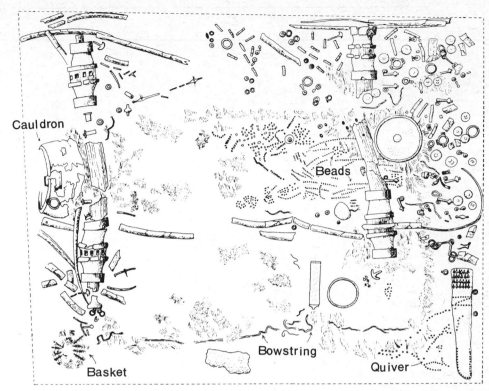

Fig. 12–2 Wagon grave in plank-built chamber, showing remains of wagon, position of male and female burials, grave goods, etc., Hallstatt D culture, sixth century B.C. (Piggott 1965:Fig. 101.)

placed a few meters apart. These *stone alignments* are best known from Brittany, France. There are enormous single stones termed *menhirs,* which were erected perhaps as shrines. Another variety of construction, the *trilothon,* features the capping of one or two vertical stones with a horizontal stone. A final type of monument consists of circular alignments of individual stones or trilothons to form an outdoor shrine or temple. These are the *henges,* the most famous of which, Stonehenge, we will discuss in somewhat greater detail below. There is no doubt that a major religious cult must have directed the efforts necessary to quarry and erect the stones, weighing up to 40 tons, which undoubtedly required much of the free time of the society. According to Piggott (1965:60), more than 5000 Megalithic tombs are known from France, 3500 on the Danish Islands, and 2000 in the British Isles.

Earlier explanations of the origins of this cult held that it was the result of diffusion from the center of civilization in the eastern Mediterranean. Renfrew's revision (1971) of European chronology, based on the recalibration of radiocarbon dates, indicates that the monuments are earlier than originally thought. They also are earliest in France; therefore their diffusion from an Aegean source is disproved.

Although the archaeological evidence is inadequate, we can make

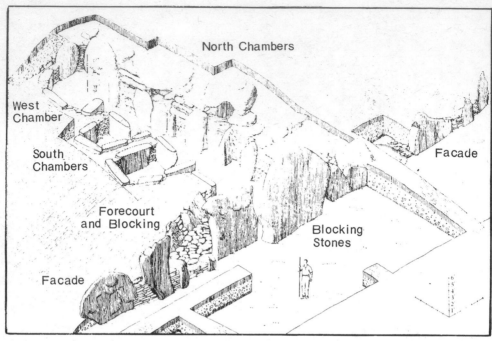

Fig. 12–3 Megalithic chambered tomb, mid third millennium B.C., at West Kennet, Wiltshire, England. (Piggott 1965:Fig. 30.)

some general statements about the religion. The objects within the tombs are those of the local cultures; thus we are not dealing with a single culture, but instead the spread of a cult with its own independent ethic. The spread of this religion is described by Childe (1958) as colonization or missionization by groups of Megalithic saints who introduced the religious concepts and determined who was to be buried within the tombs. In France, Childe notes the presence of two different levels of tombs, those for the Megalithic chiefs and inferior ones for the native Neolithic peasants. Surely burial in these tombs was a great honor, as the burials within a tomb were limited from about 8 to 40. The tombs were likely the property of specific social groups, with burial restricted to the members of one family or larger kin group.

Tombs are of two general formats: the *passage grave,* with a passage leading to a multichambered polygonal or circular room, and the *gallery grave,* without the separate entry passage. Instead there is an elaborate entrance to an oblong burial chamber.

Some of the tombs are decorated with carved or painted designs. Most of the designs are geometric in spiral, curvilinear, and rectilinear patterns. Another form of decoration consists of the symbolic representation of a female deity, a type of mother goddess. Inasmuch as some of the goddess representations are associated with those of axes, it is also thought that she may have had some connection with warfare.

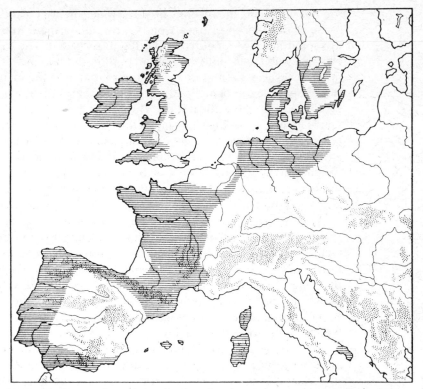

Fig. 12–4   Distribution of Megalithic chambered tombs in western Europe. (Piggott 1965:Fig. 29.)

The henges stand as the greatest examples of the Megalithic builder's skill, and of these, Stonehenge in Wiltshire, England, is the most outstanding. Harold Edgerton (1960) has ventured a reconstruction of the building techniques used at Stonehenge.

Stonehenge architects chose to build with gray sandstone slabs called sarcens, which they quarried on the Marlborough Downs. . . . Here on the Marlborough Downs about 1500 B.C., toilers lever an embedded sarcen from the earth. Their fellows, risking crushed arms or legs, thrust timbers under the stone. With the slab clear of the ground, workmen begin to shape it by heating the line of an intended cut with firebrands. Others then douse the stone with cold water to inflict internal stress. Finally, men batter the sarcen by simultaneously dropping 50-pound stone mauls. Four maul hurlers, standing on animal skins to save feet from blistering, await their foreman's shout. With arm raised, he delays until an assistant marks the traget line, which still steams from its fire-and-water bath (Edgerton 1960:848–849).

The maul hurlers then throw their stones on the line until the unwanted portion of the stone is sheared off. The quarrying was only a minor portion of the total effort involved. The quarried sarcens were then hauled on a wooden sledge over log rollers the 24 miles to the Stonehenge construction site. While long rows of men pulled on the ropes attached to the sledge, other laborers would run relays, placing the recently used log rollers in front of the advancing sledge. Once at the site, the stones were set by rolling them into position with the lower third of the stone over a pit dug to receive it. The top of the stone was elevated with levers until the bottom portion slid into the pit. The setting of the lintel stones was even more difficult, for it required the inching forward of the stones up some sort of inclined plane made of log cribbing until the stone could be aligned atop the vertical slabs. The size of the task can be appreciated when you learn that replacing some fallen lintels in 1958 required the aid of a 60-ton crane. The major circle of stones at Stonehenge once included 30 stones set in a ring 97⅓ feet across. The individual sarcens were up to 20 feet in height and weighed 40 to 50 tons. Further evidence of the skill of the builders is provided by the fact that the lintels were fitted to the uprights with mortise and tenon joints and the lintels were fitted together with a tongue and groove joint.

Outside of the circle of sarcens were two rings of holes which held smaller stones termed bluestones. These weighed up to 4 tons, but the amazing fact is that they were transported from quarries up to 250 miles away. Another feature of interest (Fig. 12–5) is an enclosing earthwork circle. Around its inside perimeter are 56 symmetrically placed small pits, called Aubrey holes, some of which are filled with cremated bone. Also around the perimeter are four upright station stones. The entrance features three uprights set in a line with parallel earthworks flanking them. At the point where the entrance meets the earthen circle are two additional uprights. The overall meaning and use of Stonehenge has been lost in antiquity. In recent centuries it has formed an important part of the Druid religion wherein each June they conduct solstice ceremonies at the site. However, we have no evidence that the Druids actually built the monument.

Stonehenge was built in three stages of construction (see Fig. 12–5). Stage I, begun about 2500 B.C. according to radiocarbon-dated features, included the enclosing ditch and embankment, the heel stone and its flanking embankments, the four station stones, and the 56 Aubrey holes. Named for the man who first studied them, the Aubrey holes are 2½ to 6 feet in diameter and from 2 to 4 feet in depth. Forming a circle 288 feet in diameter, they are filled with chalk rubble and frequently, cremated human bones. The second stage of construction, begun about 2350 B.C., included the setting up of the 82 bluestones in two rows, each stone about 6 feet apart.

Stonehenge III is the final stage of construction which includes the most dramatic portions of the monument as it is preserved today. Beginning about 2000 B.C. and continuing until 1900 B.C., the final building phase included the construction of the sarcen circle, the placement of five trilothons, a horseshoe of bluestones, and exterior to the sarcens, two circles of holes termed Y and Z holes. The total amount of construction time required was enormous. Hawkins (1965:73) has provided an estimate of the man-days required (Table 12–1).

Stonehenge has been likened to an outdoor temple, which function it

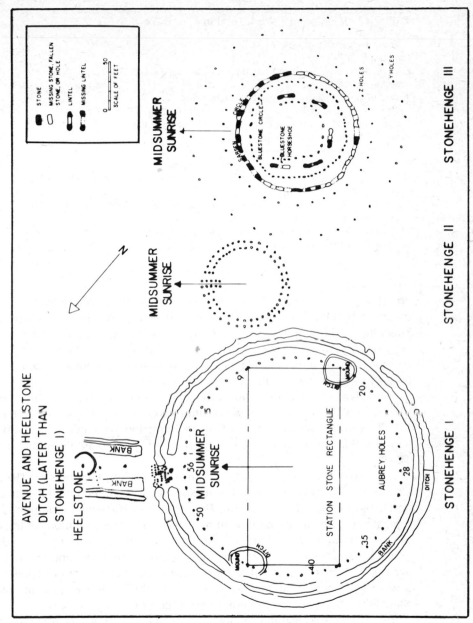

Fig. 12–5 Plans of the three major constructional periods at Stonehenge. (Compiled from Hawkins 1965:Figs. 3, 4, and 5.)

TABLE 12–1   Minimum Work Total in Man-Days

Digging ditch, making bank: 3500 cubic yards, at 1 yard per man-day	3500
Carrying for above	7000
Digging 5000 cubic yards for Avenue banks, leveling, survey, etc.	6000
Carrying for above	12,000
Transporting 80 bluestones, average weight 4 tons,	
24 miles by land at 100 men per stone, 1 mile per day	192,000
216 miles by water at 10 men per stone, 10 miles per day	17,280
Erecting Stonehenge II at 20 man-days per stone	1600
Transporting 80 sarcens, average weight 30 tons,	
20 miles by land at 700 men per stone, 1 mile per day	1,120,000
Dressing, shaping sarcens: 3 million cubic inches of rock powder at 50 cubic inches	
per man-day	60,000
Cutting with stone axes, hauling 300 logs for lattice tower, 2000 rollers, at 1 man-day	
per log	2300
Making 60,000 yards of hide rope at 1 man-day per yard	60,000
Erecting Stonehenge III at 200 man-days per stone	16,000
TOTAL MAN-DAYS	1,497,680

could well serve even if the rites were held there infrequently. Our best evidence of the use of the monument derives from recent research by Gerald Hawkins (1965) who has provided a series of reconstructions of astronomical sightings that may be taken by aligning the various stones with the position of the sun, moon, stars, and planets. On the basis of a computerized program, Hawkins asserts that the monument functioned as a type of computer used in astronomical observations. No correlations were observed for the stars and planets, but 10 sun and 14 moon positions were noted with an average error of 1.5°. The probability of such correlations being due to chance is less than one in a million (Hawkins 1965:172). The lines of sight plotted are illustrated in Figure 12–6.

Other authors, principally Thom (1967, 1971), Hutchinson (1972), and Cowan (1970), have reviewed the reasons for Megalithic circular monuments and their methods of construction. The more than 200 such monuments known typically feature circles, often with flattened sides. Interpretations of the details of these monuments include ascribing to their makers a rudimentary knowledge of trigonometry, use of a standard length of measurement, the Megalithic yard of 2.72 feet, use of a flexible compass, and even a set of beliefs leading toward Pythagorean mathematics. Certainly the evidence provides proof of Megalithic man's ability to think in abstract terms.

After the Megalithic period, the primary evidence of religion consists solely of grave offerings; later, just prior to the Roman conquest, we can distinguish a formalized religion—that of the Druids. We have little evidence that Druidism is descended from the Megalithic religion. The ancient Druids were practitioners of magic and ritual, and in Ireland they also bore arms. They foretold events through revelations received while in a trance. They made

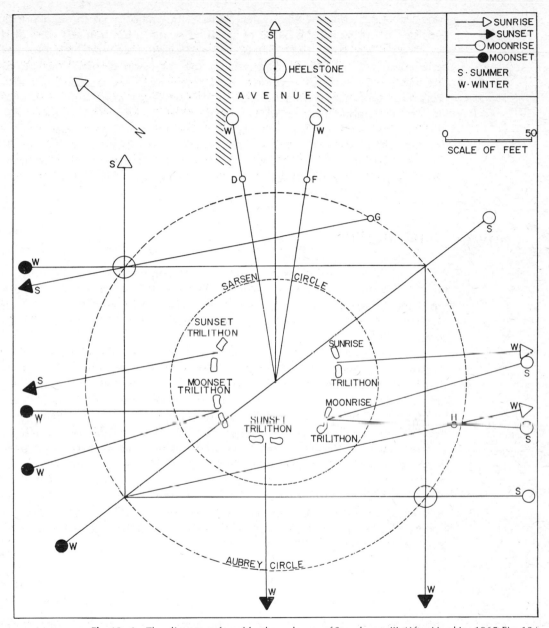

Fig. 12–6   The alignments found for the archways of Stonehenge III. (After Hawkins 1965:Fig. 12.)

votive offerings to trees and water bodies; the majority of these offerings consisted of sprinkling the blood of sacrificed animals, but humans were also occasionally sacrificed. They memorized and transmitted oral literature and believed in an afterlife as witnessed by the inclusion of numerous burial offerings. Their sacrifices were organized according to the concepts of earth, fire, and water symbolized in the sacrifices by hanging, burning, and drowning. Druids were important in secular matters, for they gave advice to the kings. There is little evidence that they functioned as a true intelligentsia, since they did not write history nor did they serve as philosophers. We know the Druids from the writings of their Roman contemporaries. Therefore we know their practices in much greater detail than would be the case if we had to rely only on archaeological evidence.

VILLAGES AND HOUSING

Archaeology is especially satisfactory as a technique for the recovery of information about prehistoric housing. We can recover evidence of house types and village patterns, and from these estimate population. During the last four millennia B.C., we have from Europe large quantitites of village remains available for study (Fig. 12–7).

The variety of housing is impressive; we have evidence of oblong houses with a porch, oval-shaped palisade units built of timber, rectangular single-roomed, square single-roomed, stone, timber framed with mud walls, pile dwellings, and so on. The majority of houses feature either log or post construction. They are arranged in villages of from 15 to 75 houses with populations of 100 to 400. The pattern was a long-standing one based on living close to one's farmland. The buildings within the village were segregated by use into houses, barns, granaries, and sheds for livestock. Frequently the houses had dual use, with part serving as stables for livestock, a pattern still used in rural Europe. The houses were from 10 by 15 feet to 15 by 30 feet. The number of acres cultivated by such a village was several hundred. The Linear Pottery villages, for example, with a population of about 400, were farming 600 acres (Piggott 1965:52).

TRADE

The evidence of trade with the Mediterranean Classical world documents the degree of interaction tempered with cultural selection that was in effect. Barbarian Europe did not seek to acquire all the luxuries available, nor did they slavishly copy all that they were exposed to. The major items acquired from the Mediterranean world were ornaments and objects manufactured of metal, especially weapons and armor. Traded in exchange were amber, tin, gold,

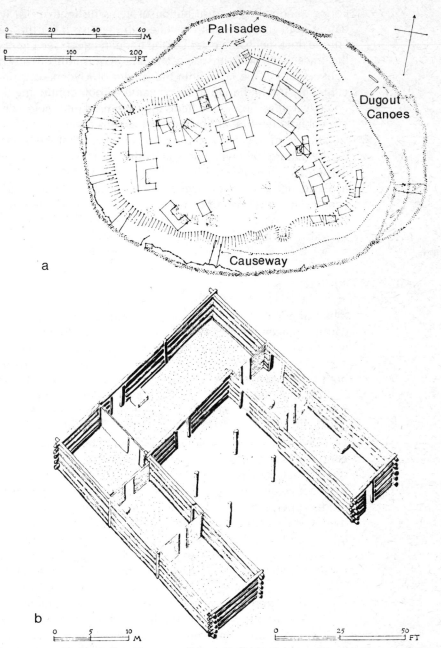

Fig. 12-7   a. Timber-built settlement on island, Urnfeld culture, twelfth to ninth century B.C., South Germany. b. Reconstructed house. (Piggott 1965:Figs. 82 and 83.)

copper, and salt. The distribution of items distinctive of Mycenaean culture, dating from the fourteenth or fifteenth century B.C., throughout continental Europe documents the extent of the trade in effect (see Fig. 9–3). The nature of the trade is clear; with respect to the acquisition of rare natural resources, continental Europe lay within the sphere of Mycenaean influence. However, culturally, the barbarian tribes remained aloof, continuing their own life style and integrating those trade items they acquired into their own system of values. We cannot therefore attribute the noncivilized nature of these tribes to cultural isolation from the civilized world. It is obvious that the barbarians were aware of the nature of civilization and simply chose to continue their peasant existence. Environmental limitations may have been of some importance, but the evidence from trade suggests that cultural selection was of equal significance. After the seventh century B.C. a major trade item from the Mediterranean was wine, as evidenced by the vessels in which it was imported as well as those for serving wine.

METALWORKING

Metal implements in barbarian Europe first appeared as items of trade. The earliest indigenous items, dating 4000 B.C., are found in the Vinča culture of the Balkans where they antedate the appearance of copperworking in the Aegean (Renfrew 1971:69). Early European centers of copperworking included both the eastern European Transylvania area and the Iberian peninsula. The earliest implements were shaft hole axes, spiral arm rings, copper discs, spiral beads, and flat ax blades. These items were traded northward as far as Denmark.

The next most significant event in the evolution of metalworking in Europe was the appearance of peoples about 2500 B.C. distinguished by a specific pottery type—the *Bell Beaker* (Fig. 12–8). The so-called Beaker folk were above all migratory traders spreading cultural traits across Europe. They used copper, and it is believed that their smiths, with their knowledge of casting, traveled with the trading bands. We do not know if their skills included mining and smelting. Their metallurgical techniques included the use of the simple open mold rather than the closed valve type. In any event their activities stimulated the use of bronze in Europe, with the exploitation of tin from Cornwall and copper from both Ireland and England. Their efforts also included the introduction of goldworking and its extraction from Irish sources.

According to Piggott (1965:102), after 2000 B.C. (now ca. 2500 B.C.) new forms of copper implements suggesting Syrian influences appear in central Europe. The new introductions feature the riveted dagger blade rather than the earlier tanged type. New ornaments include the ingot-torc and pins for garments. From this time, after about 2000 B.C., we have present a local bronze industry with uniquely European attributes. Coupled with this development was the appearance, after 1800 B.C., of increasing importation of trade items of

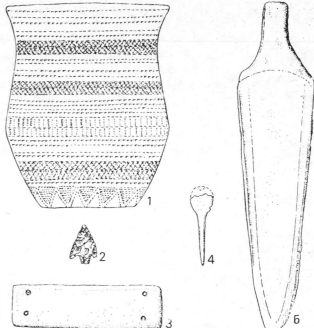

Fig. 12–8 Objects from Bell Beaker grave, beginning of second millenium B.C., at Roundway, Wiltshire, England: *1.* beaker; *2.* flint arrowhead; *3.* archer's wristguard; *4.* copper pin; *5.* copper tanged knife-dagger. (Piggott 1965: Fig. 53.)

bronze from Mycenae. The local response was the development of new forms of the introduced Mycenaean objects. These included swords, spearheads, daggers, helmets, body armor, gold cups, and other golden ornaments. By the fifteenth century B.C. the technique of annealing appears, wherein by heating and hammering, metals are beaten into sheets. The resultant thin material was then manufactured into a wide variety of bronze vessels, helmets, shields, and so forth. The major types of vessels included a bucket of the situla form, a cup with a handle, and a strainer for wine.

The appearance of iron prior to 1000 B.C. represented not an innovation of revolutionary importance but a continuation of prior cultural patterns. After the beginning of the eighth century B.C. we perceive the influx of horse bits and bridles into central Europe from the steppes to the east. These reflect influences from the Scythian culture. In the next two centuries the westward spread of wagon or cart burial occurred (see Fig. 12–2). Both of these trends suggest an invasion of central Europe by nomadic herding peoples. By the seventh century B.C., in Hallstadt burials, we have the presence of implements of iron, especially long swords.

The working of iron had a sporadic development in the Middle East. It was first used in Predynastic Egypt where meteoric iron was employed. Smelted iron dates later, after 3000 B.C. It was difficult to smelt, and the finished product was not superior to bronze; thus it remained little used except for ornaments. The first major development of iron in quantity was by the Hittites in Asia Minor about the fifteenth century B.C. From there its use gradually spread westward. A curious feature of the iron technology of all Europe, Rome included, was the fact that the tempering of iron was unknown until the eleventh century A.D.

In addition to cart fittings, including iron rims, the major uses of iron were for ornaments, fire dogs, horse trappings, shields, weapons (Fig. 12–9), axes, adzes, and other carpentry tools. If we may distinguish some innovative aspects associated with the use of iron, the foremost is perhaps its greater availability; secondly, new forms of weapons appeared, so perhaps it made for more efficient weapons; and finally, carpentry was given a dramatic boost by the availability of iron woodworking tools.

TRANSPORT

Wheeled transport by wagon or cart was the typical mode in barbarian Europe. The wheel was invented in Mesopotamia prior to 3000 B.C. Its use spread across Europe by 2500 B.C. (Fig. 12–10). Early wheels were solid, either of one piece of wood or discs made from planks. There were two forms of vehicles, the two-wheeled cart and the wagon with four wheels. There is also archaeological evidence of corduroy roads of logs built as early as 2500 B.C. The use of wheeled vehicles required proper terrain, not too hilly or boggy. Central and northern Europe possessed these qualities, with the result that wheeled vehicles aided the frequent moves of the peasant farmers. Another aspect was the associated rise in importance of draft animals, both oxen and horses with their harness trappings. In Celtic times there was a shift from the heavier wagons to the lighter two-wheeled war chariots. After 500 B.C. the typical warrior or chief's grave includes the chariot. The appearance of spokes likely derives from the need for lighter, faster chariots. Spoked wheels are a common Celtic trait dating from the last few centuries B.C.

The gauge of wagons, the distance between the wheels, was established at 3 feet 6 inches to 3 feet 9 inches; a tradition that extends from the time of Ur in Mesopotamia down to the Hallstadt wagons of the fifth and sixth centuries B.C. The later La Tene wagons shifted to a gauge of 4 feet 8½ inches which is the standard railroad gauge still in use today. Archaeological evidence for these gauges is provided by wheel ruts preserved in numerous European sites. In northern Europe we have a continuation in use of the vehicles developed in earlier periods—the sledge, wooden dugout, and skis (Fig. 12–11).

WARFARE

The practice of war by the European barbarians is known to us from the inclusions of weapons and chariots in burials, but of even greater detail are the historical accounts from Roman sources. We may infer warfare from the swords, spears, shields, helmets, and rare body armor recovered archaeologi-

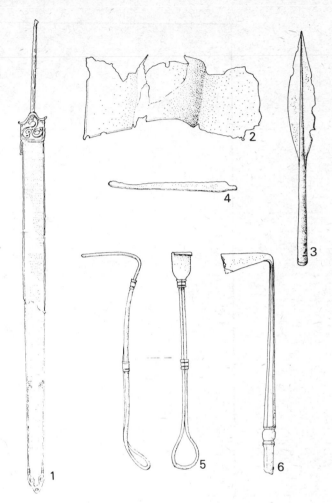

Fig. 12–9 Objects from middle La Tene grave, second century B.C., at Obermenzingen, South Germany: *1*. sword in scabbard; *2*. shield boss; *3*. spearhead; *4*. surgeon's knife; *5*. retractor; *6*. trephining saw. (Piggott 1965:Fig. 129.)

cally; but it is from the historical sources that we obtain our knowledge of the place of warfare in the society and the tactics employed. The appearance of horse trappings has led some authors to infer the use of cavalry, but in fact the horse was more typically ridden to provide access to the battlefield, with the contest consisting of individual clashes on foot.

With the transition from Hallstadt to La Tene culture about the fifth century B.C., we have the rise of chariot warfare. We quote from the description of a chariot warrior chieftain in action (Powell 1963:106–107):

The iron sword was carried in a bronze scabbard with ornamental foot or chape, and with a design in the La Tene style chased on the outer face. A dagger, similarly sheathed, might also be carried as well as a complement of spears. A few particularly wealthy chieftains possessed helmets of cap, or high conical, shape made of bronze and sometimes covered with gold worked in La Tene motifs, and embellished with coral studs. The horses were handsomely fitted out with bronze snaffle bits and harness

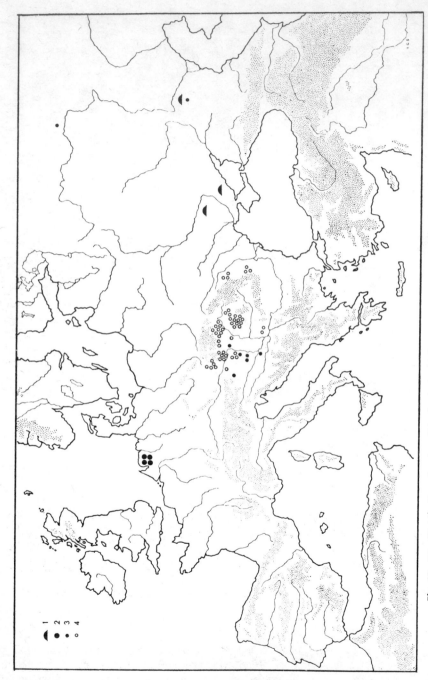

Fig. 12–10 Distribution of early solid-wheeled vehicles in Europe: *1.* vehicles in burials, third millennium B.C.; *2.* wooden wheels, ca. 2500 B.C.; *3.* models of vehicles and wheels, late third millennium B.C.; *4.* models, second millennium B.C. (Dates are recalibrated.) (Piggott 1965:Fig. 49.)

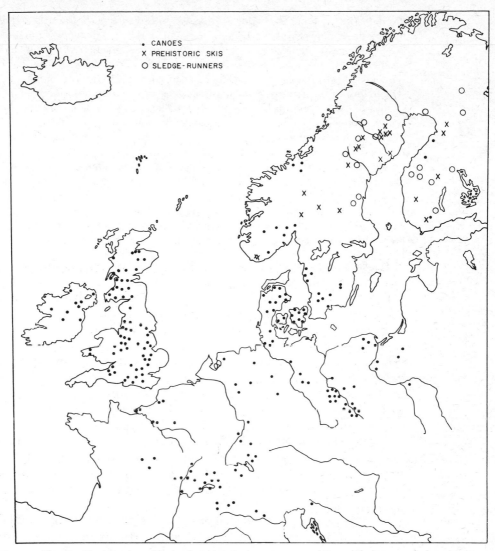

Fig. 12–11 Location of finds of prehistoric dugout canoes, skis, and sledge-runners from Norway, Finland, and Sweden. (After J. G. D. Clark 1952:Fig. 160.)

mounts, and the chariot also had bronze fittings, with iron tyres and other components. The normal metal snaffle-bit in prehistoric Europe was of the two-link type, but in Champagne, and later in Britain and Ireland, a three-link type is found which would have been less severe on the horse's mouth. This suggests the emergence of a finer breed, more sensitive to skilled control.

With Polybius, and subsequent authors, the procedure on the battlefield can be brought into view. Taking all the evidence into consideration, it may be deduced that the initial purpose of the chariot warrior was to drive furiously towards and along the front of the enemy ranks to instill terror by sight, and by the delivery of missiles, no less than by the tremendous noise that was kept up by shouting, horn blowing, and beating on the sides of the waggons drawn up to the flanks or in the rear. The warriors then descended from their chariots, which the charioteer held in readiness for a quick retreat if need be, while the warrior, with casting spear, or drawn sword, stood out to deliver a challenge to an opposing champion. The challenge was evidently in a set formula of boasts of prowess, and perhaps of lineage, incorporated in a war song. Indeed, a kind of frenzy was probably worked up. In inter-tribal fighting, it would appear that the main body of troops became involved only after this phase of individual contest, and perhaps only if one side had become certain of success in a general melee. The course of events against Roman armies must have involved the whole body of fighting men more directly, and it led to considerable modification in battle order.

The archaic mode of individual challenge, and encounter by champions, recalls the scenes in the *Iliad,* and the Celts were indeed the inheritors of that tradition which had long become outmoded south of the Balkans and of the Alps.

In Caesar's account of chariot warriors he states they ran up the pole between the horses, or at least intimidated the enemy with their agility.

The average Celtic warrior fought on foot with armament consisting of a cutting sword, one or two spears used for casting, and the long oval shield of wood with iron fittings. A unique feature was their appearance in battle naked, which was intended as an appeal for magical or supernatural protection. The horsemen practiced the decapitation of foes whose heads were displayed hanging to the horses bridles and eventually were taken home for display. By the first century B.C. we have the introduction of the sling as a weapon of war to Britain from Mediterranean sources. One result of the use of slings was the restructuring of the hilltop forts to include multiple ramparts.

The final accolade given to the successful warriors was the feasts and gifts provided by the king. Celtic feasts were renowned for gluttony and indulgence in drinking. The affairs were socially structured with the best portions rigidly allocated by rank including the presentation of the boar's head to the charioteer.

The other major evidence of warfare is defensive in nature; the hilltop forts which became common after 1000 B.C. The basic feature of their construction was the building of a timber-framed rampart covered with earth (Fig. 12–12). The fortress was located on a prominent hilltop with the rampart defenses surrounding the perimeter. Piggott (1965:204) cites the fact that the amount of timber required was substantial; for example, one small fortress utilized all the 9-inch timbers to be cut at one time from 60 acres of forest. The timbers were placed both vertically and horizontally and secured with iron nails. A unique aspect of these forts is that many of these ramparts are preserved today in vitrified form, the result of firing. Previously it was thought such firing was part of the construction process. The modern view is that all fired walls were the result of enemy attack. Constructional features present include the use of protruding bastions along the wall, in-turned gateways,

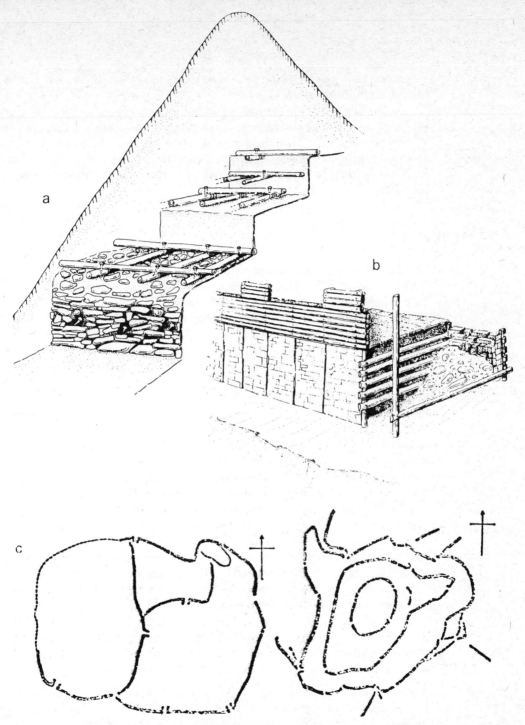

Fig. 12–12 *a.* Timber-framed wall of hill fort, of murus gallicus type with iron nails, late La Tene culture, first century B.C. *b.* Timber-framed wall of hill fort, middle La Tene culture, second century B.C. *c.* Hill forts of oppida status, Late La Tene culture, probably first century B.C., in final constructional phase. (Piggott 1965:Figs. 119, 120, and 121.)

enclosure of springs, flanking guard chambers along gateways, and late in the period, multiple ramparts.

The larger hill forts termed *oppida* by the Romans, functioned as tribal centers. One of the largest of these, Manching, Bavaria, encloses an area about 1½ miles in diameter. Within the fortresses were houses, streets, workshops, grain storage pits, and pastures for livestock. The primary use of the hill fort was for refuge in time of attack with the typical peasant living in and farming near his village.

CULTURE HISTORY

Standard references on European prehistory have dealt with the time period under review, the last 4500 years B.C., as a sequence of cultures each with its own diagnostic culture traits. Thus these works feature descriptions of the Megalithic peoples, Linear Pottery peoples, Impressed Ware peoples, Bell Beaker folk, Food Vessel people, Battle Axe people, Urnfield and Scythian cultures, plus those cultures with geographic names—Starĉevo, Chassey-Cortaillod, Wessex, Windmill Hill, Tripolye, Boian, Hallstadt, and La Tene. The result is a bewildering complexity of culture names and selected traits, which to my way of thinking, leads to confusion rather than order. For this reason then, I have followed the procedure in this chapter of emphasizing the continuity of European peasant culture rather than its discontinuities. The result is a narrative which is not chronologically oriented. It lacks the time-space coefficients of standard prehistory. Such studies cannot simply be ignored, for they form the framework upon which individual finds are arranged prior to their interpretation. These data are presented in summary form in Figures 12–13, 12–14, and 12–15. The archaeological details distinguishing these named cultures, one from the other, are frequently of minor character; for example, specific pottery types found in burials. The point of view expressed in this chapter is that we may understand the basic nature of the period without reference to these sometimes minor but nonetheless archaeologically significant diagnostics. Those wishing to explore the subject in greater detail will find numerous references on the subject available.

At this point in our discussion I can visualize no better way to dramatize the end of this period than to describe the Roman conquest of Maiden Castle between A.D. 43 and 47 (Fig. 12–16). Sir Mortimer Wheeler (1943:61–63) has reconstructed the events from the archaeological findings.

Approaching from the direction of the Isle of Wight, Vespasian's legion may be supposed to have crossed the River Frome at the only easy crossing hereabouts—where Roman and modern Dorchester were subsequently to come into being. Before the advancing troops, some 2 miles away, the sevenfold ramparts of the western gates of Dunium towered above the cornfields which probably swept, like their modern successors, up to the fringe of the defences. Whether any sort of assault was attempted upon these gates we do not at present know; their excessive strength makes it more likely that, leaving a guard upon them, Vespasian moved his main attack to the somewhat less formidable eastern end. What happened there is plain to read. First, the regiment of artillery, which normally accompanied a legion on campaign, was ordered into action, and put down a barrage of iron-shod ballista-arrows over the eastern part of the site. Following this barrage, the infantry advanced up the slope, cutting its way from rampart to rampart, tower to tower. In the innermost bay of the entrance, close outside the actual gates, a number of huts had recently been built; these were set alight, and under the rising clouds of smoke the gates were stormed and the position carried. But resistance had been obstinate and the fury of the attackers was roused. For a space, confusion and massacre dominated the scene. Men and women, young and old, were savagely cut down, before the legionnaires were called to heel and the work of systematic destruction began. That work included the uprooting of some at least of the timbers which revetted the fighting-platform on the summit of the main rampart; but above all it consisted of the demolition of the gates and the overthrow of the high stone walls which flanked the two portals. The walls were now reduced to the lowly and ruinous state in which they were discovered by the excavator nearly nineteen centuries later.

That night, when the fires of the legion shone out (we may imagine) in orderly lines across the valley, the survivors crept forth from their broken stronghold and, in the darkness, buried their dead as nearly as might be outside their tumbled gates, in that place where the ashes of their burned huts lay warm and thick upon the ground. The task was carried out anxiously and hastily and without order, but, even so, from few graves were omitted those tributes of food and drink which were the proper and traditional perquisites of the dead. At daylight on the morrow, the legion moved westward to fresh conquest, doubtless taking with it the usual levy of hostages from the vanquished.

Thereafter, saving what they could of their crops and herds, the disarmed townsfold made shift to put their house in order. Forbidden to refortify their gates, they built new roadways across the sprawling ruins, between gateless ramparts that were already fast assuming the blunted profiles that are theirs to-day. And so, for some two decades, a demilitarized Maiden Castle retained its inhabitants, or at least a nucleus of them.

So much for the story; now for its basics. First, scattered over the eastern end of Maiden Castle, mostly in and about the eastern entrance and always at the same Romano-Belgic level, were found upwards of a dozen iron arrowheads, of two types: a type with a pyramidal point, and the simple flat-bladed type with turnover socket. Arrowheads occurred at no other Iron Age level, but both types are common on Roman military sites where *ballistae* but not hand-bows are to be inferred. There, then, in the relatively small area uncovered, are the vestiges of the bombardment.

Secondly, the half-moon bay which represents the Iron Age B adaptation of the Iron Age A barbican, close outside the portals of the eastern entrance, was covered with a thick layer of ash associated with the post-holes of three or more circular or roundish huts. In and immediately below this ash were quantities of late Belgic or "Belgicizing" pottery. In the surface of the ash was similar pottery with scraps of pre-Flavian Samian. There are the burnt Belgic huts, covered by the trodden vestiges of the continued post-conquest occupation for which more tangible evidence will be offered shortly.

Thirdly, into this ash a series of graves had been roughly cut, with no regularity either of outline or of orientation, and into them had been thrown, in all manner of attitudes—crouched, extended, on the back, on the side, on the face, even sitting up—thirty-eight skeletons of men and women, young and old; sometimes two persons were

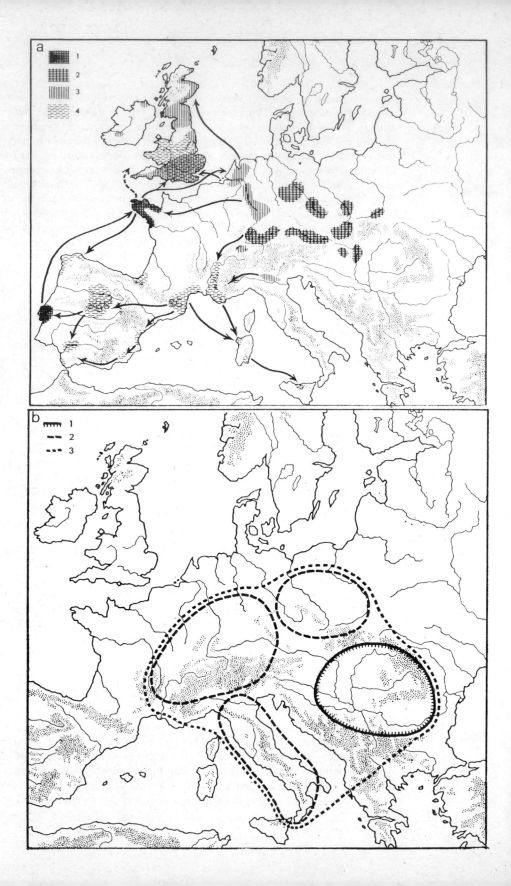

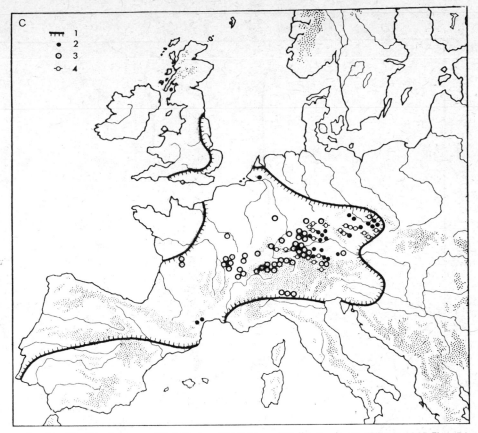

Fig. 12–13 Distributions of Bell Beaker, Urnfield, and Hallstatt cultures. (Piggott 1965:Figs. 54, 79, and 100.)

a. Distribution and movements of Bell Beaker cultures, end of third to beginning of second millennium B.C.; *1.* "Maritime" Group; *2.* Eastern and Central Groups; *3.* Netherlands, Rhenish and Austrian Groups, and Reflux derivatives; *4.* other Reflux derivatives.

b. Generalized map showing expansion of Urnfield cultures: *1.* thirteenth century B.C.; *2.* twelfth–tenth century B.C.; *3.* tenth–eighth century B.C.

c. Distribution of *1.* Hallstatt culture, seventh–fifth century B.C.; *2.* wagon-graves of Hallstatt C; *3.* wagon-graves of Hallstatt D; *4.* wagon-graves, C or D.

huddled together in the same grave. In ten cases extensive cuts were present on the skull, some on the top, some on the front, some on the back. In another case, one of the arrow-heads already described was found actually embedded in a vertebra, having entered the body from the front below the heart. The victim had been finished off with a cut on the head. Yet another skull had been pierced by an implement of square section, probably a ballistabolt. The last two and some of the swordcuts were doubtless battlewounds; but one skull, which had received no less than nine savage cuts, suggests the fury of massacre rather than the tumult of battle—a man does not stay to kill his enemy eight or nine times in the melee; and the neck of another skeleton had been dislocated, probably by hanging. Nevertheless, the dead had been buried by their friends, for most of them were accompanied by bowls, or in one case, a mug for the traditional food and drink. More notable, in two cases the dead held joints of lamb in their hands—joints chosen carefully as young and succulent. Many of the dead still wore their gear: armlets of iron or shale, an iron finger-ring, and in three cases bronze

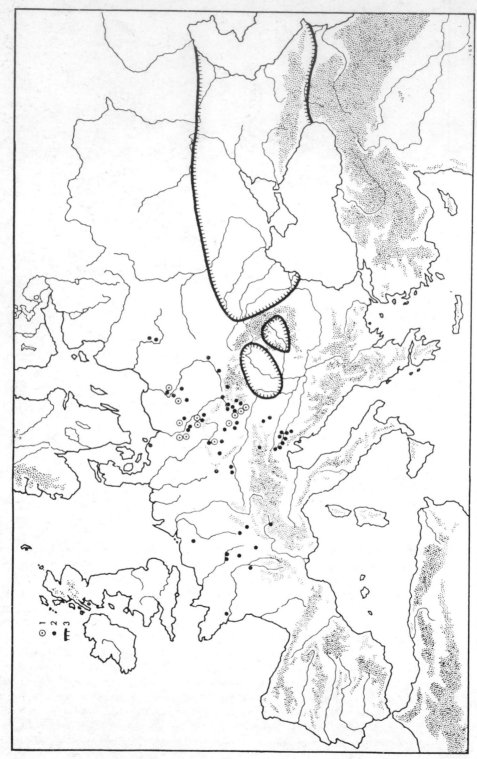

Fig. 12–14 *1.* Hill forts with evidence of Scythian attack; *2.* stray Scythian finds, mainly arrowheads; *3.* Scythian settlement areas. (Piggott:1965:Fig. 106.)

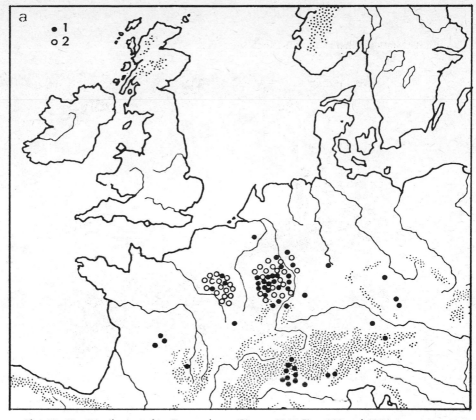

Fig. 12–15 Distribution of La Tene culture. (Piggott 1965:Figs. 118 and 134.)
a. Early La Tene culture: *1.* imported bronze wine-flagons, fifth century B.C.; *2.* chariot-burials.
b. Mature La Tene culture: *1.* La Tene culture and influences; *2.* sword scabbards in Swiss style;
3. British derivatives; *4.* many scabbards.

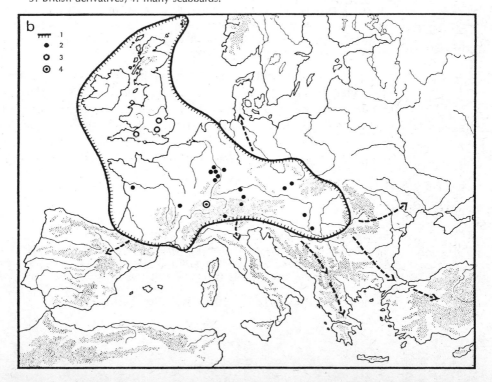

Fig. 12–16   View of Maiden Castle. (Daniel 1968:57. Crown copyright.)

toe-rings, representing a custom not previously, it seems, observed in prehistoric Britain but reminiscent of the Moslem habit of wearing toe-rings as ornaments or as preventives or cures of disease. One man lay in a double grave with an iron battle-axe, a knife and, strangely, a bronze ear-pick across his chest. The whole war cemetery as it lay exposed before us was eloquent of mingled piety and distraction; of weariness, of dread, of darkness, but yet not of complete forgetfulness. Surely no poor relic in the soil of Britain was ever more eloquent of high tragedy. . . .

The above event is symbolic in that it represents the head-on collision of two different cultural systems: barbarian Europe and the Classical world of Rome. The conflict continued for four centuries after the fall of Maiden Castle, but the latter is representative of many similar events. The cultural systems in contact were no longer able to live in peaceful and symbiotic coexistence. The European events which followed pertain to history rather than prehistory.

REFERENCES

Braidwood, R. J., 1967, *Prehistoric Men*, 7th ed. Glenview, Ill.: Scott, Foresman.
Childe, V. G., 1958, *The Prehistory of European Society*. Baltimore: Penguin.
Clark, J. G. D., 1952, *Prehistoric Europe: The Economic Basis*. London: Methuen.
Cowan, T. M., 1970, "Megalithic Rings: Their Design Construction," *Science* 168:321–325.
Daniel, G., 1968, *Man Discovers His Past*. New York: Crowell.

Edgerton, H., 1960, "New Light on an Old Riddle, Stonehenge," *National Geographic Magazine* 117(6):346–866.

Hawkes, C., and J. Hawkes, 1949, *Prehistoric Britain*. Harmondsworth, Middlesex: Pelican.

Hawkins, S., 1965, *Stonehenge Decoded*. New York: Doubleday.

Hutchinson, G. E., 1972, "Long Meg Reconsidered," *American Scientist* 60:24–31, 210–219.

Piggott, S., 1965, *Ancient Europe from the Beginnings of Agriculture to Classical Antiquity*. Chicago: Aldine.

Powell, T. G. E., 1963, *The Celts*. London: Thames and Hudson.

Renfrew, C., 1971, "Carbon 14 and the Prehistory of Europe," *Scientific American* 225(4):63–72.

Thom, A., 1967, *Megalithic Sites in Britain*. London: Oxford.

———, A., 1971, *Megalithic Lunar Observatories*. Oxford: Clarendon Press.

Wheeler, R. E. M., 1943, *Maiden Castle*. London: Dorset.

13

Early Man in
the Americas

In contrast to the Old World where we have both cultural and physical evidence of man's evolution from primate ancestors, in the New World we have evidence only of *Homo sapiens sapiens* possessing an advanced culture, a level we could term Upper Paleolithic. Thus man migrated into the New World at a date late in his total overall cultural history, bringing with him a culture as evolved as that of his Old World contemporaries. However, once into the New World, his culture rapidly adapted to the specific New World environments. The majority of archaeologists accept the view that man entered the New World by means of a migration across the Bering Strait, either at times of lowered sea level when a land bridge was present (Fig. 13–1) or during the winter when passage over ice would have been possible. There are other theories relative to the peopling of the New World, but these primarily relate to later time periods. For example, Greenman (1963) has outlined a northern

Fig. 13–1 Bering land bridge at maximum extent (shown in light gray).

Europe to Greenland to northeastern North America route which would have required boats. Pottery from Ecuador, dated 2500 B.C., features attributes similar to those of Jomon pottery of Neolithic Japan, leading Meggers, Evans, and Estrada (1965) to suggest a direct sea route from Japan at that time. The Aleutian island chain forms another suitable route. There is also the possibility of South Atlantic crossings, demonstrated by Thor Heyerdahl in his famous voyages in Ra I and II, the papyrus reed boats built according to Ancient Egyptian designs. We will not debate here the merits of these particular migration theories. At this point we are interested in the earliest migrations to the New World, and all evidence points to the Bering Strait as the initial point of entry. There is ample evidence of later movements of peoples into the New World; thus there is no need to think of a single "migration" with irreversible effects. Early migrations probably include nonprojectile-point, pebble-tool users, as well as specialized big game hunters, utilizing an Upper Paleolithic type of tool inventory. Later documented migrations include a Mesolithic culture pattern using microblades, and even later, about 3000 B.C., the arctic specialization we know as Eskimo culture.

We also have evidence of later migrations from the New World back to Siberia; therefore, the crossing of the Bering Strait was not a rare, unidirectional event. Such crossings must have occurred many times in the course of daily life in the region, since a similar environment is present on both sides of the Strait. Probably these early peoples initially entered the New World following herds of mammoths and other late Pleistocene big game animals as part of their normal migratory hunting life style (Fig. 13–2).

A MIGRATION HYPOTHESIS

The migrations of peoples following herds of game animals would have been governed to some degree by two interrelated factors: the presence of a land bridge at the Bering Strait and an open corridor between the late Pleistocene ice sheets in Canada. A correlation of these variables is attempted in the following hypothesis:

Any consideration of migrations would seem to be based on the primary variable of migration rates of the game animals that were being followed and hunted. In the present case, the primary animal was the mammoth. Analysis of the environmental needs of the mammoth should give us some clues as to movements of these animals in response to advances and retreats of late Wisconsin glaciers.

Stomach contents of mammoths preserved in frozen ground in Siberia indicate that these mammoths were subsisting on a diet of young shoots and cones of fir, pine, birch and willow trees and a broad variety of boreal meadow and tundra herbs, mosses, and grasses. If we may assume that these were the type of mammoth that early hunters followed into the New World then it is possible to conceive of these mammoths following such an environmental zone (termed Taiga-Tundra) from Siberia into Alaska through Canada and into the United States with the dependent hunters in close attendance. The time necessary to accomplish this migration need not have been great as the mammoth were almost certainly moving in direct relationship to the glacial advances and retreats, which we know to have been rapid. The natural path of this migration would conform closely to the northern boundary of the boreal forest belt of Canada and the eastern United States, an important corridor for migrations from earliest times to the present. The movements of these prey animals would have been governed by movements of the Late Wisconsin continental glaciers. In this respect two factors acting in opposition to each other are of importance: 1. Increasing glaciation would result in the lowering of sea level thus creating a land bridge across the Bering Strait. 2. Increasing glaciation would result in the coalescence of the Cordilleran and Laurentide Ice Sheets thus blocking any possible migration route between the Bering Strait and the United States. The combination of these factors clearly indicates that conditions suitable for migrations across the Bering Strait continuing southward to the United States during the Late Wisconsin must have been infrequent and of short duration. Haynes has presented the view that such an opportunity only occurred once, about 12,000 years ago. We believe that several such opportunities existed during the Late Wisconsin.

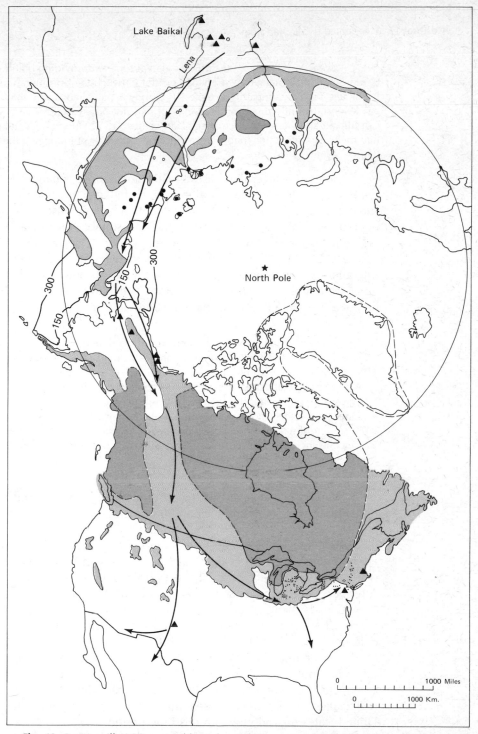

Fig. 13–2 Map illustrating possible early migration routes relative to Wisconsin glaciations, location of early sites in Siberia and America, and the Bering land bridge. Light gray indicates the maximum extent of the Wisconsin drift border. Dark gray shows the position of the Valders Age ice border as far as it is known. Large dots indicate position of frozen mammoths; circles, frozen rhinoceroses. Tiny dots show finds of fluted points in the northeastern United States. Arrows show possible migration routes. Archaeological sites are shown as triangles. (After Hester 1966:Fig. 7.)

If we may reconstruct the kind of glacial regimen providing both dry land at the Bering Strait and along a trans-Canada corridor between the Cordilleran and Laurentide Ice Sheets it would appear to be either: 1. During a glacial advance which had lowered sea level sufficiently to permit crossing but had not progressed to the point where the Cordilleran and Laurentide Ice Sheets had coalesced. 2. During a glacial retreat which had melted sufficient ice to form a corridor but had not yet inundated the Bering Strait. (Hester 1966: 135).

Sources concerning past climatic fluctuations, changes in sea level at the Bering Strait, and geological evidence of glacial advances and retreats are summarized in Figure 13–3. Agreement between these data supports our attempt to identify specific times in the past suitable for migrations.

In Figure 13–3 we can see several periods of glacial advance and retreat after 20,000 B.P. which would have fitted our criteria for possible times of migration. At this time is it possible to distinguish between these as to which times were most favorable for migration? The following statements summarize the facts available to answer our question.

1. Unless the migrants moved extremely rapidly, a time of glacial advance would have closed the trans-Canada corridor before they could move through it.
2. A glacial advance would feature increasingly severe climate.
3. A time of glacial retreat would be more favorable climatically if the migrants got across the Bering land bridge before it submerged.
4. Once across the land bridge, during a glacial retreat, migrants would have time to move into the trans-Canada corridor before glacial readvance closed it.
5. Once in the corridor, subsequent glacial advance would force the mammoths and attendant hunters rapidly to the south.

If times of glacial advance were climatically more rigorous than times of retreat then we shall consider only the times of retreat as most favorable for human migration. Viewed in this light, the most favorable time may have been the retreat beginning 15,000 years ago, for it occurred after a 2000-year interval when the land bridge was open, followed by a 1000- to 2000-year warm interval which would have permitted expansion to the south. The subsequent glacial advance between about 13,000 and 12,000 B.P. closed the trans-Canada corridor and could have forced men and animals into the central United States in time to be represented at the Clovis culture sites which have dated between 12,000 and 11,000 B.P.

The retreat beginning some 17,000 years ago may have permitted migration, but its major drawback is that the time the corridor was open was extremely short, possibly less than 1000 years. In addition, the immediate reglaciation would have closed the corridor forcing the entire Siberia-to-United-States migration within this time period.

The retreat beginning about 20,000 B.P., lasting until 18,000 B.P., (according to Fig. 13–3) probably was not favorable for migration from Alaska to the United States, since extensive ablation (melting plus evaporation) had to occur to separate the Cordilleran and Laurentide ice sheets. While this corridor may have been opened by about 18,000 B.P., the subsequent advance could have closed it almost immediately.

The retreat 12,000 years ago almost certainly could have permitted human migration, although the land bridge was open only a short time. Another time of potential migration discussed by Wendorf (1966) is that man first immigrated to the New World *prior* to the establishment of the Late Wisconsin ice sheet. He states the most probable time for this would have been between 25,000 and 18,000 B.C. when the Bering land bridge was exposed but the Canadian ice sheets were not yet in existence.

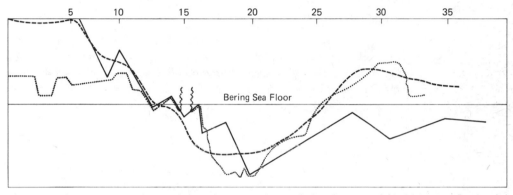

Fig. 13–3 Correlation of Late Pleistocene data with the elevation of the Bering Sea floor; solid line—glacial movements in North America after Flint (1963:Fig. 2); dashed line—sea level at the Bering Strait after Hopkins (1959:Fig. 4); dotted line—fluctuations in tree pollen in the Texas High Plains after Hafsten (1961:Fig. 34). Portions of the graphs below the Bering Sea floor line indicate times of possible land bridges at the Bering Strait, graphs above the sea floor line indicate times the land bridge was inundated. Time scale is in thousands of years before present. (After Hester 1966:Fig. 3.)

Support for these migration theories depends upon the individual researchers' views as to the significance of the land bridge and the presence of a Canadian corridor or ice barrier. It should be mentioned that evidence of a trans-Canada corridor is only now being collected.

For example, Haynes (1970:88) disagrees with the above hypothesis, citing evidence presented by Armstrong and others (1965) to the effect that the period 15,000–14,000 B.P. featured a major glacial advance, the Vashon stade, in the mountains of British Columbia. At this time I see little need to revise the present hypothesis, for what we still need are studies of the glaciation of the corridor region itself. In addition we are uncertain whether a land bridge was actually necessary or whether the glacial ice really formed a significant barrier. Stagnant glaciers can actually support pockets of vegetation; therefore man might possibly have crossed over such stable ice. Having explored these theories of early migration, we shall proceed southward to examine the earliest known evidence of man south of the glacial border.

EVIDENCE OF EARLY NEW WORLD MIGRANTS

Alex Krieger, in an article entitled "Early Man in the New World" (1964), has presented an overall summary of New World early evidence separated into three major stages: a Pre-Projectile Point stage, a Paleo-Indian stage, and a Protoarchaic stage. Not all New World early materials fit neatly into this classification, and there are disagreements among archaeologists as to the placement of specific site collections. Nonetheless Krieger's scheme is a useful summary for purposes of an overview of early New World findings.

Pre-Projectile Point Stage

Krieger defines the Pre-Projectile Point stage as featuring a low level of stoneworking technology. All tools were made by percussion flaking and are often large and heavy. A basic characteristic was the inability of the toolmakers to flatten and thin the artifacts. Other cultural traits include the occasional use of bone tools and the use of shallow basin-shaped fire hearths. No burials are known. Projectile points by definition do not occur. Sites assigned to this stage vary in their documentation as to age, and the validity of the objects termed implements are open to question—as many of the crude so-called pebble tools are difficult to distinguish from naturally broken rocks, and especially difficult when found in isolation apart from important materials, such as fossil bones, stratigraphic context, and other materials suitable for dating. The further back in time we go the less cultural material is preserved for analysis.

The above list could be greatly expanded if we wished to include all those sites claimed to be very early. Of the sites mentioned, perhaps Pikimachay Cave and Hueyatlaco are the best candidates for the earliest manifestations in the New World. We must also mention the much publicized work of L. S. B. Leakey and Ruth Simpson at Calico Hills, California. Their findings consist of stone "tools" embedded in a very ancient alluvial fan. Geologic estimates are that the age of the fan is somewhere between 50,000 and 500,000 years. Although excavated with fantastic care, the "tools" fail to convince many archaeologists of their human alteration; they may in fact be naturally broken rocks.

Paleo-Indian Stage

Implements of the Paleo-Indian stage feature finely controlled percussion flaking so that artifacts possess thin, flat cross sections. Projectile points and knives are common, and some feature added refinement achieved through pressure chipping. Numerous sites, including both the killsite and campsite varieties, are known (Fig. 13–4). Extinct fauna is commonly found in these sites. Hearth pits occur, and rarely, circles of shallow postholes suggest some type of temporary structure. A few burials have been found with red ochre sprinkled over the bones and associated stone tools, some of which had been burned. Paleo-Indian sites are much more numerous than sites of the earlier stage and indicate that a population dispersal throughout the New World had occurred by 10,000 B.P. The stage is best dated from 11,000 to about 9000 B.P. Grinding stones and bone implements are present but rare. The best known manifestations are those with bifacial fluted points, the North American Clovis or Llano culture and the later Folsom continuation of the same tradition; as well as the separate Old Cordilleran culture with its characteristic bipoint.

Protoarchaic Stage

The major diagnostic difference between the Protoarchaic stage and its antecedent Paleo-Indian stage, is the widespread occurrence of food-grinding implements. Pecking to shape artifacts for use is the most common technique used. The subsequent grinding was primarily through use. A new technique introduced was parallel flaking with pressure. A greater range in stone and bone artifacts is present, indicating a greater diversification in economy and culture. Burials were in purposefully dug graves. Radiocarbon dates on sites assigned to this stage by Krieger range from 9800 ± 500 to 5000 years B.P. (Table 13–1.)

At this point it seems appropriate to evaluate the stage classification system of Pre-Projectile Point, Paleo-Indian, and Protoarchaic proposed by Krieger. It is not an ideal system, for it tends to lump certain manifestations together while ignoring or separating others. For example, Lanning and Hammel (1961) have defined the Andean Biface Horizon, dated 11,000 to 10,000 B.P., as a South American continentwide *horizon* typified by bifacially worked lanceolate points. In Krieger's scheme, sites with Andean bifaces are assigned to both the Paleo-Indian and Protoarchaic stages, thus implying continuity through time. Furthermore there is a North American biface manifestation, the Old Cordilleran complex, which could lead to a definition of a New World Biface Horizon, a feature not emphasized by Krieger. In North America the Protoarchaic sites represent a direct continuation of the Paleo-Indian tradition, and one can emphasize either the new traits to demonstrate the Protoarchaic distinctiveness or the old traits to demonstrate the continuity of the Paleo-Indian tradition.

A final criticism concerns the presence of a microblade tradition in North America (Fig. 13–5) which is of equal antiquity to the Paleo-Indian tradition. This tradition may be traced back through eastern Siberia to obsidian-dated sites in northern Japan 14,000 to 16,000 years of age. The affinities of this Microblade tradition are clearly with the Mesolithic of the Old World. It does not fit within Krieger's scheme, even though it is an important New World manifestation.

In his excavations at Pikimachay and Pepper caves in Peru, MacNeish (1971) has developed a sequence of traditions as follows: Core Tool tradition, 25,000 to 15,000 B.P.; Flake and Bone Tool tradition, 15,000 to 12,000 B.P.; Blade, Burin, and Leaf Point tradition, 12,000–13,000 to 10,000–11,000 B.P.,

TABLE 13–1 Sites in the New World with Radiocarbon Dates Greater than 13,000 B.P.

Site	Date B.P.	Remarks and Associations
1. Trail Creek, Alaska	13,070 ± 280	Bison bone worked by man.
	15,750 ± 350	Horse bone associated with worked bison bone.
2. Lamb Spring, Colorado	13,140 ± 1000	Mammoth bone associated with worked camel toe bone.
3. Ft. Rock Cave, Oregon	13,200 ± 720	
4. Pikimachay Cave, Peru, Ayachucho Level	14,150	Core tools, flake tools, and bone tools
5. Lucy Site, New Mexico	14,300 ± 650	Caliche overlying Sandia level
6. Muaco, Venezuela	9030 ± 240	Bones
	10,490 ± 100	Soil
	14,290 ± 500	Charred bones
	16,365 ± 400	Charred bones
7. Taima Taima, Venezuela	13,010 ± 280	Bones
	14,440 ± 435	Bones
	12,580 ± 150	Soil
	11,860 ± 130	Wood
	9,650 ± 80 to 14,010 ± 140 (16 dates)	Soils
8. Wilson Butte Cave, Idaho	14,500	Skeletal fragments
9. Laguna Beach, California	17,150 ± 1470	Skull
10. Manix Lake, California	19,290 ± 400	Dates on tufa of high lake stand, crude choppers and large leaf-shaped points occur only above dated level.
	19,490 ± 400	Wood from mammoth beds
11. Santa Rosa Island, California	15,820 ± 280	Charcoal from mammoth beds
	16,700 ± 1500	Charred mammoth bones
	29,700 ± 3000	
12. Pikimachay Cave, Peru, Paccaisa Level	19,600	Crude core tools, extinct fauna

Site	Date B.P.	Remarks and Associations
13. Sandia Cave, New Mexico	20,000	Dates on tusk have been questioned (Bryan 1965:144).
14. Scripps Campus, La Jolla, California	21,500	
15. Hueyatlaco, Mexico	21,850 ± 850	Shell date, associated with butchered horse, camel, mastodon, etc. Flake or blade point industry. Recent geologic dates are of the surprising antiquity of 200,000–250,000 years.
16. Tlapacoya, Mexico	21,700 ± 500	Charcoal from hearth
	22,400 ± 2600	Charred log
	23,400 ± 950	Tree above blade
	24,000 ± 4000	Charcoal from hearth
	24,200 ± 400	Soluble organics
	24,500 ± 900	Wood
17. Old Crow, Canada	23,000–28,000	Bone tools
18. Calico Hills, California	34,000	Date is on calcium carbonate cementation in the alluvial fan. Haynes (1973) believes the "artifacts" are rocks broken by natural geologic action.
19. Lewisville, Texas	37,000	Dates are much older than Clovis point found in hearth would imply.
	38,000	Findings are controversial.
20. American Falls, Idaho	30,000	Charcoal, peat
	43,000	Bison bones have holes punched with wooden spears.

Numerous additional sites, at least several dozen, are thought to have great antiquity. This group is best summarized in Krieger (1964) and Bryan (1965). The list includes sites of undoubted importance such as Freisenhahn Cave, Texas; Sheguiandah site, Level V, Ontario; and the Camare complex, Venezuela. Other sites are less accepted, such as the San Marcos complex, Texas, and the Texas Street site, San Diego, California. These sites are not listed in Table 13–1 because none of them has radiocarbon-dated levels earlier than 13,000 B.P.

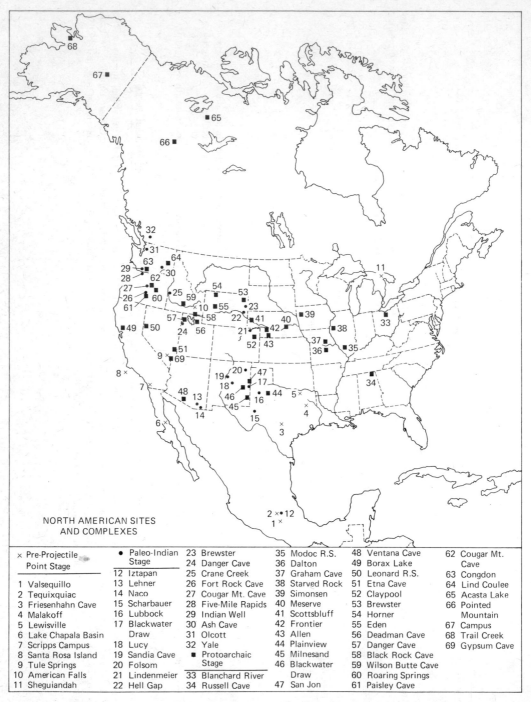

NORTH AMERICAN SITES
AND COMPLEXES

× Pre-Projectile Point Stage	• Paleo-Indian Stage	23 Brewster	35 Modoc R.S.	48 Ventana Cave	62 Cougar Mt. Cave
		24 Danger Cave	36 Dalton	49 Borax Lake	63 Congdon
	12 Iztapan	25 Crane Creek	37 Graham Cave	50 Leonard R.S.	64 Lind Coulee
1 Valsequillo	13 Lehner	26 Fort Rock Cave	38 Starved Rock	51 Etna Cave	65 Acasta Lake
2 Tequixquiac	14 Naco	27 Cougar Mt. Cave	39 Simonsen	52 Claypool	66 Pointed Mountain
3 Friesenhahn Cave	15 Scharbauer	28 Five-Mile Rapids	40 Meserve	53 Brewster	67 Campus
4 Malakoff	16 Lubbock	29 Indian Well	41 Scottsbluff	54 Horner	68 Trail Creek
5 Lewisville	17 Blackwater Draw	30 Ash Cave	42 Frontier	55 Eden	69 Gypsum Cave
6 Lake Chapala Basin	18 Lucy	31 Olcott	43 Allen	56 Deadman Cave	
7 Scripps Campus	19 Sandia Cave	32 Yale	44 Plainview	57 Danger Cave	
8 Santa Rosa Island	20 Folsom	■ Protoarchaic Stage	45 Milnesand	58 Black Rock Cave	
9 Tule Springs	21 Lindenmeier		46 Blackwater Draw	59 Wilson Butte Cave	
10 American Falls	22 Hell Gap	33 Blanchard River	47 San Jon	60 Roaring Springs	
11 Sheguiandah		34 Russell Cave		61 Paisley Cave	

Fig. 13–4 Map of major early man sites in North and South America. (Compiled from Krieger 1964:Figs. 1, 3, and 5.)

SOUTH AMERICAN
SITES AND COMPLEXES

x Pre-Projectile Point Stage	● Paleo-Indian Stage	■ Protoarchaic Stage
1 Pozo de Muáco	17 El Jobo	23 El Inga
2 Manzanillo	18 Lauricocha Caves, Level I	24 Lauricocha Caves, Levels II & III
3 Chocó	19 Quebrado de Camarones	25 Ichuña Rock Shelter
4 Garzón	20 Zuniquena	26 Ongamira Cave
5 Ghatchi I	21 Lagoa Santa Caves	27 Ayampitín
6 Jose Vieira	22 El Totoral	28 Intihuasi Cave
7 Gruta de Wabeto		29 Palli Aike Cave
8 Barracão		30 Fell's Cave
9 Quarai		
10 Catalán		
11 Ampajango		
12 Aceguá		
13 Potraro Sucio		
14 Carro de Montevideo		
15 Playa Verde		
16 Taltal		

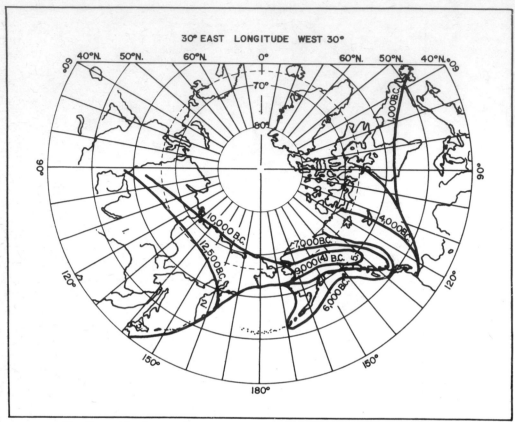

Fig. 13–5 Distribution of microblades through time and space in eastern Asia and northwestern North America.

and finally a specialized Bifacial Point tradition, 10,000–11,000 to 8000–9000 B.P. He further cites similarities with selected North American data. At this writing we have too few established sequences from other sites of the same age to permit an evaluation of the applicability of MacNeish's sequence to New World data in general.

While Krieger's classification is a useful way to categorize early data in the New World, it does not take into account all major manifestations or sites. Part of the difficulty is that we are still collecting data, much of which is poorly preserved because of its great age. More time is needed, as well as better documented information, in order to develop a better organization of New World early data.

PALEO-INDIAN PATTERNS IN NORTH AMERICA

The Paleo-Indian tradition is the earliest segment of culture history in the New World sufficiently well documented to permit a reconstruction of the life way of the people. There are several factors basic to our understanding of these early Americans:

1. The earliest migrants to North America were of *Homo sapiens sapiens* type.
2. The continent at the time provided a series of empty ecological niches which man occupied.
3. With no competitors to impede him, man spread rapidly throughout most of the continent.
4. The early migrants brought with them a big-game-hunting economy of Upper Paleolithic type.
5. The continent was well supplied with game suitable for exploitation by such an economy.

The Great Plains

The earliest Paleo-Indian cultural pattern defined in North America, the Clovis Culture, has strong affinities with a generalized Upper Paleolithic industry of the Old World (Hester 1966). We believe the bearers of this tradition migrated from Siberia following herds of mammoth and other late Pleistocene mammals. They brought with them a generalized Levalloiso-Mousterian unifacial stone industry and a simple bone-working technology. As they preyed upon the mammoths, these early peoples followed a life of restricted wandering in response to the movements of the mammoth herds. The mammoth followed the tundra environmental zone from Siberia through Alaska and Canada into the northern United States. Hunters following such game herds would have thus occupied the North American continent.

It has been assumed by researchers that this big-game-hunting economy, typified by numerous outstanding sites in the Great Plains, such as Clovis, Dent, and Lindenmeier, represented the basic environmental adaptation of the Paleo-Indians. A description of this economy is as follows:

The Paleo-Indian cultural tradition in the Great Plains

. . . was adapted to the utilization and exploitation of a savanna grassland with abundant permanent water in small ponds and streams. . . . The stream valleys sheltered galleries of juniper and oak in the valleys and along the bottoms. On this savanna landscape moved large herds of giant bison and smaller groups of other Pleistocene forms now extinct.

The correlation between type of site and site situation is striking. . . . Campsites tend to occur on ridges, dunes, or hills which overlook either a stream channel or a pond at a distance of several hundred yards to a mile. Killsites tend to occur either at the edge of former ponds or stream channels.

Attributes of a campsite include hearths, discarded food bones, chipping debris, and a full chipped and flaked tool complex. . . . The food bones are normally disarticulated and are occasionally split and charred. Seeds, grinding stones, and storage or cooking pits are rarely present. Activities identified with campsites include food preparation, working of hides, and tool manufacture. The high proportion of point bases over point tips, a common attribute of campsite lithic collections, is suggestive of repair of weapons.

Killsites are characterized by animal skeltons, frequently in high numbers, with the associated projectile points utilized to kill them plus a limited number of chipped and flaked butchering tools. Often preferred portions of the animals are missing. These body parts, presumably were cut out and taken back to nearby campsites, though hearths are occasionally present indicating that some of the kill was consumed or smoked on the spot.

One basic hunting pattern, reconstructed as follows, represents a majority of all the sites surveyed. The campsite was situated so that animals in the vicinity could be observed as they came for water. Once observed, the animals were stalked and killed as they were drinking in a stream or pond. The number of animals killed by this technique ranged from one to about thirty. Both mammoth and bison were hunted by this method.

A second pattern is the stampede. . ., the animals in this case being bison which were driven into an arroyo, stream or over a cliff, where many of the animals were crushed or drowned. The number of animals killed by this technique occasionally was as high as several hundred. . . .

The location of the projectile points in the carcasses indicates an identical method of killing for both mammoth and bison. The spears were aimed at the thoracic region with the intent to penetrate the heart, spinal cord or other vital parts. . . .

The absence of an emphasis on the hunting of horses and the absence of mammoth traps suggest that we are studying hunting techniques specifically adapted to New World conditions, rather than techniques transferred from an Old World tradition (Wendorf and Hester 1962:159).

Our best evidence for Paleo-Indian butchering techniques comes from the Olsen-Chubbock site in eastern Colorado. At this site approximately 190 bison were killed by stampeding across a small arroyo. Of the bison killed, approximately 74 percent were completely butchered and 16 percent were partially butchered. The task would have required 100 people about 2½ hours or 50 people one half day. Ten men could have completed the task in about 2 days (Wheat 1972:116). The actual butchering process has been reconstructed from the positions in which the various bones were found (Fig. 13–6). In his analysis, assuming that 50 percent of the usuable meat was preserved by drying, Wheat estimates the size of the participating group of early hunters. His estimate is 36,560 pounds of usable meat which could have been consumed by 50 persons in 73 days, 100 persons in 37 days, 150 persons in 24 days, or 200 persons in 18 days. If 100 persons had 100 dogs, the consumption could have taken place within 22 days (Wheat 1972:122). While not precise, such estimates help us understand the possible kill utilization patterns that the Paleo-Indians may have employed.

A study of sites by time period for the Llano Estacado (Texas and New Mexico) revealed 13 of Clovis age, 29 of Folsom age, and 39 of the Parallel Flaked or Plano horizon. Many of these were multicomponent sites, suggesting a continuation of the same land use pattern through several thousand years. The site data also imply a steady population increase through time.

Analysis of stone types utilized for tool manufacture at Blackwater Draw, New Mexico, and the location of the stone quarries have led to the inference that the Paleo-Indian social group, probably a small band or

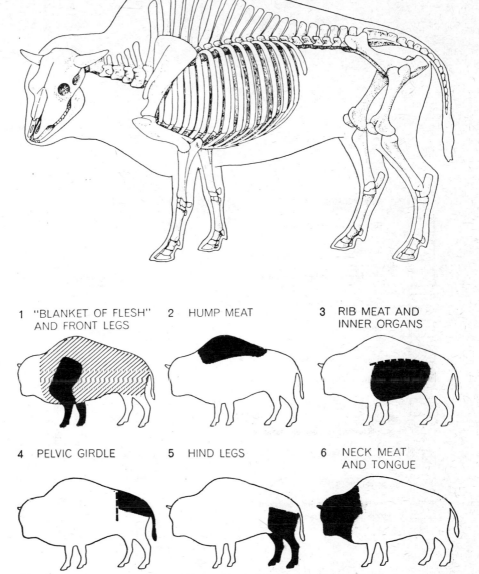

1 "BLANKET OF FLESH"   2 HUMP MEAT   3 RIB MEAT AND
   AND FRONT LEGS   INNER ORGANS

4 PELVIC GIRDLE   5 HIND LEGS   6 NECK MEAT
                                                  AND TONGUE

Fig. 13–6 Butchering methods used by the Paleo-Indians as reconstructed from the bone stratification at the Olsen-Chubbuck site and recent practices of the Plains Indians. After the carcass of the
bison (skeleton at top) had been propped up and skinned down the back, a series of "butchering
units" probably were removed in the order shown on the numbered outline figures. (Wheat
1967:52.)

Glaciated area

Exposed continental shelf

Tundra

Undifferentiated alpine formations

Temperate deciduous forest

Coniferous forest

Undifferentiated tropical deciduous forest & grassland

Temperate rainforest

Tropical rainforest

Undifferentiated Caribbean formations

Desert

Scrub steppe

Undifferentiated prairie, grassland, scrub steppe & desert

extended kin group, wandered over an area some 100 to 200 miles in diameter (Hester 1972:94).

The Northeastern United States

The vegatation of the Late Glacial period from New England to Minnesota may be summarized from the writings of Davis (1967), Watts (1967), and Ogden (1967). According to their interpretations, the succession of vegetal communi-

Fig. 13–7 The distribution of major environmental zones as reconstructed for the Wisconsin maximum and their occurrence today. (*Left*) Glacial maximum environments. (*Right*) Modern environments. (Patterson 1973:Figs. 2–1 and 2–2.)

ties, in a north-south transect south of the ice margin, consisted of a tundra zone; a zone of open spruce woodland or fir-spruce forest, a mixed forest zone of pine, oak, and elm, and finally deciduous forest (Fig. 13–7). During deglaciation in the period 12,000 to 10,000 B.P. these zones were shifting northward. Vegetal communities requiring cool and moist conditions were being replaced by communities with warmer and drier requirements. Throughout this interval of deglaciation the trend of replacement shows little evidence of reversal.

Large mammals inhabiting these environments included the musk ox; mammoth, mastodon, bison, *Cervalces* (the extinct moose), *Castoroides* (the giant beaver), and *Platygonus* and *Mylohyus* (extinct peccaries) (Fig. 13–8). Also of possible significance to human existence at this time were the marine mammals in the Great Lakes, which included whale, walrus, and seal (Griffin 1965).

The archaeological evidence from the northeastern United States consists of frequent but isolated surface finds of fluted points and rarely, campsite debris such as that at Shoop, Pennsylvania; Debert, Nova Scotia; and Bull Brook, Massachusetts. The artifactual assemblages are quite similar to those known from fluted point sites in the West such as Clovis and Lindenmeier (Hester 1966; Byers 1966). If these artifactual assemblages are similar, can we also assume the economies were similar? Faunal associations at the campsites in the Northeast are totally lacking. Bone preservation is poor in these sites; therefore archaeologists have postulated big game hunting of whatever animals are known to have lived in the vicinity. In the case of the Debert site, there were caribou, and in the Great Lakes region, the mastodon. Although the distribution of fluted points and fossil mastodons in Michigan is essentially identical (Martin 1967:Fig. 2), we lack the kind of conclusive killsite associations so typical of the Plains. To my knowledge, only one mastodon, currently being studied in Michigan, shows evidence of having been killed and butchered. On the other hand, remains of hundreds of mastodons have been found without any evidence of man.

According to recent opinions, the mastodon and other members of the Late Glacial megafauna became extinct during this interval (12,000–10,000 B.P.). As evidence, Martin (1967) has plotted the northern distribution of species of this fauna and found it to lie south of the Valders ice margin. Therefore, he argues that if these species survived later than 10,000 B.P., they would have undoubtedly moved north of this line. McMillan (1968) has reviewed the evidence for mastodons in association with Archaic artifacts and in every case has found the evidence to be suspect. He concludes that the mastodon became extinct prior to the advent of Archaic culture ca. 8500–8000 B.P.

Some authors (Mason 1962; Griffin 1965) have suggested that the Paleo-Indians arrived in the eastern United States 12,000–15,000 years ago. Mason (1962) has even hypothesized that owing to the great numbers and widespread distribution of fluted points in the East, the Paleo-Indian culture originated there and spread to the West. There is currently no radiocarbon evidence to support these views of eastern primacy. The only securely dated site is that at Debert, Nova Scotia, where 13 dates average 8635 ± 47 B.C. or 10, 585 ± 47 B.P. (Stuckenrath 1966). This dating is 600 to 1000 years later than established occupation in the Great Plains.

Evidence from Debert indicates that the local environment was quite cold. Borns (1966) states that

... by the time of the occupation of the Debert site all of the continental ice had dissipated from northern Nova Scotia, and that a Valders-age ice cap, the margin of

Fig. 13–8   Selected fauna typical of the Late Pleistocene of the New World: *Definitely associated with early man; **possibly associated with early man. The woolly rhinoceros, a typical animal of the Siberian tundra, for some reason did not cross over into North America with the rest of the tundra fauna. Current evidence is that the long-horned bison (illustrated) became extinct prior to the advent of man. Shorter horned species of bison were common prey of early man. (Martin and Guilday 1967.)

which was probably less than 60 miles to the southwest, occupied the South Mountain area, while a snow cover more extensive and persistent than presently exists covered the Cobequid Mountains approximately 5 miles to the north.

He goes on to postulate that the environment probably supported permafrost, thus implying arctic or subarctic temperatures. Of course, areas in the Northeast farther removed from the glacial margin featured a more moderate climate.

The Southeastern United States

The environment of the southeastern United States has been reconstructed by Whitehead (1965). Late Glacial (15,000–10,000 B.P.) vegetation in the Chesapeake Bay and southeastern North Carolina regions is described as a spruce, fir, pine, and birch forest, shifting to a pine dominance with spruce, birch, and alder, with oak and hickory becoming more important. The Postglacial environment (10,000 B.P.–Present) featured a gradual transformation of the "northern hardwood" forest into a forest dominated by oak, hickory, sweet gum, and many other deciduous forest species which reached a maximum about 7000 years ago. The archaeological sites are similar to those in the northeastern United States; isolated finds of fluted points are common and concentrations of occupational debris are rare. Associations with extinct fauna do not occur in these sites.

     The evidence for the economy practiced is also scanty. Williams and Stoltman (1965) hypothesize that the fluted point distribution is understandable if we assume that their makers roved the countryside hunting big game, primarily mastodon. They then "prove" their hypothesis by plotting the occurrence of mastodon remains and fluted points. Their survey does indicate regional concentrations of both mastodons and fluted points; however, the evidence is again circumstantial and does not really "prove" that the Paleo-Indians subsisted by big game hunting.

     One item of significance is that by 9000–10,000 B.P. or slightly earlier, there are several variants of fluted points with differing geographic distributions within the Southeast. This fact suggests that specific regional adaptations reflected in the cultural inventory had already occurred.

The Great Basin and the Southwest

Man's appearance in the Great Basin and the Southwest was first evidenced 10,000 to 11,000 years ago in Danger Cave, Utah; Leonard Rockshelter, Fishbone Cave, Guano Cave, and Tule Springs, Nevada; Fort Rock Cave, Oregon; and Naco and Lehner, Arizona (see Fig. 13–4). These sites include both campsites and killsites. What is most distinctive, with the exception of the Naco and Lehner sites, is the general absence of bones of extinct fauna in the levels containing artifacts. Radiocarbon dates indicate the region to have been initially occupied by man between 10,000 and 11,000 years ago or slightly earlier. Dates from Tule Springs suggest the late glacial megafauna became extinct there by 11,500 B.P. (Haynes, 1967). Abundant small bones and remains of plants indicate that food collecting and hunting were the primary economy. Quite likely seasonal wandering was the residence pattern as the inhabitants moved from one food harvest to another.

The Full Glacial climate about 20,000 B.P. resulted in a biotic zone depression of 900 to 1200 meters. The change to a warm, dry Postglacial grass and sagebrush environment seems to have occurred rather rapidly around 12,000 B.P. (Martin and Mehringer 1965:451). As a result of this early shift to Postglacial climate, Mehringer (1967) states that the environment of the Southwest, inhabited by mammoths and other large herbivores, was little different from that of today. We conclude that shortly after 11,000 B.P., the Paleo-Indians of the Great Basin gave up the hunting of big game for a food-collecting economy featuring widespread use of all available resources. In spite of the absence of documented killsites, the presence of Clovis fluted points is strong evidence of early man the hunter in the Great Basin, a point emphasized by Tuohy (1968:21). Evidence from the Southwest suggests that big game hunting persisted there until at least 9000 B.P.

The West Coast

According to Meighan (1965), the oldest sites in the West are poorly known. They are difficult to find and the cultural inventory is crude and not well dated. It is believed that the coast was settled from the interior prior to 8000 B.P. by big game hunters who had no interest in the food resources of the sea. The primary cultural material identified is the San Dieguito complex, consisting of leaf-shaped points, cutting and scraping tools, and a few grinding stones. The primary extinct animal species thought to have been man's prey is the dwarf mammoth, known from Santa Rosa Island. It appears that men hunted these animals between 12,500 and 9500 B.P. After 7500 B.P., the earlier peoples were succeeded by the La Jolla culture—a seed-grinding, small-game-hunting, shell-fish-gathering culture.

The Columbia Plateau

Three major sites in the plateau region possess cultural and environmental materials associated with radiocarbon dates. The Five Mile Rapids site at the Dalles, Oregon, has a date of 9785 ± 220 B.P. from the lowest level. The economy was of riverine type, featuring salmon fishing and bird and mammal hunting. No extinct species occur. The artifactual complex, termed the Old Cordilleran tradition, featured leaf-shaped bipoints, bolas, burins, and heavy cobble choppers. One date associated with a point of this tradition from Wilson Butte Cave in Idaho has the surprising antiquity of 14,500 ± 500 B.P. A similar site located on the Fraser River in British Columbia, the Yale site, has been dated 8150 ± 300 and 9000 ± 500 B.P.

The environment east of the Cascades, as reconstructed by Heusser (1965), included a lodgepole pine parkland during the Late Glacial, succeeded by grasses, chenopods, and composites. This transition occurred about 8000 B.P. and undoubtedly was influential in the shift to a greater reliance on fishing recorded in the later archaeological levels.

Other Areas

Evidence from other areas in North America is little known; hence, only the most outstanding examples will be cited. The Plains region of southern Canada featured a bison-hunting economy with artifacts of the Plano horizon, probably dating 8000–7000 B.P. (Wormington and Forbis 1965). Almost certainly this evidence records a late northward expansion of the economy developed in the Central Plains region.

One site, Onion Portage in northern Alaska, is of interest because of early radiocarbon dates ranging from 8100 to 7180 B.P. In general, sites from Alaska have failed to suggest great antiquity for Paleo-Indian remains, and the extinct faunal remains have not had associated cultural materials. Recent exceptions include the materials from Old Crow, Yukon, dated at more than 23,000 years and the Putu complex which possesses fluted points of Folsom type.

Conclusions

The earliest established Paleo-Indian remains are those in the Great Plains dated 12,000–11,000 B.P., although most other areas record human habitation within the next thousand years. The big-game-hunting economy established in the Plains is thought to have been practiced from the West Coast to the East Coast and south to the valley of Mexico. A detailed consideration of the data reveals little evidence outside of the Plains to prove this assumption. Much circumstantial evidence exists but validated killsites are rare.

The environmental reconstructions are quite variable not only in their specific ecological makeup but also in their indicated response to glacial fluctuations. Our major conclusion is that in every area for which we have data, at the earliest level, these data record cultural adaptations to local environments which included desert grassland, savanna grassland with gallery forests, pine parkland, boreal forest, deciduous forest, and even tundra. These adaptations record both differences in artifactual inventory and, where the evidence is present, in the nature of the food resources utilized. Since these early data record specific environmental adaptations, we may assume the evidence of the earliest migrants, when found, will date even earlier.

NORTH AMERICAN PALEO-INDIAN CHRONOLOGY
AND ARTIFACT COMPLEXES

We have so far been primarily concerned with the lifeway of the North American Paleo-Indians and their regional adaptations to the local environment. Their chronology is reasonably well established by radiocarbon dating (Fig. 13–9). In addition the artifact complexes are well known. We therefore can discuss cultural developments of the early North American Paleo-Indians with some confidence.

The Paleo-Indian artifacts are viewed as a tradition marked by continuity in form and type of most of the artifacts in the inventory. Basic implements include bifacially flaked and chipped projectile points which have a channel flake removed from each face in the early portions of the tradition—the Clovis and Folsom periods. Other elements of the tradition feature a unifacial, edge retouched, inventory of implements made on primary flakes which include side scrapers, end scrapers, knives, and gravers. Other tools include choppers, abraders, hammerstones, as well as rare occurrences of burins and core struck blades. An industry of pointed bone tools is also present. Through time the major change occurs in the form of projectile points, with the other tools remaining relatively constant (Figs. 13-10–13-13).

THE PALEO-INDIAN TRADITION IN SOUTH AMERICA

At present it is not possible to describe the Paleo-Indian way of life in South America region by region as we did for North America. South American data is scanty and is poorly dated, with the result that different scientists group the known remains differently.

The geography of South America is dominated by the presence of the Andean Chain which includes higher terrain toward the equator and diminishing elevations both to the north and south. South of 30° south latitude, the climate is increasingly conditioned by the more moderate influence of the southern ocean. In contrast to the continental climate of North America where the temperature gradient is constant (that is, as you go north the climate steadily gets colder), the South American climate is somewhat milder toward the higher latitudes. One result of these factors is the presence of a series of elevation-determined environmental zones which trend north-south for most of the length of the continent. On the other hand, as you move east or west of the Andean Chain, the environment changes radically in the space of a few miles to either tropical rain forest or shrub steppe to the east or desert to the west. This situation would have favored a rapid north-to-south dispersal of big game hunters, following game animals within these mountain environmental zones. Thus, the environmental influences permitting or limiting the expansion of

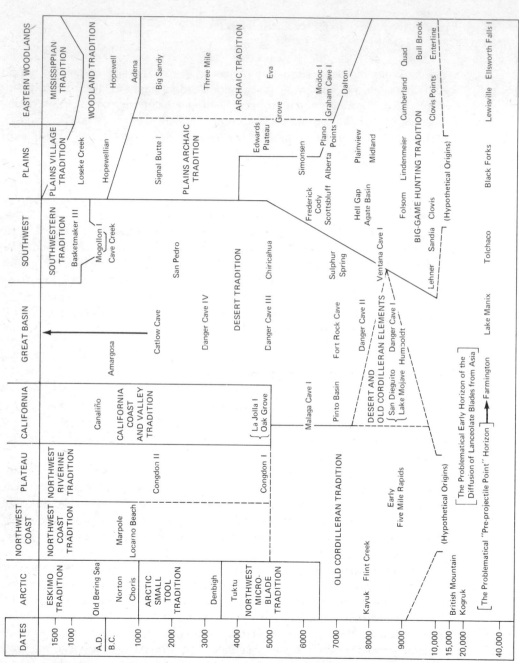

Fig. 13–9 Chronology of early North American cultures. (Willey 1966:Fig. 2–31.)

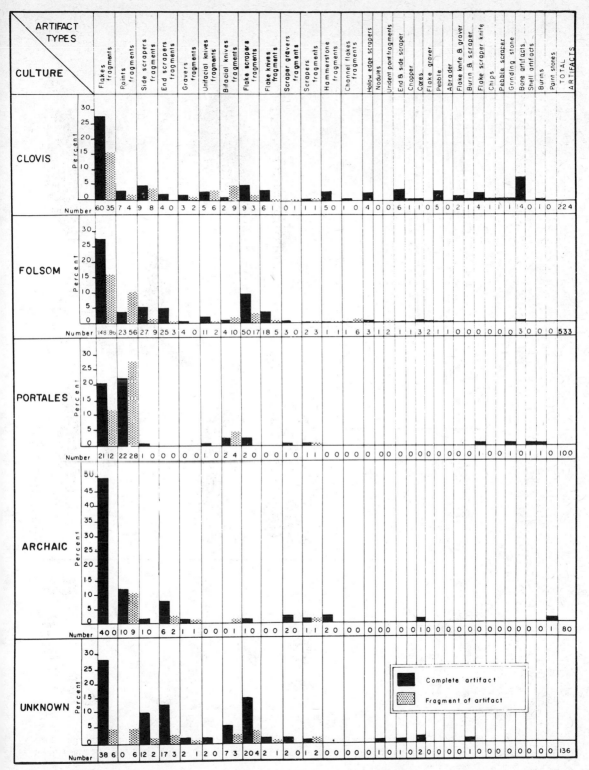

Fig. 13–10 Artifact types by culture from the stratified early man site at Blackwater Draw, New Mexico, indicating the continuity between cultural periods in the artifactual inventory. (Hester 1972:Fig. 83.)

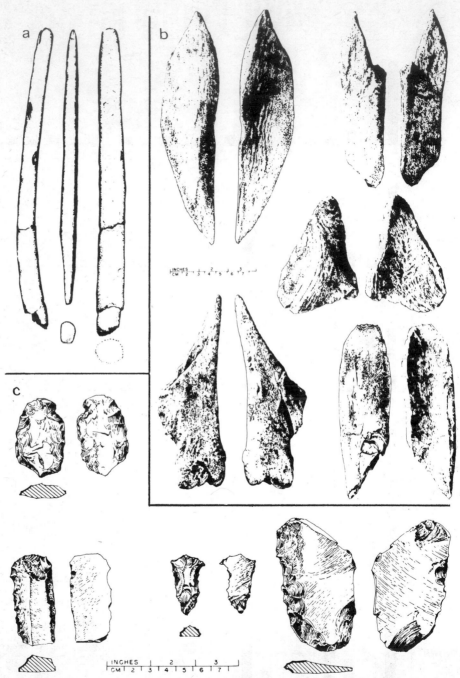

Fig. 13–11 Clovis culture bone tools: *a*. bone points or foreshafts; *b*. flaking or digging tools; *c*. Clovis period stone tools. (*a*. Sellards 1952:Fig. 14; *b*. and *c*. Hester 1972:Fig. 101 and Fig. 89 respectively.)

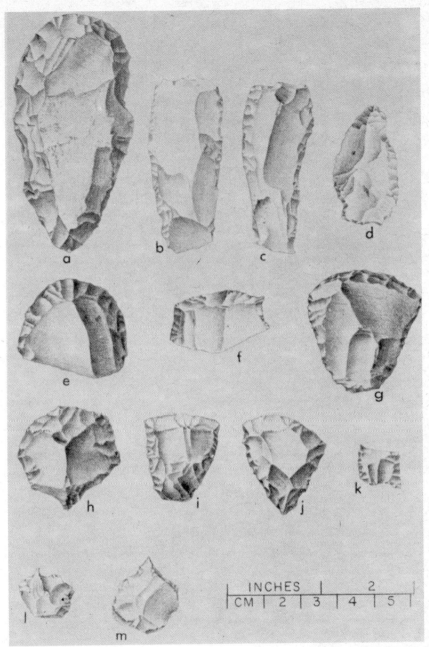

Fig. 13–12a. Typical Folsom period artifacts: *a.–c.* side scrapers; *d.* flake knife; *e.–j.* end scrapers; *k.* point made from channel flake; *l.–m.* gravers. (From Hester 1962:Fig. 9 [drawing by Hal M. Story. Courtesy of Texas Memorial Museum].)

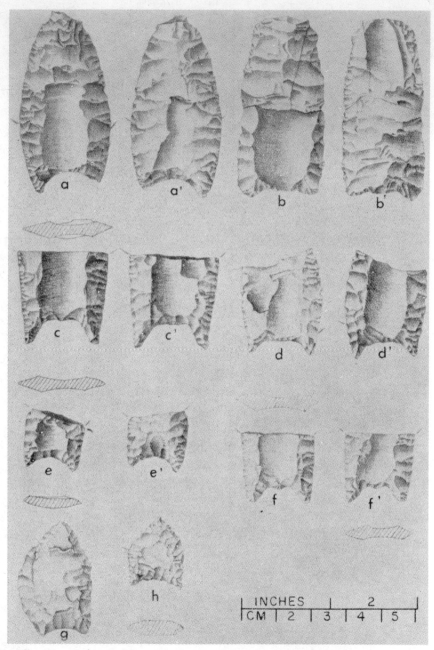

Fig. 13–12b. Folsom period projectile points illustrating both faces of each specimen: *a.* through *h*. (From Hester 1962:Fig. 4 [drawing by Hal M. Story. Courtesy of Texas Memorial Museum].)

Fig. 13–13   Sequence of Paleo-Indian projectile point types. (Photograph courtesy of James Grady.)

early man throughout the continent are obvious. Other features of the Late Pleistocene environment include a lower sea level (200 to 400 feet below present sea level), resulting in additional exposure of the continental shelves (Fig. 13–14). A second feature was the presence of high altitude lakes which are now dry or greatly reduced in size.

Sites have been plotted in relation to the position of glacial ice and tundra (Fig. 13 14). This technique reveals that the majority of sites termed Early Lithic by Lanning and Hammel (1961) or Pre-Projectile Point by Krieger (1964) lie within areas that featured ice or tundra during the glacial maximum some 18,000 to 20,000 years ago. I interpret these findings as suggesting that most of the sites termed "early" in South America postdate the glacial maximum and probably have ages of 11,000 years or younger. Pikimachay Cave is the only exception to these findings, since it seems to be securely dated to the Late Glacial. The rapid north-to-south migration down the Andean Chain is validated by the radiocarbon-dated 10,000-year-old cultural levels in Palli Aike and Fells caves, at the extreme southern tip of the continent in Tierra del Fuego.

The South American fauna in the Late Pleistocene included many exotic species: sloth, glyptodon, camels, toxodon, capybara, spectacled bear, dire wolf, puma, stegomastodon, horse, tapir, and peccary. Associations of these species in archaeological levels are rare to absent. The primary species recorded from cultural sites include guanaco, sloth, horse, and mastodon.

A chronological ordering of the South American finds is presented in Figure 13–15. In this chart the compiler, Gordon Willey (1971), has divided the earliest data into three traditions (all preprojectile point or at least nonprojectile

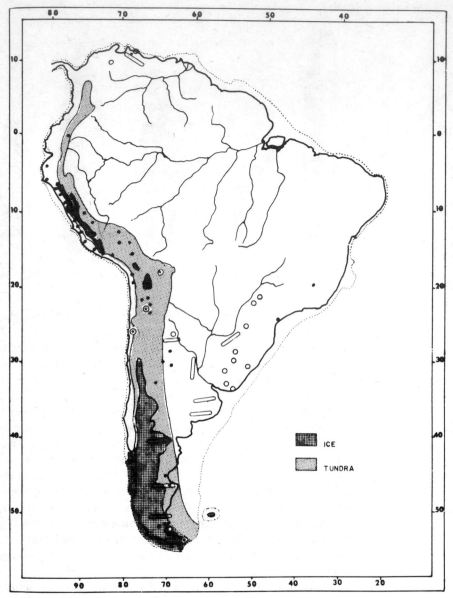

Fig. 13–14   Map illustrating correlation between early human sites in South America and Pleisto-cene glaciation: Dots—"Early Lithic" sites according to Lanning and Hammel (1961, Fig. 1); circles and ovals—"Preprojectile Point" sites listed by Krieger (1964); dots within circles—sites listed by Lanning and Hammel as "Early Lithic" and Krieger as "Preprojectile Point." Note number of sites in areas covered with ice or tundra vegetation during the glacial maximum. (Hester 1966:Fig. 4.)

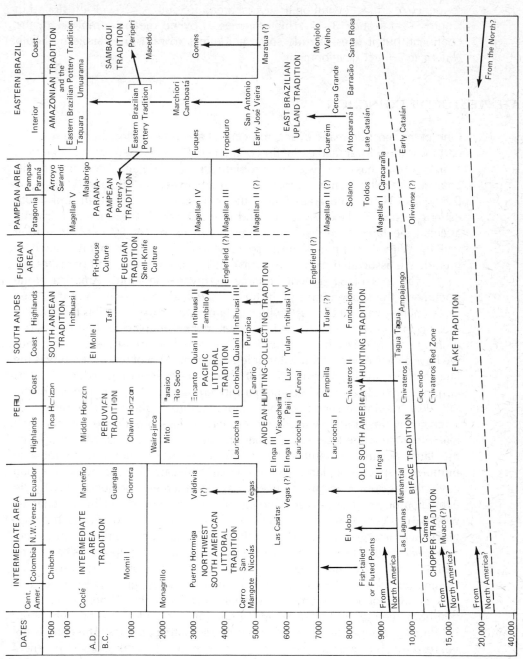

Fig. 13–15 Chronological chart of early South American phases or complexes and their affiliations with cultural traditions. (After Willey 1971:Fig. 2–2.)

point): the Flake tradition, Chopper tradition, and Biface tradition. The sequence of artifact evolution in several areas of South America is illustrated in Figures 13–16 and 13–17. This coverage is by no means complete for the continent, but it does provide some guidelines toward understanding South American artifact development.

LATE PLEISTOCENE EXTINCTION

One of the most dramatic events to occur at any time during man's tenure on earth was the widespread extinction of the Late Pleistocene mammalian fauna. Martin (1967) has reviewed the problem in some detail. According to his analysis, the extinction was rapid, occurring between 15,000 and 8,000 years B.P. (Fig. 13–18). The areas where this occurred include North and South America, New Zealand, Australia, and Madagascar. The extinction primarily affected the large herd-dwelling mammals in excess of 50 kilograms adult weight. With their primary hosts so removed, the extinction broadened to include the associated carnivores, scavengers, commensals, and parasites.

The loss of 31 genera of large herbivores in North America alone documents the scope of this prehistoric ecological catastrophy. What is even more impressive, as it contrasts with earlier periods of extinction, is that most of these animals were not replaced by other species adapted to their ecological niche. In many cases these niches have remained empty to the present. Thus we have a case of extinction without replacement. Also of unique quality is the fact that the small mammals did not suffer a corresponding reduction; they continued in existence to become our modern fauna. Only the modern bison, elk, deer, mountain sheep, caribou, mountain goat, and musk-ox remain as large herbivores, and they average considerably less in body weight than their Late Pleistocene predecessors. Further unique features cited by Martin are that the large oceanic mammals did not become extinct nor did appreciable numbers of species of plants. He thus regards the Late Pleistocene mammalian extinction as unique and imbalanced. Martin further asks the question: why did extinction occur at this time? If the extinction was related to climatic change, why did it occur when it did, after the fauna had survived several previous glacial and interglacial periods? Martin explains this unique pattern of extinction as the result of prehistoric overkill by early man. His hypothesis cannot be verified easily. Certainly man was a hunter of many of the animals which became extinct; on the other hand numerous other genera which became extinct have not been reported in association with artifacts. Other explanations that have been offered (Martin and Wright 1967) include stress brought about by climatic change, disease, and out-of-phase mating patterns. The issue is not yet resolved, but from our perspective, as we trace the cultural development of man in the New World, the extinction of the Lake Pleistocene fauna was highly significant. Man could no longer survive as a specialized big game hunter. He had to modify his economy in ways we shall examine in the chapter to follow.

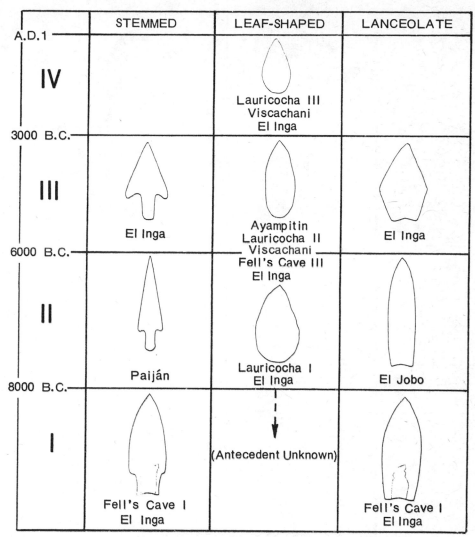

Fig. 13–16   Projectile point types from El Inga, Ecuador, with their chronological position relative to other South American projectile point types. (Mayer-Oakes 1963:121.)

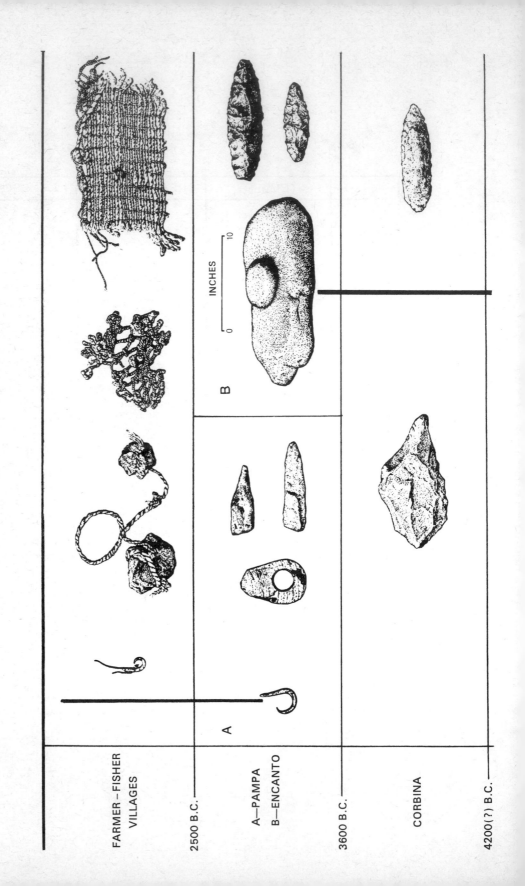

FARMER – FISHER
VILLAGES

2500 B.C.

A—PAMPA
B—ENCANTO

A

B

INCHES

0   10

3600 B.C.

CORBINA

4200(?) B.C.

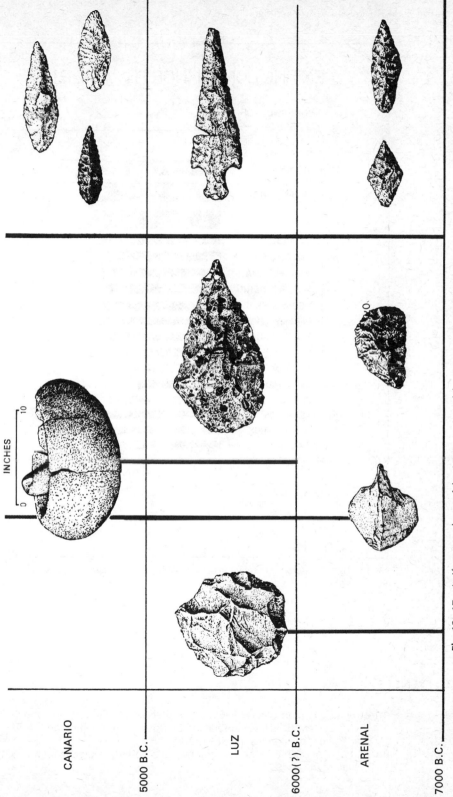

Fig. 13–17 Artifact complexes of the Ancon region of the Peruvian coast illustrating the transition from hunting-gathering cultures to those relying on fishing and finally farming. (Lanning 1965:74–75.)

CANARIO

5000 B.C.

LUZ

6000(?) B.C.

ARENAL

7000 B.C.

INCHES

10

0

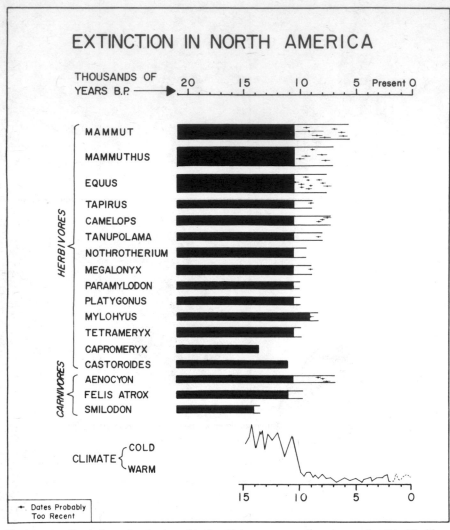

Fig. 13–18 Chronology of extinction of the late Pleistocene megafauna by species. (Modified from Martin 1967:Fig. 1.)

REFERENCES

Armstrong, J. E., and others, 1965, "Late Pleistocene Stratigraphy and Chronology in Southwestern British Columbia and Northwestern Washington," *Bulletin Geological Society of America* 76:321–330.

Borns, H. W. Jr., 1966, "The Geography of Paleo-Indian Occupation in Nova Scotia," *Quaternaria* 8:49–57.

Bryan, A. L., 1965, *Paleo-American Prehistory*. Occasional Papers of the Idaho State University Museum, No. 16.

Byers, D. S., 1966, "The Debert Archaeological Project: The Position of Debert with Respect to the Paleo-Indian Tradition," *Quaternaria* 8:33–47.

Cushing, E. J., and H. E. Wright, Jr. (eds.), 1967, *Quaternary Paleoecology*. New Haven, Conn.: Yale University Press.

Davis, M. B., 1967, "Late-Glacial Climate in Northern United States; A Comparison of New England and the Great Lakes Region," in Cushing and Wright, pp. 11–44.

Greenman, E. F., 1963, "The Upper Paleolithic in the New World," *Current Anthropology* 4(1):41–91.

Griffin, J. B., 1965, "Late Quaternary Prehistory in the Northeastern Woodlands," in Wright and Frey, pp. 655–667.

Haynes, C. V., Jr., 1967, "Quaternary Geology of the Tule Springs Area, Clark County, Nevada," in H. M. Wormington and D. Ellis (eds.), *Pleistocene Studies in Southern Nevada*. Nevada State Museum Anthropological Paper No. 13, pp. 15–104.

———, 1970, "Geochronology of Man-Mammoth Sites and Their Bearing on the Origin of the Llano Complex," in W. Dort, Jr. and J. K. Jones, Jr. (eds.), *Pleistocene and Recent Environments of the Central Great Plains*. Lawrence, Kansas: Department of Geology, University of Kansas, Special Publication 3.

———, 1973, "The Calico Site: Artifacts or Geofacts?" *Science* 181:305–310.

Hester, J. J., 1962, "A Folsom Lithic Complex from the Elida Site, Roosevelt County, New Mexico," *El Palacio* 69(2):92–113.

———, 1966a, "Origins of the Clovis Culture." XXXVI Congress International Americas Actas y Memorias, pp. 129–142.

———, 1966b, "Late Pleistocene Environments and Early Man in South America," *The American Naturalist* 100:377–388.

———, 1972, Blackwater Locality No. 1, a Stratified Early Man Site in Eastern New Mexico. Ft. Burgwin Research Center, Southern Methodist University, No. 8.

Heusser, C. J., 1965, "A Pleistocene Phytogeographical Sketch of the Pacific Northwest," in Wright and Frey, pp. 469–483.

Krieger, A., 1964, "Early Man in the New World," in J. D. Jennings and E. Norbeck (eds.), *Prehistoric Man in the New World*. Chicago: The University of Chicago Press.

Lanning, E. P., 1965, "Early Man in Peru," *Scientific American* 213(4):68–76.

———, and E. Hammel, 1961, "Early Lithic Industries of Western South America," *American Antiquity* 27(2):139–154.

MacMillan, R. B., 1968, Personal communication.

MacNeish, R. S., 1971, "Early Man in the Andes," *Scientific American* 224(4):36–46.

Martin, P. S., 1967, "Prehistoric Overkill," in Martin and Wright, pp. 75–120.

———, and P. J. Mehringer, 1965, "Pleistocene Pollen Analysis and Biogeography of the Southwest," in Wright and Frey, pp. 433–451.

———, and J. E. Guilday, 1967, "A Bestiary for Pleistocene Biologists," in Martin and Wright, pp. 1–66.

———, and H. E. Wright, Jr., (eds.), 1967, *Pleistocene Extinctions: The Search for a Cause*. New Haven, Conn.: Yale University Press.

Mason, R. J., 1962, "The Paleo-Indian Tradition in Eastern North America," *Current Anthropology* 3:227–278.

Mayer-Oakes, W. J., 1963, "Early Man in the Andes," *Scientific American* 208:117–128.

Meggers, B. J., C. Evans, and E. Estrada, 1965, *Early Formative Period of Coastal Ecuador*. Washington, D.C.: Smithsonian Institution Contributions to Anthropology I.

Mehringer, P. J., Jr., 1967, "The Environment of Extinction of the Late Pleistocene Megafauna in the Arid Southwestern United States," in Martin and Wright, pp. 247–266.

Meighan, C. W., 1965, "Pacific Coast Archaeology," in Wright and Frey, pp. 709–720.

Ogden, J. G., III, 1967, "Radiocarbon and Pollen Evidence for a Sudden Change in Climate in the Great Lakes Region Approximately 10,000 Years Ago," in Cushing and Wright, pp. 117–127.

Patterson, T. C., 1973. *America's Past: A New World Archaeology*. Glenview, Ill.: Scott, Foresman.

Sellards, E. H., 1952, *Early Man in America*. Austin: University of Texas Press.

Stuckenrath, R. J., 1966, "The Debert Archaeological Project, Nova Scotia Radiocarbon Dating," *Quaternaria* VIII (Rome).

Tuohy, D. R., 1968, "Some Early Lithic Sites in Western Nevada," in C. Irwin-Williams (ed.), *Early Man in Western North America*. Eastern New Mexico University Contributions in Anthropology 1(4):27–38.

Watts, W. A., 1967, "Late-Glacial Plant Macrofossils from Minnesota," in Cushing and Wright, pp. 89–97.

Wendorf, F., 1966, "Early Man in the New World: Problems of Migration," *The American Naturalist* 100(912):253–270.

———, and J. J. Hester, 1962, "Early Man's Utilization of the Great Plains Environment," *American Antiquity* 28(2):159–171.

Wheat, J. B., 1967, "A Paleo-Indian Bison Kill," *Scientific American* 216(1):44–52.

———, 1972, "The Olsen-Chubbock Site: A Paleo-Indian Bison Kill." Memoirs of the Society for American Archaeology, No. 26.

Whitehead, D. R., 1965, "Paleonology and Pleistocene Phytogeography of Unglaciated Eastern North America," in Wright and Frey, pp. 417–432.

Willey, G. R., 1966, *An Introduction to American Archaeology*, Vol. I. Englewood Cliffs, N.J.: Prentice-Hall.

———, 1971, *An Introduction to American Archaeology*, Vol. II. Englewood Cliffs, N.J.: Prentice-Hall.

Williams, S., and J. B. Stoltman, 1965, "An Outline of Southeastern United States Prehistory with Particular Emphasis on the Paleo-Indian Era," in Wright and Frey, pp. 669–683.

Wormington, H. M., and R. M. Forbis, 1965, *An Introduction to the Archaeology of Alberta, Canada*. Denver: Denver Museum of Natural History Proceedings, No. II.

Wright, H. E., Jr., and D. G. Frey (eds.), 1965, *The Quaternary of the United States*. Princeton, N.J.: Princeton University Press.

14

The Development of New World Cultures

In their monumental synthesis *Method and Theory in American Archaeology* Gordon Willey and Phillip Phillips (1958) have presented us with an organized view of New World culture history. Their approach consists of the definition of a series of stages. These are viewed as *levels* of similar cultural attainment, irrespective of their antiquity or geographic location. Willey and Phillips classified all New World data into five stages, which from early to late are termed Lithic, Archaic, Formative, Classic, and Postclassic. This is a generalized sequence referring to all New World developments; in fact most culture traditions did not participate in every one of these stages. Typically cultures within a region developed until a level was reached at which environmental limitations became significant. On the other hand, some cultures remained at essentially the same level over long periods of time. There are even examples of regression from one stage to a later more simplified one. Nonetheless the stage concept is useful and we will use it here.

In the Willey and Phillips classification, the Lithic stage refers to the culture of the earliest Americans which we reviewed in our last chapter. Their definition encompasses both the presumed "earliest" unspecialized core and flake industries, and those industries featuring advanced technology in stoneworking including the blade technique, bifacial flaking, and the fluting of projectile points. They state that "the Lithic is the stage of adaptation by immigrant societies to the late glacial and early postglacial climatic and physiographic conditions in the New World" (Willey and Phillips 1958:80). The earliest manifestations in every region of the New World may be assigned to this Lithic stage, even though such remains in a few areas, such as the Amazon Basin, are extremely rare.

The next stage in our sequence, the Archaic stage, is defined as "the stage of migratory hunting and gathering cultures continuing into environmental conditions approximating those of the present" (Willey and Phillips 1958:107). The Archaic was initiated after the extinction of the Late Pleistocene megafauna and was terminated in many regions by the transition to a full-fledged agricultural economy. In between these two dramatic end points the Archaic is marked by regional adaptation to local food resources of every possible type. In those situations such as the Great Basin, California, and the Northwest Coast, where agriculture was never important, Archaic cultures continued in existence until the time of historic contact. In terms of the technology, the most important criteria of the Archaic were the rise in importance of grinding and polishing in stone tool manufacture and the use of basketry. In those areas where agriculture did develop, the Archaic subsistence pattern was replaced by the rise of the Formative stage.

The New World Formative stage is the equivalent in part of the Old World Neolithic. Willey and Phillips (1958:146) define the Formative "by the presence of agriculture, or any other subsistence economy of comparable effectiveness, and by the successful integration of such an economy into well-established, sedentary village life". They further cite the fact that such societies typically feature pottery making, weaving, stone carving, and a specialized ceremonial architecture. As Willey and Phillips state, "These elements are not linked to American agriculture through any inner causality . . ." (1958:146). In a later section when we discuss the Formative stage in detail, we will attempt to factor out these interrelationships.

The Classic stage according to Willey and Phillips is defined more in terms of qualitative factors than quantitative ones. The Classic features "excellence in the great arts, climax in religious architecture, and a general florescence in material culture" (Willey and Phillips 1958:182). A further factor of overriding importance is the rise of urbanism. The Classic could fit our definition of civilization for it includes monumental public architecture, a calendrical system, writing, pervasive art styles, widespread trade in luxuries, a class or even a caste system, a formal pantheon of gods, and a priestly oligarchy. The Classic stage did not develop throughout the New World, but was restricted to

Mesoamerica and the Andean region. The reasons for this restricted geographic range are thought to be primarily environmental.

The Postclassic featured mass production of crafts, strong political control maintained by secular leaders, urbanism, military expansion, and conquest. In two cases, the Aztec and Inca, Postclassic empires were terminated by European conquest.

The Postclassic stage in Middle America and Peru is marked by the breakdown of the old regional styles of the Classic stage, by a continuing or increased emphasis upon urban living, and, inferentially, by tendencies toward militarism and secularism (Willey and Phillips 1958:193).

We have reviewed the stage classification of Willey and Phillips as an introductory scheme preparatory to our further review of New World data. The authors of this scheme contemplated additional subdivisions such as an Early and Late Archaic, Preformative, and so on, since the individuality of specific cultures made their assignment to one of the five major stages seem to be a gross oversimplification. They further recognized that other cultures could well be categorized as "belated" or "marginal." For our purposes we will follow the basic outlines of the five major stages as defined. In order to more fully communicate the evolution of culture through these stages in the New World we have included maps of the culture areas for the different time periods (Figs. 14–1 and 14–2).

The culture area concept is adapted from its use relative to modern aboriginal or ethnographic cultures. The concept is that for areas of similar environment, the cultures living therein tend to develop similar economic adaptations with more culture traits in common than these cultures share with cultures lying outside the culture area. For archaeology the concept is equally applicable. One influencing factor is that through time the environments change in climate, flora, and fauna. These environmental factors plus those of a cultural nature—that is, innovations, diffusion of culture traits, conquest, and such—lead to modifications of the boundaries of the archaeological culture areas through time. Nonetheless there is an inherent integrity in the cores of these areas; thus the culture area concept may be used in archaeology.

There is further a historical framework for each of the distinctive cultural-environmental adaptations we term a culture area. With respect to two of our defined stages, the Lithic and the Archaic, our frame of reference is continental in scope. We do not therefore define archaeological culture areas for those stages. Our culture areas (Fig. 14–2) refer to adaptations which occur later in the record when the cultural adaptations were regional in scope.

Within each culture area we utilize the concept of cultural tradition. The definition by Willey and Phillips (1958:37) is: "An archaeological tradition is a (primarily) temporal continuity represented by persistent configurations in single technologies or other systems of related forms." Such traditions, presented in phase sequence diagrams form a major archaeological method of understanding past cultures as complexes of traits with continuity through time.

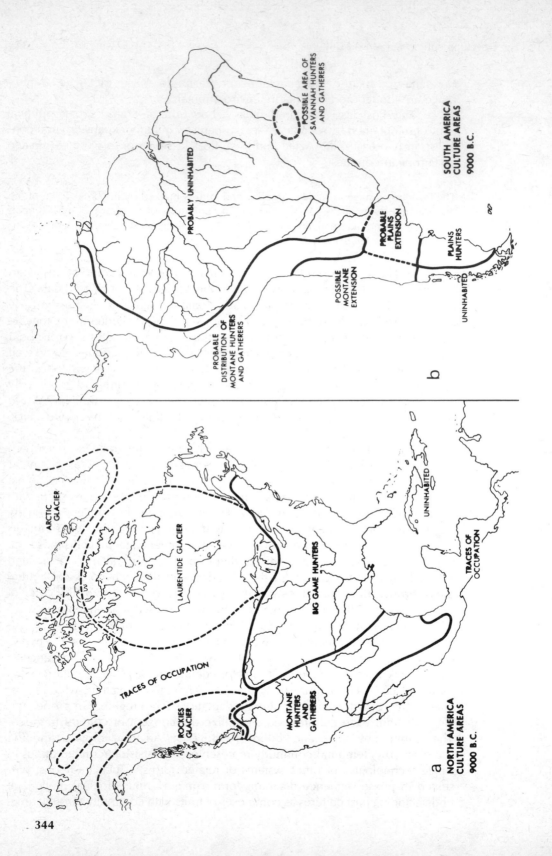

POSSIBLE AREA OF
SAVANNAH HUNTERS
AND GATHERERS

PROBABLY UNINHABITED

PROBABLE
PLAINS
EXTENSION

POSSIBLE
MONTANE
EXTENSION

PLAINS
HUNTERS

PROBABLE
DISTRIBUTION OF
MONTANE HUNTERS
AND GATHERERS

UNINHABITED

SOUTH AMERICA
CULTURE AREAS
9000 B.C.

b

ARCTIC
GLACIER

LAURENTIDE GLACIER

UNINHABITED

BIG GAME HUNTERS

TRACES OF OCCUPATION

ROCKIES
GLACIER

TRACES OF
OCCUPATION

MONTANE
HUNTERS
AND
GATHERERS

NORTH AMERICA
CULTURE AREAS
9000 B.C.

a

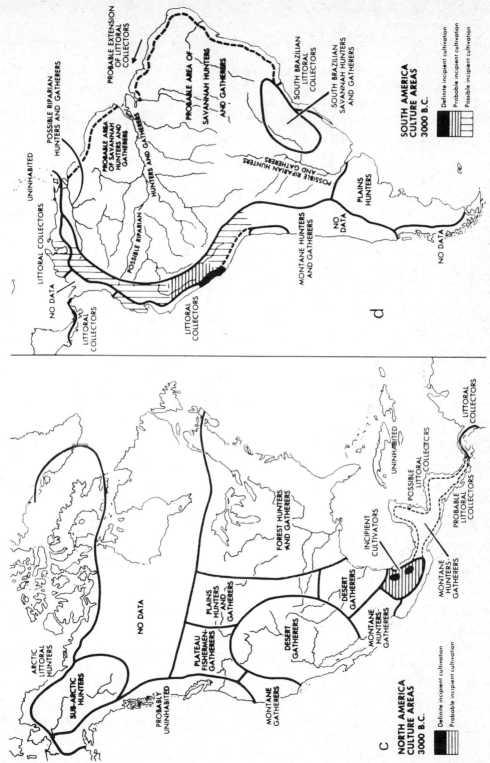

Fig. 14-1 *a.* and *b.* New World culture areas plotted for 9000 B.C.; *c.* and *d.*, for 3000 B.C. (Sanders and Marino 1970:Figs. 2 and 3.)

NORTH AMERICA CULTURE AREAS 3000 B.C.

ARCTIC LITTORAL HUNTERS

SUB-ARCTIC HUNTERS

PROBABLY UNINHABITED

NO DATA

PLATEAU FISHERMEN-GATHERERS

PLAINS HUNTERS AND GATHERERS

FOREST HUNTERS AND GATHERERS

DESERT GATHERERS

MONTANE GATHERERS

MONTANE HUNTERS-GATHERERS

DESERT GATHERERS

INCIPIENT CULTIVATORS

MONTANE HUNTERS-GATHERERS

UNINHABITED

POSSIBLE LITTORAL COLLECTORS

PROBABLE LITTORAL COLLECTORS

LITTORAL COLLECTORS

Definite incipient cultivation

Probable incipient cultivation

c

SOUTH AMERICA CULTURE AREAS 3000 B.C.

UNINHABITED

POSSIBLE RIPARIAN HUNTERS AND GATHERERS

PROBABLE EXTENSION OF LITTORAL COLLECTORS

NO DATA

LITTORAL COLLECTORS

LITTORAL COLLECTORS

POSSIBLE RIPARIAN HUNTERS AND GATHERERS

PROBABLE AREA OF SAVANNAH HUNTERS AND GATHERERS

PROBABLE AREA OF SAVANNAH HUNTERS AND GATHERERS

POSSIBLE RIPARIAN HUNTERS AND GATHERERS

SOUTH BRAZILIAN LITTORAL COLLECTORS

SOUTH BRAZILIAN SAVANNAH HUNTERS AND GATHERERS

MONTANE HUNTERS AND GATHERERS

NO DATA

PLAINS HUNTERS

NO DATA

Definite incipient cultivation

Probable incipient cultivation

Possible incipient cultivation

d

Fig. 14–2 New World archaeological culture areas ca. 3000 B.C.–A.D. 1500 (After Willey 1966 and 1971:Figs. 1–1.)

THE ARCHAIC STAGE

The concept of an Archaic stage has within recent years shifted from a concern with the types of artifacts utilized to an emphasis on life style and ecological adjustment. One reason for this shift has been greater understanding of the nature of the Archaic. Previously, when cultures were viewed primarily in terms of their artifactual inventory, the Archaic appeared to be a bewildering maze of local cultures—here using fish weirs, nets, fishhooks, and such; there using choppers and grinding stones. Attempts at chronological ordering through reference to artifact types was frustrated by the wide variety in artifact forms as well as by their limited change in form through time. A further problem concerned the apparent chronological overlap between early Archaic cultures and late Paleo-Indian manifestations. If the Archaic evolved from the Paleo-Indian tradition, then why was there such an overlap in age? Was it due to errors in dating, or could the Archaic represent direct descendents of an earlier non-Paleo-Indian tradition? Further problems derived from attempts to define the Archaic in negative terms; for example, it did not possess pottery or agriculture. As a result of these problems, the Archaic stage became the focus of a special conference at the Society for American Archaeology meetings in 1955. A publication growing out of that meeting (Byers 1959) led to the present concept of a continentwide Archaic stage.

The latter concept refers to the Archaic stage as dominated by hunting-gathering societies, each exploiting its local environment with a breadth and intensity of resource utilization previously unknown in the New World. These societies exploited the plant kingdom, especially in the gathering of seeds. Shellfish were collected in quantity, fishing became important, and no species of small mammal was ignored. As the ecological niches were systematically explored for utilizable resources, the tool inventory became increasingly varied and to some degree specialized, although numerous multipurpose tools were also in vogue.

Other characteristics of the Archaic adaptation included a band-type social organization made up of small related groups of people practicing a semisedentary life style. Termed *restricted wandering* (Beardsley and others 1955), this pattern emphasized seasonal movements of the band from one known food resource or harvest to another. The required mobility limited the quantity of cultural items that could be acquired or transported. Campsites tended to be revisited as the group moved in a yearly cycle. However the necessity to move, in order to acquire adequate food at all seasons of the year, inhibited the kinds of cultural developments that are associated with a fully sedentary life. In the Archaic then we have the formation of a life style which tended to reinforce itself. The Archaic need for mobility as well as the ability of the economy to meet current needs inhibited culture change. For these reasons, some Archaic cultures lasted into the historic period. For example, in the Great Basin there was limited culture change over 9000 to 10,000 years

(Jennings 1968:136–137). Owing to regional diversity in environments it has been possible to define separate resource utilization patterns for the Archaic. We thus have the *Primary Forest Efficiency* of the eastern United States, the *Coastal Archaic* of the Atlantic Seaboard, the *Boreal Archaic* of Massachusetts to Maine, the *Desert Culture* of the Great Basin, the *California Sequence,* and others.

Primary Forest Efficiency

Primary Forest Efficiency (Caldwell 1958) is defined as a mixed reliance on forest products—nuts, berries, fruits, and seeds, each harvested in turn—in conjunction with the hunting of deer and small mammals as well as use of riverine resources, primarily fish and the freshwater mussel. Caldwell describes this pattern as one of harmonious balance between man and his environment with increasing specialization and diversity in the tool inventory through time. Although seasonal shifts in resource harvests were the rule, the site types suggest there were base camps utilized for part of the year interspersed with use of small temporary seasonal harvest camps. By 2000 B.C. there had developed strong linkages in the cultural patterns of all eastern Archaic peoples. They had further reached the population maximum possible with the Archaic economy. The Archaic productive efficiency included the utilization of all natural resources, not just foods. For example, fiber was used extensively in matting, basketry, nets, sandals, and cordage. The resultant products led to efficiency in fishing, trapping, winnowing, storage, and transport. One aspect of cultural development not perceived in the eastern Archaic is an increase in crafts, knowledge, and general level of cultural attainment. In this area the Archaic cultures did not progress, perhaps because of the limiting factor of an economy requiring mobility.

Coastal Archaic

The Coastal Archaic, extending northward from Virginia along the Atlantic coast, contains as its basic artifact complex: "stemmed and side notched points and knives, semilunar (rocker) knives, steatite vessels (Late), choppers, grooved axes, gouges, slab milling stones, pestles, and several styles of atlatl weights" (Jennings 1968:125). An outstanding site consists of the Boylston fish weir found during excavations for a building in Boston in 1913.

The weir was constructed of sharpened wooden stakes 4 to 16 feet in length driven into a bed of blue clay 16 feet below modern sea level. Obviously sea level at that time was lower, since the weir would have been between the high and low tide lines with the tops of the stakes underwater at high tide. The 65,000 stakes, placed about 2500 B.C., had bundles of brush wedged between them to make a fence impenetrable to the fish trapped within. The two acres of area enclosed within the weir could have provided an enormous fish catch if the conditions were right. On the west coast of Canada, modern Indians used somewhat similar traps made of stone until about 40 years ago. They informed me that traps of this sort could provide up to 400 salmon in one day's catch, a total of about 2000 pounds. Such weirs were common in the Coastal Archaic and represent communal effort, rarely recorded for Archaic cultures.

Boreal Archaic

Farther north we have had distinguished another manifestation, the Boreal Archaic. Major unique traits of this Archaic culture, known from Massachusetts to Maine, are the ground and polished stone tools specialized for woodworking (Fig. 14–3). These include grooved axes, gouges, adzes, as well as ground implements for other purposes—hammerstones, plummets, animal effigies, ground slate projectile points, pendants, stone rods, and bolas stones. Chipped artifacts are primarily restricted to triangular projectile points with a stemmed and slightly convex base. Important sites include Wapanucket No. 6, Massachusetts, dated ca. 2300 B.C., and Ellsworth Falls, Maine, dated from prior to 2009 B.C. ± 310 years to 1400 B.C. ± 400 years. Similarities in tool types and ecological adaptation occur in sites as widely separated as the Ellsworth Falls sequence, Port au Choix, Newfoundland, and numerous sites on the west coast of North America from the Fraser Delta north to the Aleutians. The possibility that the Boreal Archaic extended across the entire northern forested zone of North America is strong, although it has not formally been so defined.

One feature of the Wapanucket No. 6 site was the presence of posthole patterns indicative of seven permanent structures (Fig. 14–4). Made of poles set in a circular pattern of pairs, the lodges have an entryway formed by the spiral overlapping of the wall. Other site features included numerous pits containing culturally used stones and fire hearths.

The Desert Culture

Widespread in the American Southwest, Great Basin, and northern Mexico was the Archaic culture manifestation termed the Desert Culture (Jennings and Norbeck 1955). The economy was specialized to acquire a living in a semiarid region characterized by numerous varieties of cactus, desert grasses, and shrubs. Varying by altitude, the forest species included mesquite, juniper, piñon, and on the highest mountains, pine, spruce, and fir. Surface water is rare to nonexistent and vegetation is sparse; consequently the carrying capacity of the environment in terms of flora, fauna, and man is low. The economic specializations practiced by man in this region were seed gathering and use of traps and snares to acquire small mammals, reptiles, and birds. The culture pattern is best known from numerous stratified dry cave sites in the Great Basin: Danger Cave, Ventana Cave, Lovelock Shelter, and Leonard Shelter. In the Great Basin the transition to an Archaic economy occurred early, with the extinction of the Late Pleistocene fauna by about 11,000 B.P. The same

Fig. 14–3 Artifacts of the Boreal Archaic culture. (Byers 1959:Fig. 3.)

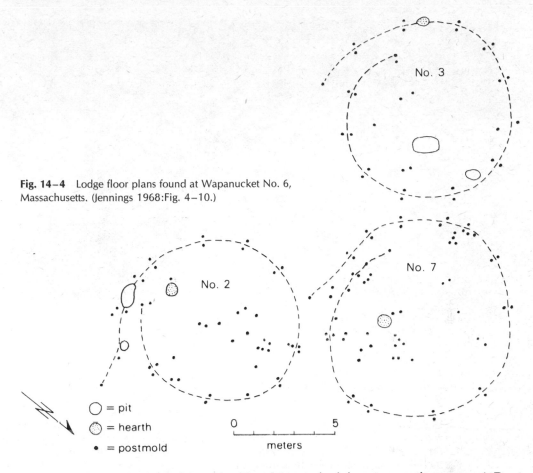

Fig. 14–4   Lodge floor plans found at Wapanucket No. 6, Massachusetts. (Jennings 1968:Fig. 4–10.)

◯ = pit
◉ = hearth
• = postmold

0   5
meters

economy persisted into the historic period of the nineteenth century A.D.— represented by the culture of the Paiute Indians. A resume of Desert Culture traits is reproduced below. We shall return to the Desert Culture later because it was upon this cultural and economic base in the states of Tamaulipas and Puebla, Mexico, that we had the development of plant domestication.

The Desert Culture is also noted for its wealth of preserved perishable artifacts and food remains (Fig. 14–5). The dry cave environments of the Desert Culture sites have preserved the best record of a total lifeway we have from the Archaic period.

TRAITS OF THE DESERT CULTURE

Time: 6000–1000 B.C., generally, and extending down to the ethnographic present in some localities.

SETTLEMENTS
1. Sparse population and small sociopolitical groups.

2. Cave and overhang locations favored for settlement.
3. Bark or grass beds.

SUBSISTENCE
4. Nonsedentary seasonal gatherers.
5. Intensive exploitation of the environ-

Fig. 14–5 Perishable artifacts typical of the Desert Culture. (Photograph courtesy of Philip M. Hobler.)

ment, nonspecialized in the sense of no major reliance on one resource, but close adaptation to everything available including small mammals such as rodents.

6. Small seed harvesting, with special techniques of preparation and cooking (parching, extensive use of flour and mush).

ARTIFACT INVENTORY

7. Basketry (twined basketry generally predominant) and cordage.
8. Netting and matting.
9. Use of fur cloth.
10. Tumplines as carrying device.
11. Sandals (at least by 7000 B.C.); moccasins rare.
12. Atlatl.
13. Use at times of pointed hardwood foreshafts for atlatl darts, without stone points.
14. Varied chipped projectile points, often relatively small in size.
15. Preferential use of basalt, quartzite, and andesite for stone tools in early stages,

later shift toward obsidian, chalcedony, and other glass-textured rocks where available.

16. Percussion chipping techniques predominate; preferential use of large flakes, cores, and spalls.
17. Flat milling stones with cobble mano (by about 7000 B.C.); basin milling stones also present.
18. A number of specialized stone tools (such as those called ovoid scrapers, choppers, pulping planes, scraper planes) of very crude "Paleolithic" appearance.
19. Digging stick.
20. Bunt points.
21. Firedrill and hearth.
22. Flat, curved wooden clubs.
23. Horn shaft wrenches.
24. Tubular pipes or sucking tubes.
25. Use of *Oliva, Olivella,* and other shell beads from the coasts of California and/or the Gulf of California.
26. Vegetable quids.
27. Dogs, at least by 4000 B.C. (Jennings 1955:70).

The California Sequence

California is a region prehistorically dominated by Archaic cultures. Within the borders of the state persisted three major economic systems. In the desert regions of southeastern California the cultural pattern was essentially that of the Desert Culture. The Topanga culture (Fig. 14–6) and the Amargosa culture are examples of desert-based, seed-gathering groups, featuring a chipped and flaked stone tool inventory in addition to reliance on the metate and mano used in grinding of the seeds collected.

Farther north in the Central Valley region the economic staple was the acorn. California peoples in this region utilized the acorn into the historic period. Little change in artifact inventory occurred between that of the early peoples and the later occupants (Fig. 14–7). A major cultural adaptation was the use of the mortar and pestle in the preparation of acorns. The latter were ground to a powder and leached to remove the tannic acid, before being made into cakes, porridge, and other foods. Other food resources were birds, fish, deer, and elk.

The Canalino sequence is a southern coastal variant using resources of the littoral environment. Major resources were shellfish, especially the California abalone and mussels. Sea mammals hunted include the sea lion, sea otter, seal, and dolphin. A final major resource were the deep-sea fish, including barracuda, tuna, and swordfish. The evidence from the coastal middens illustrates the prolific resources that were available. One aspect, typical of the central and coastal California cultures, was the fact that the abundance and stability of the food resources led to a dense population and the establishment of permanent settlements. These factors permitted California to experience one of the highest population densities known for prehistoric peoples not utilizing agriculture. Californian societies had the following social features as inferred from their cultural remains (Meighan 1959:303). The largest political unit was the village ranging up to several hundred persons. Social distinctions did exist as indicated by the preferential treatment given a few burials within each village. It is thought such class distinctions were based on personal recognition of individuals rather than on heredity. Warfare was prevalent and trophy heads were taken. However no defensive sites are known. Trade over long distances was common, with one of the favored routes including the trade of marine shells to the southwestern cultures of Arizona and New Mexico. Charmstones, quartz crystals, and sucking tubes present in Californian cultures imply that a shaman directed curing oriented religion was practiced.

Somewhat similar littoral resource users lived to the north from California throughout the Northwest Coast to southern Alaska. We will not describe their culture in detail here; however, one study (Conover 1972) provides us with perhaps the most detailed analysis available of the prehistoric food resource utilization of such peoples (Fig. 14–8).

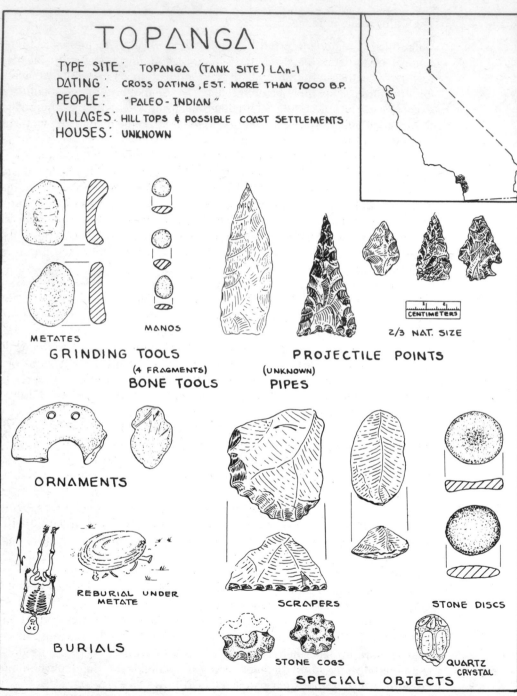

Fig. 14–6 The Topanga, an early California complex. (Meighan 1959:Fig. 1 [drawing after Treganza 1950].)

The Archaic in South America

So far in this section we have not discussed Archaic cultures of South America. This is not because such cultures did not exist; it is primarily because such cultures have not been intensively studied by archaeologists. There was a coastal fishing shellfish-gathering culture in Tierra del Fuego—the Beagle Channel sequence. Extensive shell mounds—*sambaquis*—are known from the southeast coast of Brazil. In the Carribbean there was a somewhat similar littoral economy practiced by peoples termed Meso-Indians. In the case of the Greater Antilles—Cuba, and Hispaniola—some of these peoples survived into the historic period and are known as the Ciboney Indians. Another Archaic economy practiced in South America is known from the Lomas —the foothills region of western Peru. Here the economy was made possible by the presence of winter fogs in an otherwise moistureless desert. The resultant fog vegetation supported a limited fauna which included land snails. The local cultures practiced a hunting and gathering mobile economy in many ways similar to that of the North American Desert Culture. With the drying up of the Lomas, about 5000 years ago, these people moved to the seacoast and changed their economy to fishing and incipient plant cultivation. Some of our best evidence for the early history of plant domestication in South America comes from a dry shell midden on the desert coast of Peru called Huaca Prieta. With at least 45 feet of stratified deposits, the site contained a wealth of perishable remains including gourds, squash, lima beans, canavalia beans, chiles, and cotton. The earliest domesticates appear about 2500 B.C., with corn not being in evidence until about 1500 B.C. So far we do not have as detailed a knowledge of the development of plant cultivation in South America as we do for Mesoamerica. We do know there were separate plants grown in the Andean highlands and another complex grown on the coast (Table 14–1).

THE RISE OF AGRICULTURE

The development of agriculture as a primary subsistence economy in the New World is linked especially to one plant: corn. Although numerous other domesticates were developed—and we shall review those later—it was corn that became the New World staple. Because of the importance of corn prehistorically, it assumes equal importance to archaeologists in their search for cultural origins. In a sense, primitive corn became the Holy Grail pursued by archaeologists Herbert Dick, Richard MacNeish, Douglas Byers, Kent Flannery, and Robert Lister, and botanists Paul Mangelsdorf, Walton Galinat, and Hugh Cutler. The search for the origins of corn was not easy for aboriginally corn was grown from the Dakotas south to central Chile. Somewhere within this vast heartland of the New World lay the point of origin of corn, but its location required more than 20 years of research. A primary problem was that

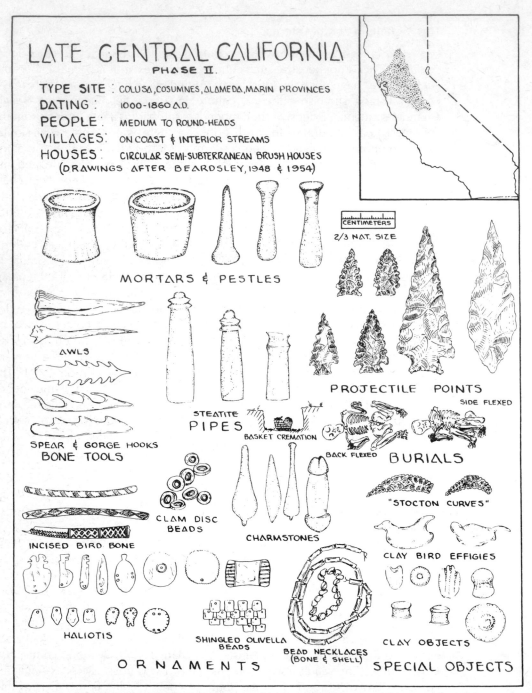

LATE CENTRAL CALIFORNIA
PHASE II.

TYPE SITE : COLUSA, COSUMNES, ALAMEDA, MARIN PROVINCES
DATING : 1000-1860 A.D.
PEOPLE : MEDIUM TO ROUND-HEADS
VILLAGES : ON COAST & INTERIOR STREAMS
HOUSES : CIRCULAR SEMI-SUBTERRANEAN BRUSH HOUSES
(DRAWINGS AFTER BEARDSLEY, 1948 & 1954)

CENTIMETERS
2/3 NAT. SIZE

MORTARS & PESTLES

AWLS

SPEAR & GORGE HOOKS
BONE TOOLS

STEATITE
PIPES

BASKET CREMATION

PROJECTILE POINTS

SIDE FLEXED

BACK FLEXED

BURIALS

CLAM DISC
BEADS

CHARMSTONES

"STOCTON CURVES"

INCISED BIRD BONE

CLAY BIRD EFFIGIES

HALIOTIS

SHINGLED OLIVELLA
BEADS

BEAD NECKLACES
(BONE & SHELL)

CLAY OBJECTS

ORNAMENTS   SPECIAL OBJECTS

Fig. 14-7   Late California complexes. (Meighan 1959:Figs. 2 and 4.)

LATE CANALIÑO

TYPE SITE : MESCALITAN ISLAND
DATING : PROTO-HISTORIC (EARLY CANALINO TO 2000 B.P.)
PEOPLE : BROADHEADS
VILLAGE LITTORAL & ISLAND
HOUSES LARGE DOME SHAPED & RUSH COVERED
    DRAWINGS AFTER   ORR ,1943; ROGERS, 1929.

MORTARS & PESTLES
GRINDING   TOOLS

SPEARHEAD   ⅔ NAT. SIZE
CENTIMETERS
PROJECTILE POINTS

FISH HOOKS
SHELL

SPANGLES & PENDANTS

LIMPET SHELL

BEADS
ORNAMENTS

PIPES

MARKERS

REBURIALS WITH WHALE BONE
BURIALS

COMAL

ARROW-SHAFT
STRAIGHTENER

WOVEN SEAGRASS

BASKET

SANDSTONE BOWL

SHELL BEAD INLAY
IN ASPHALTUM

TARRING
PEBBLES

STEATITE OLLA

WHALE   EFFIGIES

STONE DISH

PAINT MORTARS
& STONE BOWL

OLIVELLA INLAY
SANDSTONE BOWL

S P E C I A L   O B J E C T S

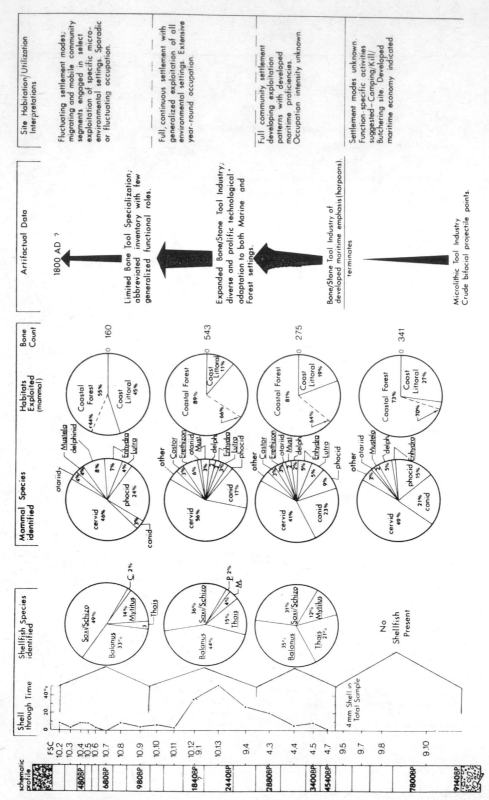

Fig. 14–8 Summary of environmental resource utilization, Namu, British Columbia. (Conover 1972:Fig. 49.)

TABLE 14–1   Principal Pre-Columbian Domesticated Plants in South America

Common Name	Occurrence
Seed Crops	
Maize	All areas.
Lupine	Highlands.
Quinoa	Highlands.
Cañahua	Highlands.
Amaranth	Highlands.
Beans	
Kidney	General.
Scarlet Runner or	
Ayecote	Cauca River.
Lima	Coast.
Jack	Coast.
Fruits	
Pineapple	Tropical.
Soursop	Lowlands.
Pepino	Temperate.
Roots	
Potato	Chile Coast and Highlands. (separate species)
Oca	Highlands.
Ulluco	Highlands.
Mashua	Highlands.
Achira	Coast; temperate valleys.
Arracacha	Temperate valleys.
Yacon	Temperate valleys.
Sweet Manioc (Yuca)	Tropical lowlands.
Peanut	Lowlands
Sweet Potato	Tropical lowlands.
Miscellaneous	
Squash	General.
Peppers, all	Medium climates.
Cacao, Chocolate Bean	Low valleys.
Cotton	Tropical Coast and Coast. (separate species)
Narcotics	
Tobacco	General and Highlands. (separate species)
Coca	Warm valleys.

(Bennett 1947:5.)

the remains of the corn plant were perishable; therefore the search was limited
to those dry cave sites where such remains would be preserved.

The history of this search has been related by Richard S. MacNeish both
in print (MacNeish 1967:3–13) and by means of a color movie, "The Origins
of Corn in Mesoamerica." The first breakthrough was the discovery of primitive
corn cobs at Bat Cave, New Mexico, in 1948. These finds by Herbert Dick

Fig. 14–9   Locations of sites with early maize in the Southwest and Mesoamerica. (After MacNeish 1967:Fig. 1.)

were submitted to Mangelsdorf for study and were subsequently verified as being ancestors of modern corn. Their age was established by radiocarbon at 3000 to 5000 years B.P. Simultaneously MacNeish was finding early corn in LaPerra cave in Tamaulipas state, northeastern Mexico. Later work in Tamaulipas suggested to MacNeish that the corn there was not the earliest domesticated. However, the Tamaulipas finds led MacNeish to shift his search farther to the south (Fig. 14–9).

In 1958 MacNeish explored caves in Guatemala and Honduras but found no corn. In 1959 MacNeish and Frederick Peterson excavated Santa

Marta Cave, Chiapas. Their finds of corn pollen there were not old enough to suggest that corn was originally domesticated that far south. The search had narrowed; as far as MacNeish was concerned, the homeland of corn had to lie between southern Tamaulipas and Chiapas. According to Mangelsdorf's studies, the best probability was that the ancestor of corn was a highland grass similar to the pod popcorn found in both Bat Cave and Tamaulipas. A study of suitable environments for early corn suggested that three regions were most probable: southern Oaxaca, the Rio Balsas region of Guerrero, and the Tehuacan Valley of Puebla. In 1959 and 1960 MacNeish visited numerous caves in Puebla and Oaxaca. Eventually he chose Coxcatlan Cave in the Tehuacan Valley as most promising. On January 27, 1960, excavations revealed a tiny corn cob about an inch in length. A month later, it was dated by C-14 at 3610 ± 250 years B.P. This early date indicated that they were on the right track. The next step was the formation of the Tehuacan Valley project of the R. S. Peabody Foundation. The project was to consist of three years of studies in the region with the goal of documenting the transition from an Archaic hunting and gathering economy to a fully agricultural one. The project was interdisciplinary, requiring analysis of the natural environment as well as specialized studies of all of the recovered ancient cultigens, corn, beans, squash, amaranth, and so on. Other studies focused on food bones, prehistoric feces, prehistoric irrigation systems, geology, and such. The goals of the project were formidable, for within Mesoamerica a wide variety of plants and animals were known to the Archaic inhabitants in their intensive use of all available resources. Table 14–2 below lists the amazing variety of plants that were eventually cultivated in Mesoamerica.

Detailed studies by Flannery (1967) of the fauna in the Tehuacan Valley sites illustrates (Fig. 14–10) the mixed reliance on a wide variety of food animals. Identification of the other major components in the diet was achieved by a combination of studies. These included study of dry vegetal parts, pollen, food bones, and coprolites. The results indicate the transition from an Archaic economy to an agricultural one was slow, requiring more than 5000 years (Fig. 14–11). In addition it was broad-based, with many different species of cultigens and wild plants being relied upon. In the New World, far from being a revolution, the development of plant cultivation was one of gradual transition in an economy already broadly based on widespread utilization of all available resources.

The development of plant cultivation in the New World has received considerable study. Mangelsdorf, MacNeish, and Willey (1971) cite a number of requisite conditions that led to this New World development. One factor was a region with great diversity in the natural vegetation. The region should also impose hardships upon its inhabitants so that acquisition of adequate foodstuffs would require intensive conscious effort. The most likely regions would be semiarid with distinct annual dry and rainy seasons. Finally, of course, we have the nature of the cultural exploitative patterns which were developed by the Archaic peoples.

Flannery (1971) has developed an explanatory model for the cultural

TABLE 14-2 Cultivated Plants of Middle America

Common Name	Common Name
Cultivated for Their Edible Seeds	Jocote
Amaranth	Coconut*
Apazote	Elderberry
Bean, Common	Guava
Bean, Lima	Guayabilla
Bean, Runner	Mammee Colorado
Bean, Tepary	Sapote, Green
Bean, Jack	Sapote, Yellow
Chia	Sapodilla
Chia Grande	Matasano
Maize	Sapote, White
Panic Grass	Nance
Peanut*	Papaya
Sunflower*	Pineapple*
Cultivated for Their Edible Roots or Tubers	Pitahaya
Coyolxochitl	Prickly Pear
Manioc	Ramon
Potato*	Sapote, Black
Sweet Potato*	*Herbs and Other Vegetables*
Yam Bean	Chaya
Cultivated for Their Edible Gourdlike Fruits	Chipilin
Chayote	Pacaya
Squash, Cushaw	Tepejilote
Squash, Summer	Tomato
Squash, Walnut	Tomato, Husk
Other Edible Fruits	Yucca
Anona	*Condiments and Other Flavorings*
Bullock's-Heart	Chili Pepper
Cherimoya*	Vanilla
Ilama	*Stimulants and Narcotics*
Soursop	Cacao
Sweetsop	Maguey
Avocado	Tobacco
Caujilote	*Fiber Plants*
Capulin Cherry	Cotton
Tejocote	Henequen
Cashew*	Maguey
Hog Plum	Sisal

*Probably not native to Mesoamerica.
(Jennings 1968:169 [modified from Mangelsdorf, MacNeish, and Willey 1964].)

adaptation to plant cultivation. In his studies of Mesoamerican food remains a number of facts are isolated: 1. Certain plants and animals were always more important than others whether they were wild or domesticated. 2. Use of these species required a procurement system which also permitted the continued survival of the species. 3. Use of these resources depended upon seasonality and scheduling. In arid Mesoamerica Flannery perceives six major procurement systems utilizing maguey, cactus fruit, tree legumes, wild grass, white-

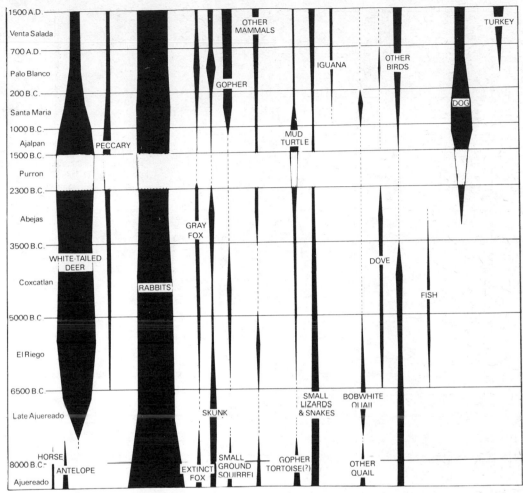

Fig. 14–10 Exploitation of the fauna by inhabitants of the Tehuacan Valley. (Flannery 1967:Fig. 95.)

tailed deer, and cottontail rabbit. He reconstructs the exploitative pattern as follows:

a. In the late dry season and early rainy season, there is a period of peak abundance of wild plant foods. These localized resources were intensively harvested, and eaten or cached as they came to maturity; this appears to have been a "macroband" activity. Because "all hands" participated in these harvests, little deer hunting was done; instead the Indians set traps in the vicinity of the plant-collecting camp, an activity which does not conflict with intensive plant harvests the way deer-hunting would.

b. In the late fall and winter, most plants have ceased to bear fruit, but deer hunting is at its best. Since this is the mating season, male deer (who normally forage by themselves) fall in with the does and fawns, making the average herd larger; and

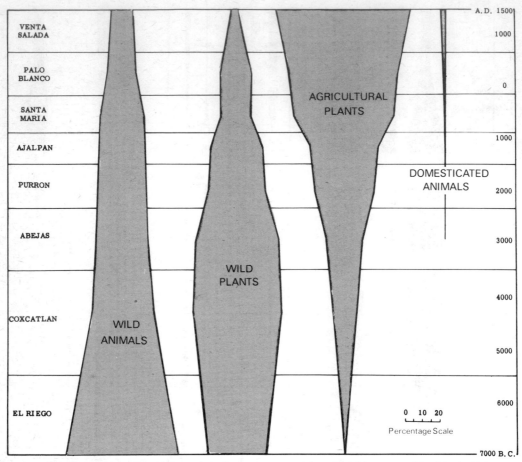

Fig. 14–11 Changing trends in the importance of the principal sources of food in the Tehuacan Valley. (MacNeish 1967:Fig. 186.)

since this is also the season when the deciduous vegetation of the highlands sheds its leaves, the deer can be more easily followed by hunters. As the dry season wears on, however, the deer grow warier and range farther and farther back into the mountains. This is the leanest time of the year in terms of plant resources, and it was evidently in this season that man turned most heavily to plants available year round, like the root of the Ceiba (which can be baked like sweet manioc) or the heart of the maguey plant (which can be roasted). These appear to have been "microband" activities.

c. By chewing roots and maguey hearts, the preceramic forager managed to last until the late spring growing season, at which point he could wallow in cactus fruit again. Essentially, his "schedule" was keyed to the seasonal availability of certain wild plants, which climaxed at those times of the year which were best suited for small-game-trapping. He scheduled his most intensive deer hunting for the seasons when big plant harvests were not a conflicting factor (Flannery 1971:91–92).

Having defined above the Archaic economy practiced in the semiarid highlands of Oaxaca and Puebla, Flannery goes on to suggest a model as to how this system might have been modified to include plant cultivation. The term proposed by Flannery is *positive feedback,* original accidental deviations which through time gradually made possible more and more reliance on certain plants. In Mesoamerica the most important such deviations were genetic changes in corn and beans. In beans, for example, the changes included increased permeability in water rendering them easier to cook and limp pods which made their harvest easier, in contrast to brittle pods such as mesquite. Corn increased its size, hybridized with its close relatives, lost the glumes, and increased numbers of kernels. Corn and beans together supplement each other nutritionally—another form of positive feedback. In Flannery's terms the positive feedback network acted as follows:

The more widespread maize cultivation, the more favorable genetic changes, the greater the yield, the higher the population, and hence the more intensive cultivation. There can be little doubt that pressures for more intensive cultivation were instrumental in perfecting early water-control systems, like well-irrigation and canal-irrigation (Flannery 1971:95).

Another aspect of the system was that the formulation of a formal planting season and harvesting season interfered with those economic activities previously scheduled at those times of the year. Therefore spring harvests of wild plants, prickly pear, and organ cactus and fall harvests of acorns, fruits, and guaves would have been reduced because of lack of available labor. Rainy season hunting of deer and peccary were also curtailed. One other feature of the cultivated plant harvests and planting would have been augmentation of band size and length of time spent together in one location. The latter is a direct causal factor leading to our next major cultural development, the Formative stage.

The history of South American domestication is currently under intensive study as the R. S. Peabody Foundation project in the Ayacucho Valley, directed by Richard S. MacNeish, is focusing their research in a way similar to their completed Tehuacan Valley studies. The South American tropical lowlands featured another agricultural crop, manioc, whose pulverized-leached pulp provided the staple food in the Amazon basin until the introduction of corn at a relatively late date in prehistory, primarily in A.D. times.

THE FORMATIVE STAGE

In their Formative stage definition, Willey and Phillips stress the appearance of agriculture and the resultant development of sedentary village life. James Ford, in his classic work *A Comparison of Formative Cultures in the Americas,* takes issue with Willey and Phillips's definition. According to Ford (1969:5) both in Mesoamerica and Peru, agriculture was practiced centuries before other Form-

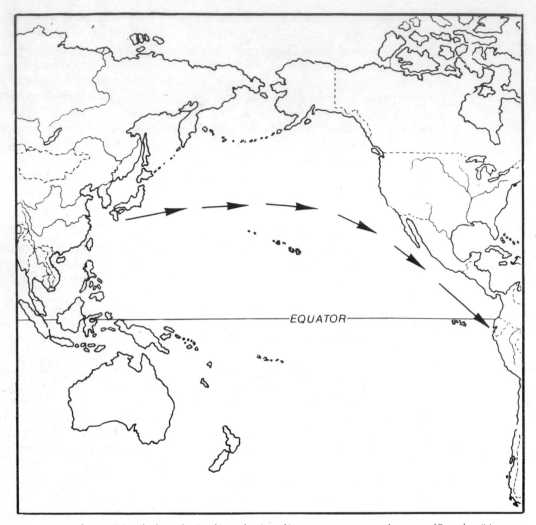

Fig. 14–12   The hypothesized introduction of Jomon type pottery to the coast of Ecuador. (Meggers, Evans, and Estrada 1965:Fig. 103.)

ative trait complexes such as ceramics or polished stone tools became common. He also is critical of the concept of "sedentary life occurring early" and chooses instead to view this "sedentism" as a process that required some time to develop. Ford also points out, correctly, that the earliest known pottery occurs in a matrix of coastal shellfish-gathering cultures on the Ecuadoran coast where, according to Meggers, Evans, and Estrada (1965:167–168), it probably was introduced from Japan (Fig. 14–12). The actual introduction of pottery is viewed as resulting from a boatload of Japanese of the Jomon culture, who were blown off course by a typhoon and who eventually drifted across the

Pacific to land in Ecuador. The new arrivals then presumably introduced pottery making to the local residents, using prior techniques and local materials. Other authors, primarily Lathrop (1967), have disputed this hypothesis on the basis that no single Jomon pattern complex is particularly similar to the earliest Valdivia complex. As Willey (1971:276) states, "If we reject the Jomon-Valdivia linkage, what then?" His answer is that while no other South American Intermediate area pottery-making culture as early as Valdivia is known, perhaps we simply need more archaeological knowledge of the Intermediate area cultures. Until that occurs, the Jomon-Valdivia linkage while not proven, is a likely possibility to be kept in mind.

We view the Formative as a developmental period within which the various elements we know as Formative came to be associated together—a process requiring considerable time. Ford (1969:5) defines the period as follows:

For these reasons it is preferable to define the Formative more loosely as the 3000 years (or less in some regions) during which the elements of ceramics, ground stone tools, handmade figurines, and manioc, and maize agriculture were being diffused and welded into the socioeconomic life of the people living in the region extending from Peru to the eastern United States. At the start of this span of years, all these people had an Archaic economy and technology; at its end they possessed the essential elements for achieving civilization.

The reasons for the development of Formative culture were undoubtedly complex. There occurred a blend of parallel independent developments region by region coupled with a widespread communications network along which ideas, objects, and their associated behavior patterns were diffused. The cultural complexity is enormous and the details of the New World Formative cultures require an individual text.

Important Formative developments occurred not only in Peru and Mesoamerica but also in the eastern United States, southwestern United States, Central America, and Columbia. Belated or marginal Formative cultures are known from the Great Plains river valleys, the Guianas, Ecuador, the mouth of the Amazon, and the southern Andes south to central Chile. The diagnostic hallmark of the Formative is reliance on agriculture as the economic mainstay. Even in Mesoamerica such reliance developed late with a fully agricultural economy not in existence until 1500–1000 B.C. In Mesoamerica domesticated animals were never particularly important as food resources, compared to the Old World Neolithic. The Mesoamerican and Southwestern domesticated animals included the dog (eaten in Mesoamerica), turkey, and parrots (kept for their feathers). Peruvian domesticated animals were primarily highland species, the llama, alpaca, and vicuña kept for their wool and meat and used for transport of goods but not ridden. One other domesticate, the guinea pig, was eaten.

Settlement patterns featured the village as the basic unit. Small clusters of individual houses were the rule, located adjacent to the fields. Basic house types included above-ground mud, stone, or wattle-and-daub-walled units with roofs of thatch or poles, grass, and earth. The typical village consisted of 6 to 10 such units. Not far away was the ceremonial center, built and used by the members of several such villages. Ceremonial centers were not universal, for within the Formative there was considerable variation. In the eastern United States the ceremonial centers consisted of specialized burial areas with burial mounds and enclosing earthen embankments. In the Southwest the ceremonial room, the kiva, was located within the village. The highest development of ceremonial centers occurred in Mesoamerica. There the center featured flat-topped platform mounds (pyramids) surmounted with a temple on top. The pyramids were arranged around a rectangular open ceremonial plaza. Associated features often included vertically set carved stone slabs, stelae, which were placed to commemorate specific dates. Frequently the date of erection was carved on these slabs.

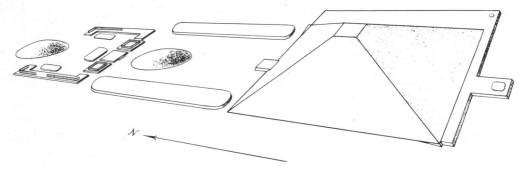

Fig. 14–13 Plan of the ceremonial center at La Venta, Tabasco, Mexico. (Willey 1966:Fig. 3–21 [redrawn from Drucker, Heizer, and Squier 1959].)

Other associated features included tombs, mosaic floors, carved stone altars, as well as residences for the priests. The earliest of these ceremonial centers is at La Venta, Tabasco (Fig. 14–13). Built about 800 B.C., the site is located on an island in the Coatzalcualcos River. It is here we perceive the earliest known evidence of hieroglyphic writing, use of stelae, and the building of a formalized ceremonial center. The site consists of earthen mounds rebuilt or added to in layers. Within the mounds, but covered with earth, are floor mosaics of blocks of serpentine in the form of jaguar masks (Fig. 14–14). Presumably these masks were immediately buried after dedication. Other important features at the site are an enclosure made of vertical basalt columns and a tomb enclosure made of the same type of columns. In addition to the beautifully carved stelae weighing up to 50 tons (Fig. 14–15), the impressive monuments include great carved stone human heads (Fig. 14–16). These heads weigh up to 15 tons and portray a distinctive race of people with down-curving mouths, shown wearing a type of helmet. Most impressive is the fact that the basalt quarry for these stones lay 60 miles upstream. Presumably the sculptured stones were floated to their positions by means of rafts. La Venta is only one of

Fig. 14–14 Jaguar mask mosaic pavement as exposed during excavation at La Venta, Tabasco, Mexico. (© National Geographic Society.)

many such ceremonial centers in Mesoamerica built during this period. Within Mesoamerica the time between 2000 B.C. and A.D. 300 (Formative stage) is termed the *Preclassic period.* During this interval there was the rise of sedentary village life, the establishment of a religious theocracy, the building of ceremonial centers, and the development of crafts including carving in jade, pottery, and such. Other developments included a growth in population, an increase in the size of ceremonial centers, and a codification of beliefs, especially in the area of religion, with the establishment of a pantheon of gods and a specialized priesthood. These religious beliefs were expressed in architecture, art, and all knowledge including astronomy and calendrical notations. The Olmec art style was widespread and its diffusion and acceptance indicates the power of the associated beliefs. These ideological concepts were what is distinctive about Mesoamerican culture. They cannot be explained as the inevitable result of the adoption of an agricultural economy. These were unique developments in New World culture history and they occurred in the Preclassic. The later Classic cultures amplified this basic Mesoamerican culture pattern but did not alter its basic configuration. Major Preclassic cultures are known from every region of Mesoamerica; the best known are the early Maya of Guatemala, the Zapotec of Oaxaca, the Olmec of the Vera Cruz coast, and the communities inhabiting the Valley of Mexico—Zacatenco, El Arbolillo, Cuicuilco, and Teotihuacan.

Fig. 14–15 Large stela from La Venta, Tabasco, Mexico. (Hester photograph, courtesy Mexican National Museum of Anthropology.)

Fig. 14–16   A great stone head from La Venta, Tabasco, Mexico. (Photograph courtesy of Mexican National Museum of Anthropology.)

Because our review of the Formative is necessarily brief, we are unable to convey to the reader the details of the various Formative cultures. We can only relate the major broad outlines of these cultural developments. Perhaps the single most important fact is that Formative cultures to the north lagged behind the Mesoamerican developments. These northern cultures did not develop the wealth of cultural detail and lacked the innovative power and vigor of the Mesoamerican societies. In addition numerous culture traits can be traced back to the south indicating that Mesoamerica functioned as a major center of diffusion. For example, in the Southwest United States there were Mesoamerican type ballcourts, use of irrigation, pyrite mirrors, copper bells, and certain ceremonial parallels, such as priests' costumes, belief in the feathered serpent, use of feathers, and even the presence of pyramids. In the eastern United States we have the northward spread of Temple Mounds after A.D. 700. These were earthen flat topped mounds of pyramidal form. A later feature was a religious cult, termed the Southern cult, which included many symbols of Mesoamerican affinity—hands, skulls, human bones, and priests in costume, some with trophy heads (Fig. 14–17). Introduced into both regions were the domesticates, corn, beans, and squash.

Another feature must be taken into account when we study the North American Formative cultures: environmental limitation. The Southwest is semi-arid and the availability of rainfall in sufficient quantity for agriculture was a continuing problem, so much so that the Puebloan religion became focused on rainfall propagation. In the Plains region the available soil for agriculture was limited to the river valley bottoms. The land used today for production of a major portion of the world's supply of wheat and corn, the rolling plains uplands, was unavailable to the prehistoric Plains inhabitants. They were unable to farm the uplands with the agricultural tools at their command, the digging stick and bison scapula hoe. It was not until the introduction of the moldboard plow in the nineteenth century A.D. that the upland sod could be effectively broken. In the eastern United States perhaps the reason for limited change lay in the less than total reliance on agriculture, resulting from the continuing productivity of the Primary Forest Efficiency.

THE ANDEAN FARMING TRADITION

In the Andean region, encompassing parts of Columbia, Ecuador, Peru, Bolivia, northwestern Argentina, and northern Chile, we had the development of a strong Formative cultural pattern. The extent to which this development was the result of influences from Mesoamerica is still under investigation. Agriculture began in the Farmer-Fisherman period after 2500 B.C. By 1000 B.C. the Andean farming tradition was fully established and formed the economic basis of all later Andean cultural developments. This tradition featured intensive agriculture of valley bottom lands watered by irrigation. Irrigation was espe-

Fig. 14-17 Symbols of the Southern cult: human hands, hearts, skulls, bones, serpents, and the taking of heads. (Willey 1966:304, 307 [after Waring and Holder 1945].)

cially important in the coastal valleys, since the coast is a desert with all rain falling on the mountains to the east and draining to the coast by means of these valleys.

Agriculture was both a male and female activity and was closely coordinated with the religion. Domesticated plants were cultivated to the limit of their ecological range and other economies, fishing, hunting, and gathering were of limited importance after the rise of agriculture. Major crops included corn, beans, squash, potatoes, quinoa, sweet potatoes, manioc, peanuts, cotton, peppers, tobacco, and coca. Agricultural implements included the digging stick (in the later periods frequently with a metal point), hoe, and stone-headed clod breaker. In addition to irrigation, agricultural practices included the use of guano fertilizer, crop rotation, and the fallowing of fields. Terraces were built, frequently stone-faced in order to more fully utilize steep slopes. Other practices included lining of some of the irrigation ditches with cut stone. Foods were preserved by drying and freezing as well as being stored in permanent granaries. From the central Andes south into Chile the highlands featured herding as an economy of importance nearly equal to farming. In some regions the elevation is so great that herding was the principal economy with agriculture being impracticable.

Pottery making was an advanced craft featuring modeled, painted, and moldmade ceramics in profusion. The ceramics, because of their realistic detail, provide us with some of the archaeological materials of greatest value in cultural reconstruction ever found anywhere in the world. From the ceramics we have learned details of social organization, political organization, religious practices, house types, disease, and sexual practices.

Weaving was an equally important craft. Peruvian textiles, preserved by virtue of their being buried in graves dug in the dry sands of the desert coast, are among the best known textiles from any prehistoric culture anywhere in the world. In terms of the technical proficiency displayed in types of weaves, fineness of weave, colors, and patterns, these textiles are unsurpassed. Weaving was done in cotton and wool, with both everyday garments and specialized wrappings for burial bundles being made. Clothing for men was a breechclout belt, slit neck shirt, shawl, and a headband. Women wore a wrap-around dress with a belt, a headband, a shoulder shawl, and bags with carrying straps.

Ornaments and implements were made of metal including gold, silver, copper, bronze, tin, and electrum. Metalworking techniques included casting, soldering, gilding, and the use of filigree. Ornamentation featured body painting, tattooing, skull deformation, inlaying of teeth, and the wearing of earplugs, noseplugs, and necklaces. Minor crafts were wood carving, the carving and painting of gourds, basketry, and the manufacture of ornaments and implements in shell, stone, and bone.

Transportation within the region was difficult because the terrain ranged within a few miles from sea level to 20,000 feet. Some of the highest areas utilized were for mining, above 15,000 feet. Major transport was on foot with the llama as the principal beast of burden. On the open sea, sailing rafts with centerboards were used. Boats of tied bundles of reeds were common on the highland lakes.

The intensive agricultural production supported a large population living in permanent houses. Houses were built of both stone and adobe brick. The village was the basic social and political unit. Each village had its own headman and worked as a cooperative labor force. Villages were organized into larger political units which through time became of increasingly larger size and complexity. Class distinctions were important and were based on wealth and political influence. Late in the tradition these class distinctions crystallized into a true caste system.

Warfare was an organized activity with a specialized warrior class and military leaders. Implements of war included the spear thrower, spear, club, sling, shield, bow and arrow, and bolas. The practice of warfare relied on use of spies, blockades, storming of fortresses, and fighting in formations.

Religion was carried out under the leadership of priests who were responsible for organizing all ritual. Most ceremonies were agricultural in nature, with another major focus being the rites associated with burial. The latter featured a public ceremony in which the corpse was wrapped in burial clothing then placed in the tomb with the appropriate grave offerings.

In the brief section above we have summarized the basic cultural pattern in existence throughout the Andean region from about 1000 B.C. until the Spanish Conquest of the Inca in A.D. 1532. The early part of this pattern was a Formative stage development with cultural dynamics similar to those of Mesoamerica. We will review the chronology and cultural details of the later portions of the Andean sequence in Chapter 16.

REFERENCES

Beardsley, R. K., and others, 1955, "Functional and Evolutionary Implications of Community Patterning," in Wauchope, pp. 129–157.

Byers, D. S., 1959, "An Introduction to Five Papers on the Archaic Stage," *American Antiquity* 24:229–232.

———, ed., 1967, *The Prehistory of the Tehuacan Valley,* Vol. I. Austin: University of Texas Press.

Caldwell, J. R., 1958, *Trend and Tradition in the Prehistory of the Eastern United States.* Washington, D.C.: American Anthropological Association, Memoir No. 88.

Callen, E. D., 1967, "Analysis of the Tehuacan Coprolites," in Byers 1967, pp. 261–289.

Conover, K. J., 1972, "Archaeological Sampling at Namu: A Problem in Settlement Reconstruction." Unpublished Ph.D. dissertation, University of Colorado.

Drucker, P., R. F. Heizer, and R. Squier, 1959, *Excavations at LaVenta, Tabasco, 1955.* Washington, D.C.: Bulletin of the Bureau of American Ethnology, No. 170.

Flannery, K. V., 1967, "The Vertebrate Fauna and Hunting Patterns," in Byers, 1967, pp. 132–177.

———, 1971, "Archaeological Systems Theory and Early Mesoamerica," in S. Struever (ed.), *Prehistoric Agriculture.* New York: Natural History Press, pp. 80–100.

Ford, J. A., 1969, *A Comparison of Formative Cultures in the Americas.* Washington, D.C.: Smithsonian Institution Press, Contributions to Anthropology, Vol. 11.

Jennings, J. D., 1955, "The American Southwest: A Problem in Cultural Isolation," in Wauchope, pp. 61–127.

———, 1968, *Prehistory of North America.* New York: McGraw-Hill.

———, and E. Norbeck, 1955, "Great Basin Prehistory: A Review," *American Antiquity* 21:1–11.

Johnson, F., 1942, *The Boylston Street Fishwir.* Andover, Mass.: Papers of the R. S. Peabody Foundation for Archaeology, Vol. 2.

Lathrop, D. W., 1967, "Review of Early Formative Period at Coastal Ecuador: Valdivia and Machalilla Phases," *American Anthropologist* 69(1):96–98.

Lilly, E., 1937, *Prehistoric Antiquities of Indiana.* Indianapolis: Indiana Historical Society.

MacNeish, R. S., 1967, "Introduction," in Byers, 1967, pp. 3–13.

Manglesdorf, P. C., R. S. MacNeish, and G. R. Willey, 1964, "Origins of Agriculture in Mesoamerica," in R. Wauchope (ed.), *Handbook of Middle American Indians.* Austin: University of Texas Press, pp. 427–445.

Meggers, B. J., C. Evans, and E. Estrada, 1965, *Early Formative Period of Coastal Ecuador.* Washington, D.C.: Smithsonian Institution, Contribution to Anthropology, Vol. 1.

Meighan, C. W., 1959, "Californian Cultures and the Concept of an Archaic Stage," *American Antiquity* 24:289–305.

Sanders, W. T., and J. Marino, 1970, *New World Prehistory.* Englewood Cliffs, N.J.: Prentice-Hall.

Stirling, M. W., 1943, *Stone Monuments of Southern Mexico.* Washington, D.C.: Bulletin of the Bureau of American Ethnology, No. 138.

Wauchope, R., (ed.), 1955, *Seminars in Archaeology.* Society for American Archaeology, Memoir No. 11.

Willey, G. R., 1966, *An Introduction to American Archaeology,* Vol. I. Englewood Cliffs, N.J.: Prentice-Hall.

——, 1971, *An Introduction to American Archaeology,* Vol. II. Englewood Cliffs, N.J.: Prentice-Hall.

——, and P. Phillips, 1958, *Method and Theory in American Archaeology.* Chicago: The University of Chicago Press.

15

Mesoamerican Civilization

THE CLASSIC PERIOD

The transition from the Formative stage (Mesoamerican Preclassic period) cultures to the Classic period cultures was gradual. It was marked more by the appearance of superlatives—in architecture, thought, writing, crafts, and so forth—rather than the appearance of new phenomena. The Classic achievements represent a cultural florescence, a time of the flowering of culture, stunning in its magnificence and variety. In this chapter I will attempt to outline the major features of the Mesoamerican Classic. The magnitude of the Classic achievement can be understood from simple statements concerning the size of the sites considered. Teotihuacan, for example, was an urban center covering 8 square miles with a population estimated at 75,000 to possibly 200,000 (Millon 1970). At Tikal the great temples on their pyramidal bases rise to a height of 60 meters above the plaza level. Monte Alban has a central plaza the size of a modern football field surrounded by a complex of buildings which has been undergoing annual excavation and restoration for more than 30 years.

In Figures 15-1–15-3 we present a set of maps locating the major sites by period and region. There are at least a hundred ceremonial centers which may be termed major and hundreds more that were of lesser size and importance. Cultural chronologies have been worked out for many of the major regions of Mesoamerica (Fig. 15–4). The regions included are the Northern Frontier and West, Central Mexico, Oaxaca, Maya Highlands, Huasteca, Central Veracruz, Southern Veracruz and Tabasco, Maya Lowlands, and the Southern Periphery. Less well known areas possessing Mesoamerican culture include Chihuahua, Guerrero, the Mexican west coast north of Colima, as well as parts of Nicaragua and Costa Rica.

The best known and most impressive regional cultures of the Classic are those of Teotihuacan in the Valley of Mexico, the Zapotec culture of the Valley of Oaxaca, the Mayan culture of the Guatemalan highlands and the Mayan culture of the Yucatecan lowlands. The wealth of the Mayan culture was so overwhelming that the Carnegie Institution established a major program of study under the leadership of Sylvanus Morley. For more than 30 years various Mayan sites were studied in detail; for example, sites of the first order of magnitude termed "metropolises" by Morley and Brainerd (1956) include Uxmal, Chichén Itzá, Tikal, and Copan. Centers of the second class termed "cities" number approximately 20. The Carnegie efforts resulted in major excavations at most of these sites. The results include not only studies of the entire cities but detailed excavation reports of individual buildings (Morris 1931; Ruppert 1935), frequently several hundred pages in length.

Prior to the detailed archaeological excavation programs of the twentieth century, there was nearly a century of explorer and antiquarian interest in Mesoamerican ruins. The Mayan country was of primary interest inasmuch as the jungle was filled with "lost cities," any one of which could provide new and unique finds. These explorations, which are still continuing, such as the recent Explorers Club-sponsored survey of Guatemalan caves, first began in 1839 with the landing at Belize, Honduras, of John Lloyd Stephens, a New York lawyer, accompanied by Frederick Catherwood, an English illustrator. Previously Stephens had had good sales of a travel book he had published in 1837 concerning his visit to Arabia and Palestine. The trip to Central America was undertaken as a result of Stephens' learning of the ancient cities to be found there and the possibility that they could form the subject of another book. Eventually published in two volumes, Stephens' *Incidents of Travel in Central America, Chiapas, and Yucatan* (1841) provides our earliest detailed descriptions of ancient Mayan ruins. Catherwood's illustrations are priceless because they were uniquely accurate copies of the ancient buildings and monuments with their, at that time, undecipherable hieroglyphs. At the time he was copying these monuments, most European illustrators were adapting aboriginal peoples and archaeological findings in their illustrations to fit preconceptions largely derived from the ancient Classical world. Catherwood's renditions were accurate and further provide us with a record of the condition of the ruins prior to modern restoration.

In the last half of the nineteenth century, explorers and students expanded our knowledge of the ancient cities, for the most part without undertaking major excavations. Including Guillelmo Dupaix, Arthur Morelet, E. George Squier, Desire Charnay, Alfred P. Maudsley, Teobert Maler, Edward H. Thompson, and others, these pioneers made known to the world the ancient splendors present in the Central American jungles (Wauchope 1965, Deuel 1967). Since their day, archaeological research has focused on problems in the following general order: 1. site location, 2. chronology based on the calendrical dates, 3. architectural studies and building reconstruction, 4. ceramic seriation, 5. radiocarbon dating and the calendrical correlation problem, 6. detailed site and regional mapping of urban developments, 7. studies of the economy, and 8. studies of social organization.

URBANISM AND SETTLEMENT PATTERN

The Classic featured the rise of urbanism for the first time in the New World. Our best evidence of urban developments comes from central Mexico. This development seems to have been environmentally conditioned, for the heavily forested jungle areas witnessed a different pattern. Our best evidence of urbanism comes from Teotihuacan. Long known as an urban center, recent studies conducted on the Teotihuacan mapping project reveal the growth of the city period by period. Teotihuacan is unique in that it was built according to an overall city plan. It was laid out within a central valley location surrounded by an encircling set of low mountains. The city plan features a major north-south street, the Street of the Dead, which runs the full length of the city. Other major structural units include an east-west street, a ceremonial center featuring many major pyramids and temples (Fig. 15–5) and an extensive residential district made up of clustered one-story apartments. There were more than 2000 such apartment compounds within the city at its maximum extent— some 20 square kilometers (8 square miles). Two opposing structures, the Ciudadela and Great Compound (Fig. 15–5, Nos. 3 and 6) face each other at the intersection of the Street of the Dead and the east-west avenue. It is believed these structures formed the bureaucratic, ceremonial, and commercial center of the ancient city. The residential units were set off into barrios or neighborhoods, some of which were segregated housing for craft specialists. The religious structures associated with these compounds imply that the local residents cooperated in ritual activities. Population in the apartment complexes is estimated at 20 to 100 persons per compound, a group likely related by kinship. Most of the workshops were for obsidian, with others for ceramics, stone, figurines, lapidary work, and work in basalt and slate. The overall impression of a basic city plan is supported by the recent detailed mapping. Planning was certainly present throughout the city and not just in the central core area.

Another major function of the city was as a marketplace and center for

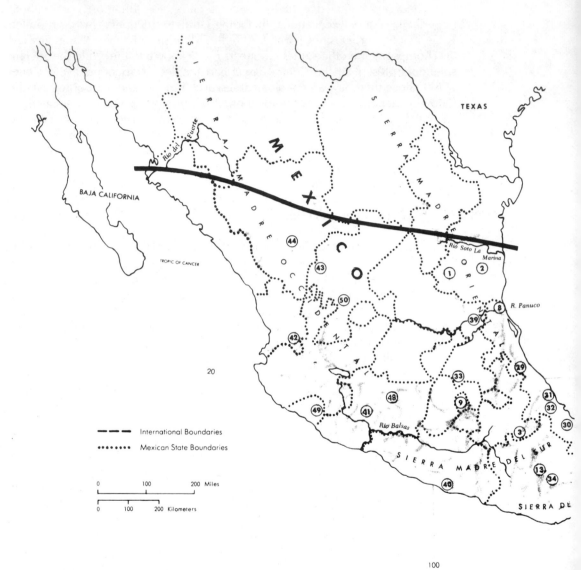

Fig. 15-1 Major sites of: *—the Preclassic period; **—Classic; ***—Postclassic. (Willey 1966:Fig. 3–10.)

Mesoamerican Archaeological Sites and Regions

1	Sierra Madre Oriental region of Tamaulipas		**18**	Altar de Sacrificios	***★★★36**	Mayapán
2	Sierra de Tamaulipas region	★★	**19**	Piedras Negras	**37**	Tulum
3	Tehuacán Valley	★★	**20**	Palenque	**38**	Yarumela
4	Islona de Chantuto		**21**	Yaxchilán	**39**	Tamuin
5	Chiapa de Corzo		**22**	Benque Viejo	**40**	Acapulco
6	Ocos		**23**	Lubaantún	**41**	Apatzingan region
★★ **7**	Kaminaljuyú	★★	**24**	Copan	**42**	Ixtlán region
8	Tampico-Panuco region		**25**	Oxxkintok	**43**	Alta Vista de Chalchuites
★★★ **9**	Valley of Mexico		**26**	Dzibilchaltún	**44**	Schroeder
★ **10**	La Venta		**27**	Cobá	**45**	Yaxuná
★ **11**	Tres Zapotes	★★	**28**	Uxmal	**46**	Zacualpa
★ **12**	San Lorenzo	★★	**29**	Tajín	**47**	Tazumal
★★ **13**	Monte Albán	★	**30**	Cerro de las Mesas	**48**	Tzintzuntzan
14	Izapa		**31**	Cempoala	**49**	Ortices
15	El Baúl		**32**	Remojadas	**50**	La Quemada
★★ **16**	Uaxactún	★★★	**33**	Tula	**51**	Rio Bec
★★ **17**	Tikal	★★★	**34**	Mitla	**52**	Xpuhil
		★★★	**35**	Chichen Itzá		

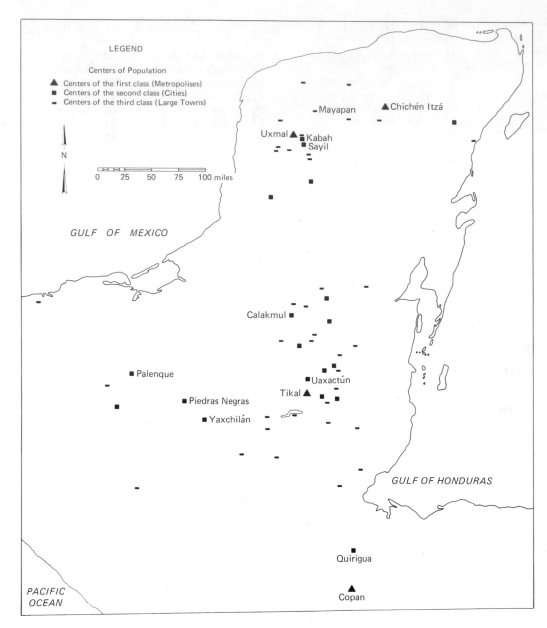

Fig. 15-2 Archaeological sites in the Mayan region. (Modified from Morley and Brainerd 1956:Plate 19.)

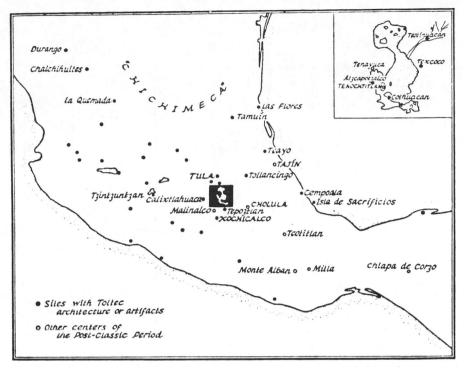

Durango •
Chalchihuites •
CHICHIMECA
la Quemada •
Tamuín •
Las Flores •
Tlayo •
o TAJÍN
TULA •
Tollancingo •
Tzintzuntzan
Calixtlahuaca •
Malinalco •
Tepoztlan
XOCHICALCO
Cempoala •
Isla de Sacrificios •
CHOLULA
Teotitlan o
Monte Alban o
o Mitla
Chiapa de Corzo

Teotihuacan
Tenayuca
Azcapotzalco
TENOCHTITLAN
Texcoco
Colhuacan

• Sites with Toltec
  architecture or artifacts

o Other centers of
  the Post-Classic Period

Fig. 15-3 Distribution of Toltec sites and other important centers of the Postclassic period. (Coe 1967b:Fig. 32.)

long distance trade. The combination of trade, religious ceremonialism, and workshops all led to an intense urbanization unique in Mesoamerica. Figures presented by Millon (1970) are that a minimal population estimate would be 75,000, with 125,000 more probable, and 200,000 not entirely unlikely. It was the most urbanized city in Mesoamerica during the Classic, and its power and influence were equally impressive. It was not until the rise of the Aztec in the Postclassic period that a comparable urban center existed in Mesoamerica.

The Mayan Settlement Pattern

The central feature of Mayan cities are the ceremonial structures faced with cut limestone masonry. They include large pyramids and platform mounds of earth and rock fill. The pyramids with temples on top are often high and steep and even with the decay of centuries are impressive indeed (Fig. 15-6).

Other major buildings included ball courts, palaces, and rarely, round buildings, some which were astronomical observatories. The basic ceremonial center plan was the rectangular plaza surrounded on three or four sides with

Chronological correlation chart

PERIODS		DATES	HUASTECA Highlands	HUASTECA Coast	CENTRAL VERACRUZ	SOUTHERN VERACRUZ-TABASCO	MAYA LOWLANDS North	MAYA LOWLANDS South	SOUTHERN PERIPHERY Honduras	SOUTHERN PERIPHERY Salvador
POSTCLASSIC	Late	1520			Cempoala IV	Soncautla	Mayapán		Naco	
			San Antonio-Los Angeles	Panuco	Cempoala III / Teayo	Upper Cerro de las Mesas				Plumbate Horizon
	Early	1200			Tajín III		Toltec Chichén	(Petén abondonment)		
		1000	San Lorenzo	Las Flores	Cempoala II					
		900			Cempoala I					
CLASSIC	Late	600	La Salta	Zaquil	Tajín II / Upper Remojadas II	Upper Tres Zapotes	Puuc-Río Bec-Chenes	Tepeu	Ulua Mayoid	Copador
	Early	500	Eslabones	Pithaya		Lower Cerro de las Mesas II	Petén Maya or Early Period	Tzakol		Esperanza-like
		300								
PRECLASSIC	Late	A.D. / B.C.		El Prisco	Tajín I	Middle Tres Zapotes	Transitional	Holmul I	Ulua Bichrome	Cerro Zapote
		300			Upper Remojadas I	Lower Cerro de las Mesas I	Yaxuná	Chicanel		
	Middle	500	Laguna	Chila	Lower Remojadas	Lower Tres Zapotes / La Venta (cer. center)	Dzibilchaltún Formative	Mamom	Playa de los Muertos	
		1000		Aguilar	Trapiche	La Venta (village)			Yarumela I	
				Ponce / Pavón						
	Early	1500	Mesa de Guaje							
			Guerra							
		2000	Flacco / Almagre / La Perra							
FOOD-COLLECTING AND INCIPIENT CULTIVATION		3000	Late Ocampo							
		4000	Nogales							
		5000	Early Ocampo							
		6000	Infiernillo							
		7000								
PALEO-INDIAN		8000	Lerma							
		9000								
		10,000	Diablo							

Mesoamerican regional chronologies chart:

PERIODS	DATES	NORTHERN FRONTIER AND WEST — Durango	Colima	Michoacan	CENTRAL MEXICO — Valley of Mexico and Environs	Tehuacán	OAXACA	MAYA HIGHLANDS AND PACIFIC SLOPES — Chiapa	Maya site
POSTCLASSIC Late	1520			Tarascan Empire	The Aztec Empire (Aztec IV)		M.A.V-Mitla	Chiapa XII	Chinautla
POSTCLASSIC Late	1200				(Aztec III)			Chiapa XI	Tohil
POSTCLASSIC Early	1000	Calera / Rio Tunal		Tarascan	(Aztec II)				
POSTCLASSIC Early	900				Chichimec and Aztec Culture / Tula-Mazapán (Aztec I)		Monte Albán IV		
CLASSIC Late	600	Las Joyas	Aztatlan		Coyotlatelco / Teotihuacán IV	Venta Salada	Monte Albán IIIB	Chiapa X	Pamplona / Amatle / Cotzumalhuapa
CLASSIC Early	500	Ayala / Alta Vista	Chametla					Chiapa IX	Esperanza / Aurora
CLASSIC Early	300		Oritices	Delicia	Teotihuacán III		Monte Albán IIIA	Chiapa VIII	
PRECLASSIC Late	A.D. / B.C.				Teotihuacán II	Palo Seco	Monte Albán II	Chiapa VII	Santa Clara
PRECLASSIC Late	300			Chupicuaro	Teotihuacán I			Chiapa VI	Arenal
PRECLASSIC Middle	300				Cuicuilco-Ticomán			Chiapa V	Izapa
PRECLASSIC Middle	500						Monte Albán I	Chiapa IV	Miraflores / Providencia / Majadas
PRECLASSIC Middle								Chiapa III	
PRECLASSIC Early	1000			El Openo	Tlatilco / Middle Zacatenco	Santa Maria		Chiapa II	Las Charcas / Conchas
PRECLASSIC Early					Early Zacatenco / El Arbolillo I	Ajalpán		Chiapa I	Arevalo / Ocos
PRECLASSIC Early	1500								
FOOD-COLLECTING AND INCIPIENT CULTIVATION	2000					Purron			Islona de Chantuto
FOOD-COLLECTING AND INCIPIENT CULTIVATION	3000					Abejas			
FOOD-COLLECTING AND INCIPIENT CULTIVATION	4000				Chalco				
FOOD-COLLECTING AND INCIPIENT CULTIVATION	5000					Coxcatlán		Santa Marta	
FOOD-COLLECTING AND INCIPIENT CULTIVATION	6000					El Riego			
FOOD-COLLECTING AND INCIPIENT CULTIVATION	7000								
PALEO-INDIAN	8000				Iztapán				
PALEO-INDIAN	9000					Ajuereado			
PALEO-INDIAN	10,000								

Fig. 15-4 Mesoamerican regional chronologies (Willey 1966:Figs. 3-8 and 3-9.)

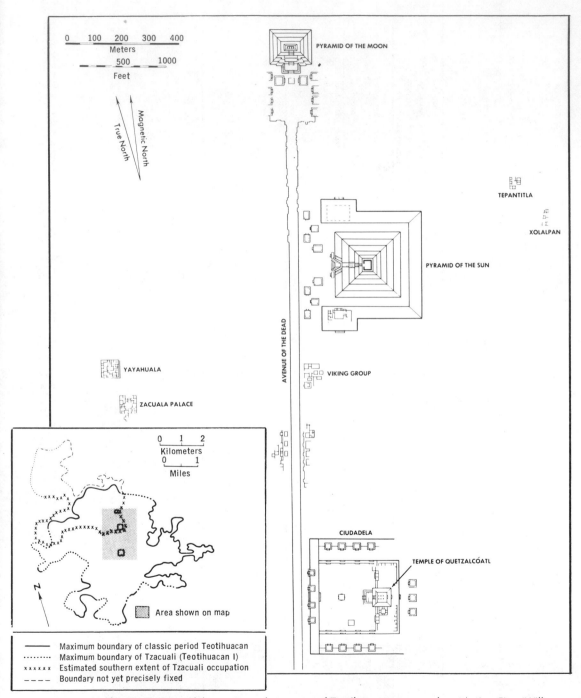

Fig. 15–5 Map of the ancient urban center of Teotihuacan, near modern Mexico City. (Willey 1966:Fig. 3–40.)

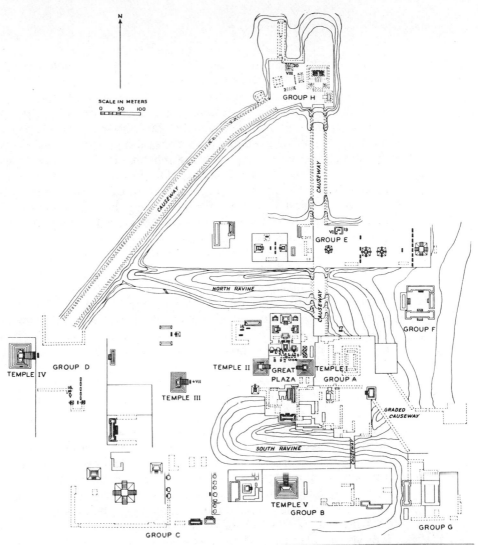

Fig. 15–6 *a.* Plan of the central section of Tikal, Guatemala. (Morley and Brainerd 1956:Plate 32.) *b.* Reconstruction drawing of one of the major temples of Tikal.
(Hester photograph, courtesy Mexican National Museum
of Anthropology.)

pyramids and platform mounds. Through time the central plazas grew by accretion until they formed a type of acropolis. Proskouriakoff (1946) has provided a reconstruction of this type of development for structure A-V at Uaxactun where eight successive stages of construction are revealed. Other features of the ceremonial centers include causeways, the erection of stelae at the base of stairways fronting on a plaza, and in Yucatan, sacred wells called cenotes. Evidence suggests that the inhabitants of the residential units, the palaces, may have been a hereditary elite. The common people primarily lived in small villages scattered throughout the farmlands. Their villages consisted of small one-room thatched structures frequently built on small earthen or stone platforms. The residents of several villages would cooperate in the building and maintenance of the regional ceremonial center.

A current controversy concerns the degree of urbanism of the major ceremonial centers. Earlier arguments asserted that the economy was based on the milpa system, a practice of clearing small fields which were farmed for two or three years and then abandoned for six to eight years. This is the modern system used in the area today, and it leads to a dispersed settlement pattern of low population density. If the milpa system was utilized prehistorically, then the ceremonial centers should not have been urban. Recent studies at Tikal, Dos Aguadas, and Barton Ramie reveal population estimates of 575 to 1600 persons per square mile, while the modern density is 25 to 100 persons per square mile (Culbert 1974:41–42). William Haviland (personal communication, 1974), who conducted the estimates at Tikal, reports there were 40,000 commoners living there. Clearly additional subsistence practices must have been employed. Culbert (1974:47–51) suggests that the elite may have enforced a shorter fallowing cycle—which would have increased yields by 28 percent at the expense of a 60 percent increase in labor. Planting of other crops besides corn could have increased the total yield. Possible food crops include yams, sweet potatoes, manioc, and the breadnut tree. The swampy areas might also have been farmed through the construction of ridged fields. While the evidence is as yet unclear, it seems that the Mayan ceremonial centers were more urban than we have previously thought.

A recent study by Marcus (1973) emphasizes the organization of the Mayan settlements into a hierarchical network. According to emblem glyphs, the four regional capitals in A.D. 731 were Copan, Tikal, Calakmul, and Palenque. In A.D. 849 the four capitals were Seibal, Tikal, Calakmul, and Moutul de San Jose. The four capitals fit the Mayan concept of the universe which was divided into four directions and the center, each with its own color, flora, fauna, and deities. Each regional capital was linked with a series of secondary centers, yielding a hexagonal settlement pattern (Fig. 15–7). The secondary centers in turn had their own satellites in a similar pattern. The pattern, while based on cosmological considerations, was also in part the result of functions to be provided by the centers—trade and transport. A final determinant was the linking of the regional capitals with the secondary centers through royal marriage alliances. Marcus further suggests that since the hexag-

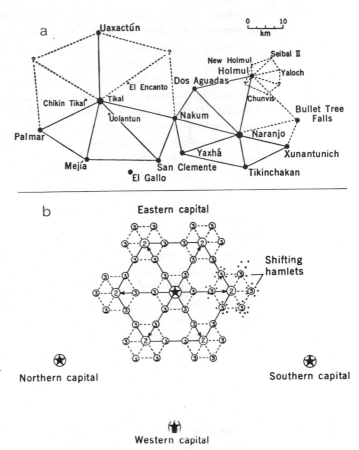

Fig. 15–7 Mayan settlement patterns. *a.* Relationships between an actual regional capital, Tikal, and its secondary centers. *b.* Schematic diagram of the Mayan settlement pattern: circled stars= regional capitals; 2s=secondary centers; 3s=tertiary centers; dots= shifting hamlets. (Marcus 1973: Figs. 6 and 8.)

onal patterns are of unequal size the relationship may have been based on population rather than geographic area. The organization within each quadrant featured a five-tier hierarchy of capital, secondary center, tertiary center, village, and hamlet. Coe (1967a) states that each community down to the village level was divided into quadrants, the *tzuculs,* wards made up of exogamous patrilineages. However, according to Haviland (personal communication), Coe's hypothesis has never been borne out.

ARCHITECTURE

Architecturally, the Mayan buildings are superlative. Many were specialized for religious functions and therefore did not need to be spacious or hospitable. Major general features of Mayan buildings were that they were thick walled, built on top of massive pyramidal platforms, and featured little interior space, with the rooms being dark, narrow, and high ceilinged (Figs. 15–8 and 15–9).

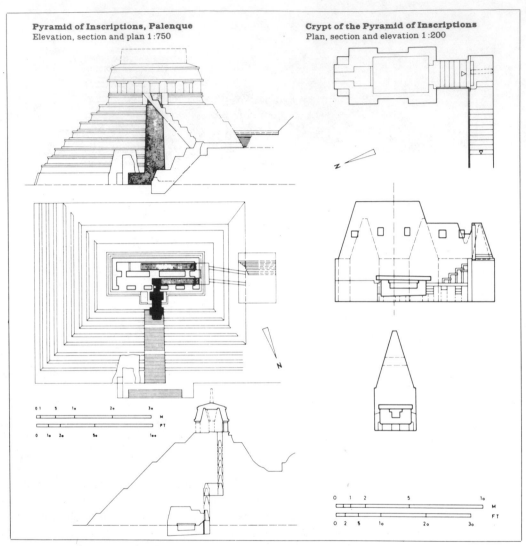

Fig. 15–8 Plan and elevations of the Pyramid of the Inscriptions, and of the crypt beneath the pyramid. (Stierlin 1964:46.)

Above the rooms extended an incredibly heavy stone roof, made necessary because of the lack of knowledge of the true arch. They used the corbeled arch made of stones cantilevered toward the center, which necessitated enormous quantities of stone. Above the roof lines so constructed were intricate decorative features including roof combs, flying facades, and sculptured friezes. Within the temples there were occasionally decorative panels, such as those in the Temple of the Foliated Cross at Palenque. These panels were carved in bas-relief or had mural paintings, of which the outstanding example is Bonampak.

Fig. 15–9 Architectural details of Mayan buildings at Uxmal, Guatemala. (*Upper left*) Ornamental facade with masks of Chac, Palace of the Governor. (*Upper right*) Corbeled arch, illustrating the mass of masonry required in the roof, Palace of the Governor. (*Above*) The Dove-Cotes Quadrangle, North Temple. (Photographs courtesy of Ken Kirkwood.)

Occasionally Mayan pyramids were also used for burial. At the Temple of the Inscriptions at Palenque a burial chamber was constructed under the pyramid with a stairway leading to the temple above (see Fig. 15–8). Within the chamber a sarcophagus with a sculptured lid enclosed the burial of a priest in costume wearing a mosaic jade mask.

Architecture in central Mexico featured a style of pyramid facade best typified at Teotihuacan but present over much of highland Mesoamerica. Termed the *Talud-Tablero* style, it consists of a stepped temple platform. The steps are made up of a sloping riser surmounted by a vertical riser with a rectangular recess (see Fig. 15–8). The center front of the pyramid featured a stairway flanked with steeply sloping abutments. This is the architectural style so common at Monte Alban and other central Mexican centers. Decorative elements at Teotihuacan feature carved stone heads of the feathered serpent and various deities, set into these wall recesses. Other elements were polychrome wall murals which have been found not only on ceremonial structures but also in the residential blocks.

ART

Mayan art was truly Classic in the sense that it was omnipresent. The media used include wall murals within tombs and temples, bas-relief carving in stone, modeled pottery, mosaic stone plaques, mosaic stone friezes on buildings, polychrome painted pottery, and painted books in hieroglyphs, called codices.

Decorative features of Mayan art include the elaborate costumes of jaguar skins, feathers, and jade ornaments worn by the priests; depicted were rulers, soldiers, war captives, and occasionally women. The art style is curvilinear and flowing, and portrays zoomorphs, plants, and water elements intertwined with the human figures and deities (Fig. 15–10). Other elements include monster figures and monster masks. Priests are shown with the characteristic sloping profile from the end of the nose to the top of the head—a profile achieved in real life by head binding with the resultant frontal deformation of the skull. The hieroglyphs were also highly artistic. In pottery the decorative motifs were similar to the wall panels. Favorite subjects were monkeys, serpents, jaguars, humans, birds, and monsters. Bands of glyphs on pottery were used as decorative borders, with some of these being pseudo-glyphs rather than symbolic in meaning. A major feature of pottery and wall mural painting was the portrayal of humans in profile. Scenes from life occur on the two of the best known murals. One features a battle scene and the other a fishing village on the seacoast. Other murals, of which those at Bonampak are best known, illustrate religious ceremonies.

In central Mexico, the Teotihuacan art style is reflected in polychrome tripod cylindrical pottery jars, jar lids painted with a fresco technique, wall murals, some ornamental carving in stone on the pyramid risers, pottery figurines, carved stone masks of humans, and giant, rather stiff human figures

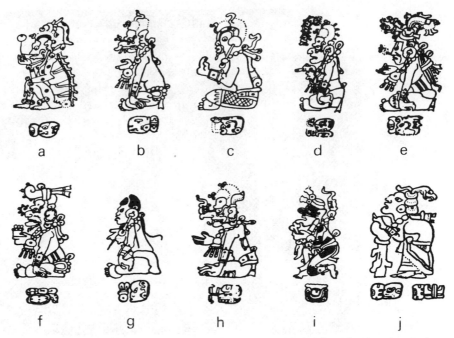

Fig. 15–10 Gods of the Maya pantheon with their name glyphs, from the Dresden Codex: a. Death God; b. Chac, the Rain God; c. North Star God; d. Itzamna; e. Maize God; f. Sun God; g. Young Moon Goddess; h. Bolon Dzacab; i. Ek Cbnab, the Merchant God; j. Ix Cbel, Goddess of Medicine. (Coe 1967a:Fig. 41.)

carved of stone. The carving consisted of crude rounding of the square stone blocks so that we can somewhat facetiously speak of sculpture in the square. Teotihuacan art, at least the smaller pieces, was widely distributed. The tripod cylinder jars were traded as far as Guatemala. A major artistic element in Teotihuacan art was the portrayal of deities, especially Tlaloc, the rain god, and Quetzalcoatl, the plumed serpent. Humans and animals were realistically portrayed. One major mural in the Temple of Agriculture depicts agricultural crops being distributed to the gods.

In the Veracruz region there was a distinctive regional culture. The principal site, El Tajin, near Papantla, features at least 60 major pyramidal mounds, the most famous of which, the Temple of the Niches, has been restored. The exterior of this pyramid is covered with small square recesses somewhat like windows in their architectural concept. There are 365 of the niches which implies a correlation between this temple and the 365-day tropical year. Tajin was influenced by the lowland Maya architectural style with its corbeled arches and elaborate roof combs. Most distinctive of Vera Cruz art are the pottery figurines, with their famous smiling heads. Other arts include elaborate stone carving of small unique items such as mirror backs, yokes, hachas, and palmas (Fig. 15–11). The following interpretation of the use of these unique items is provided by Gordon Willey (1966:143).

Fig. 15–11 Art style of the Huastec culture, Vera Cruz State, Mexico: (*left*) palma; (*right*) hacha. (Hester photographs, courtesy Mexican National Museum of Anthropology.)

The yokes, palmas, and hachas probably represent stone replicas of wooden parapher-nalia used in the ceremonial ball game. Yokes, which are large horseshoe-shaped affairs, were worn around the waist of the players as protective belts and the long thin, paddle-shaped palmas were apparently fitted into the fronts of these belts. Just what function the hachas performed is less certain; perhaps they were court markers or scoring devices used in the game. These hachas, or "thin-stone heads" as they are sometimes called, are approximately life-sized human heads or faces in profile. They were widely traded in southern Mesoamerica over routes that extended far beyond the borders of Central Veracruz into the Isthmus of Tehuantepec and down the Pacific coast of Guatemala.

In Oaxaca the major site at Monte Alban represents a Classic continua-tion of the enormous ceremonial center established there in Preclassic times (Fig. 15–12). Preclassic art at Monte Alban is noted for the spectacular bas-relief carvings on stone slabs of men in dancing positions, the so-called Danzantes; as well as hieroglyphs. Classic art at Monte Alban is best represented by the pottery urns of seated deities. Also present are carved stelae with figures and hieroglyphs. Tombs placed in terrace platforms and under patios have fresco murals with hieroglyphs, gods, and men. Pottery vessels in a variety of forms— spouted jars, floreros, candeleros, and cylinder jars—show considerable Teoti-huacan influence. After Monte Alban IIIb, the late Classic, the site was aban-

Fig. 15–12   Architecture at the great Zapotec ceremonial center, Monte Alban. (Willey 1966: Fig. 3–94.)

doned except for use as a burial place. The reasons for the abandonment of the Late Classic centers such as Monte Alban and the Mayan centers are still not fully understood (Sabloff and Willey, 1967).

KNOWLEDGE AND SCIENCE

The earliest intellectual developments in Mesoamerica including the calendar and hieroglyphic writing occurred in the Preclassic non-Mayan sites of La Venta and Monte Alban. Nonetheless by Classic times the Maya were the acknowledged leaders of Mesoamerican thought, knowledge, and science.

A major feature of Mayan knowledge was astronomy. Their astronomical knowledge has been preserved for us by means of calendrical notations on the carved stelae as well as in the codices. Among the basic calendars was the 260-day Tzolkin, which corresponds to no astronomical equivalent. Astronomically derived calendars include the 365-day tropical year, a lunar calendar based on the 29 + day lunar cycle, and a calendar that correlated five 584-day revolutions of Venus with eight 365-day years. A further refinement was the correlation of the 13 month, 20-day month, 260-day Tzolkin with the 365-day year (Fig. 15–13). This set of correlations resulted in a term of 52 years called the calendar round. The latter possessed all of the possible position variations in day and month names before the two sets of correlated day names returned to the point of origin. All of the calendars had ceremonial associations, with

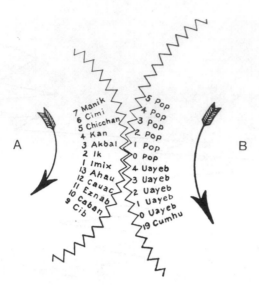

Fig. 15–13 Diagram showing the enmeshing of the 365-day calendar year (B) with the 260-day sacred year (A). (Morley and Brainerd 1956:Fig. 20.)

important dates being marked with the erection of specially inscribed monuments (Fig. 15–14).

The astronomical observations were made by means of several systems. One method utilized the alignment of two stelae with an important astronomical rising or setting (Fig. 15–15). Another more complex system, according to Morley (1946), involved viewing the solstices and equinoxes from a fixed location with the line of sight to the horizon intercepting the corner of a temple (Fig. 15–16). Another building interpreted as an observatory is the five-sided structure within the central patio at Monte Alban. A final type of observatory consisted of a round building which had narrow windows through which lines of sight to the horizon intersected important astronomical events (Fig. 15–17). The Caracol at Chichén Itzá is the best known example of such an observatory. Ruppert (1935:275) has assessed the use of the Caracol as follows:

In an analysis of the Caracol to determine the purpose for which it was built, its primary use must, *á priori,* have centered about the tower itself. The two annular chambers are of such unusual plan that for this alone the building would be given special consideration as having a specific use or purpose. Further, the spiral stairway and the upper story chamber with the shafts giving out therefrom attract particular attention and are deserving of special note and must be considered in designating a use for the structure.

The possible observatory value of the two small shafts has not been assignable. On the other hand, the window or passage to the west offers an apparent observatory value. As explained in the text, the diagonal from the inner right jamb to the outer left jamb is due west and is the line on which the sun sets at the vernal and autumnal equinox, about March 21 and September 21. Further, the diagonal from the inner left jamb to the outer right jamb is within 4°45' of the line on which the sun sets at the time of the summer solstice, about June 21. The erection of the jambs in such a position as to secure these observations could hardly have been by chance. More likely it was

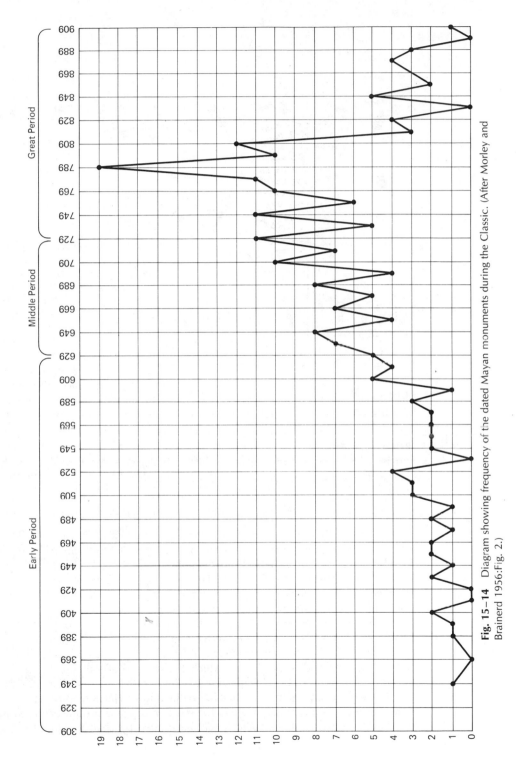

Fig. 15–14 Diagram showing frequency of the dated Mayan monuments during the Classic. (After Morley and Brainerd 1956:Fig. 2.)

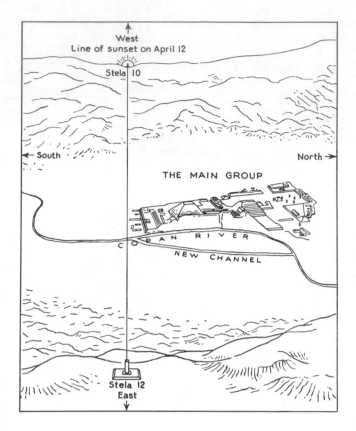

Fig. 15–15 The sundial composed of Stelae 10 and 12, Copan, Honduras. (Morley and Brainerd 1956:Fig. 4.)

planned and carefully thought out as the result of long observation of solar phenomena. If so, some observatory value must be attributed to the tower and passageway.

To suggest here that other windows and shafts existed and to speculate as to their bearing or use would be purely hypothetical. If the tower is to be considered as an astronomical observatory, may not the stylobate, which the writer has suggested may have been the first unit built on the lower platform, also have served a like purpose, as, for example, at the time of either equinox a beam of light passing between the two columns at sunset would strike upon some object placed to the east of the stylobate?

It is possible that observations made at various times of the year may have been used by the priests or leaders in advising the people of the approaching seasons with regard to agricultural pursuits or religious and civil events. May it not also be within reason to suppose that the Caracol might have served as a military or civil watch tower, or for communication by means of signals with outlying settlements?

In the writer's opinion, until such time as further proof may be forthcoming, perhaps in the discovery of another such building with the windows or shafts in a better state of preservation, any statement as to the use of the structure is conjectural.

The Mayan dates were expressed in what is termed the *Long Count* or *Initial Series calendar.* Incorporated within the Mayan system of counting time were a number of major intellectual concepts. The first of these was that the

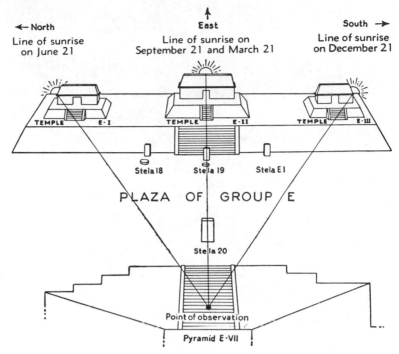

Fig. 15–16 Diagram of the astronomical observatory at Group E., Uaxactun, Peten, Guatemala, used for determining the dates of the solstices and equinoxes. (Morley and Brainerd 1956:Fig. 33.)

Maya dealt in elapsed time, with all time being reckoned from a mythical point of origin based on astronomical calculations. The origin date was 3113 B.C. a date approximately 3000 years prior to the origin of Mayan culture. Units of time were counted by means of a vigesimal system—a system based on units of 20. The various elapsed segments of time were as follows (Morley 1946:276):

20 kins	=	1 uinal or 20 days
18 uinals	=	1 tun or 360 days
20 tuns	=	1 katun or 7200 days
20 katuns	=	1 baktun or 144,000 days
20 baktuns	=	1 pictun or 2,880,000 days
20 pictuns	=	1 calabtun or 57,600,000 days
20 calabtuns	=	1 kinchiltun or 1,152,000,000 days
20 kinchiltuns	=	1 alautun or 23,040,000,000 days

The Long Count was inscribed with the introducing glyph (Fig. 15–18), followed by, from top to bottom and left to right, the various glyphs for the units of elapsed days—baktuns, katuns, tuns, uinals, and kins—followed by other glyphs with astronomical meanings. Adjacent to each time unit glyph is a number in the bar and dot system signifying the number of elapsed baktuns, katuns, and so on. The date is additive; for example, a date of 9.3.3.14.0 would

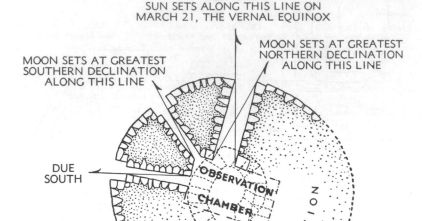

DUE WEST
SUN SETS ALONG THIS LINE ON
MARCH 21, THE VERNAL EQUINOX

MOON SETS AT GREATEST
NORTHERN DECLINATION
ALONG THIS LINE

MOON SETS AT GREATEST
SOUTHERN DECLINATION
ALONG THIS LINE

DUE
SOUTH

OBSERVATION
CHAMBER

SECTION

FALLEN

True North

Fig. 15–17 Plan of the Caracol, Chichén Itzá, Yucatan, Mexico, showing its use as an astronomical observatory. (Morley and Brainerd 1956:Fig. 32.)

read 9 baktun, 3 katun, 3 tun, 14 uinals, and 0 kin. We would add 9 × 144,000 + 3 × 7,200 + 3 × 360 + 14 × 20 + 0 × 1 to obtain the number of elapsed days since the mythical origin date of 3113 B.C.

Our explanatory example would have been an unlikely date for a Mayan monument, since most were dedicated at the ending of a specific period, especially a katun ending; therefore a typical date has zeros for the tun, uinal, and kin positions. Figure 15–14 illustrates the regularity with which monuments were erected on such even dates.

We have not as yet explained the system of bar and dot numeration. In it there was a separate shell-like symbol for zero, followed by dots from 1 to 4; units of 5 are represented by bars, 5 by one bar, 10 by two bars, and so on. The bars and dots are combined to form the intervening numbers (Fig. 15–19). Above 20 the system works as follows:

In our own decimal system, the positions to the left of the decimal point *increase by tens from right to left*—units, tens, hundreds, thousands, etc. In the Maya positional system, however, the values of the positions *increase by twenties from bottom to top, with the single exception of the third position which in counting time alone, is only 18 instead of 20 times the second* (Morley 1946:280).

We cannot translate much of the ancient writing because of the destructive acts of the Spanish after their conquest of Mexico in 1521. Long after the passing of the Classic period, the local Maya retained their codices and many

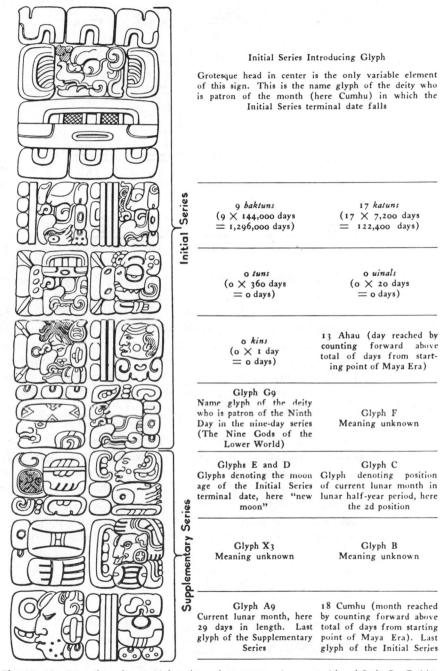

Initial Series Introducing Glyph

Grotesque head in center is the only variable element of this sign. This is the name glyph of the deity who is patron of the month (here Cumhu) in which the Initial Series terminal date falls

9 *baktuns* (9 × 144,000 days = 1,296,000 days)	17 *katuns* (17 × 7,200 days = 122,400 days)
0 *tuns* (0 × 360 days = 0 days)	0 *uinals* (0 × 20 days = 0 days)
0 *kins* (0 × 1 day = 0 days)	13 Ahau (day reached by counting forward above total of days from starting point of Maya Era)

Glyph G9
Name glyph of the deity who is patron of the Ninth Day in the nine-day series (The Nine Gods of the Lower World)

Glyph F
Meaning unknown

Glyphs E and D
Glyphs denoting the moon age of the Initial Series terminal date, here "new moon"

Glyph C
Glyph denoting position of current lunar month in lunar half-year period, here the 2d position

Glyph X3
Meaning unknown

Glyph B
Meaning unknown

Glyph A9
Current lunar month, here 29 days in length. Last glyph of the Supplementary Series

18 Cumhu (month reached by counting forward above total of days from starting point of Maya Era). Last glyph of the Initial Series

Fig. 15–18 Examples of an initial and supplementary series: east side of Stela E., Quirigua, Department of Izabal, Guatemala. (Morley and Brainerd 1956:Fig. 25.)

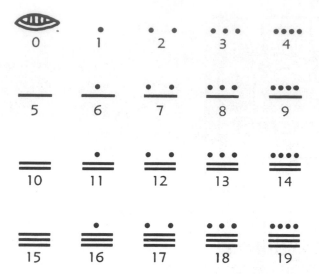

Fig. 15–19 Glyphs for the numbers 0 and 1 to 19 inclusive, in the Mayan bar-and-dot notation, the Maya "Roman Notation" (Morley and Brainerd 1956:Fig. 23.)

of the old traditions. After the Conquest the Spanish ordered these "works of the devil" burned. The result was an enormous loss of traditional Mayan knowledge. Currently, through aid of computers, major efforts at deciphering the known inscriptions are underway. Experts differ as to what was recorded in the glyphs. J. Eric Thompson, the leading scholar of Mayan epigraphy, asserts the inscriptions deal only with time, astronomy, ceremonies, gods, and astrological matters. Tatiana Proskouriakoff suggests that the glyphs also record the dynastic succession of the hereditary elite and other historical events.

One other result of the Spanish conquest was the provision of a means of correlating the Mayan calendar with the Christian calendar. After the peak of the Classic period, about A.D. 900, the Long Count system of numeration fell into disuse and was replaced by a type of shorthand, the *Short Count,* which did not enumerate all of the elapsed time units. Shortly after the Spanish Conquest, Bishop Landa of Yucatan correlated some of the post-Conquest Short Count dates with specific dates in the Christian calendar. On the basis of Landa's information two correlations have been proposed: the Goodman-Martinez-Thompson correlation (GMT) and the Spinden correlation. Named after the modern scholars responsible for them, these correlations are 260 years apart, with the Spinden correlation the earlier. Numerous radiocarbon dates on wooden lintels from Tikal carved with Long Count dates support the GMT correlation.

SOCIAL ORGANIZATION

It is assumed that scientific knowledge in Mayan society was possessed by a selected few individuals. These were the educated elite who made all the astronomical observations and calculations, wrote the codices, and at least supervised the sculpturing of the inscribed monuments. The common people were primarily the farmers and common laborers.

We perceive from the wall murals that status was stratified, at least in part, by dress, with the priests and officials dignified by beautiful costumes while the common people and captives are shown wearing only breechclouts. Authority and political control was vested in the priest-rulers. Recent research implies that the priests were members of a hereditary elite that ruled with despotic power. Their control over the common people lay in their ability to foretell astronomical events: the rising and setting of the sun, moon, and planets at critical positions, and eclipses. Further power lay in the relationships between the Maya and their gods. Mayan religion emphasized man's dependence on the gods, but they could be influenced by prayer, fasting, and propitiation, all areas in which the priests could exercise influence. The gods even required human sacrifice, which, although probably infrequent, is represented in glyphs (Fig. 15–20). All of our knowledge of ancient Mayan social organization, religion, scientific achievements, and so forth is inhibited by the fact that 75 percent of the hieroglyphic writing is yet to be translated.

HISTORICAL DEVELOPMENT

The Classic was a time of development of great regional cultures. Ceremonialism may be construed as the major overriding theme of the period with other emphases on knowledge, elitism, trade, commerce, and warfare. Regional alliances, confederacies, or other political ties do not seem to have developed. Each center featured an increasing florescence in culture until approximately A.D. 900 in the Maya region, somewhat earlier at Teotihuacan. In the Maya region, after A.D. 900, the building of ceremonial centers, carving of stelae (at least dated ones), and other evidences of the Classic culture came to an abrupt end over the southern portion of the region. Originally archaeologists felt this cessation was followed by a mass movement of Maya to Sayil, Kabah, Uxmal, and other cities to the north. Recent workers are split on this issue. Some support the migration concept; others believe the northern cities witnessed a similar end of the Classic culture. The issue is as yet unresolved. Reasons for the Mayan downfall are not yet understood. Various theories advanced are: a revolt against the elite, environmental limitations of the slash-and-burn system, inadequate soils to support a large population, and a regional water shortage. Most plausible would be a combination of several such causes (Culbert 1974). At approximately the same time there was abandonment of other major centers including Teotihuacan, Monte Alban, and Tajin. The Classic, for whatever reasons, was at an end. Slyvanus Morley in his work, *The Ancient Maya,* enumerated the major achievements or superlatives of that most classic of Classic civilizations. We reproduce a number of these superlatives in Table 15–1. These of course relate in part to Morley's value judgments, but nonetheless it is an interesting way to categorize a culture.

Fig. 15–20 Scenes of human sacrifice as represented on the monuments, codices, and wall paintings. (Morley and Brainerd 1956:Plate 28.)

TABLE 15–1   Selection of Maya Superlatives

Kind of Superlative	Example
Oldest city.	Tikal
Largest city.	Tikal
City where astronomy reached its highest development.	Copan
City where stone sculpture reached its highest development.	Piedras Negras
City where stucco modeling reached its highest development.	Palenque
City where wood carving reached its highest development.	Tikal
City where architecture reached its highest development.	Uxmal
City having largest ball court.	Chichén Itzá
City having earliest astronomical observatory.	Uaxactun
City having the most stelae.	Calakmul; 103 stelae (79 sculptured, 24 plain)
Oldest construction.	Stucco-covered pyramid, E-VII-sub, Uaxactun
Highest building.	Temple IV, Tikal, height 229 feet
Oldest dated object.	The Leyden Plate, of jade, dating from 8.14.1.3.12, or A.D. 320
Oldest dated stone sculpture.	Stela 9, Uaxactun, dating from 8.14.10.13.15, or A.D. 328
Largest block of stone ever quarried by the ancient Maya.	Stela E, Quirigua, height 35 feet, weight about 65 tons
Most beautiful example of low-relief sculpture.	Tablet in Temple of the Cross, Palenque
Most important mathematical monument.	Stela 10, Tikal. The number of days recorded here involves eight orders of units or 1,841,641,600 days, or 5,042,277 years.
Longest inscription in the Maya hieroglyphic writing.	Hieroglyphic Stairway leading to Temple 26, Copan. This inscription contains some 2500 individual hieroglyphs.
Most beautiful hieroglyphs ever carved on stone by the Maya.	Inscription on Stela F, Quirigua
Hieroglyphic inscription having the greatest number of initial series.	Hieroglyphic Stairway leading to Temple 26, Copan; 18 initial series
Latest dated object in the Old Empire.	Jade pendant, Tzibanche, dating from 10.4.0.0.0 or A.D. 909

(Morley 1946: facing p. 448.)

THE POSTCLASSIC PERIOD

An additional problem facing Classic civilizations was the encroachment of barbarian invaders from the north. The earliest city to be so attacked was Teotihuacan which fell about A.D. 600. Over the succeeding 300 years the other Classic centers collapsed for one reason or another. The transition to the

Postclassic was marked by the disintegration of the Classic cultures: the ceremonial centers were abandoned; their peoples moved away or at least no longer contributed their labor toward the building of temples or sculpturing of monuments; and so forth. The appearance of the Chichimecs, the wild tribes of the north, was not the cause of the disintegration of the Classic cultures; they merely were able to take advantage of the situation because of the existing internal weaknesses in the old theocratic system. The parallels with the fall of the Roman Empire are numerous. The Postclassic was therefore a time of cultural change in which the old established order was first replaced with chaos, out of which grew a new culture type with new centers, a new type of leadership, and a new social organization. The major changes included a shift to militarism and violence with new gods of war enshrined. These gods, because of their violent nature, required increasing quantities of sacrifices, especially human, for their appeasement. With the Postclassic the center of cultural development shifted to central Mexico, never to return to the Maya lowlands. Throughout Mesoamerica then, the old traditions were altered but not completely severed. Many traditions did continue, although modified, and the new emphases probably were much more important to the rulers, priests, and warriors than to the common people.

The Chichimecs were former Desert Culture hunters and gatherers living on the northern frontier of Mesoamerica in a situation analogous to that of the barbarian Germanic tribes living on the frontier of Rome. Through time, in ways which are more surmised than a matter of historical record, these peoples became knowledgable in the patterns of Mesoamerican civilization. They moved southward, possibly with drought forcing them out of their homeland, settled down, and took up Mesoamerican farming practices. One late group of Chichimecs, the group we know as Aztec, first appeared in the Valley of Mexico about A.D. 1320 and settled next to civilized peoples known as Culhuas. The Aztec initially served as mercenary soldiers for the Culhuas but within a hundred years came to dominate them, more parallels with Rome. However we are ahead of our story, for there were numerous significant Postclassic developments prior to the Aztec.

TULA OF THE TOLTECS

The earliest of the Chichimecs to make significant contributions were the peoples we know as the Toltec. They settled at Tula, Hidalgo, about A.D. 900; Dutton (1955:247) gives A.D. 856. They built a substantial city located on a bluff for its defensive properties (Fig. 15–21). The city center is about one square kilometer with numerous mounds scattered over the adjacent hills. The city, while of undoubted importance, was not an urban center of the scope of Teotihuacan. The architecture is basically a continuation of the *talud-tablero* tradition of central Mexico. Two major pyramids flank a central patio. Adjacent

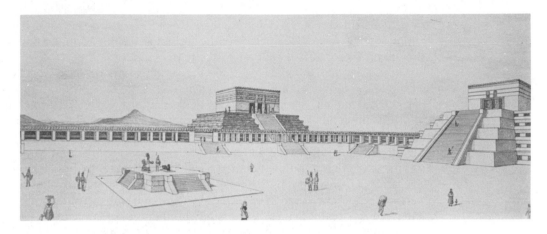

Fig. 15–21   Tula of the Toltecs. (*Above*) Reconstruction drawing of the main plaza at Tula. (Drawing courtesy of the Mexican National Museum of Anthropology.) (*Below*) The major pyramid at Tula. (Photograph courtesy of Philip M. Hobler.)

to the pyramids are unique additions in the form of a colonnade and a structure with more such columns, the Palace of the Columns. To the north is a second plaza with an I-shaped ball court along its north side.

According to Dutton (1955:246) the architecture of Tula was both ambitious and poorly built, for the builders utilized large rocks without mortar as the central nucleus of the walls. Wall decorations were of stucco and sculptured stone relief. The weakness of the internal structure led to considerable damage and subsequent repair through time. The buildings were constructed to impress rather than endure.

The sculptural tradition included a style which was bold but lacking in detail, hence lacking realism. Bas-relief carving was used extensively on the stone columns and the pyramid walls. Especially diagnostic to Toltec sculpture are the famous caryatid figures. These are by definition human figures used as support columns. At Tula the figures (Fig. 15–22) are those of a Toltec warrior.

Each caryatid was made of four sections, which fit one onto another, reaching a total height of 12 feet. Each represents a richly attired warrior, with a headdress, the decoration of which simulates a band ornamented with stars, topped with plumes. The star band is tied at the back of the head by two small knots, with short, fringed ends which drop freely. The lower set extends over a triangular-shaped element which forms the back of the headdress, and this too is fringed. The whole ornament is secured at the nape of the neck by means of ties, from which are suspended the two ends of the fastening ribbon, each with "swallow tail" notches. The human figure was colored red, and the face had a painted decoration: it is probable that the hollowed out sockets of the eyes had originally been inlaid with some appropriate material. The hair is indicated by engraved vertical lines, which extend across the forehead from side to side. As adornments, the personages wear rectangular ear ornaments, a great chest ornament in the form of a stylized butterfly, necklaces of beads, a girdle whose rear fastening shows an enormous buckle or circular shield—a representation of the sun. In the center is a human face, with vertical tablet earplugs, like the main figure, and this is surrounded by a panel in which are four snakes, each identified as a *xiuhcoatl*—turquois serpent, or fire serpent—separated by radial belts, or solar rays.

Further adorning these figures are: a triangular-shaped loin cloth; a girdle tied in front with ends that fall with the V-notches showing plainly over the loincloth; bracelets, anklets, and sandals decorated with plumed serpents. Each figure is in the same position, and is armed with an *atlatl*, or dart thrower, which is grasped in the right hand, while the left hand holds the darts and a characteristic curved weapon—effective both as fending club and combat implement. A long, feather ornament falls from the left shoulder, over the darts, and from which the hand is extended to grasp the curved weapon, over the front of which is a large, oval-shaped ornament with stepped spiral decoration. At the shoulder of the figure is a design, conical above and with three triangles pendent from a medial band, reaching to a second band (Dutton 1955:204).

Other items unique to Toltec architecture are the Atlantean figures and standard bearers (Fig. 15–22). The former consist of small human figures 30 inches in height with arms upstretched. These were used as support columns for altars. The standard bearers possess cupped hands with a hole drilled therein for the staff of a flag. At Tula one of these was positioned at each end of

Fig. 15–22 *(Upper left)* Caryatids, *(right)* standard bearer; *(left)* Atlantean figures. (Hester photographs, courtesy Mexican National Museum of Anthropology.)

the long wall (131 feet) adjacent to pyramid B. Decorative friezes on the wall show a serpent devouring a human skeleton; hence its assigned name, the Serpent Wall. Other frieze elements repeated on the tablero sections (vertical portions) of the wall and the pyramid walls are eagles or vultures eating human hearts, human skulls, squared spirals, jaguars, and monster masks.

The square warrior columns of the same height as the caryatids were also in four sections. Each column has similar elements on each face: warriors, a collection of weapons such as atlatls or darts, a symbol representing a "terrestrial belt" indicated by an eye and an upper mandible, and finally a panel combining the warrior, war equipment, and terrestrial belt. We have described the Tula architectural features in some detail, since they also occur at the Mayan site of Chichén Itzá, some 600 miles to the east.

After the Spanish Conquest, the Aztec related to Spanish historians the legends of their people and those of other central Mexican groups. According to these legends, soon after the founding of Tula, there arose two factions. One followed the political leader or king, Topiltzin, who was dedicated to the peaceful god, Quetzalcoatl, the feathered serpent. The other faction swore allegiance to the new god of war and death, Tezcatlipoca, the smoking mirror. The followers of Tezcatlipoca were victorious, and Topiltzin and his followers were driven out of Tula about A.D. 987. According to legend they traveled to the south and east where they set sail with the promise to return. Although we are not sure that Topiltzin was the Mexican leader who conquered Yucatan—a fact mentioned in the Mayan histories—we can identify architecturally Mexican elements in Yucatan, especially at Chichén Itzá (Fig. 15–23).

After the defeat and exodus of Topiltzin and his followers from Tula, the Toltecs that remained there assumed cultural and military leadership of central Mexico. Their empire continued for 200 years until it also was destroyed violently about A.D. 1156 or 1168 (Coe 1967b:138).

THE MEXICAN PERIOD AT CHICHÉN ITZÁ

In the traditional histories of the Maya, the so-called Books of Chilam Balam, preserved since the Spanish Conquest, there are references to the arrival in Yucatan of a man named Kukulcan, or feathered serpent, about the year A.D. 987. There is some confusion about the date, owing to use of the Mayan Short Count at this time. Each Short Count cycle always ended on the same named day. Therefore events on specific dates in the Short Count system could refer to more than one possible true date separated by 256¼ years. If we accept the A.D. 987 dating of Kukulcan's arrival, then his party could have been the displaced group of Toltecs led by Topiltzin. The major events are recorded in wall murals in the Temple of the Warriors. The Toltecs arrived by sea. In the first mural they are shown offshore in boats scouting a Mayan seaside village. A second mural illustrates a battle on the water, the losing Maya on rafts and the Toltec in canoes. The next mural (Fig. 15–24) shows the battle is carried to the land where fighting takes place in the houses and temples. The Maya are defeated again and their leaders are sacrificed. The Toltec then imposed leadership on northern Yucatan. Their capital city was established at Chichén Itzá where new architectural styles—actually those common at Tula—were introduced. The new architectural style represented a combination of the old northern Mayan Puuc style and the Toltec elements. Columns became important, being used inside rooms to provide greater interior space. Colonnades, nearly identical to those at Tula (Fig. 15–25), were added. Further additions include the decorative friezes of repeated skulls, serpents, and such.

Specific major structures of the Mexican period are the giant pyramid dedicated to Kukulcan the "Castillo" and the Temple of the Warriors (Fig.

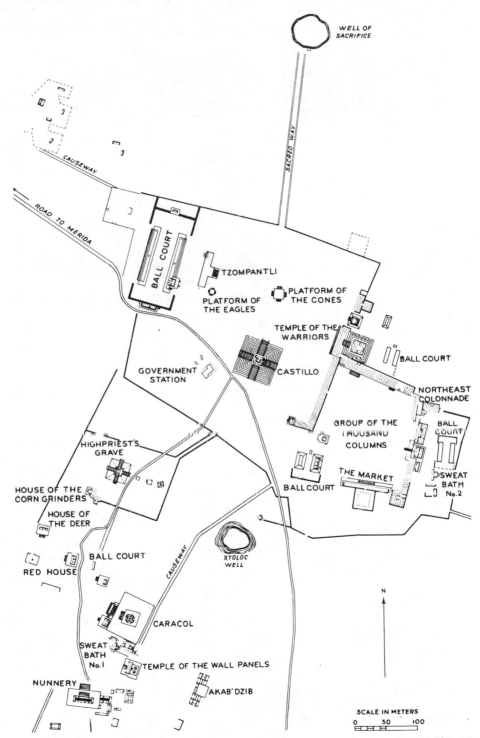

Fig. 15–23 Map of the central section of Chichén Itzá, Yucatan, Mexico. (Morris 1931:Plate 3.)

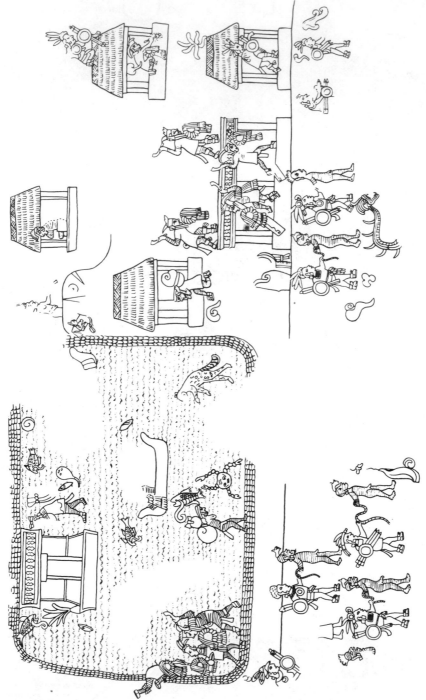

Fig. 15-24 Battle scene from the wall painting in the Temple of the Warriors, Chichén Itzá, Yucatan, Mexico. (Morley and Brainerd 1956:Plate 25.)

Fig. 15-25   Temple of the Warriors, general view showing the northwest colonnade in foreground. (Photograph courtesy of Ken Kirkwood.)

15–25), a structure similar to the Pyramid B complex at Tula but larger. Inside the Temple of the Warriors is another temple, the Temple of the Chacmool. A most interesting feature of the latter structure is that within it is an altar in Toltec style set upon Atlantean figures. Curiously, the Atlantean figures were set several inches into the floor as if they were too tall for use in the small interior temple. This fact has led me to speculate that possibly the altar with its Atlantean figures was actually transported from Tula by the Toltec to be reinstalled at Chichén Itzá. Proof that such in fact happened could rest on mineralological identification of the stone utilized. Other major buildings of the period include the beautiful ball court, the largest in Mesoamerica, flanked by temples within which are murals and bas-reliefs depicting Toltec life and scenes of battle.

A further Toltec contribution to Mayan life was human sacrifice. The Tzompantli, or skull platform, supported racks upon which the heads of the sacrificed were placed. The platform itself is decorated with a frieze of skulls impaled on stakes. Human sacrifice was also accomplished by the throwing of humans alive into the sacred cenote. According to Bishop Landa, one typical time for such sacrifices was during drought. The cenote has been dredged, and we now know that most of the victims were adult males although children and women were also sacrificed. A wealth of other sacrifices, including gold and jade ornaments, pottery, and copal incense, has been recovered from the cenote. One further indication of sacrifice consists of reliefs on the ball court

Fig. 15–26. (*Top*) The Caracol or Observatory at Chichén Itzá, Yucatan, Mexico. (*Left*) Wall ornament, a mask of Chac within a snake's mouth, Temple of the Warriors, Chichén Itzá, Yucatan, Mexico. (Photographs courtesy of Ken Kirkwood.)

depicting the decapitation of a ball player. One can only assume that playing the ball game was a very serious matter indeed.

Another diagnostic trait of the Mexican period is the presence of a specific type of glazed pottery termed *Plumbate Ware*. Plumbate was unique in its non-central-Mexican point of origin. Manufactured in kilns near the Guatemala-Chiapas border, Plumbate was widely traded throughout the Yucatan Peninsula and effectively serves as a chronological marker.

According to the chronicles Chichén Itzá was abandoned on the Short Count date of Katun 6 ahau (now correlated with A.D. 1224) and the Toltec were no longer important in Mayan history.

Following the Mexican period in Yucatan we have the legendary migrations of the Itzá (Fig. 15–27). In their wanderings the Itzá moved across Yucatan to Lake Peten Itzá then east to British Honduras. They then turned north under the leadership of a man known as Kukulcan II. In Katun 4 ahau (A.D. 1224–1244) they reached Chichén Itzá which they proceeded to occupy as squatters. They founded the city of Mayapan in Katun 13 ahau (A.D. 1263–1283) which after A.D. 1283 became the capital of Yucatan. The city was an urban community consisting of numerous house mounds within an enclosing city wall. Within the wall were approximately 2000 houses with 11,000 to 12,000 inhabitants. The city was without an internal plan.

The late Postclassic in Yucatan is marked with strife between the ruling families. The last such revolt at Mayapan in Katun 9 ahau (A.D. 1441–1461) resulted in the destruction of the city and its abandonment. The Itzá left Yucatan and wandered back to Lake Peten Itzá where they established a new capital at Tayasal on an island in the lake. Here they remained, continuing the Maya traditions in a limited way, until they were conquered by the Spanish. The Postclassic in Yucatan, far from having a dramatic ending, simply drifted farther and farther into the jungle to be lost to history. In place of the Itzá dynasty in Yucatan there were left 16 rival city-states, each weak and faltering in its ability to continue basic Mayan traditions, yet ready to war with each other. This situation existed until the Spanish Conquest at which time we pick up the story of the Mayan culture from the writings of Bishop Landa and other historical sources. The single most dramatic event of the Spanish-Mayan confrontation was of course the public burning of the codices. Even though the classic Mayan culture, religion, and so forth were greatly reduced, the people still had in their possession the ancient hieroglyphic codices. Owing to the Spanish zeal in eradicating "works of the devil," only three have survived.

THE AZTEC EMPIRE

The Aztec were another one of the Chichimec tribes that left their hunting and gathering desert existence to settle in the Valley of Mexico, that great central Mexican center of culture from Preclassic times to the present (Fig. 15–28).

Aztec legends state they began their wanderings about A.D. 1168 (Vaillant 1950:97). At first they lived on an island in a lake in western Mexico.

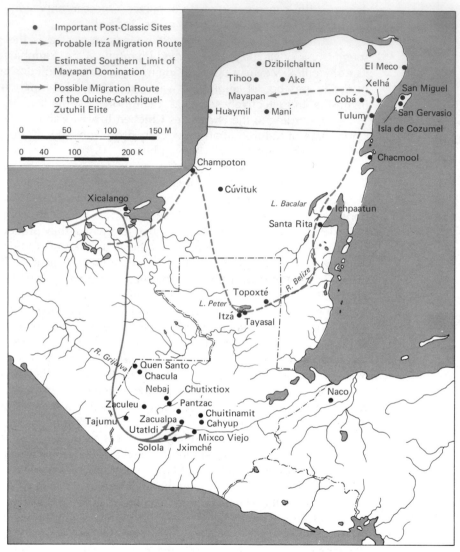

Fig. 15–27 Map illustrating the legendary wanderings of the Itzá. (Coe 1969:Fig. 28.)

On the nearby shore in a cave they acquired their god Huilzilopochtli, whom they then carried with them in their wanderings. According to the annals the Aztec or Tenochcas were among the last of the wild tribes to enter the Valley of Mexico about A.D. 1215. They are described as quarrelsome, cruel, unfaithful to their word, and women-stealers. They were brave, disdaining death and practicing warfare as a means of support. Their garments were of palm fiber and their sandals of straw—truly an impoverished group. They moved from place to place within the Valley of Mexico, eventually settling on Chapultepec Hill where they began to take up farming. Life during the thirteenth century in

Fig. 15–28 The lakes, islands, and principal archaeological sites in the Valley of Mexico. (Bernal 1963:Fig. 32.)

the Valley of Mexico included a delicate balance of power between the various tribes. Alliances between these tribes were formed at times to curb aggressive neighbors. The Tenochcas took part in these affairs and became noted for their prowess in warfare. In one battle the Culhuas and Tenochcas fought the Xochimilcas. The former were successful and took many prisoners. The Culhua chief, Coxcox, asked the Tenochcas why they had taken no prisoners. The Tenochcas then pointed out that 30 of the prisoners had an ear cut off and that they possessed the missing ears. The prestige so acquired led the Tenochcas to ask for Coxcox's daughter to marry their chief. Their wish was granted, and overjoyed, the Tenochcas sacrificed the girl to their gods. The ceremony that followed, to which they invited the girl's father, involved a priest wearing the girls' skin to impersonate a nature goddess. Needless to say Coxcox was horrified and with his warriors drove out the Tenochcas, who fled to an island in the middle of Lake Texcoco which was already a refuge for dissidents from the mainland. The events we have described took place sometime between 1299 and 1323 (Bernal 1963:89). A result of these events was that Chalpultepec was abandoned and a new city called Tenochtitlán was founded on the island in the lake. After the establishment of Tenochtitlán, the Aztec petitioned the Culhuas for a chief, a wish that was granted. They then allied themselves with the Tepanecs against the Culhuas whom they destroyed in 1367. Later, in 1428

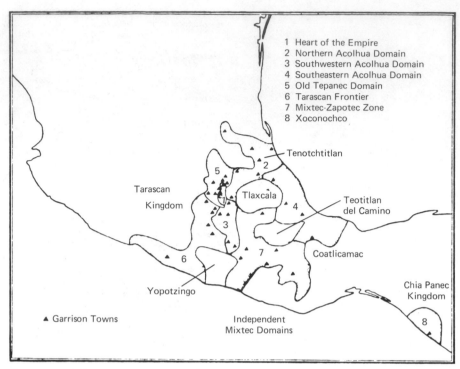

1 Heart of the Empire
2 Northern Acolhua Domain
3 Southwestern Acolhua Domain
4 Southeastern Acolhua Domain
5 Old Tepanec Domain
6 Tarascan Frontier
7 Mixtec-Zapotec Zone
8 Xoconochco

Tenotchtitlan

Tarascan
Kingdom

Tlaxcala

Teotitlan
del Camino

Coatlicamac

Chia Panec
Kingdom

Yopotzingo

▲ Garrison Towns

Independent
Mixtec Domains

Fig. 15–29   Extent of the Aztec Empire in 1520 with the provinces into which the Aztec domains were organized. (Coe 1967b:Fig. 37.)

the Aztec turned on the Tepanecs and with the assistance of Texcoco and Tacuba destroyed forever the power of the Tepanecs of Azcapotzalco. In 1434 the triple alliance was formed, uniting the most powerful cities in the political expansion which we know as the Aztec Empire (Fig. 15–29). The Aztec Empire was never as well integrated or dominant as the Inca Empire in Peru. The Aztec were unable to subjugate some of their neighbors; for example, their enemies the Tarascans were as close as 40 miles to the west of Tenochtitlán. The Tlascallans in Puebla state were also traditional enemies who remained unconquered.

Aztec Life

The Aztec in a series of political maneuvers assumed the role of legal descendents of the Culhuas, the Valley group who claimed to be the direct descendents of the Toltecs of Tula. Thus by these political acts the Aztec purported to continue the Toltec traditions. In fact many of the cultural traits *can* be traced to Toltec origins. The architecture, for example, especially at Tenotchtitlán, shows strong Toltec affinities (Fig. 15–30).

Fig. 15–30 Reconstruction of the main square of Tenochtitlán. (Hester photograph, courtesy Mexican National Museum of Anthropology.)

The economy featured *chinampa* farming, an extremely productive system, based upon the building of rafts in the lake covered with earth and muck from the lake bottom. Through time the chinampas gradually became permanently fixed to the lake floor. Other major aspects of the Aztec economy relate to the strategic location of Tenochtitlán. Situated in the center of the lake and ringed with cities on the mainland, the city formed a natural trade center. Transport was by canoe as well as by means of five causeways that connected the city to the mainland. Trade extended widely beyond the city to the farthest extent of the empire. A special group of merchants, known as *pochteca,* traveled as far as Panama on trading missions. In addition they served as messengers and spies because of their opportunities to observe and trade with distant tribes. Within the city, major crafts included jewelry making, pottery manufacture, the working of feathers into garments, and metalworking. The primary market for these goods consisted of the aristocracy.

Aztec social organization was based upon a system of clans called *calpulli.* The common people belonged to the calpulli and each of these had lands in specific sections of the city farmed by the calpulli members. Each of the 20 clans had its own temple and market; an intriguing thought is the possibility that such a system was a legacy from the ancient civilization at Teotihuacan.

Social classes included slaves (the lowest class) who were primarily prisoners of war, the common people, and classes distinguished by profession—the warriors, bureaucrats, artisans, merchants, and priests. Service to the state was rewarded with special status, and even merchants were so dignified. Most notable are the warrior orders—the eagle and jaguar knights (Fig. 15–31). Rule was by an emperor selected from a royal lineage by a council of high officials. He was semidivine and ruled with considerable autonomy. All of the officials had large private land holdings from which they received income. In addition, tribute was exacted from subject tribes.

Fig. 15–31 An eagle knight, member of an Aztec Military Society. (Hester photograph, courtesy Mexican National Museum of Anthropology.)

As in the Inca Empire, warfare provided the most common method of achieving status. We base our knowledge of Aztec life and customs on a series of historical records dating soon after the Spanish Conquest. Therefore, our knowledge is actually ethnographic rather than archaeological. The most important reference is the Florentine codex which provides us with numerous illustrations of the various aspects of Aztec life (Dibble and Anderson 1957) (Fig. 15–32).

Aztec Religion

The integrative mechanism within Aztec society—the beliefs and justification for major areas of activity—was derived from their religion. They not only emphasized the typical Postclassic focus on violence and death but intensified this aspect into an obsession with meeting the dictates of bloodthirsty gods. The primary deities were Huitzilopotchtli, Quetzalcoatl, and Tezcatlipoca, but the Aztec pantheon provided a wealth of deities hardly equaled by any other society known to history. According to Vaillant (1944), there were 3 "great gods, 4 creative deities, 15 fertility gods, 6 rain gods, 3 fire gods, 4 pulque gods, 12 planetary and stellar gods, 6 earth gods, 6 variants of the great gods, and 4 others. There were also gods of death, the day hours, night hours, days, and weeks."

The religion was based upon the concept that Huitzilopotchtli, the sun or giver of life, must be nourished by human blood. Sacrifice was carried out by the priests dressed in black. They practiced penance by slashing their own ears with obsidian knives to provide blood. Sacrifices of humans were carried out in

Fig. 15—32 Scenes from the Florentine Codex. (Dibble and Anderson:Figs. 49, 50, 51, and 55.)

front of the temples on the tops of the pyramids. Stone boxes containing fire received the hearts of the sacrificed, and then the body was thrown down the steps of the pyramid. The total number of sacrifices eventually required is almost beyond belief. In one three-day ceremony late in the Aztec reign, 40,000 victims were sacrificed and their skulls placed upon the Tzompantli. Another method of sacrifice consisted of a gladiatorial contest between a captured warrior armed with a dummy weapon set with feathers instead of obsidian blades, and an Aztec knight armed with real weapons. The contest took place upon a circular stone, the stone of Tizoc, to which the captive was tied. Some sharing of beliefs was held by the nearby tribes, since captives believed that such a death was glorious and the sacrificed was united with Huitzilopotchtli. Another major religious feature was the ceremonial rebuilding of the pyramids and the destruction of all household items at the end of each 52-year cycle.

Aztec Archaeology

We do not have the wealth of archaeological materials available from the Aztecs as one might expect. The primary cause of this lack was the systematic destruction of Tenochtitlán by Cortez who then rebuilt his capital on top of the

Fig. 15–33   Chart showing the nature of Aztec archaeological materials. (Vaillant 1950:Plate 29.)

ruins. Subsequent excavations for building foundations and the recent subway system have revealed bits and pieces of the ancient Aztec splendor. Some of the best preserved Aztec remains lie outside the former capital city—at Tena-yuca, at Malinalco where a temple was cut into the living rock, as well as canals for gardens and baths cut into bed rock near Texcoco by its famous ruler Nezahualcoyotl. Basic Aztec archaeological materials are illustrated in Figure 15–33. Pottery consisted of a series of black-on-orange types derived from the Mazapan wares of the late Teotihuacan-Toltec era. Aztec stone carving is

Fig. 15–34 Coatlicue, Mother of the Gods, the principal Aztec goddess. (Hester photograph, courtesy Mexican National Museum of Anthropology.)

spectacular in its conception. Known sculptures emphasize carving in the round in a representational style of the various deities, boxes for sacrificed hearts, the famous calendar stone (which is the Aztec concept of the cosmos), the sacrificial altars, and so on. Perhaps most impressive is the twin snake-headed Coatlicue, mother of the gods, with her necklace of skulls and hearts and legs with claws (Fig. 15–34).

THE SPANISH CONQUEST

Cortez landed on the Vera Cruz coast in the year 1519, having been since his teens one of the band of disinherited, gold-crazy, religiously inspired adventurers known to history as conquistadores. Rapacious, without fear, and believing that their mission to conquer and convert the Indians was divinely sanctioned, such men were to achieve military miracles in the New World.

The Spanish arrived at a time most propitious for attack. For one reason the neighboring tribes, long oppressed by the Aztec with their demands for tribute and sacrificial victims, were ready for revolt. The Aztec leader Montezuma was further seeking guidance from his soothsayers. Numerous ill omens were noted: a column of fire seen at midnight, the destruction of a temple by lightning without thunder, sudden waves on the lake, and others. Most impressive was a bird caught by hunters which had a mirror on its head. In the mirror Montezuma perceived an army of armed men mounted on the backs of deer.

In addition to the right time, the Spanish had on their side advantages in military aims and techniques. The Aztec fought for ceremonial reasons with their primary goal the taking of prisoners for sacrifice. The Spanish fought to conquer, using to their advantage cavalry, armor, cannons, swords and muskets. The Aztec battles were fought in a mass attack, while the smaller Spanish forces were disciplined and, moving from point to point upon orders, achieved superiority of arms in whichever vicinity they were in.

Although the Spanish forces were pitifully small, Cortez achieved a psychological advantage by burning his ships so that his men had no choice—they could only advance. He further met an Indian woman named Malinche on the coast, who became his mistress and interpreter. Through her he learned of the desires for revolt. He marched inland joined with allies from Cempoala, the Totonac capital, and by the Tlaxcalans. Vacillating and indecisive, Montezuma permitted the Spanish to enter Tenochtitlán where they were quartered in part of the royal palace. They reciprocated by kidnapping him and soon after he was killed, either by the Spanish or by his own people—the record is unclear. In the subsequent great Aztec uprising known as the Noche Triste, the Spanish were driven from the city, with severe fighting occurring at breaks in the causeways made by the Aztec. More than two thirds of the Spanish were killed. Retreating to Tlaxcala, the Spanish rested and were reinforced with new Spanish troops from Cuba. Over a period of seven months they built an armada of 13 small boats. The following year the Spanish returned to Tenochtitlán with 50,000 Tlaxcalan allies and fought a great battle on the lake. The Aztecs in canoes were no match for the Spanish; their valiant leader Cuahtemoc was captured, and on August 13, 1521, the Aztec surrendered. To provide a fitting end to our discussion of the Postclassic in Mesoamerica we provide the following quote from the historian of the conquistadores, Bernal Diaz de Castillo, who witnessed this culture at its height and in its defeat.

Everywhere the Conquerors beheld the evidence of a crowded and thriving population, exceeding all they had yet seen. The temples and principal buildings of the cities were covered with a hard white stucco, which glistened like enamel in the level beams of the morning. The margin of the great basin was more thickly gemmed, than that of Chalco, with towns and hamlets. The water was darkened by swarms of canoes filled with Indians, who clambered up the sides of the causeway, and gazed with curious astonishment on the strangers. And here, also, they beheld those fairy islands of flowers, overshadowed occasionally by trees of considerable size, rising and falling with the gentle undulation of the billows. At the distance of half a league from the capital, they

encountered a solid work or curtain of stone, which traversed the dike. It was twelve feet high, was strengthened by towers at the extremities, and in the centre was a battlemented gate-way, which opened a passage to the troops. It was called the Fort of Xoloc, and became memorable in aftertimes as the position occupied by Cortés in the famous siege of Mexico.

Here they were met by several hundred Aztec chiefs, who came out to announce the approach of Montezuma, and to welcome the Spaniards to his capital. They were dressed in the fanciful gala costume of the country, with the *maxtlatl,* or cotton sash, around their loins, and a broad mantle of the same material, or of the brilliant feather embroidery, flowing gracefully down their shoulders. On their necks and arms they displayed collars and bracelets of turquoise mosaic, with which delicate plumage was curiously mingled, while their ears, under-lips, and occasionally their noses, were garnished with pendants formed of precious stones, or crescents of fine gold. As each cacique made the usual formal salutation of the country separately to the general, the tedious ceremony delayed the march more than an hour. After this, the army experienced no further interruption till it reached a bridge near the gates of the city. It was built of wood, since replaced by one of stone, and was thrown across an opening of the dike, which furnished an outlet to the waters, when agitated by the winds, or swollen by a sudden influx in the rainy season. It was a draw-bridge; and the Spaniards, as they crossed it, felt how truly they were committing themselves to the mercy of Montezuma, who, by thus cutting off their communications with the country, might hold them prisoners in his capital.

In the midst of these unpleasant reflections, they beheld the glittering retinue of the emperor emerging from the great street which led then, as it still does, through the heart of the city. Amidst a crowd of Indian nobles, preceded by three officers of state, bearing golden wands, they saw the royal palanquin blazing with burnished gold, it was borne on the shoulders of nobles, and over it a canopy of gaudy feather-work, powdered with jewels, and fringed with silver, was supported by four attendants of the same rank. They were bare-footed, and walked with a slow, measured pace, and with eyes bent on the ground. When the train had come within a convenient distance, it halted, and Montezuma, descending from his litter, came forward leaning on the arms of the lords of Tezcuco and Iztapalapan, his nephew and brother, both of whom, as we have seen, had already been made known to the Spaniards. As the monarch advanced under the canopy, the obsequious attendants strewed the ground with cotton tapestry, that his imperial feet might not be contaminated by the rude soil. His subjects of high and low degree, who lined the sides of the causeway, bent forward with their eyes fastened on the ground as he passed, and some of the humbler class prostrated themselves before him. Such was the homage paid to the Indian despot, showing that the lavish forms of Oriental adulation were to be found among the rude inhabitants of the Western World.

Montezuma wore the girdle and ample square cloak, *tilmatli,* of his nation. It was made of the finest cotton, with the embroidered ends gathered in a knot round his neck. His feet were defended by sandals having soles of gold, and the leathern thongs which bound them to his ankles were embossed with the same metal. Both the cloak and sandals were sprinkled with pearls and precious stones, among which the emerald and the *chalchivitl*—a green stone of higher estimation than any other among the Aztecs—were conspicuous. On his head he wore no other ornament than a *panache* of plumes of the royal green which floated down his back, the badge of military, rather than of regal, rank.

He was at this time about forty years of age. His person was tall and thin, but not ill-made. His hair, which was black and straight, was not very long; to wear it short was considered unbecoming persons of rank. His beard was thin; his complexion somewhat paler than is often found in his dusky, or rather copper-colored race. His features, though serious in their expression, did not wear the look of melancholy, indeed, of dejection, which characterizes his portrait, and which may well have settled on them at a later period. He moved with dignity, and his whole demeanor, tempered by an expression of benignity not to have been anticipated from the reports circulated of his character, was worthy of a great prince.—Such is the portrait left to us of the celebrated Indian emperor, in this his first interview with the white men. (Prescott 1856:296–298.)

REFERENCES

Bernal, I., 1963, *Mexico before Cortez*. New York: Doubleday.

Coe, M. D., 1967a, *The Maya*. New York: Praeger.

————, 1967b, *Mexico*. New York: Praeger.

Culbert, T. P., 1974, *The Lost Civilization: The Story of the Classic Maya,* New York: Harper & Row.

Deuel, L., 1967, *Conquistadores without Swords: Archaeologists in the Americas*. New York: St. Martins.

Dibble, Charles E., and Arthur J. O. Anderson (trans.), *Florentine Codex,* Parts V and VI, No. 14. Salt Lake City: School of American Research, University of Utah.

Dutton, B. P., 1955, "Tula of the Toltecs," *El Palacio* 62(7–8):195–251.

————, 1956, "A Brief Discussion of Chichén Itzá," *El Palacio* 63(7–8):202–232.

Leonard, J. N., 1967, *Ancient America*. New York: Time/Life Books.

Marcus, J., 1973, "Territorial Organization of the Lowland Classic Maya," *Science* 180:911–916.

Marquina, I., 1951, *Arquitectura Prehispanica*. Mexico City: Memorias del Instituto Nacional de Antropologia e Historia, No. 1.

Millon, R., 1970, "Teotihuacan: Completion of Map of Giant Ancient City in the Valley of Mexico," *Science* 170:1077–1082.

Morley, S., 1946, *The Ancient Maya*. Stanford, Calif.: Stanford University Press.

————, and G. Brainerd, 1956, *The Ancient Maya,* 3d edition. Stanford, Calif.: Stanford University Press.

Morris, E. H., 1931, *The Temple of the Warriors at Chichén Itzá, Yucatan*. Washington, D.C.: Carnegie Institute of Washington Publications, No. 406.

Prescott, W. H., 1843, *The Conquest of Mexico,* Modern Library ed. New York: Random House.

Proskouriakoff, T., 1946, *An Album of Maya Architecture*. Washington, D.C.: Carnegie Institute of Washington Publications, No. 558.

Ruppert, K., 1935, *The Caracol at Chichén Itzá*. Washington, D.C.: Carnegie Institute of Washington Publications, No. 454.

Sabloff, J. A., and G. R. Willey, 1967, "The Collapse of Maya Civilization in the Southern Lowlands: A Consideration of History and Process," *Southwestern Journal of Anthropology* 23:311–336.

Stephens, J. H., 1841, *Incidents of Travel in Central America, Chiapas, and Yucatan,* 2 vols. New York: Harper & Row.

Stierlin, H., 1964, *Living Architecture: Mayan*. New York: Grosset & Dunlap.

Vaillant, G. C., 1944, *The Aztecs of Mexico*. Harmondsworth, Middlesex: Pelican.

————, 1950, *The Aztecs of Mexico*. Suffolk: Pelican.

Wauchope, R., 1965, *They Found the Buried Cities,* Chicago: The University of Chicago Press.

Willey, G. R., 1966, *An Introduction to American Archaeology,* Vol. 1. Englewood Cliffs, N.J.: Prentice-Hall.

Andean Civilization

The Andean sequence constitutes a series of major cultural developments paralleling somewhat those of Mesoamerica. We have in the Andean region, especially Peru, a sequence that begins with Preceramic periods, evolving into a period of experimentation with plant domestication and leading to full-fledged irrigation agriculture. The sequence may be subdivided into the major categories of Archaic, Formative, Classic, and Postclassic (Fig. 16–1).

The Andean developments are so similar to those of Mesoamerica that it has led to Julian Steward's description (1957) of the *multilinear evolution* concept in which similar cultural patterns evolve in regions with similar environmental and historical factors. The Andean pattern is so similar to that of Mesoamerica in chronology, general cultural evolution, and even in cultural details—species of plants cultivated and design styles—that the possibility of

ROWE-LANNING (Willey 1971)	DATES	BENNETT AND BIRD (1964 REV.)	BUSHNELL (1963 REV.)	MASON (1957)	STEWARD AND FARON (1959)	COLLIER (1962)	KIDDER (1964)
LATE HORIZON	1534 / 1476	Imperialists	POST-CLASSIC — Inca	Imperialists	Inca Empire	Postclassic	New Kingdoms and Empires
LATE INTERMEDIATE PERIOD	1000	City Builders	City Builder	Urbanist	Cyclical Conquests		
MIDDLE HORIZON	600	Expansionists	Early	Expansionist			
EARLY INTERMEDIATE PERIOD	200 A.D.	Mastercraftsmen	Classic	Florescent	Regional States (Florescent)	Classic	Regional States (Florescent)
	200 B.C.	Experimenters	(Late)	Experimental		(Late)	Regional States (Formative)
EARLY HORIZON	900	Cultists	Formative (Early)	Cultist	Formative (Theocratic States)	Formative (Early)	Cultist Temple Centers
INITIAL PERIOD	1800	Early Farmers	Early Farmers	Formative	Incipient Farming	Initial Ceramic	Horticultural
PRECERAMIC PERIODS VI	2500			Early Agricultural		Preceramic	Villages
V	4200	Hunters	Early Hunters		Hunters, Gatherers, Fishers		
IV	6000						
III	8000						
II	9500						
I							

Left-side brackets (Rowe-Lanning): POSTCLASSIC, CLASSIC, PRECLASSIC, ARCHAIC

Fig. 16–1 Chart illustrating the correspondence between the Andean chronologies proposed by various researchers and the Mesoamerican sequence. (Modified from Willey 1971:Fig. 3–6.)

direct historical contacts between Mesoamerican and Andean area cannot be ignored. On the other hand positive proof that such contacts occurred is lacking.

A basic integrative factor present in Andean archaeology is the feature termed *Horizon style*. Horizon styles are decorative elements which occur together on a variety of media, such as pottery, stone sculpture, weaving, bone carving, and metalwork. A further feature of the styles which makes them of incalculable archaeological value is the fact that these styles are noted for their rapid spread and their brief duration in time. The Horizon styles therefore are useful as chronological markers. They serve to correlate local archaeological sequences one with the other. Through time from early to late, the major Horizon styles are Chavin, White on Red, Negative Painted, Tiahuanaco-Huari, Interlocking, and Inca (see Fig. 16–1). In brief, Horizon styles are distinctive in character, widespread geographically, and of brief duration. They further serve to provide Andean archaeology with a portion of its unique quality.

The Andean region is dominated by the Andean Mountain chain rising to 20,000 feet near the equator and diminishing in elevation both to the north and the south. The central region within which most of Andean culture developed includes Peru and portions of Ecuador and Bolivia. This area may be subdivided into six major regions (Fig. 16–2) termed the North, Central, and Southern Highlands and the North, Central, and South Coasts. The highlands include the mountains, high plateaus, and mountain valleys primarily at elevations of 9000 feet or above. The climate is equitable with adequate rainfall in the lower portions. The climate changes to a cold steppe regime in elevations of 11,000–14,000 feet; higher still lie alpine tundra and snowfields. The coastal region is a desert. Rainfall occurs inland in the mountains and returns to the sea by means of a series of 40 or more short, steep, parallel river valleys (Fig. 16–2). The combination of no rain on the coast and the availability of surface water only in the valleys early led to dependence on irrigation. A further bonus is the preservation of perishable materials. The coastal aridity permits the recovery, through archaeological methods, of as complete a record of prehistoric life style as found anywhere in the world. Only Egypt, Mesopotamia, and the American Southwest have similar optimum conditions for preservation coupled with an outstanding culture.

Our discussion of Andean culture history will follow the sequence of periods outlined by Willey (1971:86). His first five Preceramic periods have already been summarized previously. We begin our coverage with the Preceramic Period VI findings at Huaca Prieta and other coastal shell middens and continue through the Inca Empire. A number of authors have reviewed the Andean evidence and subdivided it into major periods. Figure 16–1 presents a resume of these classifications which should aid in your understanding of the terms utilized by the various authors.

The periods have been defined by Willey (1971:86) as follows:

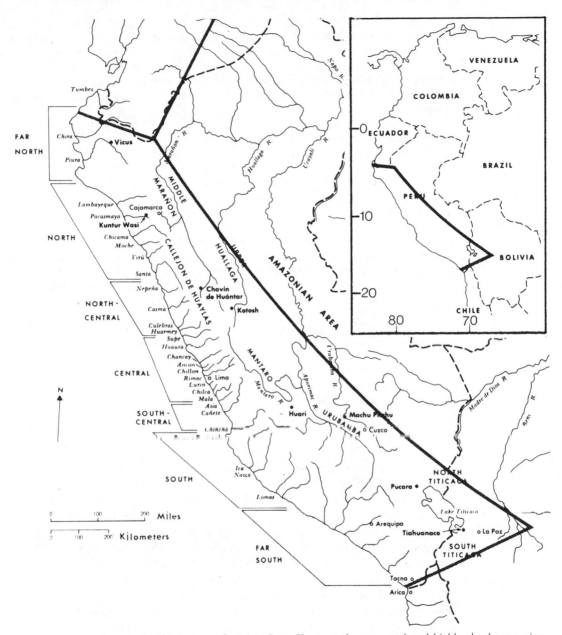

Fig. 16–2   The regions of ancient Peru. The map shows coastal and highland subareas, river valleys of the coast, some modern cities, and in the highlands certain archaeological sites. Inset shows the area within its South American setting. (Willey 1971:Fig. 3–1.)

Preceramic Period VI (2500–1800 B.C.). On the coast this period saw the continuity and enrichment of the Pacific Littoral tradition cultures. Populations increased. In the last centuries of the period the Pacific Littoral tradition began to be transformed into the Peruvian tradition. This transformation or transition was marked by the appearance of large habitation sites, sizable public or ceremonial constructions, and the first appearance of maize cultivation. The period closes with the appearance of pottery.

The Initial Period (1800–900 B.C.). This is the first ceramic period in the Peruvian area archaeological sequence. It is also here considered as marking the emergence of the Peruvian cultural tradition. As has already been noted, it begins with the appearance of pottery. It closes with the first appearances of the Chavin art style.

The Early Horizon (900–200 B.C.). The Early Horizon is the period of the Chavin style and its immediate derivatives. The Chavin style is not represented in all parts of the area, but cultures in subareas and regions where the style is not present may be assigned to the 900–200 B.C. period by cross dating.

The Early Intermediate Period (200 B.C.–A.D. 600). This period opens with the various new subareal ceramic and art styles that replace Chavin and Chavin-influenced ones. It closes with the appearance of the Tiahuanaco and Huari horizon styles.

The Middle Horizon (A.D. 600–1000). The Middle Horizon is the time of the Tiahuanaco- and Huari-derived styles and their propagation throughout most of the Peruvian area. It closes with the emergence, once more, of subareal styles.

The Late Intermediate Period (A.D. 1000–1476). This period, intermediate between the Middle and Late Horizons, is characterized by a series of late ceramic and art styles—and by a series of corresponding late states or kingdoms.

The Late Horizon (A.D. 1476–1534). The Late Horizon begins with the expansion of the Inca style and culture—and with the expansion of Inca militarism and the Inca state—in the late fifteenth century. It closes with the downfall of this empire and the ascendancy of the Spanish conquerors under Pizarro.

The extremely brief resume, period by period, taken from Willey's work permits us to proceed in much the same manner as we did in the preceding chapter. Our concern is to present a synthesis of the major diagnostic features of each period rather than review the regional sequences in detail. The basic cultural pattern shared by all periods is the Andean Farming Tradition described in detail in Chapter 14. In this chapter we will focus on those elements that are unique to each period. Much of the chronology and understanding of Andean archaeology is based on cemetery excavations. Owing to the spectacular remains preserved in the cemeteries—ceramics and weaving—major excavations were carried out early in the twentieth century prior to the advent of modern excavation techniques. While the remains preserved in museums today are spectacular, the information associated with them concerning their age and associations is often less impressive. As a result, reexamination of the regional chronologies is a current focus of interest of archaeologists working in the area. In the absence of firm stratigraphic controls the Horizon styles were utilized as a means of site and regional correlation. In the absence of an independent dating technique such as radiocarbon, the Horizon styles were more or less assumed to appear simultaneously wherever they

occur. The reasoning is circular: the styles are assumed to be contemporaneous, and therefore wherever they occur, the cultural layers containing them are believed to be of equivalent age.

The earliest unique cultural manifestations, the Chavin period occurred within the Early Horizon (900–200 B.C.). The Chavin period (named after the typesite, Chavin de Huantar, in the Northern Highlands) is marked by a Horizon style of the same name (Fig. 16–3). In the highlands the Horizon style is present in stone sculpture and other media. On the coast it is present in pottery as well as weaving and metalwork. The style consists of abstract curvilinear representations of a feline or anthropomorphized feline. The single diagnostic feature uniformly present is overlapping canine teeth (Fig. 16–3). Other elements of the style include men, demons, jaguars, eagles, serpents, caimen, and other beasts (Willey 1971:116). The style further features eyes in which the pupils are located at the top of the orbit. The style is symmetrically balanced with numerous repeated elements that are clearly intended as decorative rather than representational. A stylistic analogy that comes to mind are the Buddhas of North India and adjacent China with many arms. The style is contemporaneous with the Olmec culture of the Mesoamerican Preclassic which featured the jaguar mouth art motif. It is tempting to suggest a historical connection on this basis but in fact the similarities between the two styles are more general than specific.

An even more suggestive correlation with Mesoamerica may be made with the carved vertical stone slabs set around the temple at Cerro Sechin in the Casma Valley, northern Peru (Fig. 16–4). The age of the site is uncertain but it is assigned by Willey (1971:112) to the preChavin Initial period. At Cerro Sechin these slabs have been deeply carved with individual human figures in profile. The similarities of these figures to the Danzantes of Monte Alban, Oaxaca, which are of similar age, is indeed striking. Such carved slabs are rare in both Mesoamerica and the Andean area. The Sechin style features warriors or dignitaries carrying maces, seminude or dismembered men, and geometric elements (Willey 1971:112).

Bennett and Bird (1964) have given the term *cultist* to the Chavin period, for they infer that the art style was associated with the peaceful dissemination of a religious cult which became nearly pan-Andean in scope. The period is marked by a rather sudden flowering of culture. The crafts include outstanding pottery, weaving, and even metalworking. There is evidence in the refuse deposits and cemeteries of a population increase. The appearance of temples signifies a formalized religion as well as a social organization capable of scheduling the construction of public buildings. The appearance of the art style was sudden, without obvious antecedents, unless it may be traced to Cerro Sechin. The style was superimposed upon a number of local cultures, each of which was evolving toward similar cultural goals sharing the common Andean Farming Tradition. Locations of sites at this time in places later abandoned, because they were too swampy or too arid, implies that agricultural techniques were as yet imperfectly developed.

Fig. 16—3 The Chavin Horizon style in different media: a. Lanzon in the temple interior; b. carving on Raimondi stone, Chavin de Huantar; c. Paracas vessel. (Willey 1971:Figs. 3–38, 3–39, 3–40.)

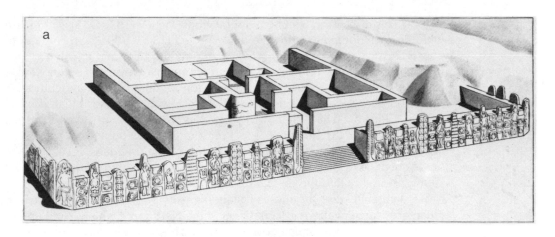

Fig. 16–4 Major stylistic elements from Cerro Sechin: *a.* the temple of Sechin, Casma Valley showing the placement of the standing figures; *b.* details of individual figures from Sechin. (Willey 1971:Figs. 3–30 and 3–31 [redrawn from Tello 1956].)

In his discussion of cultural innovations, Willey (1970:115) is impressed with the developments during the Initial period (1800–900 B.C.). He cites the appearance of plant cultivation, increase in the number and the size of sites, florescence in crafts, and ceremonial structures. However he is unwilling to assert that all these developments were the logical outgrowth of agriculture. He points out that sedentism and population increase first were initiated by the coastal fishing and shellfish-gathering peoples. Thus there was already a social tradition of communal living in effect prior to the development of agriculture. Food debris from Chavin sites, especially the coastal middens, reveal reliance on seafoods as well as the peanut, warty squash, and avocados. There is a strong possibility that the dog was domesticated and the llama kept.

In architecture the most outstanding example is the site of Chavin de Huantar. At an elevation of 10,000 feet in the Northern Highlands of Peru, the Chavin ceremonial complex covers an area 210-meters square. The site constructions consist of a series of rectangular platform mounds with remains of rectangular buildings on top (Fig. 16–5). The platforms contain within them stone-slab-lined galleries and rectangular rooms on three levels connected by stairways and inclines. Interior ventilator shafts provide air to underground galleries and rooms. The exterior facing stones were well cut pieces of granite. Also attached to the platform exterior was a set of human and animal heads sculptured in the round and tenoned into the wall. Other stone sculptures at the site include a cornice carved with figures in relief, carved stone slabs set into the exterior walls, lintels, and columns. Set within one of the galleries inside the platform is the Great Image or Lanzon (see Fig. 16-3), a carved stone slab of prism form. It is carved in bas-relief in the form of an anthropomorphic figure with the Chavin-style fangs, hair represented by snakes, ornaments in the ears, and a necklace as well as a girdle of combined serpent-jaguar faces. The Great Image is presumed to have represented a supreme deity placed in a setting deliberately calculated to inspire awe.

The Chavin style changes through time, with the Great Image being an early more representational figure. The Raimondi Stone (see Fig. 16–3) is typical of the later more abstract style. According to John Rowe, Chavin de Huantar included in addition to the ceremonial center an associated residential area plus several nearby villages. Presumably these villages shared in the maintenance and use of the ceremonial center. The pottery is similar to that of the North Coast.

The best known Chavin period pottery is that from the North Coast Cupisnique culture. Typically the pottery is black to brown and highly polished. It features the unique Peruvian vessel form, the stirrup spouted vessel (Fig. 16–6, Nos. 44 and 27), so typical from this period and throughout the entire Peruvian ceramic tradition. Cupisnique pottery is famous for its realistic modeling of plants, animals, humans, and buildings. This tradition of realism in pottery continued throughout the Peruvian cultural sequence, providing us with a wealth of information about their prehistoric life style. Cupisnique

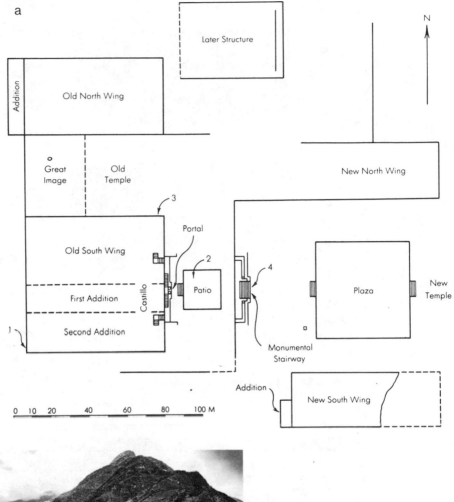

Fig. 16–5 Chavin de Huantar, type site of the Chavin Horizon. *a*. Plan. (Willey 1971:Fig. 3–36.) *b*. View of southeast corner of Chavin Temple, Peru. (Courtesy of the American Museum of Natural History.)

	NORTH HIGHLANDS	FAR NORTH COAST	NORTH COAST	CENTRAL COAST	SOUTH COAST	SOUTH HIGHLANDS
INCA HORIZON	Inca-Cajamarca 735	Tallan 734	Inca-Chimu 745	Inca-Pachacamac 755	Ica-Inca 763	Imperial Inca 704
LATE PERIOD	Cajamarca 583	Lambayeque 608	Chimu 647	Chancay 662	Ica 686	Selda 552
WARI HORIZON	Wari-Recuay 225	Wari-Lambayeque 510	North Coast Wari 578	Huara 560	South Coast Wari 523	Wari 507
EARLY PERIOD	Recuay 220	Vicus Negative 175	Mochica 283	Early Lima 553	Nazca 426	Tiahuanaco 544
CHAVIN HORIZON	Chavin 22	Chongoyape 44	Cupisnique 27	Ancon 30	Paracas-Chavinoid 322	Chavinoid 74

Fig. 16–6 Representative Peruvian ceramic styles by time period. (Sawyer 1968:Terminal Plate.)

pottery is common and usually intact, for vessels were placed in graves as burial offerings. Other decorative techniques include the use of zoned decoration, incising, punctations, and other surface manipulations.

The coast sites also possess temples, of lesser size than Chavin de Huantar but nonetheless impressive. As their major building material they used adobe, made into bricks of conical form. Typical platforms were up to 170 meters square and 30 meters in height. They had as decoration adobe sculptures in Chavin style, some also painted. Domestic architecture was simple with circular and rectangular stone platforms upon which the houses were built. The houses were of adobe with thatch roofs. Metalworking also appears at this time on the North Coast. Manufacturing techniques were limited to soldering, hammering, annealing, and repoussé decoration. Items were of thin gold and include crowns, ornaments, ear spools, tweezers, and pins found as grave offerings. The repoussé decoration is clearly in the Chavin style.

Chavin influence is seen elsewhere, including the Paracas pottery of the South Coast. The excellently made Paracas wares also include evidence of a non-Chavin tradition. Important ceramic traits are the double spout and bridge bottle (Fig. 16–6, No. 322), red slipped decoration, negative painting, whistling bottles, and an emphasis on polychrome painted decoration. Paracas burials include excellent examples of weaving. The painted pottery designs and those of the textiles are similar.

In textiles, the spindle whorl and heddle loom first appear. All weaving was in cotton and included plain weave tapestries, weft stripes, fringes, tassels, and embroidery. Clothing included belts, breechclouts, a head cloth, and featured body painting as well as the wearing of rings, bracelets, ear plugs, and necklaces of bone, turquoise, lapis lazuli, shell, gold, and iron pyrites. Personal beauty was also enhanced by artificial skull deformation.

In review we may categorize Chavin culture as based upon, but not originating, a settled farming way of life. The presence of separate identifiable cultural patterns such as the Paracas pottery is indicative of local autonomy. The Chavin religion, about which we know little, was the only unifying element in the Andean area and its influence was limited to the far North Coast, Southern Highlands, and South Coast. The absence of fortifications implies a peaceful spread of a religious cult based upon worship of an anthropomorphized feline deity. There was no overall political unity and the social organization consisted of family units organized into small villages. The major integrative force in the society was the religion.

THE EARLY INTERMEDIATE PERIOD

In the period 200 B.C.–A.D. 600, within the Andean area we have the development of a series of cultures noted for their originality and regionalistic, almost nationalistic, focus. This is the period within which Bennett and Bird (1964) perceive two levels: an early period termed "Experimenter" followed by a truly Classic manifestation termed "Mastercraftsmen." According to Bennett and Bird it was during the Experimenter period that perfection was acquired in crafts, building, and agricultural methods. Perhaps the deliberate intention to "experiment," they imply, is overstated; nonetheless this is the time of achievement of control of the environment through irrigation farming. The period was marked by two Horizon styles in pottery: the White on Red and Negative Painted. The Mastercraftsmen, by definition, excelled in crafts and experienced a cultural florescence comparable to the Mesoamerican Classic. Willey (1971:131) prefers to lump these entities into one larger grouping, the "Early Intermediate period," the basic qualities of which he identifies as: the formation of separate states or kingdoms, achievement of a population maximum, regionalized art styles, great valley irrigation systems, the first appearance of interregional warfare, intensive craft specialization, marked distinctions in social class, and finally the appearance of true cities, those communities in excess of 5000 population.

The White on Red and Negative Painted Horizon Styles

The Salinar and Gallinazo pottery styles, which feature the White on Red Horizon on the North Coast, continue the previous incised decoration which often outlines the white painted areas. Applique is also used. The Chavin motif is no longer present; instead designs are simple geometric lines and dots. Life modeling continues, and two new vessel forms are introduced: the handle and spout bottle and the figure-handle and spout vessel. Stirrup spout vessels continue in vogue.

Gallinazo pottery has some elements of the White on Red style but more commonly features the Negative Painted style (see Fig. 16–6, No. 175). The latter utilizes a resist-dye painting in which a dull black paint contrasts with the lighter base color of the vessel. Modeling is even more common than in the Salinar pottery. Inasmuch as Gallinazo cultural levels are stratigraphically above those of the Salinar culture, it is apparent that the change from the White on Red Horizon to the Negative Painted Horizon also is indicative of a chronological difference between the two styles. Salinar house types continued to be built on platform mounds or terraces with the house walls of conical adobes. Some rooms were agglutinated into small compounds. Small flat-topped platform mounds scattered throughout the valley probably served as local worship centers. On the tops of nearby hills, walled fortifications represent the earliest evidence of warfare recorded in ancient Peru.

The main site at Gallinazo is considerably larger than previous communities. The total site area ranges from 2 to 6 square kilometers depending upon one's definition of how concentrated the population must be to be included. The population is estimated at 5000 to 10,000 persons, living in clusters of adobe apartments, although Wendell Bennett, the excavator, estimated that 20,000 rooms occur within the area adjacent to the ceremonial center. The latter is dominated by a pyramid 25 meters in height associated with smaller pyramids, platforms, and a walled courtyard. Probably Gallinazo served as the capital of its valley, the Viru, with numerous other small settlements within the valley being occupied simultaneously. The Salinar-Gallinazo sequence is the cultural antecedent of the great Mochica civilization of the North Coast, one of the most outstanding cultures ever to exist in aboriginal America.

Mochica Civilization

We could rely upon Mochica ceramics as the sole means of acquiring information and still be able to reconstruct a creditable version of their life style. The modeled ceramics are so realistic and portray such a wealth of cultural detail, in combination with their realistically painted pottery, that they permit a glimpse into every aspect of ancient Mochica society and life. The Mochica consisted of the inheritors of the North Coast cultural traditions. With their main site at Moche, they expanded beyond their home valley to dominate the North Coast. The emphases in the pottery, mural art, and fortifications imply that this expansion was based upon actual conquest of adjacent valleys.

Architecture featured massive adobe brick ceremonial structures, the most impressive of which, the Huaca del Sol at Moche, is a terraced and truncated pyramid 228 by 136 meters with a maximum height of 41 meters. The Huaca del Sol functioned as a platform for one or more temples while the nearby Huaca de la Luna, a terraced platform abutting a hillside, included residences, probably of the ruling elite.

The Mochica were highly concerned with personal status. The portrait-head vessels record the actual countenances of individuals, each of whom may be identified as to his real life importance because of the geographic distribution of his portrait vessels. In addition, status was further identified by the type of headdress worn. Mochica society was male dominated and militaristic. Other aspects of Mochica society delineated by ceramics include molded animals, plants, demons, house types, and scenes from daily life including sexual practices, hunting, fishing, punishment of prisoners, religious ceremonies, and burial scenes. A further ramification on some painted vessels are scenes of men carrying small bags of beans marked with crosses and dots. It has been suggested that the beans may have served as symbolic ideographs, which if not an actual language, could have served as memory aids in the transmission of messages.

The grave offerings provide a wealth of cultural objects. Graves have been found on top of pyramids, in cemeteries, as well as in locations adjacent to the farmed portions of the valleys. Graves were rectangular pits with the burials in an extended position. Some grave pits were roofed with adobes. The graves feature offerings differing according to the status of the individual buried therein. Burial items include the stirrup spouted vessels, ornaments of gold, copper, silver, and inlaid bone. For the first time we have the widespread use of metal in utilitarian implements as well as in ornaments. Copper was used for axes, spears, helmets, and the points for digging sticks. Metalworking techniques included alloying, casting, and gilding.

With respect to our coverage of the Mochica we cite their achievements as a major regional culture with a strong political organization as well as the infinite variety and accuracy of their modeled ceramics. No other ancient culture surpasses the skill of the Mochica in the manufacture of modeled pottery.

Nazca Culture

The South Coast is known for the development at this time of a culture termed Nazca, after a valley of the same name. A direct outgrowth of the preceding Paracas culture, Nazca culture is world famous for its polychrome painted ceramics. The Nazca ceramic decorations (see Fig. 16–6, No. 426) include designs present earlier on Paracas textiles. New designs include a cat demon, bird, fish, and animal designs. The pottery is noted for its fired pigments, in contrast to the earlier unfired Paracas pigments. Nazca pots are known to have as many as 11 colors, although 4 or 5 are most common—red, black, white, gray, orange, and shades of each. Major vessel forms are the double spouted bottle with bridge between the spouts and open bowls. The design style of the pottery shares many features with the textiles of the famed Paracas Necropolis mummy bundles (Fig. 16–7). The textiles, which were specially manufactured to be used as mummy wrappings, feature a wide variety of weaves including brocade, double cloth, tapestry, gauze, lace, and weft stripe. These textiles are among the highest quality ever manufactured in the world at any time period. Woven of llama wool and cotton, the textiles feature a background color of black, red, or green with embroidered designs in the same elements as the pottery. The weaving is further enhanced by the wide range of dyes used; 190 shades or hues are known.

Architecture and settlement patterns of the South Coast are less well known, owing to the focus of the excavators on the recovery of burials. Large towns or cities did exist at this time on the South Coast. For example at Cahuachi, in the Nazca Valley, a platform was surmounted with a temple of wedge-shaped adobes. Nearby is a ridge covered with walled courts and rooms. Perhaps the best known Nazca features are the strange patterns or drawings on the ground made by removing stones from the surface. The patterns so made are thought to be of Nazca origin, since they are of design elements common to Nazca ceramics and textiles. The designs include primarily geometric elements and animal figures. Their abstract design and large size, necessitating an aerial vantage point to best perceive them in entirety, have led recent authors to ascribe to them mystical meanings. For example Von Däniken in his book and movie, *Chariots of the Gods,* claims they are the work of extraterrestrial beings.

With our discussion of Nazca culture we bring to a close our review of

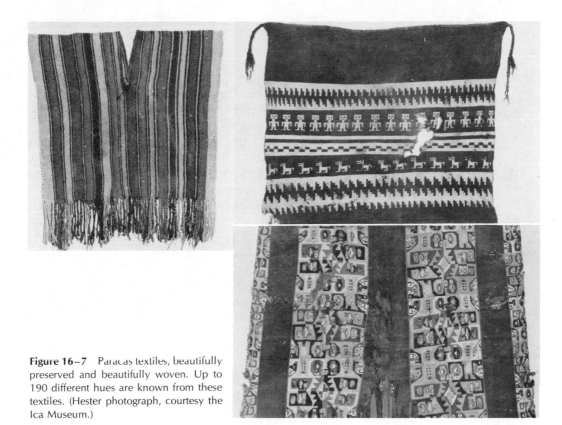

Figure 16-7 Paracas textiles, beautifully preserved and beautifully woven. Up to 190 different hues are known from these textiles. (Hester photograph, courtesy the Ica Museum.)

the Early Intermediate period. However, we have not mentioned simultaneous developments in the Andean highlands. In the highlands we had the establishment of centers during this time period at Huari, Pucara, and Tiahuanaco. These came to dominate Andean civilization in the next major period, the Middle Horizon.

A summary of the Early Intermediate period would emphasize the development of population centers (if not actual urbanism), the rise of military power, the development of regionally oriented city-states, and a wealth of cultural detail only achieved by true civilization. The regionalism of the design styles and media emphasized is self-evident proof of the absence of any overall political or religious integration.

THE MIDDLE HORIZON (A.D. 600–1000)

The Middle Horizon marks a turning point in Andean archaeology. No longer were the regional cultures content to remain within their own valleys, developing their own regional style in crafts, practicing their own religion, and largely ignoring the endeavors of the regional cultures in the nearby valleys. In this period there developed for the first time an attempt at imperialism. Two cultural centers—Tiahuanaco, in the Southern Highlands at the southern end of Lake Titicaca (see Fig. 16–2), and Huari in the Central Highlands—extended their cultural influence outward by colonization and conquest. Bennett and Bird (1964) term the period *expansionist,* which is certainly an appropriate term. If our archaeological knowledge was more complete we could identify in this period antecedents of the later Inca expansion. The period may be described as evidencing a concern for the manipulation of man-hour units and political organization of peoples. The major known entity of this period is Tiahuanaco culture largely because of the spectacular site of the same name. Recent research suggests that Huari was of nearly equal importance but it is as yet less well known.

Tiahuanaco

Tiahuanaco is manifest by a major ceremonial center and a Horizon style of the same name. The art style is primarily represented in stone carving, architecture, and ceramics. In ceramics the style exhibits polychrome painting in white, black, and red (Fig. 16–8). Ceramics are highly polished with a red slip and designs outlined in black. The basic feature of the style is a standing anthropomorphic deity facing forward and clasping a staff in each hand. The overlapping canine teeth recur as a motif. Other motifs include heads of birds and animals, running figures in profile wearing a cape and bird mask, repeated profile figures of pumas and condors, and repeated geometric designs, circles, dots, and crosses. The design style is frequently stylized to the point that the deity figure is represented only by the face, with the body made up of geometric elements.

The Tiahuanaco style spread as a complex, thus implying concommitant political and military unity. Early in the period the Tiahuanaco style was disseminated northward to Huari which then began its own consolidation and expansion. The Tiahuanaco style and empire is therefore primarily limited to the southern Andes, including southern Bolivia, the south coast of Peru, and the Atacama desert region of northern Chile.

The site of Tiahuanaco consists of a major ceremonial center built at an elevation of 14,000 feet. Because this elevation is too high for most crops, except quinoa, potatoes, and oca, there was considerable reliance on herding. The environmentally limited economy probably was responsible for the site construction pattern and use. The site was probably not a residential center for the populace. Archaeologists believe the site was constructed at intervals, perhaps during religious pilgrimages, at which time the regional population accumulated materials used during the rest of the year by a small group of skilled construction workers. The site was never finished. The building of sections at intervals would explain the presence of structural units which are internally organized but are not arranged into an overall site plan.

Fig. 16–8 Ceramic vessel typical of the Tiahuanaco Horizon style. (Hester photograph, courtesy the Ica Museum.)

There are four major structural units and several smaller ones. The largest consists of a natural mound made into a pyramid 210 meters square and 15 meters in height, on top of which are house foundations. Also associated is a water reservoir. The unit may also have served as a fortress. Another unit features a stone-faced earthen platform 135 by 130 meters with an inner courtyard. Associated are stone statues and a monolithic gateway. The other structural units are similar but smaller. Carving in the round is suggested, but actually the technique employed consists of bas-relief carving on four sides on slabs weighing up to 100 tons. The monolithic gateways are most impressive (Fig. 16–9). These were made by carving a doorway through giant stone slabs. The gateways are decorated by friezes of bas-relief carving in the Tiahuanaco style. The friezes are carved with stiff human figures, pumas, and condors in profile. The largest gateway, called the Gateway of the Sun, has located above the doorway a deity termed the Gateway God, which faces frontward clasping a staff in each hand. He is a variant of the anthropomorphic deity with a headdress of snakes and a jaguar-style mouth.

Our knowledge of Tiahuanaco is limited because of the lack of major excavations. We do know something of the architectural stoneworking, since it is exposed. Stone for sculptures and construction was imported from quarries 5 kilometers distant. Building blocks were fitted together by cutting notches or grooves into the edges of adjacent blocks. Into the grooves were fitted copper clamps of either T or I shape. Some of the carved heads were separately carved and then tenoned into walls. Building stones were further finished by grinding of the surface. Ceramics are well fired and highly polished. Principal vessel

Fig. 16–9   Monolith gateway at Tiahuanaco. (Willey 1971:Fig. 3–90.)

forms include flaring sided goblets, open bowls, and bowls with annular bases. Although up to eight colors of paint were used, most pottery is black, white, and red.

In the highlands, sites of Tiahuanaco culture are represented by cemeteries, stone building units, and stone sculpture. Sites on the coast are primarily represented by cemeteries. It is from the coast, where preservation is so good, that we have most of our evidence of the textiles. Tiahuanaco textiles are well made, especially tapestries; the decoration includes use of the Tiahuanaco Horizon style.

Several styles of burial were practiced. On the Central Coast the burials are in pits; mummies are wrapped in special burial garments with an attached mask of clay, metal, or wood. The South Coast burials are in large pottery urns. In the highlands burials were placed in boxes lined with stone slabs.

The Tiahuanaco cultural expansion shows evidence of not being well organized or enduring. In terms of cultural dynamics the period seems to have been confused, with earlier buildings on the coast being reused and some valley bottom irrigation systems in temporary disuse. At the end of the period there is evidence of reorganization with some coastal sites featuring villages made up of clusters of rectangular enclosures. Late in the period the Tiahuanaco Horizon style was replaced by local styles featuring the geometric designs of the Black, White, and Red Horizon.

Huari

Huari archaeology is not that well known, due primarily to only recent recognition of its importance as a cultural center. Much of the Huari sphere of influence was interpreted previously as Tiahuanacoid, since Huari materials incorporate elements derived from the Tiahuanaco style. According to Willey (1971:160–161), we may infer from ceramics the following developments in the Huari region: Tiahuanaco influences first appear in early Middle Horizon times at Conchopata, a shrine near Huari. Votive urns at Conchopata feature depictions of the Gateway God plus additional elements which are locally distinctive. Willey suggests that missionaries from Tiahuanaco introduced these religious concepts to the Central Highlands. Shortly thereafter, the style is apparent also at Huari where it gives rise to later ceramic styles termed Chakipampa B and Vinaque. These latter styles were widely traded to the north and west. Everywhere they occur it appears their trade was associated with high prestige or military conquest. In any event these became the styles associated with the local rulers. Vinaque pottery, which features the derived Tiahuanaco-style deities and animals, is most common in spouted bottles, keros, beakers, face-neck jars, and anthropomorphic jars. Most evidences of Huari influence are indicated in ceramics by a fusion of Huari elements with those of the prior local style—Nazca, Pachacamac, Mochica, and so forth. At the end of the Vinaque period the city of Huari was abandoned, possibly as a result of attack. The Huari influence was then replaced with a reassertion of local regional cultures.

Viewed primarily from the perspective of ceramic analyses, the Tiahuanaco-Huari influences can be described as, first, the introduction of new ideas with little change in the prior cultural patterns. A second phase was dramatic change in both the old and new ideas with subsequent fusion. Finally there was the development of new styles out of the fused elements, followed by some reassertion of the old local styles. We may infer that major social changes accompanied the pottery changes. These changes are most evident on the North Coast where Mochica settlements and religious centers were abandoned and new cities were built inside poured-adobe rectangular walled compounds. The building of walled urban communities is a practice which came to dominate the succeeding period, the Late Intermediate period.

THE LATE INTERMEDIATE PERIOD

After A.D. 1000 the major developments in Andean prehistory shifted back to the North Coast, the location of the great Chimu kingdom. At its greatest expansion it extended 600 miles from north to south. Other kingdoms of this period are less well known: the Cuismanu of the Central Coast, the Chuquismancu located farther south, and the Chincha of the South Coast. In the highlands we have the earliest evidence of the Inca as a regional culture at Cuzco. In the Southern Highlands there is a continuation of a local culture at Tiahuanaco. It is from this time period that we have our earliest historical evidence—legends transcribed from the Inca by the Spanish after the Conquest.

Termed "City Builder" by Bennett and Bird (1964), this period is noted for the rise of local city-states in all of the Andean subregions. Major features expressed by all of these cultures are planned urban communities, a population increase, strong political organization, mass production of crafts with a decrease in artistic skill, and a concern for the manipulation of large amounts of labor through the authority vested in the government. Our review of this period will consider only the Chimu kingdom as an example.

Chan Chan and the Chimu Kingdom

The Chimu capital at Chan Chan, located in the arid Moche Valley only a kilometer from the sea, is the largest and most impressive city of the period. Chan Chan, only currently being mapped in detail, is made up of 10 residential units. These quadrangles are enclosed by walls still standing to a height of 12 or more meters. The very thick walls are made up of a combination of poured adobe and adobe brick. Within these compound walls (Fig. 16–10) are enclosed residential areas, the largest being 375 by 480 meters. The enclosed structures include gabled houses, sunken gardens, stone-lined water reservoirs, courtyards, small rooms, streets, pyramids, stairways, terraces, and tombs. Between the 10 quadrangles lay irrigated fields, cemeteries, small buildings, and reed marshes. No population estimate seems reliable until after the current mapping project has been completed. The area of the city has been estimated at from 6 square miles (Willey 1971) to 11 square miles (Bennett and Bird 1964). The size and decoration of the dwelling units plus grave contents indicate that the Chimu were powerful and wealthy. One major function of the quadrangles was to provide housing for the ruling class. The city is of the type Schaedel (1951) terms *urban elite center,* which included the functions of political administrative center, religious center, and urban life. Some other sites, without the elaborate courtyards and fine residences, provided the more plebeian housing of the common people. It is assumed that these *urban lay centers* were tributary to and under the political authority of the *urban elite centers,* of which Chan Chan was the largest and finest.

Major features of interest typical of Chan Chan are the arabesque wall murals carved in the adobe walls (Fig. 16–11). The decorations are geometric in concept, even though they include repeated figures of men, deities, and animals. It has also been suggested that the quadrangles had further social connotations; that is, that they functioned as *barrios,* semiautonomous units based on kinship or craft specialization. The parallels with the residential areas at Teotihuacan suggest that a similar type of urban pattern was in effect. From

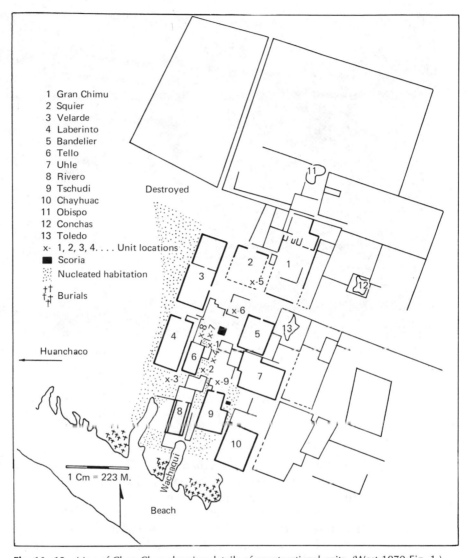

1 Gran Chimu
2 Squier
3 Velarde
4 Laberinto
5 Bandelier
6 Tello
7 Uhle
8 Rivero
9 Tschudi
10 Chayhuac
11 Obispo
12 Conchas
13 Toledo
x- 1, 2, 3, 4. . . . Unit locations
■ Scoria
Nucleated habitation
Burials

Destroyed

Huanchaco

1 Cm = 223 M.

Wachaqui

Beach

Fig. 16–10   Map of Chan Chan showing details of constructional units. (West 1970:Fig. 1.)

this period we have evidence of a highway system which may have actually been initiated during Middle Horizon times. It was augmented and maintained by the Chimu, finally to become part of the later, and much more famous, Inca system of roads.

Chimu pottery is a mold-made blackware which, in vessel forms and style, represents a continuation of the earlier Mochica-modeled tradition. Chimu ceramics on the other hand, because of their emphasis on mass production, represent a major reduction in ceramic skills. The emphasis is on quantity, not quality. The forms—the stirrup-spout vessels, figure-bridge-spout

Fig. 16–11 Wall sculpture at Chan Chan. (Hester photograph.)

types, and the modeled houses, humans, animals, and so on—are all continuations of earlier North Coast pottery themes. Chimu art is well known, owing to the excellent preservation within the burials. There are woven patterned textiles, painted textiles, wood carvings, and metalwork. The latter features silver and gold used for ornaments and domestic service, in addition to quantities of the new alloy, bronze, which came into widespread use at this time for weapons and utilitarian implements.

One outstanding feature of the Central Coast is the famous fortress of Paramonga. Although militarism was not as important in the Late Intermediate period as in the Mesoamerican Postclassic, it was nonetheless present. The later Inca were not responsible for the introduction of militarism into the Andean region; they simply perfected an already existing militaristic tradition. Other cultures of the Late Intermediate period are less well known. It is these lesser cultures of the Chincha, Ica, Rimac, and many other valleys which were subjugated by the Inca in their imperial expansion.

THE INCA: THE LATE HORIZON A.D. 1476–1534

The Inca rise to power parallels that of the Aztec. In a brief period of time they changed from one of the lesser city states or an even less formalized status, as the ruling lineage of one of the mountain valley cities, to the greatest political empire in the ancient New World. The transition was rapid and was due to tight political control and the development of an impressive military organization.

Our sources of information on the Inca are many. We have available the wealth of contemporary historical accounts of the Spanish Conquest of the Inca and the Postconquest period written by Spanish conquistadores, priests, early travelers, and some Inca educated in Europe. Further sources relevant to the history of the Inca Empire are the legends that were transcribed after the Spanish Conquest. Finally we have Inca archaeological remains. The archaeological materials include ceramics, buildings, textiles, metal objects and some specialized stone tools. Factors governing the archaeological information are 1. massive overbuilding in the late Imperial period, which obliterated or concealed earlier remains, and 2. Spanish destruction of objects, primarily those of metal, which were melted into bullion.

The geographic extent of the Inca Empire is known, but its population has been variously estimated at from 1.5 million to 6 million. A major unknown factor is the population reduction caused by the Spanish Conquest. The census of 1571 reported 1.5 million, but the population may have exceeded 3.5 million during the height of the empire. Between 1250–1532, 12 Inca rulers are known but the first 8 are legendary. These rulers probably refer to a local Cuzco ruling clan. Rulers with known reigns begin in 1438 with the ninth Inca; therefore the empire lasted only 94 years. The conquest of Andean tribes and the establishment of the empire primarily occurred after 1470 (Fig. 16–12). Expansion was brought about through the desire for economic gain and for strengthening the ruling class. Victory was due to superior organization and numerical superiority on the battlefield. After capture of a region a census was taken and a relief map was modeled in clay. Villages were often moved en masse as a means to reduce the possibility of revolt. Sometimes new Inca rulers were installed, but often local rulers were kept, with their sons being taken as hostages to Cuzco. Then the new areas were connected by roads to the existing empire.

During the Inca period there was little change in the prior agricultural economy. The Inca broke first ground prior to planting when the priests felt it was propitious. Personal service was taxed, with the people farming the lands of the church and state. Taxes were in terms of manpower labor units. The labor system was a pyramid with the ruling family at the top. Their foods are the same as those of Peruvian Indians today—corn and potato soup, corn bread, corn beer, and dried llama meat. The food surplus of each district was stored in state granaries and used to support the aristocracy, priests, army, and all public laborers.

The society featured three castes: the Inca, the original conquerors and original rulers of conquered territory, and the commoners. Privileges were very important, with the upper class controlling all high posts, performing no labor, and receiving all of the education.

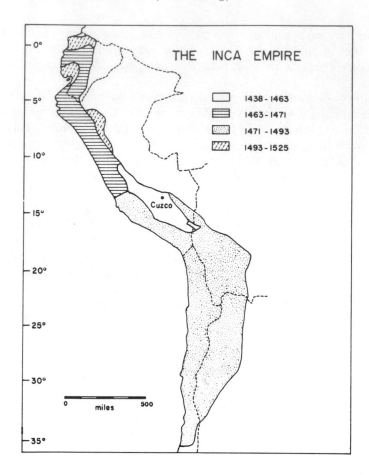

THE INCA EMPIRE

☐	1438 - 1463
☰	1463 - 1471
▦	1471 - 1493
▨	1493 - 1525

Cuzco

0   miles   500

Fig. 16–12 Map illustrating the expansion of the Inca Empire through time. (Patterson 1973:Fig. 5–3.)

Inca Archaeology

Inca materials mark the end of all archaeological sequences. Inca is the third horizon style to cover the entire Peru-Bolivia region. Most areas have both pure Inca-style artifacts and Inca-influenced local materials. The Cuzco area was the main center, a fact confirmed archaeologically as well as historically. Ceramics are the best Inca diagnostic trait but textiles, metalwork, and architecture were also well made. Textiles and ceramics seem the result of mass production. The building style suggests an emphasis on organized unit labor.

Little is known of the origin of the Inca style, for excavations have not revealed much material ancestral to Inca. According to tradition, the Inca occupied the Cuzco region for at least three centuries. The period from 1200 to 1438 is termed Early Inca. Burials of this period are flexed and cloth wrapped and placed in beehive-shaped masonry tombs with corbeled vaults. For the

Panoramic view of Machu Picchu. (Hester photograph.)

Agricultural terraces at Machu Picchu. (Hester photograph.)

The Inca fortress of Sacsahuaman near Cuzco. (Photograph courtesy of Ken Kirkwood.)

Monolithic masonry at the Inca fortress of Sacsahuaman, showing a stone with 10 angles. Note the close fit of the joints. (Photograph courtesy of Ken Kirkwood.)

Fig. 16–13 Inca architectural and masonry styles.

Early Inca period we have few objects of metal. Bone is common as are slate knives. The ceramics have carelessly painted linear and geometric designs in black, white, and red.

The late Inca archaeological period covers the time of political expansion. Most artifacts and ruins pertain to this late period; thus it is best known (Fig. 16–13).

The Inca Achievement

The 90+ years of the Inca Empire formed the most significant period in all of Andean culture history. The entire Andean culture was given a new orientation which has continued to the present. Thus modern Peruvian Indian history and culture begins with Pachacuti, the founder of the Inca Empire, rather than the Spanish Conquest. At the time of the Inca conquest the area was populated by a large number of small tribal groups. They shared many elements of culture, but differences were also numerous. The Inca eliminated most of these differences by unifying the language, life, and institutions of a vast region. For example, today, five sixths of all Indians speak Quechua; the other sixth speak Aymara. The continuity of Incan administrative policy was more an inevitable result than an intentional policy on the part of the Spanish. Thus there is today a feeling of solidarity among the Andean Indians. They share a belief in a common cultural heritage—a true Inca legacy.

REFERENCES

Bennett, W. and J. Bird, 1964, *Andean Culture History,* 2d ed., New York: Natural History Press.

Bushnell, G. H. S., 1963, *Peru.* New York: Praeger.

Patterson, T. C., 1973, *America's Past: A New World Archaeology.* Glenview, Ill.: Scott, Foresman.

Posnansky, A., 1945, *Tiahuanaco: The Cradle of American Man.* New York: Augustin.

Sawyer, A. R., 1968, *Mastercraftsmen of Ancient Peru.* New York: Solomon R. Guggenheim Foundation.

Schaedel, R., 1951, "Major Ceremonial and Population Centers in Northern Peru," in *Civilizations of Ancient America: Selected Papers of the XXIX International Congress of Americanists.* Chicago: The University of Chicago Press, pp. 232–243.

Steward, J., 1957, *Theory of Culture Change.* Urbana: University of Illinois Press.

Von Däniken, E., 1970, *Chariots of the Gods.* New York: Putnam.

West, M., 1970, "Community Settlement Patterns at Chan Chan, Peru," *American Antiquity* 35:74–86.

Willey, G. R., 1971, *An Introduction to American Archaeology,* Vol. 2. Englewood Cliffs, N.J.: Prentice-Hall.

17

Other New World Cultures

The record of man's occupation of the New World after 3000 B.C. shows increasing specialization, region by region, based on more intensive utilization of local resources. Such specialization with increasing adaptation to local environments had the result that local cultures diverged from each other. For the data after 3000 B.C. it is no longer possible to categorize continentwide stages. We must instead rely on the concept of *culture area:* within each major geographic region there is a tendency for cultures to be more alike and somewhat distinct from those cultures of surrounding regions. Major regional specializations identified by 3000 B.C. in North America include Arctic Littoral Hunters, Subarctic Littoral Hunters, Northwest Coast Forest Littoral Hunters, Fishers, and Gatherers, Plateau Fishermen-Gatherers, Desert Gatherers, Plains Hunter-Gatherers, Plains Village Farmers, Southwestern Farmers, Eastern Farmers and Hunter-Gatherers, Montane Hunters and Gatherers, Incipient Cultivators (in Mexico), and Littoral Collectors.

South American data is less well known but identified economic strategies specific to regions at 3000 B.C. include Littoral Collectors, Riparian Hunters and Gatherers, Montane Hunters and Gatherers, Savanna Hunters and Gatherers, and Plains Hunters (see Fig. 14–2).

By 1000 B.C. the situation had changed to include new centers of incipient cultivation in the North American Southwest and Mississippi River Valley. Farming was by this time widespread in Mesoamerica; in South America there had developed a farming tradition in the Andean Region as well as a distinct tropical farming pattern (Fig. 17–1). Major changes after A.D. 300 include expansion of the areas farmed in both North and South America and widespread settlement of the Caribbean Islands by Littoral Collectors (Fig. 17–2).

By A.D. 1500 the areas farmed had expanded to the limits of the environments suitable for cultivation. This expansion progressed through time at the expense of the areas inhabited by Hunters and Gatherers. By A.D. 1500 (Fig. 17–3) we can view New World Hunters and Gatherers as marginal peoples pushed into or at least permitted to occupy the less desirable areas. Most of these hunting-gathering peoples remained at a stage of cultural complexity little different from that achieved during the pre-3000 B.C. Archaic stage. The exceptions to this trend include the Northwest Coast of North America where the intense productivity of the open sea, littoral, and coast forest provided a food surplus and thus development of a high culture. The Great Plains of North America, with its enormous carrying capacity of buffalo, permitted a similar food surplus. That culture, exploiting the great herds, is an example of a cultural stage termed *climax hunting* (Hester 1962). In both of these examples the food-getting mechanisms were highly efficient, rivaling the productivity of farming as an economy. A summary of New World economic adaptations by time and geographic region is given on the back endpaper. While admittedly brief, this summary provides a unifying conceptual framework for all New World prehistorical data. We will now proceed to a brief description of these economic adaptations. We have already discussed several of these adaptations in earlier chapters and will not repeat them here. They include Desert Gatherers, Incipient Cultivators, Mesoamerican Farmers, Eastern Forest Hunter-Gatherers, and Andean Farmers.

NORTH AMERICA

Arctic Littoral Hunters

Early in Arctic prehistory we have a somewhat poorly known manifestation represented by a Mesolithic-type industry using microblades. Although our evidence concerning their economic adaptation is scanty, what is available

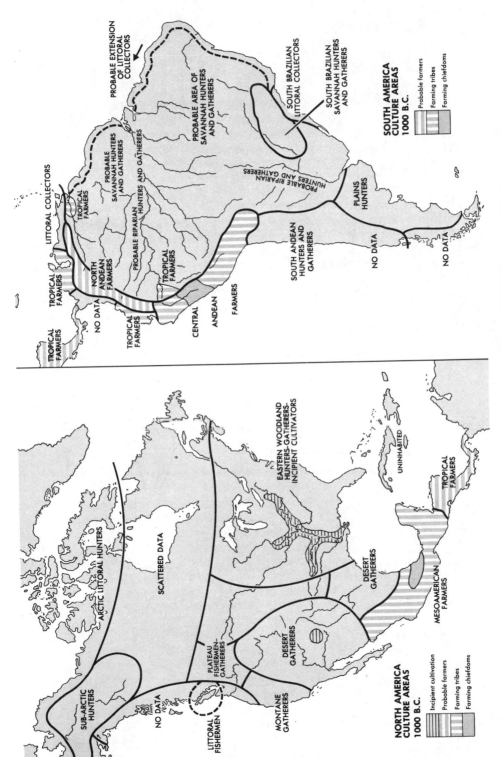

Fig. 17-1 New World culture areas, North and South America at 1000 B.C. (Sanders and Marino 1970:Fig. 4.)

Within the image:

NORTH AMERICA CULTURE AREAS 1000 B.C.

Incipient cultivation
Probable farmers
Probable tribes
Farming chiefdoms

SUB-ARCTIC HUNTERS
ARCTIC LITTORAL HUNTERS
SCATTERED DATA
EASTERN WOODLAND HUNTERS-GATHERERS-INCIPIENT CULTIVATORS
UNINHABITED
TROPICAL FARMERS
DESERT GATHERERS
MESOAMERICAN FARMERS
DESERT GATHERERS
MONTANE GATHERERS
PLATEAU FISHERMEN-GATHERERS
NO DATA
LITTORAL FISHERMEN

SOUTH AMERICA CULTURE AREAS 1000 B.C.

Probable farmers
Farming tribes
Farming chiefdoms

PROBABLE EXTENSION OF LITTORAL COLLECTORS
SOUTH BRAZILIAN LITTORAL COLLECTORS
SOUTH BRAZILIAN SAVANNAH HUNTERS AND GATHERERS
PROBABLE AREA OF SAVANNAH HUNTERS AND GATHERERS
LITTORAL COLLECTORS
TROPICAL FARMERS
PROBABLE SAVANNAH HUNTERS AND GATHERERS
PROBABLE RIPARIAN HUNTERS AND GATHERERS
PROBABLE RIPARIAN HUNTERS AND GATHERERS
TROPICAL FARMERS
NORTH ANDEAN FARMERS
NO DATA
TROPICAL FARMERS
TROPICAL FARMERS
CENTRAL ANDEAN FARMERS
SOUTH ANDEAN HUNTERS AND GATHERERS
PLAINS HUNTERS
NO DATA
NO DATA

457

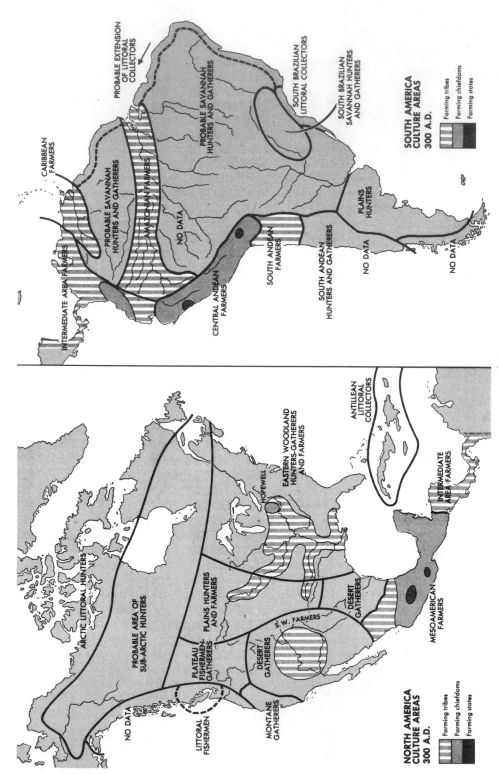

Fig. 17-2 New World culture areas, North and South America at A.D. 300. (Sanders and Marino 1970:Fig. 5.)

SOUTH AMERICA CULTURE AREAS 300 A.D.

Farming tribes
Farming chiefdoms
Farming states

CARIBBEAN FARMERS

PROBABLE EXTENSION OF LITTORAL COLLECTORS

SOUTH BRAZILIAN LITTORAL COLLECTORS

SOUTH BRAZILIAN SAVANNAH HUNTERS AND GATHERERS

PROBABLE SAVANNAH HUNTERS AND GATHERERS

AMAZONIAN FARMERS

PROBABLE SAVANNAH HUNTERS AND GATHERERS

NO DATA

INTERMEDIATE AREA FARMERS

CENTRAL ANDEAN FARMERS

SOUTH ANDEAN FARMERS

SOUTH ANDEAN HUNTERS AND GATHERERS

PLAINS HUNTERS

NO DATA

NO DATA

NORTH AMERICA CULTURE AREAS 300 A.D.

Farming tribes
Farming chiefdoms
Farming states

ARCTIC LITTORAL HUNTERS

PROBABLE AREA OF SUB-ARCTIC HUNTERS

NO DATA

PLATEAU FISHERMEN-GATHERERS

LITTORAL FISHERMEN

MONTANE GATHERERS

DESERT GATHERERS

S.W. FARMERS

PLAINS HUNTERS AND FARMERS

HOPEWELL

EASTERN WOODLAND HUNTERS-GATHERERS AND FARMERS

ANTILLEAN LITTORAL COLLECTORS

DESERT GATHERERS

INTERMEDIATE AREA FARMERS

MESOAMERICAN FARMERS

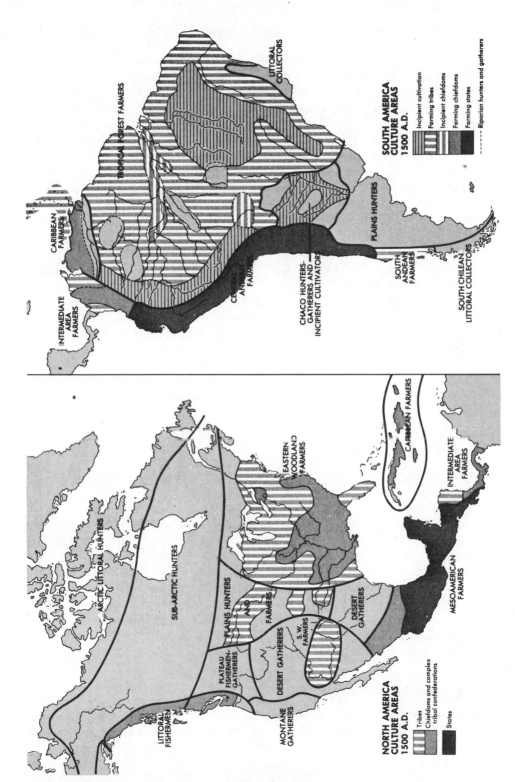

Fig. 17-3 New World culture areas, North and South America ca at A.D. 1500. (Sanders and Marino 1970:Fig. 6.)

459

suggests that these peoples were inland hunters of caribou and, farther south, deer.

After about 3000 B.C. we have the initiation of the Eskimo Tradition with its specialization for life on the Arctic littoral. Eskimo resource utilization included sea mammal hunting, both from boats and through holes in the ice. The species hunted were primarily the walrus and seal. Other reliance was on whaling, fishing, trapping of small mammals, hunting of birds, and gathering of sea bird eggs. The food resources were adequate to support a sparse population, but the adaptation required intense knowledge of game habits, the weather, and ice conditions in order to survive. Also necessary were efficient game-taking devices, the most important of which was the socketed, detachable, toggling harpoon head attached to a line with floats. Use of such a composite weapon provided both the killing and retention capability necessary to hunt and retrieve sea mammals. The intense winter cold required warm permanent houses of sod, stone, bone, and driftwood construction heated by use of the seal oil lamp. Other adaptations to cold included use of tailored fur clothing and consumption of large amounts of animal fat. Survival was further achieved through use of dog sleds in winter with overnight stops in the easily built snow igloo. Winter villages were permanent and located on the coast. The summer dwellings were portable skin tents, permitting movement into the interior for hunting at the time of the annual caribou migration. Social organization was clearly limited by the nonavailability of a food surplus. Bands were small and governed by a head man. The possibility of winter isolation and starvation led to practices of abandonment of the aged and, rarely, cannibalism.

Subarctic Littoral Hunters

South of the Tundra the interior of Canada features boreal forest. Poor in natural resources, this area seemingly has always featured sparse population. The major food resource was the caribou which follows an annual pattern of migration making kills at certain spots at certain times of the year relatively easy. Major hunting techniques included use of the bow and arrow combined with stalking. Other food getting procedures relied on traps or snares. Our archaeological evidence is scanty and comprises small collections of implements from widely scattered sites. Ethnographic information indicates these peoples, primarily Athabaskans, adapted to the cold winters through use of log houses, snowshoes, and dog toboggans. Summer living featured use of bark houses, bark canoes, and a migratory life combining hunting with gathering of berries and other plant foods.

Northwest Coast Littoral Hunters, Fishers, and Gatherers

The Northwest Coast environment is characterized by heavy coastal rain forest and an extensive highly involuted coastline. Food resources available to the prehistoric inhabitants were many and easily obtained. Beginning as early as 2500 B.C. and continuing to the nineteenth century A.D., the economy was one of mixed reliance on fishing at the mouths of salmon streams during the annual spawning season; shellfish gathering; inland hunting of deer, caribou, moose, and mountain goat; bottom fishing for cod and halibut in the shallow bays; and offshore harpooning from boats of sea lions, seals, porpoises, and larger whales. Subsistence was varied emphasizing seasonal harvests, some of which required seasonal transhumance. Examples include seaweed gathering, fur seal hunting, and camping at the mouths of the salmon streams. Houses were large rectangular dwellings built of posts and split planks obtained from the local straight grained red cedar. Extended families lived within these 30-by-60-feet structures. When the village moved, the planks were sometimes taken with them. During the winter season—a period of almost incessant cold rain—life focused on wood carving and an elaborate ceremonial calendar. Such noneconomic activities could be afforded because of the wealth of stored food. Salmon and clams were smoked for preservation and strips of halibut were dried. Herring eggs and fish oil were stored in wooden boxes for later consumption. The wealth of food available on the Northwest Coast permitted the growth of one of the most highly developed cultures anywhere in the world not based on an agricultural economy. The technology associated with food getting included dugout canoes, fish weirs, fish lines with composite hooks, harpoons, fixed barbed point spears, dip nets, and the use of rakes to pull surface schooling fish into canoes.

Californian Specializations

The Littoral Collectors of California were more limited in their resources than were peoples living farther north. Major resources included deepsea fish, sea birds, and shellfish, especially abalone and crabs.

Inland, the California Montane food collectors specialized in the gathering of acorns and pine nuts. The abundance of wild grass seeds and nuts was such that a high population density was possible and bands lived in permanent villages. Collecting expeditions went out from the villages to harvest the local wild plants. Even though the carrying capacity of the land was high in terms of nonagricultural productivity, band size was still limited to a few hundred persons. Social organization included fraternities, although in terms of complexity, California bands were not as advanced as those of the Northwest Coast. Through time California cultures remained at an Archaic level. Those cultures are discussed in greater detail in Chapter 14.

Plateau Fishermen-Gatherers

Basic environmental resources in the Interior Plateau region included the annual salmon run, sturgeon, deer, and the root of the camas plant. In the higher mountains elk, mountain goat, and bighorn sheep were also available.

Fishing by netting or spearing salmon as they swam upstream over rapids formed the base for a long-term economy in the region dating back to ca. 9000 B.C. Artifacts associated include bone points, ground edge cobbles, and bipoints typical of the Old Cordilleran Culture. Between 5000 and 1000 B.C. Plateau prehistory is poorly known. After A.D. 500 there appears a regional culture distinctive of the area. Termed the Northwest Riverine Tradition, this culture featured permanent villages in the river valleys with major reliance on fishing. The tool inventory included a complex of ground-stone woodworking tools, probably introduced from the north after 1000 B.C. Other trends through time include increasing trade with the Northwest Coast littoral peoples and the introduction of specific Northwest Coast traits, including house types and burial patterns.

Plains Hunter-Gatherers

Plains cultures possessed a nomadic life adjusted to reliance on the migratory herds of buffalo. The pattern emerged during the Paleo-Indian period. There is a Plains Archaic period, but sites are few and during the period human occupation was at a minimum. Later occupation, 3000–500 B.C., featured use of rock shelters and open campsites. The artifact inventory included chipped-stone skin-dressing tools as well as bone fleshers. Primary food animals included buffalo, deer, and antelope, as well as birds, reptiles, and fresh water mussels. Site features are limited to fire hearths and excavated storage pits. A typical hunting technique was the use of the stampede to drive herds of buffalo over a cliff—the so-called "buffalo jump." The migratory bison hunters' life style is best known to us from historical accounts rather than from archaeological investigations. An eyewitness account of one such group was recorded by Castaneda, the chronicler of Coronado's expedition of 1539–1541.

After seventeen days of travel, I came upon a rancheria of the Indians who follow these cattle. These natives are called Querechos. They do not cultivate the land, but eat raw meat and drink the blood of the cattle they kill. They dress in the skins of the cattle, with which all the people in this land clothe themselves, and they have very well-constructed tents, made with tanned and greased cowhides, in which they live and which they take along as they follow the cattle. They have dogs which they load to carry their tents, poles, and belongings (Hammond and Rey 1940:186).

Plains Village Farmers

The majority of archaeology in the Plains is derived from the sedentary riverine villages of the Missouri River drainage. These developed in A.D. times after the introduction of corn horticulture. Farming was conducted in small plots in the valley bottoms and the villages were constructed on the first terrace above the river. Houses were of the earth lodge type and featured a semisubterranean excavated floor, wooden support posts, and a cribbed log superstructure, with the entire dwelling then covered with earth. Villages ranged from a few houses up to a maximum of 200. Another feature common to these sites was the widespread use within and between the houses of bell-shaped undercut storage pits. Community labor was used in the excavation of defensive moats around the villages and the erection of a wooden palisade, sometimes featuring bastians. The economy was mixed, with fall hunts for buffalo augmenting the farm produce.

Southwestern Farmers

Following the development of plant cultivation in Mesoamerica, its practice with specific cultigens spread northward into the Southwest. Although our earliest occurrences of corn date prior to 3000 B.C., the corn, beans, squash agricultural economy did not substantially alter the Southwestern life style until the first centuries A.D. The initial pattern established was that of small sedentary villages made up of semisubterranean to subterranean pithouses. Pottery was introduced and a distinct Southwestern cultural tradition was formed. Later developments included the use of a separate and architecturally distinct subterranean ceremonial structure: the kiva. After about A.D. 1000 the house type changed to surface units made up of contiguous masonry rooms: the pueblo. In the northern Southwest between A.D. 1100 and 1300 there occurred a climax in architecture, with large villages containing up to 3000 people living in multistory units of up to five stories.

The social organization and culture of these peoples has persisted to the present and is characterized by a strong religion, which emphasizes keeping in harmony with nature by means of ceremonies and prayers for rain. Individual aggressiveness is minimized and the relationships between individuals are highly structured according to their roles as members of numerous cross-cutting secret societies.

In southern Arizona the initial settlements were confined to the major river valleys and feature use of irrigation with a major system of canals. Mexican trait introductions were strong and, besides the food plants, included iron pyrite mosaic mirrors, copper bells, carved stone palettes, and pottery styles. There was much trade in shell bracelets and other shell ornaments. Architectural introductions include the ball court and even flat-topped pyramidal mounds. The Hohokam culture, as it is termed, flourished from about 300 B.C. to A.D. 1400 before the large settlements were abandoned. The probable cause of abandonment was the silting up of the canals and progressive salinization of the fields. At the height of the occupation the canals were up to 75 miles in length and 30 feet in width. The maintenance of a system of this magnitude required community control of labor. Nonetheless there is no evidence of the cultural attributes we ascribe to civilization, and we must therefore view the Hohokam culture as another manifestation of the New World Formative stage.

Eastern Farmers and Hunter-Gatherers

In Chapter 14 we described the economy of the Archaic peoples of the Eastern Woodlands of the United States. Termed *primary forest efficiency,* this economy focused on a mixed reliance on the hunting and gathering of a wide variety of locally available foods. Late in the Archaic period, after 2000 B.C., there occurred the introduction of limited cultivation of plants and the use of pottery. After those introductions these previously semisedentary peoples began to live in permanent villages along the major river valleys. These later occupants have been classified into two major cultural traditions: the Woodland Tradition, dated 1000 B.C.–A.D. 700, and the Mississippian Tradition, A.D. 700–1700.

The Woodland Tradition has as its major distinguishing characteristic the use of a gray friable pottery, surface-decorated with cord marking or impressions of fabrics. The cord marking was done with a cord-wrapped paddle while the clay was still damp. Vessel forms were simple, primarily globular jars. Other major features were burial mounds and earthworks. The latter features were associated with an elaborate pattern of ceremonial treatment of the dead. The most outstanding developments of this cultural pattern are known from the Ohio River Valley.

During the earlier portion of this tradition, termed Burial Mound I, 1000–300 B.C., the economy featured cultivation of sunflower, marsh elder, squash, gourd, and chenopod. Gordon Willey (1966:268) states that corn found in a Burial Mound II context, 300 B.C.–A.D. 700, indicates a long period of antecedent development. Therefore even though no corn has been found in Burial Mound I levels, it was probably grown at that time.

The most distinctive Burial Mound I culture is that termed Adena. It featured conical burial mounds up to 20 meters in height. Surrounding clusters of these mounds were earthen enclosures up to 100 meters in diameter. Within the mounds were rectangular log tombs placed within a pit. Inside the tombs were two or three extended burials covered with red ochre. Sometimes the tombs were burned before being covered with the earthen mound. Another burial pattern featured cremation in clay basins. With both types, elaborate offerings of grave goods were included. The artifacts included ground and polished stone celts, gorgets, boatstones, effigy pipes, and stone tablets with carved curvilinear designs. Ornaments of copper were used as well as copper axes. Villages were simple pole and thatch structures grouped in clusters of two to five. Probably several such villages supported a single burial complex.

The Burial Mound II period is best known from the Hopewell culture, also well represented in the Ohio River Valley. Hopewell represents a continuation of the Woodland cultural pattern but is more elaborate. The major distinctions from Adena lie in the burial rites. The Hopewell culture was further disseminated widely into adjacent regions; this expansion is viewed as having been spread by an elite. Certainly social stratification is evident in the burial patterns. Three fourths of the dead were cremated, while burial in log tombs was reserved for a minority. The log tombs held enormous quantities of grave goods including thousands of freshwater pearls, chipped arrowheads, effigy pipes, copper ornaments, and cutouts of sheet mica in the form of heads, hands, swastikas, animal claws, and geometrics. The earthworks were larger and more elaborate than those of the Adena culture. They included up to 100 acres and had walls up to 5 meters in height. Another new feature was the fortification of hilltops. Hopewell culture emphasized wealth conspicuously consumed in the burial ceremonies. Many of the objects so consumed were made from materials traded over great distances. The Hopewell culture may thus be viewed as indicative of a cultural climax, although there is no evidence of urbanism and the overall level of attainment is that of the Formative stage.

The Mississippian tradition, A.D. 700–1700, is not a simple continuation of Woodland traits. The differences suggest that there were major influences spreading up the Mississippi Valley from Mesoamerica. Although intervening areas in northern Mexico and southern Texas show little evidence of such cultural transmission, the new traits are definitely of Mesoamerican affinity. These introductions include rectangular, flat-topped platform mounds arranged around rectangular open plazas. Formerly called *temple mounds,* these structures served as bases for both temples and the houses of the chiefs. The structures themselves were of pole and thatch. The largest site known is Cahokia, located within the suburbs of the present city of St. Louis. Numerous mounds are known, the largest of which, Monk's Mound, measures 200 by 300 meters by 30 meters in height. According to Willey (1966:298), 80 mounds are known within a 3 to 4 mile radius, and approximately 200 more smaller mounds are estimated to have been destroyed by recent plowing. Recent studies at Cahokia by Melvin Fowler have been concerned with mapping the entire site from early aerial photographs, estimating its maximum population (perhaps as much as 40,000 people at its peak), and excavating incredibly elaborate burials featuring large numbers of individuals buried as accompaniment to other persons of obvious high status. Notwithstanding the size and complexity of sites such as Cahokia, Mississippian culture is also assigned to the Formative stage.

The Mississippian culture spread up the river systems into Wisconsin and to the southeast as far as Tennessee, Alabama, and Georgia. In these remote locations the Mississippian communities featured palisaded earthworks and appear to represent intrusive communities surrounded by other peoples still practicing a Woodland culture life style. The Mississippian culture featured as one of its dominant elements the Southern cult, which we have mentioned previously as a possible extension of Mesoamerican ceremonialism. The end of the Mississippian tradition is marked by a smooth transition to the cultures of the historic tribes of the Southeastern United States. Whereas numerous cultural traditions persisted into the historic contacts of DeSoto and others, the period of florescence began to wane after A.D. 1200. Nonetheless as late as A.D. 1700, the Natchez maintained a ceremonial center with temple mounds and burial mounds. They further had a stratified society with nobles and commoners.

SOUTH AMERICA

Our knowledge of South American prehistoric economic systems is less than that for North America. Few sites outside of the Andean region have been excavated in detail. Three primary economies may be isolated: hunting-gathering, incipient agriculture, and tropical forest slash-and-burn agriculture.

Hunters and Gatherers

Primary areas where hunting and gathering was practiced included the savanna areas, the deciduous forests of the Brazilian and Guiana highlands, and the pampas. Typical strategies were the hunting of deer and guanaco with the bow and bolas, the gathering of wild seeds, roots, and other plants, fishing done with the bow, and on the coast, shellfish gathering. Shelters were sometimes caves; otherwise windbreaks made of skins were used. The camps were occupied only as long as food was locally available. Due to the meager cultural inventory, plus the added difficulty of site location in areas now densely vegetated, most site data is limited to tools of chipped stone, bone, and shell. The largest social groups were the bands of guanaco hunters in the pampas where the availability of game permitted groups in excess of 100 people. Elsewhere the low carrying capacity of the tropical forest environment limited population. The tropical forest pattern featured seasonal camps along the rivers with a rainy season dispersal of smaller groups who moved out into the savanna grasslands for collecting purposes.

Incipient Cultivators

The tropical forest pattern described above was modified by the addition of limited cultivation, primarily of bitter manioc. The use of cultigens was simply added to the already existing mixed hunting and gathering economy. Villages were small, probably consisting of several extended families. Pottery was introduced and features soft gray to brown surface textured wares.

Tropical Forest Slash-and-Burn Agriculturalists

According to Meggers (1954), the tropical forest, evaluated in terms of its agricultural potential, is a limiting environment which only permits or gives rise to cultures existing at a subsistence level. The agricultural system is based on the cutting and burning of small areas to prepare plots for planting. Major crops are manioc, and in A.D. times, corn. Villages were small, located on the river banks, and were frequently moved as the fields were exhausted after four to six years. There was no permanent architecture and no elaborate social organization or religion. Transportation was by dugout canoe on the network of rivers.

The pottery continues the tradition of incised decorated wares. Other artifacts include basketry, textiles, and implements of ground stone. The mixed hunting and gathering economy was also continued. Fishing employed the use of poison. The house type was pole and thatch and included single family units as well as large rectangular communal houses. There was some preference for secondary burial in pottery urns. For the most part tropical agriculturalists date after A.D. 500, although some pottery manioc griddles in Venezuela are dated as early as 1000 B.C. About A.D. 500 there began the spread of tropical agricultural peoples to the Antilles where they replaced the earlier shellfish-gathering littoral inhabitants termed Meso-Indians.

In general we may summarize South American cultures as possessing little in the way of elaborate social organization, architecture, and crafts in all of those areas lying beyond the Andean chain.

REFERENCES

Hammond, G. P., and A. Rey, 1940, *Narratives of the Coronado Expedition 1540–1542*. Albuquerque: University of New Mexico Press.

Hester, J. J., 1962, "A Comparative Typology of New World Cultures," *American Anthropologist* 64(5):1001–1015.

Meggers, B. J., 1954, "Environmental Limitation on the Development of Culture," *American Anthropologist* 56:801–824.

Sanders, W., and J. Marino, 1970, *New World Prehistory*. Englewood Cliffs, N.J.: Prentice-Hall.

Willey, G. R., 1966, *An Introduction to American Archaeology,* Vol. 1. Englewood Cliffs, N.J.: Prentice-Hall.

Name Index

Text folios are in roman type; figure folios are in italic type.

469

Subject Index

Text folios are in roman type; figure folios are in italic type.

473

THE CHRONOLOGY OF

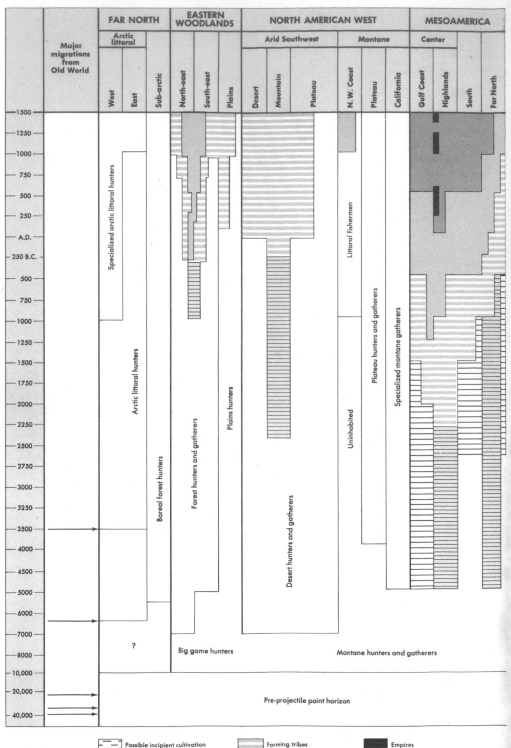

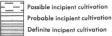